Materiality and Aesthetics in
Archaic and Classical Greek Poetry

Ancient Cultures, New Materialisms

Series Editors: Lilah Grace Canevaro, University of Edinburgh and Melissa Mueller, University of Massachusetts, Amherst

Reconsidering the ancient world through the lens of New Materialism
From archaeological sites to papyri and manuscripts, we experience the ancient world through its material remains. This materiality may be tangible: from vases to votive offerings and statues to spearheads. It might be the text as object or the object in the text. The New Materialisms have transformed the way we conceive of the material world – but how and to what extent might they be applied to ancient cultures?
Books in this series will showcase the potential applications of New Materialism within Classics, giving us a new way to look at ancient texts, ancient objects and ancient world-views.

Books available:
Amy Lather, *Materiality and Aesthetics in Archaic and Classical Greek Poetry*

Visit our website at edinburghuniversitypress.com/series-ancient-cultures-new-materialisms to find out more

Materiality and Aesthetics in Archaic and Classical Greek Poetry

Amy Lather

EDINBURGH
University Press

Edinburgh University Press is one of the leading university presses in the UK. We publish academic books and journals in our selected subject areas across the humanities and social sciences, combining cutting-edge scholarship with high editorial and production values to produce academic works of lasting importance. For more information visit our website: edinburghuniversitypress.com

Edinburgh University Press Ltd
The Tun – Holyrood Road, 12(2f) Jackson's Entry, Edinburgh EH8 8PJ

Typeset in 10/14 Ehrhardt by
Servis Filmsetting Ltd, Stockport, Cheshire

A CIP record for this book is available from the British Library

ISBN 978 1 4744 6235 8 (hardback)
ISBN 978 1 4744 6237 2 (webready PDF)
ISBN 978 1 4744 6238 9 (epub)

Contents

List of Illustrations	vii
Acknowledgements	ix
Note on the Text	xi
Introduction	1
1. A Beautiful Mind: Patterns of Thought and the Decoration of Textiles	18
Poikilia, Polychromy and Perception	20
Sensing Fabric in the Acropolis Korai	29
Visualising Fabric and Constructing Images in Vase Painting	45
Putting the 'Hand' into Handicraft: *Poikilia* and (Feminine) Thought Patterns	54
2. Brazen Charm: The Vitality of Archaic Armour	64
Affective Armour	66
Bronze as Light	69
Heavy Metal: The Sound of Battle	74
Bodies Nonhuman and Superhuman	77
A Wall of Armour, a Human Boulder and Brazen Voices	81
The Armour of Achilles and Blazing Weaponry	85
Life in/of Metal	91
3. Mind Tools: Art, Artifice and Animation	95
Paradoxical *Poikilia*: Labyrinthine Passageways	98
Poikilia in Miniature	101
A Wonder to Behold: Pandora in the *Theogony*	104
Intelligent Things	108

Hephaestus' Tools 111
The Ships of the Phaeacians and Other 'Smart' Objects 115
Conclusion: *Poikilia* and the Riddle of Speech 122

4. The Protean Shape of Lyric *Poikilia* 127
The Imaginative Matter of *Poikilia*: Scintillating Objects in Sappho,
Alcman and Anacreon 132
Pindaric *Poikilia* and the Victorious Imagination 141
Pythian 8, *Pythian* 10 and *Olympian* 1 143
Olympian 6, *Nemean* 5 and *Nemean* 4 150
Visible and Audible Movement: *Poikilia*'s Scintillating Shape 155

5. *Mētis* and the Mechanics of the Mind 162
Crafting Cognition with Prometheus 166
Mētis, the Mother of Invention 172
Social Media and the Embodiment(s) of *Poikilomētis*: A Viewing Guide 185
Conclusions 194

6. The Materiality of Feminine Guile 196
Hera and the *Kestos Himas* 197
Goddesses in Disguise and Divine Assemblages 201
Aphrodite's Seductive Assemblage in the *Homeric Hymn to Aphrodite* 206
Pandora as *Dolos* 209
Killer Style and Tragic *Poikilia*: Clytemnestra and Medea 211
Conclusions 221

Conclusions 223

Bibliography 230
Index Locorum 256
Subject index 264

List of Illustrations

1.1. Amphora by Exekias, depicting Achilles and Ajax playing a game
      (c. 550–540 BCE)   22
1.2. Peplos kore (Acropolis 679) (c. 530 BCE)   31
1.3. Reconstruction of polychromy on Peplos kore (c. 530 BCE)   32
1.4. Acropolis kore 675 (510–500 BCE)   35
1.5. Acropolis kore 682 (525 BCE)   37
1.6. Acropolis kore 594 (c. 500 BCE)   41
1.7. Detail of Acropolis kore 594 (c. 500 BCE)   42
1.8. Side view of Acropolis kore 675 (510–500 BCE)   43
1.9. Sophilos Dinos depicting wedding procession of Peleus and Thetis
      (c. 580–570 BCE)   47
1.10. Amphora by Exekias with man and woman on a chariot (c. 540 BCE)   49
1.11. Amphora by Amasis painter portraying Dionysus and maenads
      (mid-sixth century BCE)   50
1.12. Amphora attributed to the Andocides and Lysippides painters
      portraying Ajax and Achilles (c. 525–520 BCE)   53

This book is dedicated to the memory of my grandfather,
James Patrick Collins, Jr, for his endless love and support, and for always
letting me get 'just one more book'.

Acknowledgements

My penchant for all things glittery, fancy and altogether *poikila* began early in life, but first became a scholarly interest in 2014 as a dissertation project. Thus this book has been in the making – in one form or another – since 2014, and it is my privilege to have so many to thank for their help and support along the way. First, I owe an enormous debt of gratitude to Deborah Beck, my dissertation supervisor at the University of Texas at Austin, who has been unflagging in her help with this project at every step of the way. My dissertation committee members at UT Austin – Lesley Dean-Jones, Paula Perlman and Stephen White – were each instrumental in shaping and improving this work in its dissertation form. Pauline LeVen, my outside dissertation reader, was also enormously generous with the time and energy she devoted to strengthening this work. I am also grateful to my colleagues at Wake Forest University for their patience, humour and support. Finally, I am tremendously thankful to the series editors, Lilah Grace Canevaro and Melissa Mueller, who offered so much feedback and guidance throughout the process of writing this book. The editorial staff of Edinburgh University Press, and especially the sharp eye of Fiona Sewell, have also saved me from numerous infelicities.

The College of Liberal Arts as well as the Humanities Institute at Wake Forest University have generously provided much support for this project's completion, and I also want to extend my gratitude to the Center for Hellenic Studies for granting me a fellowship that enabled me to finish my manuscript.

I want to thank (in alphabetical order) the many friends and colleagues who have enriched this work: Emily Austin, Stephen Blair, Jacqueline DiBiasie-Sammons, Dean Franco, T. H. M. Gellar-Goad, Elena Giusti, Ayelet Haimson-Lushkov, Paul Hay, Caitlin Hines, Jonatan Mars, Alyce Miller, Gregory Nagy, John Oksanish, Chuck Oughton, Julie Pechanek, Mary L. B. Pendergraft, Verity Platt, Evan

Rap, Andrew Riggsby, Julia Scarborough, Michael Sloan, Alex Walthall, Brian Warren and Colin Yarbrough. A special thanks is owed to my friend Katherine McKeon, whose excitement for this book's publication has been a constant source of encouragement.

Finally, to my family: thank you for your patience and love.

Note on the Text

Unless otherwise noted, the Greek texts used are from the *Oxford Classical Text* editions. The abbreviations of ancient authors and works follow those of the *Oxford Classical Dictionary* (2012), 4th edition, edited by Simon Hornblower, Antony Spawforth and Esther Eidinow.

For the reader's ease, in Greek quotations I underline forms of *poikil-/* as well as its English translation. Unless otherwise noted, all translations are my own.

Introduction

THINGS MAKE US who we are. Humans have never ceased to wonder about the significance and impact of the objects that surround us, a tendency that is particularly marked in today's era of 'smart' devices. Advances in technology, however, have always marched in lockstep with worries about their effects on the human mind and body – for example, how smartphones shorten attention spans and diminish social bonds. At the same time, however, recent research in neuroscience and philosophy of mind has illuminated the extent to which our cognitive architecture interacts with and even depends upon its physical environs.[1] Whether we like it or not, it seems increasingly plausible that being human means being intimately bound to the nonhuman, inanimate things that surround us.[2]

Moreover, we *like* things – how they look and feel as much as how they make *us* look and feel. Aesthetics thus has as much to do with art as it is part of our lived experience, as recent critical shifts have shown in the form of 'everyday' aesthetics and the new materialisms.[3] While the former seeks to expand the scope of aesthetics

---

[1] Clark, a leading proponent of the extended mind hypothesis, in his 1997, 2003 and 2008 works explores in great detail the levels and forms of interaction between cognitive processes and external stimuli.

[2] For different formulations of this point from the perspectives of anthropology, archaeology, philosophy and sociology see e.g. Appadurai 1986, Hodder 2012, Latour 2013, Malafouris 2013 and the essays compiled in Grusin 2015. In the field of classical archaeology in particular see the groundbreaking study of Hamilakis 2013.

[3] Pioneering studies in 'everyday' aesthetics are Dewey 1934, Berleant 1970, Mandoki 2007, Saito 2007, Miller 2010. For the new materialist correlate see especially Bennett 2001 and 2010 as well as the essays collected in Coole and Frost 2010 and Iovino and Oppermann 2014. On new materialisms and embodiment in the field of classics in particular, see now

outside the exclusive sphere of the fine arts to include everyday objects and materials within the purview of aesthetic experience, the new materialisms – broadly construed – aim to formulate a less anthropocentric worldview that adequately accounts for the influence of nonhuman substances on human life and thought. What both fields share in common, however, is an awareness that things are able to affect our thinking because of how their material components attract and engage our senses, and that the values we attach to such experiences can affect our behaviour in profound and man-ifold ways. The disciplines of archaeology and anthropology have proven especially fruitful for putting into practice the new materialists' interest in de-centring the human subject and orienting attention towards the dynamic relations between per-sons and things. Numerous recent works in these fields have developed approaches to material culture that articulate the agency of matter in shaping human practices and values,[4] but the field of literary studies has likewise exhibited a 'material turn' thanks in no small part to Bill Brown's 'thing theory' as articulated in a seminal 2001 essay.[5] Things of the past, present and (imagined) future – in both their material realia and their literary and artistic representations – are experiencing a renaissance.

Taking its cue from the ever-increasing scholarly interest in the relationships between human and nonhuman entities, this book investigates how minds and things interact by focusing on a concept that looms large in ancient Greek aesthetics: *poikilia*.[6] This term provides a useful rubric for teasing out the relations between materiality and human thought precisely because its semantic range from its earliest attestations onwards encompasses both artefacts and mental processes.[7] In Homer,

Telò and Mueller 2018 as well as Gaifman, Platt and Squire 2018. See too Canevaro 2019, which provides a useful survey of recent studies of materialisms in classics.

[4] Gell 1998 remains a seminal study in this regard, and I list here those more recent con-tributions that have been the most influential on this study: Renfrew and Zubrow 1994, DeMarrais, Gosden and Renfrew 2004, Boivin 2008, Malafouris and Renfrew 2010, Johannsen, Jessen and Jensen 2012.

[5] While the 2001 essay formally introduces the theoretical contours that Brown adopts in his approach to literary things, see also his 1996, 2003 and 2015 for extensive studies of objects in the American literary imagination.

[6] I thus share the aims of Bielfeldt 2014 and 2018, who articulates her study of the relation-ship between Roman lampstands and slaves as an attempt 'to uncover how objects are expe-rienced as material and ontological presences while hermeneutically contextualizing the meanings and values that objects were assigned by their makers, handles and beholders', 2018: 424. For comparable approaches to the role and construction of objects and material-ity in Greek thought, see especially Grethlein 2008 and 2020, Whitley 2013, Purves 2015, Mueller 2016a, Telò and Mueller 2018, Canevaro 2018.

[7] A note on terminology: while the differences between 'thing', 'object' and 'artefact' are non-trivial and have been the subject of lively philosophical debate, these distinctions fall

for instance, Odysseus is *poikilomētis*, 'with cunning mind', but so too are precious textiles as well as bronze armament *poikilos*, 'elaborately wrought'. Thus, to the ancient Greek mind, objects and minds exhibit a commonality that is perceptible enough to be classified with the same word. And this in turn implies that the application of the terminology of *poikilia* is not bound to the modern Cartesian dichotomy between (abstract) minds and (concrete) things.[8] Instead, the entities marked in terms of *poikilia* participate in a fluid economy of exchange between minds, bodies and things. Indeed, it is this fluidity that, as I will argue, accounts for the aesthetic value afforded to *poikilia* in archaic and classical Greek thought.[9]

There are distinct advantages to focusing on an aesthetic concept that spans multiple material registers (metal, fabric, music etc.) rather than looking at just one specific type of object or material. In doing so we will gain a better understanding of: (1) how the ancient Greek mind, in applying the same terminology to a wide variety of things, conceived of the relationality between different kinds of artefacts; and (2) how the perception and effects of *poikilia* remained constant or changed across different media. Moreover, since there exists a verbal form of *poikilia* in addition to the adjective and noun, I also explore the processes involved in the construction of artefacts. It thus becomes possible to discern not only how persons interact with and respond to the finished products named in terms of *poikilia*, but also how human

outside the purview of my argument and, accordingly, I use these terms interchangeably to refer to various sorts of nonhuman entities, although I reserve 'thing' and 'object' for material ones (as opposed to e.g. language and music). I use the term 'material' in a similarly broad fashion, designed to encompass all phenomena with sensuous, perceptible properties, including those of the human body.

[8] Indeed, the different Greek terms for cognitive or emotional faculties (e.g. *thumos, psuchē*) also raise problems for this dichotomy, as words like these frequently imply a bodily element to mental states. I will not rely on a single translation for such terms, and instead translate each of them as seems most appropriate for the contexts in which they appear (e.g. 'mind' versus 'heart').

[9] Ancient aesthetics has recently witnessed an explosion of scholarly interest under the influence of Porter 2010's groundbreaking study (see also his 2016 work, which concentrates on the sublime in particular). Wiley has also recently (2015) published a *Companion to Ancient Aesthetics* edited by Destrée and Murray, and Sluiter and Rosen 2012 presents a variety of contributions focused on aesthetic value in antiquity. See also Halliwell 2011, Peponi 2012, Liebert 2017 and Grethlein 2017 for studies of different kinds of aesthetic experiences and responses in ancient Greek thought.

Following Porter's exploration of the materialist and sensuous dimensions of ancient aesthetics, and in step with the 'sensory turn' that the humanities has experienced, numerous studies devoted to the senses have also been published recently, most notably Routledge's series 'The Senses in Antiquity', which includes volumes concentrating on each of the canonical five senses as well as one on synaesthesia.

cognitive and physical characteristics mingle with material elements in the creation of such products.

In its interest in aesthetic experience as a form of interaction between humans and things, this study joins the growing body of work in the humanities devoted to uncovering the specific ways in which humans make sense of things, and conversely, how things make sense of *us* – how they make us who we are as individuals, societies and epochs. This book intertwines two strands of thought by considering how matter impinges *on* or even constitutes human thought and activity as well as how human cognitive processes develop and evolve *from* their interactions with things. Literary representations of material objects and human experiences of those objects have much to divulge about the contours of the human mind and body as perceived by authors working in different periods and genres. Conversely, the philological approach adopted here also ensures an equal attention to the ways in which texts manage to impart meaning and agency to material substances. Broadly speaking, then, the analyses offered in each chapter are informed by embodied theories of mind as well as by various inflections of the new materialisms.[10]

While the 'new materialisms' is a label applied to a heterogeneous body of humanistic scholarship, one recurrent feature is a concern with the ontological distinctions between humans, persons, things and materials. And in the context of the *poikilia* word group, which encompasses all manner of beings both living and nonliving, material and immaterial, organic and inorganic, the interstices and slippages between these categories will prove an omnipresent theme. My readings reveal that Jane Bennett's 2010 concept of vital or 'vibrant' materialism is especially pertinent to *poikilia*. By 'vibrant' Bennett denotes the affective liveliness of the material – the capacity for nonhuman substances to colour and shape human experience of the world. As she puts it, to focus attention on material things in this way is to 'highlight the extent to which human being and thinghood overlap, the extent to which the us and the it slip-slide into each other. One moral of the story is that we are also nonhuman and that things, too, are vital players in the world' (2010: 4).[11]

In this vein, the interpretations offered here will attend not only to the effects of things on humans and so to the agentive capacities of material, but also to the inter-

---

[10] Thus while Porter's 2010 work did much to draw attention to the prominence of matter and materiality in the ancient Greek imaginary, my approach differs from his in its application of contemporary cognitive models and theories to ancient sources.

[11] Bennett's influence on the new materialisms can be felt in Coole and Frost 2010's introduction to this body of theory, who note that 'materiality is always something more than "mere" matter: an excess, force, vitality, relationality, or difference that renders matter active, self-creative, productive, unpredictable', 9.

mingling of the human and nonhuman elements at work in portrayals of cognition and perception. Throughout this book we will encounter objects and materials that are vital as well as vibrant. I adopt the terms 'vital' or 'vitality/vitalism' and 'vibrant' or 'vibrancy' to mean two different things. By 'vital' or 'vitality/vitalism' I refer specifically to the agentive and affective capacities of things as manifested in their evocation of affects, emotions and other kinds of human responses. On the other hand, 'vibrant' or 'vibrancy' will single out the appearance or impression *of* vitality in objects: that is, how the sensuous, aesthetic qualities of materials – including that of *poikilia* – signal their own agentive capacities.

While the approach of the new materialisms seeks to destabilise the hierarchy of agency between persons and things and between human and nonhuman, the embodied approach to cognition challenges the conception of thought as a brain-bound process. In recent decades a number of theories of embedded, enactive, extended and/or embodied ('4E') cognition have emerged, but they are united in their attempt to unpack how the brain responds to and engages with forces outside the skull – whether those happen to be bodily senses or features of the external world. What vital materialism and embodied cognition have in common is the desire to challenge the Cartesian dualism that places material things and mental processes in opposition. Broadly speaking, embodied cognition insists that mental activity is bound up with the workings of the body. This correspondingly entails that cognition is also dependent on the interactions of the body with its surrounding physical environment, including the material entities therein.

Two inflections of embodied cognition will prove especially pertinent to the cognitive facets of *poikilia*: enactive perception and extended mind on the one hand and material engagement on the other.[12] Enactive perception and extended mind, as articulated by Alva Noë and Andy Clark respectively, argue that sense perception and higher-order thinking (for instance, mathematical calculation) are born out of our dynamic, embodied engagement with the things populating our everyday worlds. While Noë's enactive account explores in depth the contribution of our sensorimotor skills to our qualitative experience of the phenomenal world, Clark's work concentrates on the tools and external 'props' (including language itself) that guide and structure thought. Indeed, Clark's conclusion to his 2008 work, *Supersizing the Mind: Embodiment, Action, and Cognitive Extension*, sounds remarkably in tune with the new materialists' interest in the intermingling between bodies and things:

---

[12] In the past decade a number of scholars have fruitfully pursued a variety of cognitive approaches to the classics, e.g. the essays collected in Meineck, Short and Devereaux 2018 and Lauwers, Schwall and Opsomer 2018 as well as Grethlein and Huitink 2017, Budelmann and LeVen 2014, Meineck 2012.

> Confronted by the kaleidoscope of cases encountered in the previous chapters, the proper response is to see mind and intelligence themselves as mechanically realized by complex, shifting mixtures of energetic and dynamic coupling, internal and external forms of representation and computation, epistemically potent forms of bodily action, and the canny exploitation of a variety of extrabodily props, aids, and scaffolding. Minds like ours emerge from this colorful flux as surprisingly seamless wholes: adaptively potent mashups extruded from a dizzying motley of heterogeneous elements and processes. (219)

Such philosophical accounts of 4E cognition, by illuminating the specific ways in which our physical environs can guide and enhance human thought processes, will thus provide useful models for the interplay between cognitive activity and material qualities so often attributed to *poikilia*: for instance, the persistent relations drawn between cunning, deception and textiles.

Conversely, Lambros Malafouris's theory of material engagement stresses how the objects in our environment are not just cognitive aids, but help to *constitute* thought. He argues, for instance, that the Linear B tablets were not simply passive vehicles for transmitting thought in the form of linguistic signs, but that these tablets, in their sensuous and spatial dimensions, actively shaped and transformed the task of recording and memorialising data: 'thinking is not simply a matter of reading a series of meaningful linguistic signs inscribed on the surface of a tablet, but also a matter of meaningfully engaging with the tablet itself as a material sign' (2013: 238). Malafouris's theory of material engagement will help to uncover how the sensuous qualities particular to certain materials (e.g. fabric, music, metal) can alter and shape the course of human engagement with that material.

As the above discussion makes clear, the intellectual orientation of this study is eclectic by design. By drawing on theoretical stances and terminology from both the new materialisms and accounts of embodied cognition, my goal is to elucidate as much as possible the sheer variety of forms – material and immaterial – that *poikilia* was thought to be able to assume in archaic and classical sources. Portrayals of *poikilia* in the literary and material record offer insight as to the media in which this quality could materialise as well as the effects of these materialisations on humans. At the same time, as is especially clear from literary representations, descriptions of *poikilia* themselves reveal the ways in which ancient sources conceptualised the relations between human bodies, minds and material things.

A brief look at one of the most famous objects in Western literature – the shield of Achilles – will preview the combined theoretical approach employed here.[13] The

---

[13] The bibliography on this ekphrasis is vast and continues to grow, but see Squire 2013 n.1 for a helpful and wide-ranging summary of the major studies devoted to this passage. I

ekphrasis devoted to Hephaestus' creation of Achilles' shield in *Iliad* 18 is the earliest and lengthiest meditation in Greek literature on the relationship between materiality, perception and cognition.[14] By verbally depicting the creation of a wondrously animate material object, the shield's ekphrasis takes as its central focus the fluid boundaries between humans and objects that have been scrutinised by the new materialists and theorists of embodied cognition. In this way, the passage vividly illustrates the kinds of human–material relations that will be parsed in each of the subsequent chapters: (1) the dynamism of matter and its perception; (2) the cognitive impact of material objects; (3) the manifestation of vitality in materials; and (4) the intersection of minds and materials embodied in the language used to describe objects.

One defining feature of this ekphrasis, as commentators both ancient and modern have observed, is that it describes the images wrought on the shield as though the figures are living beings. It thus literally depicts a form of vital materialism by imagining how a material thing (a 'shield both great and mighty', σάκος μέγα τε στιβαρόν τε, 18.478) can come to life. Most often, the vitality of the shield's imagery consists in its kinetic aspect: the figures portrayed within are not just lifelike in appearance, but seem to actually move of their own accord. People dance (18.494–5, 571–2, 594–5), engage in battle (18.516–40), plough and harvest (18.542–6, 550–6, 565–8), and, in general, behave like real human beings. Moreover, the shield's imagery is not just a visual phenomenon, but invokes the entire sensorium: sounds, textures, smells and tastes are all inscribed into its surface. Music plays (18.495, 569–70); people sing (18.493, 570–1) and speak (18.499–502); stones are polished (18.504); fields are soft (18.541) as are clothes (18.595); wine is honeysweet (18.545), so too is harvested fruit (18.568).[15] In addition, the shield's images represent the full gamut of human

highlight the following works as particularly apropos of my analysis here: Squire 2013 examines the legacy and influence of the Homeric ekphrasis in later Greek and Roman art and literature; Steiner 2001: 20–2 and Francis 2009 situate the ekphrasis within the wider context of archaic conceptions of images and likenesses; de Jong 2011, Heffernan 1993: 10–22 and Becker 1990 and 1995 focus on the metapoetic significance of the ekphrasis scene; while Scully 2003, Taplin 1980 and Hubbard 1992 concentrate on the poetics of the shield's description. See also Webb 2009 for the authoritative study of ekphrasis writ large in ancient thought and rhetoric.

[14] cf. Brown 2015: 1–8, who likewise opens his book on the object–thing relationship in art and literature with an 'overture' on this ekphrasis because, 'The poem repeatedly clarifies that Achilles' Shield is at once a static object and a living thing, just as it marks and celebrates the phantasmagoric oscillation between forms and materials . . . Homer's distribution of vitality extends beyond the immortal and the mortal – to the artifactual', 2.

[15] On the interpretation of the animate aspects of the shield in ancient commentary and exegesis, see Culhed 2014.

affect and emotion: there is joy (18.571–2), wonder (18.495–6), delight (18.603–5) as well as carnage (18.513–40) and conflict (18.497–500). In their sensory and affective plenitude, then, the shield's images seem to embody the richness of lived human experience.[16]

Having recourse to the entire sensorium in the portrayal of each image, the language of the ekphrasis poses the question of what it would mean for an image to come alive rather than be merely lifelike.[17] The only thing, after all, that distinguishes the figures in the shield from the characters of the surrounding epic narrative is that the former happen to appear within the description of the shield. For at the same time as the narrator insists on the sensuous and affective liveliness of the shield's imagery, he also repeatedly reminds his audience of the fact that these are images and not real beings by referring to the shield's material basis and Hephaestus' ongoing construction of it.

For instance, with the repetition of ἐν δ' throughout the passage, the narrator juxtaposes the material basis of the shield with the liveliness of the images contained therein. By relating how Hephaestus 'puts in/on' each scene, the narrator imputes a nonhuman, inanimate quality to the shield's materiality by portraying it as the passive vehicle for the lifelike scenes Hephaestus imposes on it. Indeed, the friction between the shield's appearance of life and its metallic quality is cited explicitly as the source of its wondrousness. At 18.549–50 the narrator remarks that 'the field grew dark behind them [the ploughmen], and seemed as though it had been ploughed although it was rendered in gold: such was the wonder that was wrought' (ἡ δὲ μελαίν' ὄπισθεν, ἀρηρομένη δὲ ἐῴκει, / χρυσείη περ ἐοῦσα· τὸ δὴ θαῦμα τέτυκτο). This interjection on the part of the narrator identifies the dialectic between vibrancy (the apparition of the ploughed field and the human activity therein) and materiality (the gold of the shield) that is operative throughout the shield's description. The twofold focus on the lifelike aspect of the shield as well as the nonhumanness of its material draws attention to the distinction between living beings and objects only to collapse them. The ekphrasis thus configures a complex and heterogeneous ontology for the shield. And in its handling of the entanglements between materiality, vitality and the language thereof, it provides an apt introduction to this study's examination of the mind–material interactions categorised under the rubric of *poikilia*.[18]

---

[16] cf. Hubbard 1992: 'The world of the shield is therefore not only the world of Homer's time, but the world as seen and represented through the various poetic arts as well as the visual arts', 29.

[17] cf. Steiner 2001: 'throughout his account [the Homeric ekphrasis] he underscores the paradox of representations that straddle the divisions between art and life, now talking of the images as though they were alive, now calling attention to the craftsmanship involved', 21.

[18] Here and throughout, I use the term 'entanglement' in the sense formulated by Ian Hodder,

That this collapse between humans and materials occurs within an ekphrasis that has been densely analysed for its entwining of verbal and visual media draws attention to the fact that the only distinguishing feature between animate beings and inanimate materials in the shield is a verbal one.[19] And in what follows, I want to suggest that the verbal–visual dialectic staged in the ekphrasis can be read as an analogue for the relation between humans and materials. More specifically, the concept of material agency – by which I mean the capacity for nonhuman entities to independently shape, constrain and/or enhance human thought and activity – will impart a new and richer understanding of the narrator's recourse to both verbal and plastic media.[20] This is because, as many critics have pointed out, the interplay between the verbal (the words of the narrator) and the visual or plastic (the work of craftsmen like Hephaestus) is generated from the ekphrasis' meditation on the distinctive affordances of words on the one hand and materials on the other.[21] The ekphrasis, I suggest, poses an ontological question of whether and how it would be possible in either medium to distinguish lively materials from living beings. And it is in the penultimate scene depicted on the shield that this question becomes the most pointed. In a complex layering of language, images

who neatly summarises how this term captures the mutual dependencies between persons and things: 'The distinctive aspect of entanglement derives from the attention given to the term "depend" in the relationships between things and between humans and things' (2012: 112). As Malafouris 2013: 33–4 details, his material engagement theory (and my own approach here) has much in common with Hodder's theory of entanglement, but focuses less on social processes and more on the 'process and making of the human mind', 34.

[19] On the dynamic between verbal and visual media staged in the ekphrasis see especially Squire 2013: 158–61, Francis 2009: 9–13 and Becker 1990 and 2003.

[20] My approach to material agency is thus much in line with Bielfeldt 2018's explanation of her approach to the intertwining of humans and objects: 'material things that engage people in a physical way and, in doing so, prompt them to reflect on the bodily conditions of human perception, existence, and history', 421. For a good summary of various formulations of 'material agency' and their relative strengths and weaknesses, see especially Johannsen 2012, who concludes that, 'archaeology may be much better off settling for a much simpler, more restricted and less ambitious concept of *agency* and allowing its attempts to capture the causal complexity of human cultural life to be structured not by the endless elaboration of one concept but by its interplay with many other important notions, like . . . activity, artefact, body, cognition, emotion, environment, history, inheritance, network, power, practice, sociality, structure, technology, and many more', 340.

[21] cf. Francis 2009: 'By the nature of his description, Homer invites comparison between the visual image of the shield and the words he uses to describe it, which communicate knowledge that the images cannot. Yet both images and words are the poet's creations, so that the result is a complex mirroring not only of the visual and verbal representation of the shield but also of the making of the shield and the making of the poem itself', 17.

and materials, Hephaestus' activity of *poikilia* consists in his crafting an image of dancing youths:

ἐν δὲ χορὸν <u>ποίκιλλε</u> περικλυτὸς ἀμφιγυήεις,
τῷ ἴκελον οἷόν ποτ' ἐνὶ Κνωσῷ εὐρείη
Δαίδαλος ἤσκησεν καλλιπλοκάμῳ Ἀριάδνῃ.
ἔνθα μὲν ἠΐθεοι καὶ παρθένοι ἀλφεσίβοιαι
ὀρχεῦντ' ἀλλήλων ἐπὶ καρπῷ χεῖρας ἔχοντες.

And in it the renowned, lame-footed god was <u>crafting</u> a dance floor, like the one that Daidalos once fashioned for fair-haired Ariadne in broad Knossos. And there youths and desirable maidens were dancing, holding one another on their wrists. (*Il.* 18.590–4)

This is the only time in the ekphrasis that the terminology of *poikilia* appears at all, and its appearance in this penultimate scene marks a change from the ekphrasis' previous characterisations of Hephaestus' work in terms of *daidal/* (479, 482), *poiē/* (490, 573, 587) or *tithē/* (541, 550, 561).[22] It is also the only time in archaic epic that the verbal form of ποικίλλω appears. So too is the beginning of the shield's creation highlighted with the use of the rare verb δαιδάλλω (πάντοσε δαιδάλλων, 18.479), which occurs only one other time in Homeric epic (*Od.* 23.200).[23] While the adjectival forms of each word (*daidal/* and *poikil/*) are common throughout Homer, where they describe aesthetic attributes of objects, their unusual verbal forms appear only in the context of an ekphrasis, which by definition involves the interplay between plastic and verbal media. This invites further scrutiny. Given the adjective's prominence as an attribute of Homeric objects, the use here of the verbal form of ποίκιλλε seems designed to encapsulate a paradox that operates throughout the ekphrasis: namely, how and where to distinguish the visual qualities imagined to exist in the shield from the verbal aspects of its description. In other words, does the *poikilia* picked out by this verb characterise the image within the shield, or the story of the image that is communicated by the narrator? The use of the verb ποικίλλω thus poses the question of where, or to whom, to ascribe agency: is it the narrator, Hephaestus and/or the shield itself that generates the object's wondrous effects?

The intricacy and beauty of the scene denoted by ποίκιλλε indeed conforms with other uses of this terminology in Homer. First, Hephaestus crafts a 'dance floor' (ἐν

[22] Here I disagree with Morris 1992, who claims that the narrator uses ποικίλλω only 'after exhausting the repertoire of verbs appropriate to the craftsmanship of Hephaistos', 13.
[23] On the significance of *daidal/* here see especially Morris 1992: 11–13.

δὲ χορὸν <u>ποίκιλλε</u> περικλυτὸς ἀμφιγυήεις, 590) populated by dancing youths (ἔνθα μὲν ἠΐθεοι καὶ παρθένοι ἀλφεσίβοιαι / ὀρχεῦντ᾽, 593–4) surrounded by an admiring crowd of onlookers (πολλὸς δ᾽ ἱμερόεντα χορὸν περιίσταθ᾽ ὅμιλος / τερπόμενοι, 604–5). Here too, as in the description of the ploughed field discussed above, the narrator makes the materiality of the shield a source of its visual interest: the dancers are clad in 'fine linen' and 'well-made chitons faintly glistening with oil' (τῶν δ᾽ αἳ μὲν λεπτὰς ὀθόνας ἔχον, οἳ δὲ χιτῶνας / εἵατ᾽ ἐϋννήτους, ἦκα στίλβοντας ἐλαίῳ, 595–6). The apparition of fabric occurs in spite of the fact that the shield is comprised solely of metal, to which the next verses seem to allude in relating that the young men in the image carry 'golden daggers suspended from silver sword-belts' (οἳ δὲ μαχαίρας εἶχον χρυσείας ἐξ ἀργυρέων τελαμώνων, 596–7). It is unclear whether the 'golden' of the daggers is meant to refer to their appearance or to their material composition, but the very ambiguity of its referent – as in the use of ποίκιλλε – points up the seamlessness of the blend between the material constitution of the shield and the language of its description. The close intermingling effected in the language of these verses – between the material qualities of the shield (the 'golden' daggers) and the attributes of the image as it appears to the narrator (the appearance of linen and shining chitons) – makes it impossible to ascribe a uniform ontology to the shield, comprised as it is of both language and material substances, of human and nonhuman forces.

The vibrancy of this scene, as elsewhere in the ekphrasis, is also expressed in the fact that it is not inert and static, but dynamic and energetic. This is because the progression of the dance movements also manifests in the image, as the narrator conveys how the dancers first move in a circular fashion (οἳ δ᾽ ὁτὲ μὲν θρέξασκον ἐπισταμένοισι πόδεσσι / ῥεῖα μάλ᾽, 599–600) and then in rows (ἄλλοτε δ᾽ αὖ θρέξασκον ἐπὶ στίχας ἀλλήλοισι, 602). And the dynamism of this scene is reflected in the very language used to describe it. That the construction of this scene is characterised with the verbal form of *poikilia* (ἐν δὲ χορὸν <u>ποίκιλλε</u>, 590) in the imperfect tense creates a temporal and aspectual congruity between Hephaestus' activity of crafting the image and the activities of the figures within the scene, which are also described in the imperfect.

While the use of the imperfect tense predominates in Homeric epic, the appearance of this tense within the ekphrasis imparts to it a special significance because it emphasises how the narrator is describing not just an object, but the process of *creating* one.[24] The progressive aspect of the verbal form that predominates throughout the

---

[24] cf. Francis 2009, 'The principal focus of the poet's descriptive energy is on the shield, and the context of the description is not a static appreciation of the completed work but rather the dynamic process of the god fabricating it. The emphasis is on the making, yet it

ekphrasis (ἐτίθει, 'he was placing' at 18.541, 550, 561), in conjunction with the use of the same tense in the description of the figures within each scene, creates the impression that the images delineated by Hephaestus come to life and move even as he is still in the process of generating them.[25] And this correlation between the progressive aspect of Hephaestus' making and the dynamism visible in each image in turn frames the audience's *perception* of the shield as an equally dynamic and enactive process. This is because the effect of emphasising the progression of the shield's creation is to also underscore how each scene comes into being and comes before the audience's eyes coterminously with Hephaestus' construction of it. And by portraying the creation as well as the perception of the shield as a continuously unfolding process, the narrator ascribes a form of vitality to the shield that consists in its being not fixed or unmoving, but an active kind of becoming.

The vitality of the shield emerges from the grammar of its description, but becomes even more starkly visible in its impact on humans. Both within and outside of the ekphrasis proper, significant emphasis is allocated to the cognitive effects of Hephaestus' creation. Most prominent of these is *thauma*: Hephaestus promises Thetis that the shield will evoke *thauma*, 'wonder', in anyone who sees it (θαυμάσσεται, ὅς κεν ἴδηται, *Il.* 18.467). As Christine Hunzinger has well shown, *thauma* occupies an ambiguous place in archaic aesthetics precisely because of its essentially paradoxical nature, as a response that arises in the space between the perception of objects or phenomena and the perceiver's awareness of that perception.[26] As Raymond Prier has shown in his 1989 study of the language of sight and wonder in Homer, the poet does not distinguish between a viewing subject and a viewed object: instead, Prier identifies 'relational projections' between the 'this' and the

is not even so much the making of the shield per se as it is the god's creation of the images ornamenting it', 9. This aspect of the shield is also something that Lessing 1984: 91–103 dwells on in his essay on the aesthetic principles of poetry versus painting. For discussion of Lessing's contributions to contemporary understanding of this ekphrasis see especially Squire 2013: 160–1.

[25] cf. Webb 2009: 69–70 on this ekphrasis as an example of an *ekphrasis tropou*, which she defines as '[a] class of subject matter which abolishes any strict boundary between "objects" and "actions"', 69.

[26] 'Resulting from the conjunction of a perceived object and the perception that the subject trains upon it, *thauma* is neither an objective quality of the world nor a feeling separable, for the subject, from the perception of an "outside" . . . *thauma* is situated in this "in-between", external to the being perceiving it but constructed by his subjective perception' (Hunzinger 2015: 424). See also the penetrating comments of Neer 2010, developed from Prier 1989: 'As for wonder, it forms a hinge or joint linking the poles of "this" and "that". The word *thauma*, "wonder", is itself intermediate between the two. It does not simply name a class of objects, but also a state of mind', 2010: 67.

'that' operative in Homeric depictions of sight and seeing.[27] The 'this' he defines as the outward movements of the gaze ('grasping, darting sight', 116), while the 'that' consists in the appearance emanating from persons or things (its 'divine', 'outer' appearance, ibid.). On this view, then, the *thauma* said to be induced by the shield is a response that itself reproduces the ontological blurring between material objects and human beings that is already inscribed within the surface of the shield.

Hephaestus' promise to evoke wonder is then vividly borne out in the following book of the *Iliad*. When Thetis presents Achilles' new armour, it 'rings out' (τὰ δ' ἀνέβραχε δαίδαλα πάντα, 19.13) and causes the Myrmidons to tremble. So profound, in fact, is their trepidation that they cannot even look at the arms (Μυρμιδόνας δ' ἄρα πάντας ἕλε τρόμος, οὐδέ τις ἔτλη / ἄντην εἰσιδέειν, ἀλλ' ἔτρεσαν, 19.14–15). Achilles, on the other hand, is filled simultaneously with wrath (ὡς εἶδ', ὥς μιν μᾶλλον ἔδυ χόλος, 19.16) and with pleasure (τέρπετο δ' ἐν χείρεσσιν ἔχων θεοῦ ἀγλαὰ δῶρα. / αὐτὰρ ἐπεὶ φρεσὶν ᾗσι τετάρπετο δαίδαλα λεύσσων, 19.18–19). The shield – a nonhuman substance – thus acts as a vector of human emotional and affective response.[28] It is significant too that these responses are brought about because of the sensuous properties of the shield (and not, for instance, from viewers' interpretation of the scenes therein): it 'rings out' (τὰ δ' ἀνέβραχε δαίδαλα πάντα, 19.13), emits 'a beam like that of the moon' (αὐτὰρ ἔπειτα σάκος μέγα τε στιβαρόν τε / εἵλετο, τοῦ δ' ἀπάνευθε σέλας γένετ' ἠΰτε μήνης, 19.373–4) and is something that Achilles touches (τέρπετο δ' ἐν χείρεσσιν ἔχων) and gazes at (δαίδαλα λεύσσων) (19.18–19). In the highly sensuous encounters portrayed in these passages, the shield vividly typifies material agency in the sense in which it is articulated by Nicole Boivin, who defines it as, 'the means by which the material world plays an active role in constituting human society *because of its material qualities*' (2008: 27, emphasis added).

As we have seen, one feature consistently alluded to as the source of the shield's marvellousness is its presentation of the animate within a material surface: the figures

---

[27] Prier 1989: 19: 'While we cannot describe the archaic worldview in terms of a conscious subject against a derived, abstracted, intentioned object, it is possible to describe the places and at least partial parameters of experience in terms of the *relational* projections from the point or intention of the "this" and the relational projections emanating from the "other" or "that".'

[28] See Telò and Mueller 2018: 3 for an apt illustration of the relationship between the new materialisms and the so-called 'affective turn' in the humanities, 'This attention to nonhuman actors can, in turn, lead to a different outlook on the human subject in Greek tragedy, one that challenges the individual's bodily and psychological autonomy through consideration of emotions as a complex of material intensities that move beyond bodily borders, consciousness and unconsciousness.'

and objects portrayed within 'look like' their real-world counterparts in spite of their different material composition. But the penultimate scene of the dance performance articulates still another form of resemblance at work in the shield. Unique to this section of the ekphrasis is the narrator's recourse to two different similes in close succession: one that characterises Hephaestus' work of crafting the image and one that characterises the movements of the dancers. This imparts a further complexity to this scene that throws into high relief the relation between Hephaestus' craftsmanship and that of the Homeric poet.

First, Hephaestus' *choros* is said to be like the one Daidalos made for Ariadne (τῷ ἴκελον οἷόν ποτ' ἐνὶ Κνωσῷ εὐρείῃ / Δαίδαλος ἤσκησεν καλλιπλοκάμῳ Ἀριάδνῃ).[29] This simile is thus unusual in its comparison of a god to a mortal, but the reference to Daidalos also recalls the earlier characterisation of Hephaestus' images and image-making with the terminology of *daidal/*. As Michael Squire has recently argued, the effect of these repeated evocations of the mythological craftsman known for bringing his statues to life 'resonates with the poet's own "daedalic" language for verbally delineating the visual nature of the shield' (2013: 160). And here, this 'daedalic' language consists in the simile itself, whose deployment specifically in order to evoke Daidalos points up how the device of the simile is one way that the narrator parallels in language the kind of image-making effected by craftsmen like Hephaestus and Daidalos.[30]

The comparison of Hephaestus to a sculptor famous for his incredibly lifelike statues is of a piece with the ekphrasis' persistent attention to the interplay between vitality and matter that can be communicated in the verbal as well as the plastic arts. In this context, however, the narrator's evocation of Daidalos imagines how the living beings dancing in the chorus can resemble works of craftsmanship, rather than how images on the shield (like that of the ploughed field) resemble their real-life counterparts. Mark Edwards, for instance, has suggested that this is the significance

---

[29] The interpretation of *choros* in this particular line is problematic because it is unclear what kind of *choros* Daidalos is supposed to have fashioned for Ariadne. Various interpretations have been put forth suggesting that it could refer to a dancing floor, a dancing place or an actual chorus of dancers. Since I am only interested in the *choros* as it is portrayed within the shield and not its specific precedent in one of Daidalos' creations, I translate *choros* simply as 'dance floor'. For the interpretation of the term as a dancing floor, see the Homeric Scholia A, b, T ad Σ 590 (IV.564); as a dance hall, cf. Paus. 9.40.3 and the Homer scholia T ad Σ 590(c). Alternatively, Kurke 2013: 158 proposes that the term could also be understood as referring to a chorus of animated statues of the sort that Daidalos was famous for creating; cf. Frontisi-Ducroux 1975: 64–71, 135–7.

[30] On the imagistic quality of Homeric similes see especially Minchin 2001 and Becker 1995: 49–50 on the relation between the shield ekphrasis and similes elsewhere in Homer.

of the verb ποικίλλω here: 'Possibly the word hints that this picture is more in the nature of a decorative frieze, like the rows of identical figures on Geometric vases, than a real-life episode like the others on the shield' (1991 ad 18.590–2). Similarly, Leslie Kurke has proposed that the reference to Daidalos' chorus intimates that this was 'a "chorus" of animated statues that moved and danced in unison, wrought of precious metal just like the dancers on Hephaestus' shield' (2013: 158).[31] The dancers on the shield, in their beautiful, shining clothing, thus visualise how living beings can take on the qualities of crafted objects.[32] This, too, is the idea conveyed by the second simile adduced in this passage.

The second simile compares the movements of the chorus crafted by Hephaestus to another form of craftsmanship: that of a potter at his wheel. More specifically, the dexterity of the chorus' feet is compared to that of a potter's hands:

οἳ δ᾽ ὁτὲ μὲν θρέξασκον ἐπισταμένοισι πόδεσσι
ῥεῖα μάλ᾽, ὡς ὅτε τις τροχὸν ἄρμενον ἐν παλάμῃσιν
ἑζόμενος κεραμεὺς πειρήσεται, αἴ κε θέῃσιν

And they were running in circles very nimbly with their cunning feet, as when a potter sits with a wheel fitted in his hands and tests it to see if it will run. (599–601)

The use of ἐπιστάμενος to characterise the dancers' feet is unusual, as elsewhere the term in Homer only describes people.[33] In its transference to feet, these limbs are personified as possessing a unique form of intelligence that manifests itself in their dexterous movements. By extension, too, are the hands of the potter (ἐν παλάμῃσιν) allotted an analogous cognitive skill, made visible in his 'testing' the run of his wheel.[34] This use of ἐπιστάμενος thus depicts skill not as a brain-bound faculty, but as a kinetic and bodily activity – an idea that, as we will see, is prominent in portrayals of *poikilia*'s fabrication.

Like the comparison to Daidalos a few verses earlier, that the dancing is compared

---

[31] Kurke nicely captures the oscillation between crafted objects and living beings conveyed in the dancers' description: 'the represented dancers instead emerge as "real" human beings, only to be assimilated once again to objects of craft with the diadems, golden daggers, and silver belts of lines 597–8, and the simile of the potter's wheel in lines 600–1' (2013: 158).

[32] For a fuller elaboration of this idea see especially Steiner 2001 passim (especially pp. 95–104 and 186–98).

[33] Edwards 1991 ad 18.599–602.

[34] On the significance of gesture in Homeric epic more broadly see especially Purves 2019. On the cognitive role of the hands in particular and their importance for human evolution see the fascinating study of Lundborg 2013.

to a craftsman at work underscores how the beauty of the chorus is such that they resemble finely crafted objects. This simile reinforces the potential overlap between artefacts and living beings expressed in the earlier simile's evocation of Daidalos. The dancers are portrayed both in the shield and in its description like living beings, possessed of the ability to act and move (similar to the other figures contained within the shield). Simultaneously, however, their radiance and skilful movements are evocative of the sorts of wondrous and lifelike objects crafted by Daidalos as well as by Hephaestus himself. The narrator thus employs the simile of the potter at his wheel to layer image (of the shield's creation) upon image (of the penultimate scene depicted on the shield) upon image (of the potter's activity evoked by the dancers' portrayal within the shield) and, in doing so, encapsulates the play between matter and vitality that, as I have argued, is operative throughout the ekphrasis. More specifically, these two similes in combination deal directly with an idea that runs implicitly throughout this passage: namely, that human bodies are themselves material, sensuous beings, not unlike their counterparts in the plastic arts.[35]

In its beauty and in its conceptual complexity, the penultimate scene in the ekphrasis illuminates the key facets of *poikilia* that will be explored in the following chapters. First, insofar as the ekphrasis of the shield dramatises the literal animation of metal, the passage as a whole offers a lengthy meditation on the potential for matter to acquire vitality. The passage intimates throughout that humans and material things need not exist in a dichotomous and hierarchical relationship, but can intersect and interact in much the same way as the verbal and visual arts do. The continual slippage between living beings and lifelike images staged in the language of the shield's description, moreover, ultimately suggests that this ontological indeterminacy is what gives the shield its marvellous power. As the subsequent chapters will disclose, the entanglement between human and nonhuman entities so densely inscribed in the shield's ekphrasis will prove to be a prominent locus of aesthetic value in archaic and classical texts and art.

The first chapter's concentration on the *poikilia* of fabric will take up the dynamism of matter and perception that, in the ekphrasis, is visible in the animate quality of the images themselves as well as in the progressive aspect of the verbs used within its description. The second chapter focuses in particular on the cognitive life of metal substances by identifying the different forms of agency located in this material across a variety of Homeric battle scenes. The third chapter investigates from a different angle the ontological fluidity of metal delineated in the second by focusing

---

[35] On this point (the materiality of the human body) see especially Bennett 2010: 111–13, on how 'Materiality is a rubric that tends to horizontalize the relations between humans, biota, and abiota', 112.

on representations of lifelike and living metallic artefacts in Homer and Hesiod. These accounts of automata imagine different ways in which cognitive processes may extend out of the brain and into the world within forms of technology. The fourth chapter will delve deeper into the affective and poetic character of *poikilia* by investigating the allure exercised by this quality across a variety of objects invoked by the likes of Sappho and Pindar. The fifth and sixth chapters are devoted to the intersection of *poikilia* and cunning or deceit, and the aim in each is to elucidate not only how *poikilia* names the extension of mental qualities into the phenomenal world, but also how this extension breaks down along gendered lines: feminine minds, as Chapter 6 details, manifest and use *poikilia* in a manner distinct from male ones. For while the masculine figures that are the focus of Chapter 5 deploy their cunning in their fashioning of objects and ruses, feminine characters do not create but *manipulate* objects in such a way as to deceive their targets.

The conclusion returns to the issue of language and materiality by focusing on *poikilia*'s role as a critical term for capturing the complexities of music and other aesthetic phenomena. There it will become clear how the mind–material interactivity intrinsic to *poikilia* (an interactivity whose contours the preceding chapters have delineated) lends its terminology a particular aptitude for identifying the characteristics and effects of complex phenomena. By looking in particular at Plato's repeated evocations of *poikilia* in the *Republic*, this section ties together a number of ideas addressed individually in each of the preceding chapters: the forms of material agency embodied in artefacts named with *poikilia*, the effects of those artefacts on human thought and perception, and the role of language in explicating the relations between human minds and bodies on the one hand and sensuous forms of *poikilia* on the other.

1   A Beautiful Mind: Patterns of Thought and the Decoration of Textiles

THE CONCEPT OF *poikilia* finds its most ample reification in fabric. In texts as well as in statuary and painting, garments (especially those on female figures) often display a degree of complex ornamentation that is intrinsic to *poikilia*. Since *poikilia* is most often associated with cloth from its earliest attestations onwards, it is fitting to begin a study of the material and cognitive dimensions of *poikilia* with a focus on the textilic. This is also a thread which the final chapter will pick up again in its exploration of *poikilia* in the textiles of Greek tragedy. And this close relationship between *poikilia* and fabric finds expression in the etymology of the *poikilia* word family itself. The earliest linguistic predecessors of the root *poikil/* denoted activities of manual craftsmanship as well as the decorated textiles that were the products of such techniques.[1] Thus the linguistic origins of *poikilia* already reveal this concept's basis in particular kinds of material products *and* in the processes that create such products.

From an etymological perspective, then, *poikilia* is situated at the intersection between embodied processes (like weaving) and the perception of specific kinds of materials (like fabric). This chapter, therefore, seeks to address the following points of inquiry: how and why, exactly, was *poikilia* thought to enhance the appearance of textiles? In order to approach this question, I draw on a variety of contemporary theories and terms, and these will continue to inform our readings in subsequent chapters. For what makes *poikilia* apt for bridging the ancient–modern divide is

---

[1] See Chantraine 1968: 923–4; cf. Bader 1987. Chantraine translates **peik-/pik-*as 'piquer, marquer', 'to stitch, to mark', cf. Sanskrit *péśa* ('to ornament', 'to adorn') and the Avestan *paēsa*, which also refers to adornment. The same root appears in Linear B as *po-ki-ro-nu-ka*, where it is used to describe the decorated borders (*o-nu-ka*) of garments (KN Ld 579.a, L 598, cf. Chadwick and Baumbach 1963: 226–7, 237).

that both ancient sources and modern theories grapple with how the human brain responds to and evaluates complex perceptual stimuli. The *poikilia* of fabric provides a particularly good example of just such a stimulus, since, as the first section of this chapter will show, the quality of *poikilia* was recognised even in antiquity to have peculiar visual effects.

By looking at examples from vase painting, statuary and texts, we will find here that the *poikilia* of fabric (and its concomitant effects) was conceptualised in a variety of ways that testify to the rich cognitive life of this material.[2] And taken together, these distinctive manifestations of *poikilia* make plain that this quality was valued not for the sake of mere decoration, but because of how *poikilia* enhanced sensory experience.[3] Decorated cloth will emerge as a multifaceted form of materiality, one that both reflects and invites engagement with human agents. My central claim here is that the perception as well as the production of *poikilia* in fabric can be charac-terised as an enactive process in which minds, bodies (particularly feminine bodies) and material things play equally important roles in the construction of *poikilia*'s experience. The perception of *poikilia* will turn out to be (to borrow the phrasing of O'Regan and Noë 2001 in their characterisation of visual perception writ large) 'something we *do*' rather than something that happens *to* a human perceiver.[4] As we

---

[2] In using the phrase 'cognitive life' in this way I am adopting the terminology and method-ology espoused by Malafouris and Renfrew 2010, who identify the cognitive life of things as: (1) the fluid and relational dynamic between humans and inanimate objects ('Things have a cognitive life because intelligence exists primarily as an enactive relation between and among people and things, not as a within-intracranial representation', 4); and (2) the capacity for things to have agency and thus shape human activity and thought ('[the term "cognitive life of things"] is introduced to counteract the prevailing assumption that only humans have cognitive lives, or agency', 5).

[3] This chapter's interest in the function and effects of non-figural designs across a variety of media is thus aligned with the focus of Dietrich and Squire 2018's volume on ornament and figure in ancient Greek and Roman art. They identify one of their central questions as, 'If classical traditions of image-making are recurrently celebrated for their mimetic natural-ism, what role should we ascribe to visual components that exceed, defy or destabilise that figurative dimension? Can we talk about "ornament" as a meaningful (which is to say, per-haps, meaning*less*) category in Greek and Roman Art?', (2, emphasis in original). Similarly, see also Platt and Squire 2017, which investigates how frames and framing devices interact with figural imagery in Graeco-Roman art forms, as well as Swift 2009's study of Roman decoration and its social functions.

[4] O'Regan and Noë 2001's 'A sensorimotor account of vision and visual consciousness' is a foundational article for Noë 2004's *Action in Perception*, which elaborates on the enactivist theory of perception formulated in the 2001 publication. This is a theory that Noë expands on in a slightly different direction in his 2012 book, which focuses on the relationship between sensorimotor presence and intentionality.

will see, the intricate fabric patterning captured by the terminology of *poikilia* fosters particular ways of viewing the objects in which this decoration appears, analogous to the way that the weaving of *poikilia* implicates both cognitive and bodily dimensions of the weaver.

In the first section of this chapter I establish the relationship between polychromy and *poikilia* in fabric. In doing so I will demonstrate how the quality of *poikilia* in this medium prompted reflection in ancient sources on the nature of colour perception. And this scrutiny devoted to the scintillating effects associated with *poikilia* in fabric is borne out in the material and literary records, where *poikilia* is likewise a source of heightened visual interest. Further, the intricate designs denoted by *poikilia* make this a fruitful concept to consider in light of recent theories of perception that stress the active and embodied component of vision, especially in relation to complex phenomena. For this reason, I then turn in the next two sections to case studies in statuary and vase painting. While sculpture and painting render *poikilia* in manners distinct to each medium, in both forms the elaborate, geometric patterning of garments plays an integral role in guiding viewers in the construction of the larger images in which they appear. In this sense, the examples adduced in these sections encourage an enactive approach to perception, and in the last section I identify a corollary to this mode of perception in the literary descriptions of *poikilia*'s production. As will become clear from these passages, no hard and fast distinction between the mental and manual applies to the weaving of *poikilia*. Instead, the appearance of this quality in fabric provided tangible testimony of the cognitive and physical processes that went into its production.

Poikilia, Polychromy and Perception

In the literary and epigraphic record, the terminology of *poikilia* consistently serves to mark out textiles that are elaborately patterned or ornamented. In Homer, for instance, Andromache 'works in <u>brightly hued</u> flowers' (ἐν δὲ θρόνα <u>ποικίλ</u>' ἔπασσε, *Il.* 22.440–1) into her weaving and Athena is said to wear a *poikilos peplos* that she 'made herself with her own hands' (ὅν ῥ' αὐτὴ ποιήσατο καὶ κάμε χερσίν, *Il.* 5.735 = *Il.* 8.386). That this quality makes fabric particularly valuable and therefore worthy of dedicating to a goddess is also reflected in the word's prominence in temple inventories. For instance, a fourth-century inventory from the Heraion on Samos

The conclusions drawn here are also very much in line with those of Hölscher 2018: 330, who throughout this monograph emphasises the reciprocal relationship between ancient viewers and images: 'in antiquity the appropriate way of dealing with images was not pure viewing and interpreting images but actively participating in the world and life of images'.

(c. 346–345 BCE) includes a 'cloak interwoven with gold and having a golden myrtle' (κιθωνίσκος χρυσῶι πεποικιλμένος μύρτον χρύσεον ἔχων, *IG* II 6, 1, 261.17–18), a formulation that indicates how the process denoted by the participle 'interwoven' (πεποικιλμένος) consisted in the decoration of fabric with additional precious material like gold.[5] Likewise, in the Brauron clothing catalogues, an inscription listing the vestments dedicated to Artemis Brauronia in 446 (*IG* II 754.8–9 = Michel, no. 819, 8–9) records a cloak (χιθωνίσκος) that is 'entirely decorated' (περιποίκιλος), with the prefix περί suggesting that the whole garment was adorned. More specifically, the adjective probably refers to the *grammata* (which could denote either letters or images) that were woven into the fabric (γράμμ[ματ]α ἐ|νυφασμένα, 3). And *poikilia*'s connection to the divine is not unique to written testimonia. As we will see, the lavish decoration of the Acropolis korai likewise attests to *poikilia*'s efficacy as a feature of those objects designed to delight the gods: *agalmata*.

As the participle 'woven in' (ἐνυφασμένα) suggests in the entry from the Brauron clothing catalogues, the patterning characterised as *poikilia* probably involved the intertwining of different-coloured threads rather than the superaddition of decoration onto pre-existing fabric.[6] The result could be a luminous, even glittering aspect, as is clear from two Homeric descriptions of 'decorated robes', *poikiloi peploi*. Helen and Hecuba each offer up a *peplos* that is 'most beautiful and ample in its decoration' (ὃς κάλλιστος ἔην ποικίλμασιν ἠδὲ μέγιστος, *Il.* 6.294–5 and *Od.* 15.106–8) and 'shines like a star' (ἀστὴρ δ᾽ ὣς ἀπέλαμπεν, *Il.* 6.295 and *Od.* 15.108). The idea that intricate patterning could lend fabric such an aspect finds illustration in the material record, particularly in one of the most famous works attributed to Exekias (Fig. 1.1). In this black-figure amphora from the mid-sixth century, Achilles and Ajax play a board game, each clad in an intricately patterned cloak. The unique designs of each one – formed from countless tiny geometric shapes incised into black slip – create myriad points of white light that indeed make each garment seem to glitter in the manner envisioned in the Homeric simile 'shone like a star'.[7]

That *poikilia* in textiles can produce such an effect chimes with Aristotle's discussion of the vagaries of colour perception, where the polychromy of textiles is

---

[5] See, most recently, Brøns 2017 on textile dedications in Greek sanctuaries from the seventh to first centuries BCE.

[6] On the prevalence of weaving as opposed to embroidery in Greek textile production, see especially Wace 1948, Barber 1991: 359 n. 2, Lee 2015: 15, and Dross-Krüpe and Paetz gen. Schieck 2014. While I am convinced by these arguments, my analysis here is nonetheless not affected by whether *poikilia* was achieved entirely by weaving or whether such a process included something more akin to embroidery.

[7] cf. Fowler 1984: 136, who was the first to my knowledge to link the lyric poets' delight in *poikilia* with the depiction of ornamented textiles in vase paintings.

Figure 1.1 Amphora by Exekias, depicting Achilles and Ajax playing a game (c. 550-540 BCE).
Photo: Image by Wikimedia Commons user Sailko, shared under the CC BY-SA 3.0 licence

held up as an example of the illusory effects that result from colours in combination. In *Meteorologica*, he claims that a rainbow only *appears* to exhibit a streak of a yellowy-orange and that this is an optical illusion generated by the juxtaposition of red and green: 'The yellowy colour appears to be there because it appears between the others, for red seems light alongside green' (τὸ δὲ ξανθὸν φαίνεται διὰ τὸ παρ' ἄλληλα φαίνεσθαι. τὸ γὰρ φοινικοῦν παρὰ τὸ πράσινον λευκὸν φαίνεται, *Mete.* 375a6–8).[8] That this effect was thought to be prominent in textiles is marked by the fact that Aristotle goes on to cite the use of dyes in fabric as further illustration of this kind of illusion:

γίγνεται δὲ τοῦτο τὸ πάθος καταφανὲς καὶ ἐπὶ τῶν ἀνθῶν· ἐν γὰρ τοῖς ὑφάσμασιν καὶ <u>ποικίλμασιν</u> ἀμύθητον διαφέρει τῇ φαντασίᾳ ἄλλα παρ' ἄλλα τιθέμενα τῶν

---

[8] For a fuller explanation of the optical illusion to which Aristotle here refers, see Keuls 1997: 141–2, who sees Aristotle's remark here as a description of the effects of optical fusion. On differing conceptualisations of the rainbow in ancient Graeco-Roman thought, see especially Bradley 2009: 36–55 and also the discussion by Grand-Clément 2011: 10–11 and 415–17.

χρωμάτων, οἷον καὶ τὰ πορφύρα ἐν λευκοῖς ἢ μέλασιν ἐρίοις, ἔτι δ ἐν αὐγῇ τοιαδὶ ἢ τοιαδί· διὸ καὶ οἱ <u>ποικιλταί</u> φασι διαμαρτάνειν ἐργαζόμενοι πρὸς τὸν λύχνον πολλάκις τῶν ἀνθῶν, λαμβάνοντες ἕτερα ἀνθ᾽ ἑτέρων.

The same effect is visible in dyes. For the placement of different colours along-side others in woven and <u>decorated textiles</u> (ποικίλμασιν) produces an indescrib-able (ἀμύθητον) difference in the appearance (φαντασίᾳ) of their colours, such as purple against white versus black; and a similar difference occurs when colours appear in one kind of light or another. For this reason, <u>pattern weavers</u> (ποικιλταί) say that they often make mistakes in the dyes when working in lamplight and end up choosing the wrong colours. (*Mete.* 375a22–8)

It is telling that Aristotle refers specifically to the *poikilia* of textiles as an example of the impressionistic nature of colour perception, because this suggests that their phenomenological effects were distinctive and well known enough to elucidate his broader point. The pseudo-Aristotelian author of the *De Coloribus* is even more explicit about the visual effects produced by polychromy in textiles. Like Aristotle, this author testifies that the illusory nature of colour perception is particularly appar-ent when colours are combined with one another. Artificial dyes in fabric are again used to elaborate this point:

βάπτεται δὲ καὶ τὰ μέλανα τῶν ἐρίων, οὐ μὴν ὁμοίως γε τῷ χρώματι γίγνεται λαμπρά, διὰ τὸ βάπτεσθαι τοὺς πόρους αὐτῶν εἰς τοὺς τῶν ἀνθῶν εἰσιόντας, τὰ δὲ μεταξὺ διαστήματα τῆς τριχὸς μηδεμίαν λαμβάνειν βαφήν. ταῦτα λευκὰ μὲν ὄντα, καὶ παρ᾽ ἄλληλα κείμενα τοῖς χρώμασι, ποιεῖ πάντα φαίνεσθαι τὰ ἄνθη λαμπρότερα· τὰ μέλανα δὲ τοὐναντίον σκιερὰ καὶ ζοφώδη. διὸ καὶ τὸ καλούμενον ὄρφνιον εὐανθέστερον γίνεται τῶν μελάνων ἢ τῶν λευκῶν· οὕτω γὰρ ἀκρατέστερον αὐτῶν φαίνεται τὸ ἄνθος, κεραννύμενον ταῖς τοῦ μέλανος αὐγαῖς. (794a32–794b7)

When black fleeces are dyed they do not become uniformly bright in colour, because their passages are dyed when the dye enters into them, but the spaces in between the hair receive no dye. These being white, when they lay side by side with the colours (of the dyes), they make the dyes appear brighter. Conversely, the black parts are shadowy and dark. For this reason, that which is called brown-grey becomes brighter on black wool rather than on white. For in this case the dye appears purer from being mixed with the rays of the black. (trans. Hett 1936, slightly modified)

According to this text, the imposition of colours against a dark or light background in turn can enhance their brightness and make the whole object appear 'more luminous' (λαμπρότερα). The author here thus elucidates the 'indescribable difference' (ἀμύθητον διαφέρει, 375a23) alluded to in the passage from the *Meteorologica* quoted above. Further, like Aristotle, the author of *De Coloribus* clearly recognises that the variable nature of colour perception is particularly marked in the perception of multiple colours in juxtaposition.

Testimony from other sources suggests that the value afforded to *poikilia* in textiles may have derived precisely from its scintillating visual aspect. Plato, for instance, famously denigrates *poikilia* in numerous works for its sensuous appeal, as in the *Hippias Major*, where 'fancy, decorative stuff' (τὰ ποικίλματα) is classed among those objects whose visual allure is such as to suggest that 'the beautiful' (τὸ καλόν) consists in that 'which pleases through sight or hearing' (τὸ καλόν ἐστι τὸ δι' ἀκοῆς τε καὶ δι' ὄψεως ἡδύ, 298a1–3). Even more pointed in its critique of sensuous pleasure is Plato's adoption of the image of the 'multicoloured cloak' in *Republic* 8 as a paradigm of the illusory appeal of democracy,

> ὥσπερ ἱμάτιον <u>ποικίλον</u> πᾶσιν ἄνθεσι <u>πεποικιλμένον</u>, οὕτω καὶ αὕτη πᾶσιν ἤθεσιν <u>πεποικιλμένη</u> καλλίστη ἂν φαίνοιτο. καὶ ἴσως μέν, ἦν δ' ἐγώ, καὶ ταύτην, ὥσπερ οἱ παῖδές τε καὶ αἱ γυναῖκες τὰ <u>ποικίλα</u> θεώμενοι, καλλίστην ἂν πολλοὶ κρίνειαν.

> 'Just like a <u>multicoloured</u> cloak <u>brightly decorated</u> with all kinds of flowers, so this state <u>adorned</u> with all kinds of characters would appear to be the finest. Perhaps too', I said, 'many would judge it to be so, just as children and women do when they see <u>intricate fabric work</u>.' (557c5–9)

As is clear from the fact that a *himation poikilon* would only *appear* to be the most beautiful (καλλίστη ἂν φαίνοιτο) – and only to women and children at that – the *poikilia* of fabric is thus a site of censure for Plato because it is not only merely sensuous but also a *deceptive* form of beauty.[9] Plato's remarks here are significant because he makes explicit the idea that the *poikilia* of fabric has the capacity to captivate the senses and, therefore, the judgement (καλλίστην ἂν πολλοὶ κρίνειαν) of viewers. Plato thus implicitly recognises that there is a cognitive dimension to *poikilia* in textiles and is critical of the effect of *poikilia* insofar as it focuses its audience's attention on material and perceptual properties rather than the metaphysical world of the Forms.

As Plato indicates elsewhere, however, sensuous forms of *poikilia* can be mar-

---

[9] cf. Porter 2010: 87, who classifies the Platonic aesthetic as a 'minimalist' one.

shalled in the service of higher-order thinking.[10] This is because the material realia of *poikilia* in all their captivating, sensuous appeal *do* reflect, albeit distantly, the imperceptible Forms. In *Republic* 7, for example, Plato invokes the *poikilia* in the night sky as an illustration of the kind of beauty that is merely apparent:

ταῦτα μὲν τὰ ἐν τῷ οὐρανῷ <u>ποικίλματα</u>, ἐπείπερ ἐν ὁρατῷ <u>πεποίκιλται</u>, κάλλιστα μὲν ἡγεῖσθαι καὶ ἀκριβέστατα τῶν τοιούτων ἔχειν, τῶν δὲ ἀληθινῶν πολὺ ἐνδεῖν,

These stars that <u>adorn</u> the heavens, since they <u>ornament</u> the visible sky, we think they're the most beautiful and perfect examples of their kind. And yet they fall far short of the real ones. (*Resp.* 529c8–d2)

Socrates' point here is to emphasise how the visible *poikilia* of the night sky is in fact only a dim reflection of the Forms underlying the planets and stars: the mathematical laws that account for their shapes and the physical laws governing their movements and speeds (*Resp.* 529d). Nonetheless, he maintains that the visible complexity of the sky – its *poikilia* – can provide a useful paradigm for the study of these laws (*Resp.* 529d6–7).[11] As it is used in the context of the *Republic* 7 passage, the image of the *poikilia* of the night sky illustrates how even the beauty and complexity found in the night sky are an artificial reality, one that is merely an imperfect representation of the eternal forms. As in the examples from the *Meteorologica* and *De Coloribus* cited above, the body's senses can (mis)construe reality as it is filtered through these *poikilia*-enhanced images. As a characteristic of both observable, material phenomena and of the complexities of perception itself, these examples make particularly vivid how *poikilia* is equally at home in matter and in mind.

Nor is Plato unique in making *poikilia* a defining feature of celestial phenomena.

---

[10] On this point see also Nightingale 2018, who focuses specifically on *poikilia* in the *Phaedo* and *Timaeus*.

[11] Similarly, in the *Timaeus*, *poikilia* is a quality that Timaeus identifies as inherent in the nature of number and astronomy. The movements of the planets, for instance, evince complex patterns that Timaeus dubs in terms of *poikilia* ('For they do not know that the wanderings of the planets, which are hard to calculate and of wondrous <u>complexity</u>, constitute time', οὐκ ἴσασι χρόνον ὄντα τὰς τούτων πλάνας, πλήθει μὲν ἀμηχάνῳ χρωμένας, <u>πεποικιλμένας</u> θαυμαστῶς, 39d1–2). As Timaeus goes on to make clear, the elaborate patterns – the *poikilia* – that govern the movements of the stars and planets typify a way in which the perceptible universe assimilates itself (ὁμοιότατον ᾖ) to its 'perfect and intelligible' creator, the Living Creature (ὡς ὁμοιότατον ᾖ τῷ τελέῳ καὶ νοητῷ ζῴῳ, 39d10). On the vision of aesthetics formulated in the *Timaeus*, see especially Nightingale 2018, who characterises it as one that is 'at once simple and extravagant' (351).

Earlier authors recognised an affinity between the luminosity of *poikilia* in fabric and that of the night sky. We saw above how Homer described Helen's and Hecuba's *peploi* as 'shining like stars', but even more pointed in its assimilation of fabric to sky is a fragment of Critias, which identifies the 'starry body of heaven' as the 'beautiful, elaborate handiwork of Cronos, the skilled craftsman' (τό τ' ἀστερωπὸν οὐρανοῦ δέμας, / Χρόνου καλὸν ποίκιλμα τέκτονος σοφοῦ, 88 [81] DK fr. 26, 33–4). The aptitude of *poikilia* in fabric for capturing the appearance of the heavens is confirmed by similar depictions elsewhere. For example, both Aeschylus and Euripides characterise the night sky as a form of *poikilia*: in [Aesch.] *PV*, Night is named with the epithet ποικιλείμων 'arrayed in spangled garb' (24), and Euripides' *Helen* alludes to the 'brocade of the stars' (ἀστέρων ποικίλματα, 1096). These examples, which suggest that the *poikilia* of fabric provided a fitting medium through which to capture the appearance of the night sky, thus accord with Socrates' identification of *poikilia* as an illuminating paradigm ('Its complexity can be used as a paradigm for the heavens', τῇ περὶ τὸν οὐρανὸν ποικιλίᾳ παραδείγμασι χρηστέον, *Resp.* 529d6–7). But in using the *poikilia* of fabric in this way, these passages testify to the fecundity of textilic *poikilia* for generating the sort of metaphorical imagery that features most prominently in Pindar (discussed in Chapter 4), who links the fabrication of *poikilia* with the process of song-making itself.[12]

Each of the passages discussed in this section – from Homer's description of *poikiloi peploi* 'shining like stars' to Plato's citation of *poikilia* as an imperfect manifestation of the Forms – treats the *poikilia* of fabric as both material and cognitive, as something that embodies the scintillating and even illusory effects of sense perception. Further, these examples impute a form of agency to the *poikilia* of fabric in its capacity to beguile the perceiver by making material realia seem somehow other than what they are: whether 'shining like stars' (Homer), or producing different colours from the dyes used therein (Aristotle and pseudo-Aristotle), or by erroneously seeming to be 'the most beautiful' (Plato). Taken together, then, these passages provide a good indication of how complexity in polychromy and design shaped the unique visual experience of *poikilia*.

In the remainder of this chapter, I turn to how the complexities native to *poikilia*'s experience exemplify what the art historian Barbara Maria Stafford has identified in her 2007 book *Echo Objects* as 'the cognitive work of images'. According to Stafford,

---

[12] See e.g. *Ol.* 6.86–7, 'Weaving an elaborate song for spearmen' (ἀνδράσιν αἰχματαῖσι πλέκων / ποικίλον ὕμνον, 86–7), *Nem.* 8.14–15, 'Bearing a Lydian *mitra*, resoundingly adorned' (φέρων / Λυδίαν μίτραν καναχηδὰ πεποικιλμέναν), and Pind. fr. 194 .2–3, 'Let us build an elaborate ornament, resounding with words' (τειχίζωμεν ἤδη ποικίλον / κόσμον αὐδάεντα λόγων).

the act of looking at images and patterns, 'does not just make our complex environment simpler to ingest. It makes aspects of the world perceptually salient and cognitively distinctive for us . . . they model how stimuli self-assemble and summon us to the analogous higher-order labor of unification' (2007: 207).[13] The images expressed in material forms, in other words, are but concrete manifestations of the mechanisms and strategies by which human brains make sense of the baffling array of sensory stimuli in which the body is constantly immersed.[14] And this process of sense-making is clearest in the case of vision, since, as the philosopher of mind Andy Clark has discussed, the human visual system must rely on highly selective usage of its perceptual resources in order to garner a coherent picture of the surrounding environment. This is because 'the human visual system supports only a small area of high-resolution processing, corresponding to the fraction of the visual field that falls into central focus' (Clark 2003: 63). Nonetheless, our lived experience of visual perception is markedly unlike this limited foveal perspective.

To articulate this mismatch between experience and physical reality, the philosopher Alva Noë has put it as follows: 'on the basis of relatively information-poor patterns of light striking the retina, we are able to enjoy colorful, detailed, high-resolution, picture-like visual experiences' (2004: 49). Noë's enactivist account of perception offers one solution to the apparent discrepancy between the physics of vision and its qualitative experience. The enactivist view posits that perception, including vision, is an embodied task predicated on ongoing and active interaction between the perceiver and her environment. For Noë, visual perception feels comprehensive only because of our implicit awareness that moving our eyes, heads or bodies will enable us to bring different parts of our visual field into focus.[15]

---

[13] cf. Stafford: 2007: 73: 'The compound symbol . . . concretely manifests the way in which the brain-mind associates the structural figments coming from various sensory inputs and that get retrieved and linked across two brain hemispheres. The sympathetic symbol is thus the external image of an inborn framing device, the universal organizational template in which and by which myriad patterns get encapsulated bit by bit.'

[14] cf. Malafouris 2013: 204, who comes to a similar conclusion in his analysis of Palaeolithic images: 'Through the process of "picturing", the underlying mechanisms of human perception were transformed into an object *for* perception and contemplation. Those invisible mechanisms became perceivable visual patterns arrayed and combined in real time and space. In this sense, the image offered a new mode of epistemic access to the world of visual experience.'

[15] As Noë puts it (2004: 63), 'In general, our sense of the perceptual presence of the detailed world does not consist in our representation of all the detail in consciousness now. Rather, it consists in our access now to all of the detail, and to our knowledge that we have this access. This knowledge takes the form of our comfortable mastery of the rules of sensorimotor dependence.'

An example first formulated by Daniel Dennett in 1991 and cited by Noë in his own 2004 study is especially pertinent to *poikilia* because it addresses how humans can have the accurate impression of seeing the entirety of a series of repeated images in spite of our limited foveal range. Dennett imagines a room wallpapered with hundreds of identical photographic portraits of Marilyn Monroe. A spectator would be able to correctly identify the room as being covered in identical portraits even at a single glance because of the brain's ability to 'fill in' its blind spots:

> Having identified a single Marilyn, and having received no information to the effect that the other blobs are not Marilyns, it [the brain] jumps to the conclusion that the rest are Marilyns, and labels the whole region 'more Marilyns' without any further rendering of Marilyn at all. (Dennett 1991: 355)[16]

This example provides an illuminating counterpoint to the representation of *poikilia* in vase painting and statuary, where this quality is often manifested in the combination of *different* repeating patterns. As I will argue, the juxtaposition of distinct repeating images is revealingly *un*like the Marilyn Monroe wallpaper because it slows down perception by preventing the brain from 'filling in' its blind spots. Instead, it encourages and even requires a viewer to examine the vase image or statue more fully in order for the complexity of its design to become clear.

The enactivist account of vision will thus provide a useful heuristic framework for analysing the effect of *poikilia* in fabric because the examples in this chapter all engage, in distinctive ways, with how the decoration of textiles may attract and manipulate perception. In so doing, the intricate ornamentation of *poikilia* in fabric across different media (texts, painting, statuary) prompts the kind of dynamic and embodied engagement ascribed by the enactivist account to *all* forms of perception. And given that weaving was predominantly women's work, together with the fact that it is women with whom fabulously decorated textiles are most frequently associated, there emerges a distinctively gendered dimension to the perceptual and cognitive processes described here. The picture of *poikilia* that forms from this chapter thus suggests that women were thought to provoke and engage the senses in a peculiarly feminine way – one that relies on intricate ornamentation both to attract and hold the viewer's gaze *and* to preserve the complex movements and planning that went into the creation of such fabric.

[16] cf. Noë 2004: 55's summary of Dennett's claim: 'When you enter the room, it looks to you as if you see that the wall is covered with Marilyns. But you certainly don't foveate each of them in series; owing to the limitations of foveal and parafoveal vision, you don't take them *all* in all at once' (emphasis in original).

Sensing Fabric in the Acropolis Korai

The Acropolis korai as a group are distinctive for the intricate patterning in the sculpted and incised pleats of their garments as well as in the painted decoration on this fabric. Each kore exhibits a unique combination of motifs and patterns that in literary sources could be characterised in terms of *poikilia*.[17] This quality is especially prominent in the polychromy that remains visible on many of these figures even today, allowing for modern attempts at reconstruction of their original appearances. In spite of the idiosyncratic nature of each kore's appearance, though, their precise identities remain obscure.[18] But whether they are meant to represent real individuals or generic, anonymous young women or goddesses, what is abundantly clear from the korai is that they are *agalmata* in the most immediate sense of the term: objects designed to delight.[19] And the ample patterns of colour, line and texture that inhere in each kore are fundamental to the operations of the korai as *agalmata*.[20]

There is a vast bibliography devoted to the interpretation of the Acropolis korai as a group, and the variety of scholarly perspectives these artefacts invite (e.g. aesthetics, history of clothing, art history, religion) testifies to the fascination they have exerted over the modern imagination. This group of maidens does make obvious the prominence of decorated fabric and clothing in the archaic aesthetic imagination.

---

[17] cf. Dietrich 2017: 279, who likewise associates *poikilia* with the 'frontal density of detail' observable on Acropolis kore 675, and Stieber 2004: 135, who characterises the korai as 'living ποικίλα ('variegated ornaments').

[18] Barrow 2015: 95–7 and Stieber 2004: 13–41 offer lucid summaries of the issues involved in the identification of the korai and the dominant scholars and publications devoted to the interpretation of these figures. See too the helpful table of Keesling 2009: 91 that summarises these scholarly trends.

[19] cf. Gaifman and Platt 2018: 412, who note that 'The significance of the *kore* as object is thus fundamentally bound to the kind of body that it depicts – itself an "object" traded for its social value.' Stieber 2004: 21–4, on the other hand, resists the use of the term *agalma* in relation to the korai because it suggests that they represent generic types. In using this term myself, I am not denying to the korai their individual distinctive features, but instead adopt the term to focus attention on the reciprocal and interactive relationship suggested by *agalma*.

[20] See Grand-Clément 2011: 281–5 on the relationship between the korai's decorations and their status as *agalmata*, especially p. 284: 'These depictions of young women reveal, even more so than the *kouroi*, the profundity of the *agalma*, an object invested with power, which seduces with the shimmering of its colors and which exhibits a certain social status.' ('Ces images de jeunes filles révèlent, davantage encore que les *kouroi*, la nature profonde de l'*agalma*, un objet investi de pouvoirs, qui séduit par le chatoiement de ses couleurs et qui manifeste un certain statut social.') In what follows, my aim is to supplement this interpretation by defining how, precisely, this 'shimmering' (chatoiement) operated on the gaze.

Indeed, the intensity of attention devoted to the formal features of their garments in modern scholarship testifies to the efficacy of this decoration for capturing attention.[21] Moreover, the placement of the korai on the Acropolis, together with the lavishness of their clothing, recalls the description of Athena's association with *poikilia* discussed above, the goddess who is herself a master artisan of *poikilia* in fabric, fashioning a *poikilos peplos* that she 'made herself with her own hands' (ὅν ῥ' αὐτὴ ποιήσατο καὶ κάμε χερσίν, *Il.* 5.735 = *Il.* 8.386). The elaborately worked *peplos* offered annually to Athena (and woven by young women like the korai) provided further recognition of the deity's penchant for richly worked fabric. Given this nexus of relations between Athena, textile *poikilia* and young women, the decorated fabric of the korai acquires greater significance in its capacity to materialise the deity's signature handiwork. In so doing, these figures become objects of delight for their human as well as their divine audiences.

One of the best known of Vinzenz Brinkmann's reconstructions of polychromy in sculpture is the so-called Peplos kore, dated to c. 530 BCE (Figs 1.2 and 1.3). The draping of her garment is comparatively simple, but was dyed in rich hues and patterned with elaborate friezes. This is particularly evident from her waist downwards, where panels of animals seem to have formed a vertical axis progressing from below her navel to her ankles. If this reconstruction is reasonably accurate, the Peplos kore would recall the similar animal friezes that appear in the garments on the Sophilos Dinos, discussed below.[22] But in the Peplos kore, the significant difference is that this patterning does not cover the garment, as in the vase painting examples, but forms a column descending from her navel. In spite of this difference, however, her garment's decorations engage a viewer's gaze in a highly specific way. Because this patterning is confined to her lower half, the gaze is drawn to her pelvic region and, as Richard Neer has argued, the profusion of creatures represented in her garment may have suggested fertility: 'the parted folds of cloth reveal hidden depths, full of life' (2010: 121). While this is one plausible way to interpret this patterning's significance, more generally this reading illustrates well how deeply the decoration of the kore shapes how it is perceived. What Neer's suggestive reading reveals, in other words, is how the structure and contents of the garment's patterning seem designed to prompt a viewer to perceive and respond to this kore in a particular way.[23]

---

[21] See e.g. Richter 1968, Ridgway 1977, Harrison 1991, Karakasi 2003, Stieber 2004: 42–82, Dietrich 2017.

[22] On the relation between these two vases see Osborne 1998: 88–95, and Brinkmann 2007: 46–8 on the animal friezes used on the Peplos kore.

[23] cf. the conclusions drawn by Hölscher 2018: 331 in his wide-ranging study of visuality and visual power in antiquity: 'Images are present for *potential* perception. In this sense, people interact with images in similar ways as with other human beings, cultural objects, and

Figure 1.2 Peplos kore (Acropolis 679) (c. 530 BCE). Photo: Image by Wikimedia Commons user Marsyas, shared under the CC BY-SA 3.0 license

Figure 1.3 Reconstruction of polychromy on Peplos kore. Photo: Image by Wikimedia Commons user G.dallorto, shared under the CC BY-SA 3.0 licence

If we accept the argument advanced by Brinkmann as well as by Brunilde Ridgway and Catherine Keesling that the Peplos kore is in fact a representation of a deity (most likely Artemis, based on the animals that figure on her gown as well as the types of objects she could have held on the basis of extant drill holes), then the Peplos kore offers an illustrative example of a confluence between a deity and their representation.[24] As Ridgway has proposed, the Peplos kore may be understood not as a mimetic portrayal of a goddess, but instead as an image of an image, 'a marble replica of the venerable image of some powerful goddess' (1977: 61). Seen in this way, the Peplos kore is suggestive of how decorative elements like the images on her skirt can compel a unique kind of engagement on the part of viewers, in which what presents itself to the gaze is a layering of images that have to be actively pieced together: each figure in each frieze on the skirt, the combination of these motifs, their relationship to the objects held by the kore, and the representation of a divine image embodied in the figure as a whole. Thus what the Peplos kore may reveal is a different kind of divine epiphany, one that unfolds not in a dazzling blaze but in protracted visual exploration.

Until very recently, the emphasis on drapery and decoration that is so visible in archaic korai had been interpreted as a failure of realism because of the way these features often both occlude the appearance of the human form underneath *and* fail to represent clothing accurately.[25] For when the archaic korai are compared with, for instance, the female figures on the Parthenon's east pediment, exhibiting in their clinging garments the so-called 'wet' look that characterises high classical sculpted drapery, the Acropolis korai seem to belong to a more primitive category of representation, one that has not yet succeeded in representing clothing and the human body realistically. By contrast, in the fifth century, as Richard Neer has summarised it, 'Classical drapery insists that *there is something beneath the carved surface*' (2010: 124, emphasis in original). Numerous important correctives have been applied to this teleological interpretation of archaic and classical statuary in recent years,[26] but the comparison between the archaic and classical stages in the representation of the

natural surroundings: being aware of their existence and reacting to their presence in more or less specific ways.'

[24] See Keesling 2003 and Brinkmann 2007. For the most recent and high-definition reconstruction of Brinkmann's 'Artemis Tauropolos', see https://buntegoetter.liebieghaus.de/en/.

[25] cf. Neer 2010: 121 on Acropolis kore 594: 'Over the upper body there is a rich confection of patterned folds that barely hangs together as the *mimesis* of real cloth.' Donohue 2005: 155–201 offers an excellent summary and analysis of the various modern interpretations devoted to archaic and classical Greek constructions of female clothing in statuary. See especially her comments on p. 191: 'the desire to trace an overall evolution in what is perceived as a "naturalistic" rendering of drapery and body has resulted in a confusion between effects specific to particular garments and general stylistic features'. See also the earlier work of Morizot 1974, who likewise drew attention to the fallacious tendency to interpret sculpted garments as attempts at faithful reproductions of real-life garments.

[26] See, most recently, e.g. Spivey 1996: 15–53, Neer 2002: 105–41, Donohue 2005, Tanner 2006: 31–96, Squire 2013: 32–68.

female form remains instructive because it enables us to discern the distinctive ways in which the materiality of fabric is deployed within the same (marble) medium. The korai that I will focus on below, which all date between 525 and 500 BCE, exhibit the *poikilia* of fabric in the form of the profuse textural as well as visual details that complicate and prolong the viewing experience. These examples thus disclose how the *poikilia* of fabric could enliven the perception of figures like the korai not through their naturalistic aspect, but by the effects of their sensuous complexity.[27] Accordingly, the examples I will concentrate on have been selected because they evince the clearest extant variety of multisensory details.

Kore 675 (510–500 BCE) (Fig. 1.4) is a case in point, embodying a number of features that also define several of her fellow roughly contemporary korai (especially kore 594 as well as 674). First, the chromatic contrast in her dress remains at least partly visible to modern viewers, an aspect which has been lost in many other korai. She is clad in a dark-hued chiton, over which is arranged a richly patterned and elaborately draped himation. The dark painted border at the hem of her himation as well as the dark blue patterned border on her chiton (the paryphe) are the most visible features of her chromatic aspect, but more subtle and intricate patterns reveal themselves even within each of the himation's pleats. Each design painted onto the borders and folds of her himation and chiton is distinct from the others. Comprised of minutely rendered meanders, crosses, four-pointed stars and rosettes, they are rendered predominantly in red and blue.[28] In addition to this array of designs, the fact that one of the most amply decorated areas is the border of her himation means that it cannot form a continuous, repeating frieze, but is distilled into a series of separate images by the pleats of the garment. The colour and shape of this decoration as it is refracted through the sculpted pleats of her himation thus add a further level of detail to the visual complexity already apparent in the texture of the kore's garments, a complexity that could be characterised as fractal in its structuring.[29]

An even richer array of patterns remains visible on Kore 682 (525 BCE) (Fig. 1.5),

---

[27] For a different but compatible reading of the interaction between the painted and sculpted elements of this kore, Dietrich 2017: 298–302 notes how the carved drapery of kore 675 and others 'serves as a sort of *tabula rasa* for additional painterly decoration', 299. According to this view, this disregard for coherence between these features of the kore is a way that the sculptor makes the statue 'openly display the process of figuration' itself (298).

[28] cf. Brinkmann and Wünsche 2004: no. 96.

[29] This interpretation builds on the analysis of Dietrich 2018a, who identifies a 'fractal structure' (177) in the endlessly repeating pleats of Acropolis kore 672's clothing and defines it as, 'this almost fractal structure of repeated deviation (that together constitutes ever-new patterns on a smaller scale' (187). The same adjective could just as aptly be applied to the repetition of painted geometric motifs that appear on many of the korai's garments.

Figure 1.4 Acropolis kore 675 (510–500 BCE). © Acropolis Museum, Photo: Socratis Mavrommatis

whose chiton is bisected with a paryphe of dark blue meanders interspersed with four-pointed stars that disappears beneath her himation precisely at the centre of her chest. This patterning on her chiton is thus framed by the sharply pleated diagonal lines of folds in her himation, and each of these pleats in turn is inscribed with alternating crosses and four-squares. The decoration on the hem of her sleeve remains visible, too, in the form of a series of dotted squares. As in kore 675, the texturing of her garments in the form of sculpted pleats and incised lines means that, even in areas adorned with the same pattern (as in the hem of her himation), no two sections are quite the same. Instead, different sections and quantities of the design appear depending on the section of cloth in which they are placed. In the himation, this effect is enhanced by the slight asymmetry effected in the garment's draping, as the section over her right shoulder drapes vertically, while the left is pulled off slightly to the side.

Each decorated area on each kore thus confronts the viewer with a distinctive visual stimulus that showcases an effect that has been well described by Alfred Gell (and one that has been corroborated in more recent accounts of image-making like that of Stafford 2007). In his 1998 work, Gell posits the concept of the 'technology of enchantment', which claims that the addition of complex surface decoration to objects allows them to achieve a form of agency because of the cognitive effects elicited by such stimuli.[30] While Gell's approach is avowedly anthropocentric (e.g. in contending that the exchange of elaborately patterned objects between individuals expresses the interaction's 'binding social force'), he nonetheless accurately identifies the force exerted by elaborate designs in noting how such surfaces 'slow perception down, or even halt it, so that the decorated object is never fully possessed at all, but is always in the process of becoming possessed' (1998: 81). A similar effect of slowing down perception is operative, I suggest, in the korai, whose vivid polychromatic decorations serve to draw the eye over the surface of each one's clothing in order to confront its full complexity. The perception of such objects would thus theoretically produce the opposite effect to the 'filling-in' phenomenon illustrated with Daniel Dennett's Marilyn Monroe wallpaper example discussed above: instead of assuming an identical series of images as in that instance, the eye, in the case of the korai, is compelled to *keep* looking in order to trace out the different contours of the pattern.[31]

[30] See Gell 1992: 'The technology of enchantment and the enchantment of technology', as well as Gell 1998 for a comprehensive elaboration of the interactions described in the 1992 essay. See also Osborne and Tanner 2008: 1–27 as well as Chua and Elliott 2013 for recent reappraisals of Gell's theory and methodology.

[31] This idea is compatible with the kind of agency attributed to archaic viewers by Dietrich 2018b, who argues that the 'iconographic under-determination' of archaic imagery 'allocates an essential role to the viewer as the true agent of identification' (481). I am suggesting here that these korai similarly invite and rely on the viewer's agency in responding to their

Figure 1.5 Acropolis kore 682 (525 BCE). © Acropolis Museum, Photo: Yiannis Koulelis

This is because the inclusion of micro patterns within the larger framework of each kore's clothing means that it is impossible to apprehend every detail of each figure in a single glance. Instead, the additional complexity imposed by the designs and colour within the texture of their clothing creates manifold visual registers. Based on reconstructions of these patterns, it becomes clear that a viewer's gaze would have had to rove up, down and around in order to perceive the myriad distinctive aspects of each kore's front.[32] And in this sense, the perception of these korai invites a dynamic and embodied form of visual perception: the *poikilia* inscribed in their clothing only becomes apparent when the eye can move continuously over the painted and carved surface.[33]

Moreover, it is significant that the coloration and texture of the korai's garments work to provoke the sense of vision as well as touch. And the korai's evocation of multiple senses may be understood in light of Gabrielle Starr's research into the impact of multisensory language (2013: 113–15).[34] Adopting a neuroscientific approach to literary study, she demonstrates how the evocation of multiple sensory modalities fuels aesthetic pleasure precisely by putting the senses in competition. She finds evidence for this view in the cognitive phenomenon of disinhibition, in which the repeated experience of a pair of sensations in tandem ultimately causes one of these stimuli to be experienced more profoundly, and therefore more pleasurably, than the other. She goes on to suggest that complex works of visual art function similarly by enhancing visual experience through the inhibition of other senses (such as hearing). This model provides a useful frame of interpretation for the complex interplay of texture and colour visible in the Acropolis korai. Since texture is both a tactile and a visible quality, this combination may have contributed to a viewer's

elaborate aspects in a manner aligned with Elsner 2006: 83's apt summation: 'one thing that is quite definite about the archaic image is its existential confrontation with the viewer – its intrusion into the viewer's own space and time, its rupture of that space and time with a being once perhaps from this world but now in another'.

[32] Neer 2010: 105–35 has identified a similar strategy at work in forms of diaphanous drapery in archaic and classical statuary, a strategy which promotes a different but no less active way of viewing by compelling the gaze to 'see through' garments to the bodily form underneath.

[33] cf. Cook 2018: 885, who identifies a similar process at work in Impressionism: 'Monet's "Water Lilies" moves the viewer to the position necessary to take the large painting in. She must stand back; she must squint. Bringing the flowers into being, the viewer becomes aware of the operation of her visual system – the work necessary to turn color and shape into an image; it wasn't just there, out there in the world for the artist to capture, it had to be actively composed by the viewer.'

[34] Using Keats's 'Ode on a Grecian Urn' as her case study, Starr concludes, 'the pleasures of thought and of perception may be felt for vivid readers because of the competition between ideas, emotions, and sensations' (2013: 113).

experience of the korai by enhancing the pleasure of their visual encounter through the evocation of sensory competition between the domains of sight and touch.

Moreover, there is a further sensuous quality suggested by the korai's representations of elaborate garments: that of smell. This is because there are indications in both the material and literary record that real fabric may have been treated with scent. Therefore, the representation of such textiles in the korai as well as in vase painting may have evoked such an association. A red-figure oenochoe (420–410 BCE) attributed to the painter Meidias, for instance, depicts women engaged in perfuming richly patterned garments, and there are several allusions to the fragrance of garments in archaic poetry.[35] Thus even though the korai themselves were not imbued with scent in the same way, the prominent elaboration of their garments may have at least created an association with the fragrances that probably inhered in real textiles. In addition, the association with fragrance would have been bolstered by the fruits and wreaths that the korai may have held.[36] Taken together, these features are suggestive of a richly multisensory context for the korai, an aspect that would only heighten the liveliness of each kore's material presence.

To return to kore 675 in particular, the dense pleating of the himation is no mere decorative feature, but plays a crucial role in compelling a viewer's eye movements by creating a strong vertical axis between the figure's head and body.[37] But as the vertical lines of her himation converge with the three carefully placed strands of hair that fall down symmetrically over each shoulder, the asymmetry of the lines of her clothing becomes more apparent by contrast: the pieces of hair immediately to either

---

[35] e.g. θυώδεα εἵματ', *Od.* 21.52; ὀδμὴ δ' ἱμερόεσσα θυηέντων ἀπὸ πέπλων/σκίδνατο, *Hom. Hymn Dem.* 277–8, cf. *Il.* 6.288, θάλαμον κηώεντα. It is clear, on the other hand, that women did use perfumed garments during the Anthesteria (see Lee 2015: 222 with fig. 7.14), the preparations for which may be what the Meidias oenochoe depicts. See Lee 2015: 256–7 for extensive bibliography on all aspects of the ancient uses and production of perfume, and Janko 1992 ad *Il.* 14. 172–4 as well as Shelmerdine 1985: 128–30 on the practice of treating cloth with oil, which is explicitly described at *Od.* 7.107 (καιρουσσέων δ' ὀθονέων ἀπολείβεται ὑγρὸν ἔλαιον).

[36] See especially Keesling 2003: 144–9 for catalogue and discussion of the handheld objects associated with the korai.

[37] For compelling arguments challenging the idea that archaic korai's dress is purely 'ornamental', see especially Dietrich 2011, 2017 and 2018a. While his interpretations concentrate on how the korai complicate any clear-cut distinction between ornamental and figurative as well as formal and naturalistic, my own argument is nonetheless compatible with his because it offers a sensory and cognitive perspective on the same features of the korai that he analyses.

side of her face descend straight down, highlighting the oblique angles at which her himation and skirt drape.[38]

The careful design of the draping of garments visible in kore 675 is apparent in numerous other archaic korai, as well. For instance, the chiton of kore 594 (c. 500 BCE) (Figs 1.6 and 1.7) is incised with wavy vertical lines, and her himation and epiblēma (the additional outer garment worn over her shoulders) likewise exhibit a profusion of crisp pleats falling in sharp vertical lines over her midsection. Her outstretched right arm, however, creates a ripple of folds in her himation, in turn generating a set of smooth concentric curves that form a striking asymmetry with the sharp lines of her himation and chiton. Similarly, the border on her himation and epiblēma has been painstakingly elaborated into neat, rippling plastic folds that cascade down each side of her midsection and so frame the bold meander pattern that bisects her lower half. The overall effect is of a dense, richly varied texture that capitalises on the natural malleability of the represented material (fabric) in order to enliven the texture of the marble garments.

Korai 594 and 675 are a particularly good pair with which to gauge how the sculpting of fabric affected their viewing experience because of the radically different treatments afforded to the *back* of each figure. While the texture of the garments as well as the hair on kore 675 (Fig. 1.8) are almost entirely unformed at the back (although the general contours of the body are rendered), on kore 594 the folds of the epiblēma drape in evenly spaced wavy lines across her back.[39] Like the rippling lines of the himation below her outstretched arm, which suggest the movement of the fabric in response to this gesture, the draping of the himation on the kore's back gives the impression that it hangs loosely over her shoulders. The comparison between the treatments of each kore's reverse side thus reveals two different possibilities for imagining the *poikilia* of fabric qua marble: kore 594 renders the garments' texture

---

[38] See also Dietrich 2018a on the mismatch between the symmetry of strands of hair versus the asymmetrical lines of clothing visible in the korai (concentrating in particular on Acropolis kore 672). He convincingly demonstrates that the highly symmetrical features typically associated with ornament were not consciously adopted by the korai's sculptors.

[39] See Dietrich 2017: 274–81 for a fresh and convincing interpretation of this apparent juxtaposition between Kore 675's front and back. Instead of assuming that this kore was only designed to be seen from the front, he proposes that, 'in a very concrete sense, the plain, uncoloured surface of the statue's back frames the elaborate surface carving and polychromy of its front' (280). The reading I offer here is indebted to and compatible with his innovative approach to this kore's decoration, but whereas his study focuses on how 'the object draws attention to its own artifice, involving the viewer in the process of transforming stone into a lifelike figure' (281), I confine myself here to a focus on how and to what effect the materiality of fabric is construed in each kore.

Figure 1.6 Acropolis kore 594 (c. 500 BCE). © Acropolis Museum, Photo: Yiannis Koulelis

Figure 1.7 Detail of Acropolis kore 594 (c. 500 BCE). © Acropolis Museum,
Photo: Socratis Mavrommatis

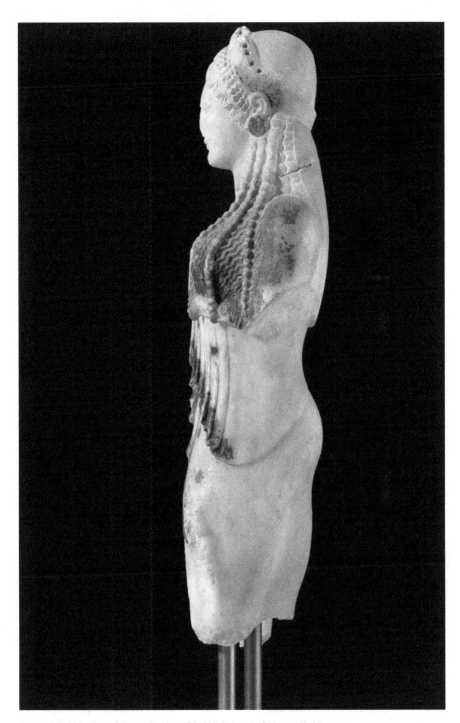

Figure 1.8 Side view of Acropolis kore 675 (510-500 BCE). © Acropolis Museum,
Photo: Socratis Mavrommatis

not only in three dimensions but in a 360-degree viewing experience, whereas kore 675 introduces a different kind of variety into the *poikilia* by generating a literally arresting juxtaposition between the treatments of her front and back.

In the domain of sculpture, as embodied in these Acropolis korai, the representation of fabricated forms of *poikilia* fostered a multisensory and dynamic perception of the clothed female form. For when the elaborate decoration of their clothing is interpreted in light of contemporary theories about how humans process complex sensory data, it becomes clear that the lavish visual and tactile details of the korai's drapery were no mere decorative elements. Instead, by slowing down and complicating the viewing process, the quality of *poikilia* served to stimulate and mobilise the senses. To encounter one of these korai, then, was to be drawn into a sphere of *poikilia* dominated by Athena herself, one in which the korai's capacity to delight the goddess qua *agalmata* may have consisted in part in the active sensory exploration that these figures evoke in their spectators.[40]

The dynamic mode of perception operative in the korai is also consonant with archaic descriptions of superlative feminine beauty, which likewise stress the arresting quality of highly adorned women.[41] Analogous to Homer's attestation that *poikiloi peploi* could 'shine like stars' (ἀστὴρ δ' ὣς ἀπέλαμπεν, *Il.* 6.295; *Od.* 15.108), Aphrodite's epiphany to Anchises in the *Homeric Hymn to Aphrodite* recounts the scintillating effect of her *poikilia*:

Ἀγχίσης δ' ὁρόων ἐφράζετο θάμβαινέν τε,
εἶδός τε μέγεθός τε καὶ εἵματα σιγαλόεντα,
πέπλον μὲν γὰρ ἕστο φαεινότερον πυρὸς αὐγῆς,
εἶχε δ' ἐπιγναμπτὰς ἕλικας κάλυκάς τε φαεινάς,
ὅρμοι δ' ἀμφ' ἁπαλῆι δειρῆι περικαλλέες ἦσαν
καλοὶ χρύσειοι παμποίκιλοι· ὡς δὲ σελήνη
στήθεσιν ἀμφ' ἁπαλοῖσιν ἐλάμπετο, θαῦμα ἰδέσθαι.
Ἀγχίσην δ' ἔρος εἶλεν, ἔπος δέ μιν ἀντίον ηὔδα·

---

[40] In this context it is also relevant to note the dedication of korai by 'craftsmen', *banausoi*, a point that Keesling 2003 (especially pp. 69–75) has rightly emphasised. For given Athena's patronage of the crafts writ large, the dedication of korai that exhibit both the elaboration of textiles and the arresting capacity of skilfully crafted artefacts would reflect the reciprocal relationship between Athena and those who practise manual craftsmanship.

[41] cf. Steiner 2001: 94–104 and 234–8 on the affinities between texts and statuary in their representations of divinities and divine epiphanies, e.g. 'In their conceits, the poets anticipate and match the strategies adopted by statue-makers when they come to fashion images that are supremely beautiful, larger-than-life, and shining with an otherworldly radiance' (99).

And Anchises, looking at her, marked her well and marvelled at her form and stature and her shining clothes, for she was clad in a robe more radiant than a beam of fire, and she had on twisted bracelets and shining earrings, and about her soft breast were exceedingly beautiful necklaces, lovely, golden, and highly wrought. And these shone like the moon around her tender chest, a wonder to behold. And desire took hold of Anchises, and he spoke to her. (84–91)

This is a passage to which I will return in more detail in Chapter 6, but it is also illustrative in the context of the korai I have been discussing here. For this description emphasises the spectacular and awe-inspiring quality of Aphrodite's accoutrements by relaying how the goddess manifests herself to Anchises as an amalgam of the visually dazzling qualities emanating from her jewellery and clothing (conveyed by σιγαλόεντα, φαεινότερον, φαεινάς, ἐλάμπετο).[42] More specifically, it is her 'highly wrought necklaces' (ὅρμοι παμποίκιλοι) that seem to have the most striking effect, because the fact that these are the last item mentioned before Anchises is overwhelmed with desire suggests that they are a peculiarly powerful component of her adornment.[43] In addition, the 'glowing' (ἐλάμπετο) and 'moonlike' (ὡς δὲ σελήνη) appearance of this jewellery 'around her tender chest' makes her 'a wonder to behold' (θαῦμα ἰδέσθαι) in a way that is evocative of similarly awe-inspiring works of craftsmanship like Achilles' shield. Thus Aphrodite, like the Acropolis korai discussed already, makes herself an object of visual fascination through the *poikilia* of her adornment. And the slippage that becomes apparent in these examples between the perception of female bodies and their adornment will also feature in the next section, which investigates representations of textilic *poikilia* in vase painting.

Visualising Fabric and Constructing Images in Vase Painting

That *poikilia* was a recognisable feature of vase painting and may have had a special affinity with black-figure vase painting in particular is encapsulated in Pindar's description of Panathenaic amphorae as *pampoikiloi*, 'highly decorated' (ἐν ἀγγέων ἔρκεσιν παμποικίλοις, *Nem.* 10.36).[44] And in vase painting of the archaic and early

---

[42] cf. Platt 2011: 68–9: 'By a process of synecdoche the poet merges the shining qualities of precious metals with the radiance of Aphrodite's body in such a way that the material and divine are inexorably blurred.'

[43] cf. Putnam 1960: 81: 'They [the *hormoi*] receive the place of extreme importance in the catalogue of Aphrodite's garments and seem to be the most seductive, for they appear at the culminating point in the description, just before the poet tells us that love seized Anchises.'

[44] On this characterisation of the Panathenaic amphorae see also Grand-Clément 2011: 433–4 and Neer 2002: 34.

classical period, *poikilia* is clearly visible not only in decorated garments, but also in the combination of ornamental and figural elements.[45] The latter help to create miniature and distinctive foci of attention that seem ideally suited for humans' highly selective visual apparatus. Nor is this a strategy unique to painting, since the organisation of and the very patterns and designs that appear in painted garments seem likely to have been borrowed from actual textiles. As John Boardman has noted (2001: 17), the repeating patterns of shapes like the meander, swastika and key as well as the cross-hatching that appear prominently on geometric pottery were most likely influenced by designs familiar from weaving.[46] For instance, an eighth-century dish from Cyprus actually depicts fabric on a loom patterned with the very sorts of designs that dominate the pottery of this period. However similar the designs used in both painting and textiles, though, the difference in the medium of representation (clay and paint for vases versus fabric for actual textiles) will prove significant by revealing how each medium placed constraints on as well as generated new possibilities for representing *poikilia*. In other words, it is in painting that we can begin to see more clearly how the materiality of a particular artistic form can shape the way in which the effect of *poikilia* was produced and the role that it plays therein.[47] In the case of black-figure painting in particular, the *poikilia* of fabric proves instrumental to making human forms visible as such in addition to distinguishing figures from one another and from other non-figural forms. In this sense, the decorative element of *poikilia* plays a crucial role in delineating the figural as such.[48]

For instance, on the Sophilos Dinos (Fig. 1.9), the uppermost frieze depicts the wedding procession of Peleus and Thetis and portrays female figures clad in

---

[45] On the relationship between figural and decorative elements in the construction of pictorial space in vase painting, see especially Hurwit 1992 as well as the more recent contributions of Dietrich 2010, Marconi 2017, Neer 2018a and Grethlein 2018. On the subject of *poikilia* in particular and its expression in vase painting, see especially Neer 2002: 54–77 and Kei 2011.

[46] See also Barber 1991: 363–72 on the intersections between vase painting and textile-weaving.

[47] A similar approach to the relationship between materiality and figural representation informs Platt 2018's study of Roman painting.

[48] cf. Neer 2018a: 210–15, especially 210, where he notes that, 'Many Geometric artefacts are, in fact, *incipiently iconic*' (emphasis in original). See also Hurwit's 1992 analysis of floral and vegetal motifs, which concludes: 'And in the subversion of the traditional, conventional relationship between image and ornament on the Greek vase – in the self-conscious claim that there is no difference, or that one may leak into or fuse with the other – it is the status of representation that suffers, for it is exposed as artificial, too. It is, then, not just the ornamentality of nature that is the point; it is the artificiality of representation itself' (71). Similarly, Dietrich 2010 concludes that seemingly decorative elements are just as constitutive of pictorial space as figures.

Figure 1.9 Sophilos Dinos depicting wedding procession of Peleus and Thetis (c. 580-570 BCE).
© The Trustees of the British Museum

white robes patterned with animal friezes rendered in black silhouette. Several of the animals rendered on these garments are the same as those featured in the lower friezes on the vase, which consist of images of animals both real and imaginary. This doubling of the same pattern at both the macro (on a frieze of the vase) and micro (on the panels of a figure's garment) levels is clearest on the garment worn by the figure labelled as Hebe, since her dress includes precisely the same combination of real and fantastical animals that occupy the lower registers of the vase. By reproducing the vase's lower series of animal friezes in miniature throughout the garments that appear in the horizontal plane of the top frieze, the painter uses the space of the painted textile to create a vertical axis between the horizontal planes of the vase's upper and lower friezes. In this way, the Sophilos painter inscribes a pattern for viewing the vase by directing the viewer's gaze both horizontally and vertically over its surface.[49] Further, by making the goddesses depicted in this frieze sites of pictorial elaboration through the embellishment of their garments, the Sophilos painter demonstrates how painted human figures can become visible as such precisely through their representation as surfaces that contain the kind of complex imagery familiar from textiles.[50]

The importance of textile decoration for delineating the human form in black-figure images is clear even in portrayals of women, where the conventional addition of white slip to female figures already provides a means of distinguishing feminine entities. For instance, in another amphora attributed to Exekias (Fig. 1.10), a man and a woman on a chariot stand directly opposite another woman, who extends a hand to the woman holding the reins of the chariot. Each woman wears a chiton with all-over chequerboard decoration: the one on the left rendered in repeating meanders, while the torso of the woman on the right displays a repeating circle pattern. In the woman on the left, the meander pattern is interrupted by a curving black line: the edge of the chariot. In this way, the patterning helps to create visual depth, for this design works to clearly demarcate the woman as standing inside the chariot.[51] The contribution of textile decoration to the construction of visual depth is even clearer in the woman on the right. Here, it becomes obvious that the woman is standing behind the two horses pulling the chariot because the patterning on her lower half, which consists in two vertical bands of swastika figures and two horizontal meander borders, clearly distinguishes the woman from the chariots and horses. Without this decoration, it would be difficult indeed for a viewer to discern the lower half of this figure.

A similar effect is observable in a mid-sixth-century amphora attributed to the Amasis painter (Fig. 1.11). Here, the patterning in the garments of two maenads distinguishes their two otherwise symmetrical figures from one another. Further, the decoration of their garments contributes to the symmetry of the image as a whole, as the patterns within each textile seem to extend into the ivy wands held by each. By contrast, the figure of Dionysus is characterised by strong vertical lines in both his garments and the lines of his hair, forming a counterpoint to the horizontal axis created by the extension of the maenads' dress patterns into their wands of ivy. Similarly, since each maenad holds an animal (one a hare, the other a fawn), the

---

[49] See the essays collected in Platt and Squire 2017, which explore in depth the relationship between images and framing devices deployed in Graeco-Roman art.

[50] cf. Osborne 1998: 94. See also Fanfani and Harlizius-Klück 2016: 89–96, who argue that this patterning of borders and friezes on this vase provides a good illustration of weaving technology's far-reaching influence.

[51] On the differences in black- and red-figure in depicting pictorial space see also Neer 2002: 36–8 and Dietrich 2010.

Figure 1.10 Amphora by Exekias with man and woman on a chariot (c. 540 BCE).
Metropolitan Museum of Art

lines and spirals embedded in the fabric appear analogous to the spots covering each animal. Indeed, that the maenad in the foreground also wears a leopard skin makes this mix between the patterns of fabric and animal skin even more blended, since the hide of this animal is not immediately distinguishable from the decorations of her garment.[52] Thus the *poikilia* visible in this vase's textiles and in their combination

[52] cf. Osborne 1998: 103, who characterises these animals as 'simple further elaborations of her costume'.

Figure 1.11 Amphora by Amasis painter depicting Dionysus and maenads (mid-sixth century BCE). Paris: Cabinet des Medailles, Bibliothèque Nationale

with the other decorative motifs provides an illustration of a larger concept inform-ing the image: the hybridity of Dionysian worship finds visual expression here in the compression of naturally occurring and artificially created patterns into a single surface.[53]

While examples of elaborate garment decoration in black-figure could be mul-tiplied, I have focused on this selection of examples because they best illuminate a

[53] cf. Carpenter 1986: 90 on the significance of this scene in the history of Dionysian imagery: 'It seems that women here have become central to the meaning of a Dionysian scene . . . Suddenly the women have attributes that give them an identity, and suddenly they are unambiguously connected with the god who welcomes them.'

particular kind of relationship between the *poikilia* of painting and textiles.[54] This relationship becomes clear from the fact that the depiction of textiles in black-figure images does not serve merely as a decorative flourish, but functions as a way to articulate and distinguish the contours of different human bodies. This is because the use of textiles to construct images in the manner described above can be explained at least in part by the constraints as well as the possibilities imposed by the black-figure technique. For given that figures had to be depicted in silhouette with the outlines incised, the decoration of figures' clothing was one way to clearly articulate human figures from one another and from the rest of the pictorial space.[55] And in this sense, the *poikilia* of painted textiles not only is constitutive of a certain type of viewing experience, but also reflects the interactivity between the painter and the materials of his craft.[56]

Since the decoration of clothing in black-figure vase painting depended on the painter's facility with the incision technique, the depiction of such garments could also be a site for showcasing the virtuosity of the painter. As an illustration of this point, this is J. D. Beazley's characterisation of Exekias' rendering of the Achilles and Ajax scene discussed above: 'In this picture, with its profusion of minute incised detail in hair, armour, and mantles, the black-figure *technique* reaches its acme, or even passes it' (1986: 60, emphasis in original).[57] The emanation of *poikilia* from the clothing of painted figures can thus also be read as a vivid illustration of the

---

[54] See also Lissarrague 2018 on the function of decorated armour in vase painting, an analysis which also bears on the next chapter's focus on metal: 'L'ornement fait partie de l'image et ajoute prestige et éclat aux objects auxquels il s'applique' (139).

[55] cf. Osborne 1998: 142: 'Because of the variety of tones and textures of line it [red-figure] could deploy, and particularly the dense and wiry relief line, it was much easier in red- than in black-figure painting to keep overlapping figures distinct.'

[56] The effect of the medium (black-figure painting) on the painter's method of representation that I am proposing here is much in line with Malafouris 2013's analysis of the relationship between the written contents of Linear B tablets and their medium of preservation in small clay files: 'It is clear that in this case the cognitive process does not simply involve the internal representation of symbols via the Linear B code in order to produce the outcome that we see inscribed in the tablets. The cognitive process of producing the file also involves physical manipulation of the properties of the representational medium as a material object in real time and space.' As he goes on to argue, the recording of data in this particular medium in turn affected the way the process of remembering was conceptualised: 'in the case of the Linear B it was not simply information that was externalized but also the *actual processing of that information*' (2013: 73, emphasis added).

[57] cf. Osborne 1998: 135 on the relationship between the black-figure technique and the depiction of textiles therein: 'Incised lines could convey the patterning of textiles in a striking way, but they could not convey interior contours to nearly such good effect.'

engagement between the materiality of the pot and its imagery and the potter's handicraft.

The development of the red-figure technique created new possibilities for the elaboration of textiles and thus for showcasing the virtuosity of the painter. This shift is nicely illustrated in the few bilingual vases that are extant, which depict the same scene in red- and black-figure on opposite sides of the vessel. As Richard Neer has argued, *poikilia* is especially apparent in bilingual vases because of the heightened visual complexity that results from the combination of painting techniques on the same vessel:

> Neither side of a bilingual amphora is necessarily superior to the other; rather, the point seems to be that to have both versions, positive and negative, is desirable. There is a virtual deadlock in such instances, as though technical extravagance – mere visual richness – were an end in itself. (2002: 33)[58]

Seen in this way, bilingual vases exploit the very kind of 'technical extravagance' and 'visual richness' that was often concentrated in textile representations on black-figure vases like those discussed above. For instance, an Attic amphora attributed to the Andocides and Lysippides painters portrays the same scene discussed earlier, of Achilles and Ajax playing a board game (Fig. 1.12). Both figures are wearing the same garments on each side of the vessel, including intricately patterned cloaks like those on the Exekias amphora. But the effect of rendering this same scene in both red- and black-figure underscores the distinctive means of portraying *poikilia* afforded by each technique. The cloaks on the black-figure side evince a luminous aspect because of their incision in white, an effect that is heightened by the three-pointed starburst motifs inscribed on each cloak. On the red-figure side, the patterning on each figure's garments is no less elaborate, but depicted at a smaller scale and in much more minute detail, due to its creation by means of brushstrokes rather than chiselling.[59] Both sides also incorporate red detailing, lending a polychromatic aspect

---

[58] Neer goes on to contend that the eventual shift away from black- to red-figure may thus be interpreted as symptomatic of a desire to cultivate a wider variety of forms of *poikilia* in vase painting, a corrective to a traditional view that understands the shift to red-figure as indication of an increased interest in the naturalistic representation of human forms and pictorial space; cf. Neer 2002: 32. Whether or not one accepts this interpretation, what his reading underscores is the wide variety of visual effects that could be created by and through *poikilia* in vase painting.

[59] cf. Boardman 2001: 79 on the new possibilities afforded by the red-figure technique: 'Different degrees of intensity of line were possible: standard, dilute, and the so-called relief line which was crisp and dark, standing proud of the surface of the vase to catch

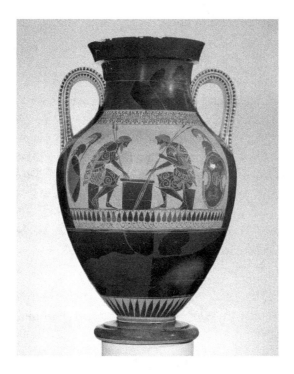

Figure 1.12a and b Amphora attributed to the Andocides and Lysippides painters portraying Achilles and Ajax (c. 525–520 BCE). Photography © Museum of Fine Arts, Boston

to the whole in addition to the contrast obtained from the juxtaposition of red- and black-figure. And given that the clothing in each technique is afforded the most lavish amount of detail in both scenes, this amphora makes each painting technique's distinctive means of elaborating textiles a focal point of the vessel.

In this section, I have suggested that the representation of *poikilia* in garments rendered in black-figure complicates any straightforward distinction between ornament and figure.[60] This is because the elaboration of textiles was no mere decorative feature, but functioned as a means by which human forms could be delineated in the black-figure technique.[61] And given that the reproduction of *poikilia* in garments in painting was in part a reflection of the constraints associated with black-figure, these representations therefore visualise the dexterity and skill of the painter in his ability to render such fine detail by means of minute incisions. Likewise, in the next section, we will see how literary depictions of women's weaving construe *poikilia* as a quality that clearly visualises human–material interaction.

Putting the 'Hand' into Handicraft: *Poikilia* and (Feminine) Thought Patterns

The vivid sensory effects conjured by the textiles we have seen so far recall Empedocles' discussion of how polychromy can lend a lifelike aspect to votive statues, *anathēmata*:

> ὡς δ' ὁπόταν γραφέες ἀναθήματα <u>ποικίλλωσιν</u>
> ἀνέρες ἀμφὶ τέχνης ὑπὸ μήτιος εὖ δεδαῶτε,
> οἵ τ' ἐπεὶ οὖν μάρψωσι πολύχροα φάρμακα χερσίν,
> ἁρμονίῃ μείξαντε τὰ μὲν πλέω, ἄλλα δ' ἐλάσσω,
> ἐκ τῶν εἴδεα πᾶσιν ἀλίγκια πορσύνοισι

> As when painters are <u>decorating</u> offerings, men through cunning well skilled in their craft – when they actually seize pigments of many colours in their hands,

reflected light, and often used to outline figures, rather as incision had been used by some black figure painters to mark contours off from the reddish background.'

[60] The reading advanced here is thus indebted to Dietrich and Squire 2018's recent collection of essays devoted to this topic.

[61] cf. the comments of Mackay 2010: 332 in her study of Exekias, where she notes that the decorations 'contribute to the variegation of the silhouettes and the impression of a decorative texture, almost filigree-like, that engages the viewer's eye, causing the gaze to rove over the deceptively simple composition by which it is then captured and subtly manipulated'.

mixing in harmony more of some and less of others, they produce from them forms resembling all things.[62]

Poikilia is not just equated here with the appearance of multiple colours, but is conceived as a manual process involving the mixture of different hues to produce a lifelike aspect. In this way, Empedocles alludes to how the painter's art of mixing colour (ἀμφὶ τέχνης ὑπὸ μήτιος εὖ δεδαῶτε) can serve to reproduce the visual qualities found in living things (εἴδεα πᾶσιν ἀλίγκια πορσύνοισι). It is significant, too, that Empedocles refers to this process specifically in the context of dedications to the gods, *anathēmata*, because this recalls the *poikilia* of the Acropolis korai and this quality's relevance to the korai's votive function. Empedocles thus explicitly affirms the unique potential of *poikilia* to enliven figures (in this case, by making them more lifelike) and, in so doing, make a dedication, an *anathēma*, a source of delight, an *agalma*.

Moreover, as more than one commentator has observed, by referring to colours in terms of *pharmaka*, Empedocles also intimates the magical or supernatural quality that attends such reproductions of nature.[63] As in Homer's allusions to Helen and Andromache 'working in' (ἐμπάσσω) images into their textiles, a verb which likewise evokes the use of *pharmaka* as I discuss below, Empedocles emphasises the bodily element to the use of *pharmaka* in referring to how painters physically 'seize pigments of many colours in their hands' (μάρψωσι πολύχροα φάρμακα χερσίν) in order to blend them in different proportions (ἁρμονίηι μείξαντε). Thus, as in the creation of images and patterns in textiles, it is the artist's manipulation of colour blends, rather than the colours themselves, that allow for discernible images to emerge out of these combinations (ἐκ τῶν εἴδεα).

In linking the skilful blending of colour with the decoration of lifelike votive offerings (ἀναθήματα ποικίλλωσιν), Empedocles testifies to the vivifying effect of colour, an idea that finds numerous parallels in later sources.[64] For instance, in Euripides' *Helen*, Helen wishes that her beauty could be 'rubbed off' her visage (εἴθ' ἐξαλειφθεῖσ' ὡς ἄγαλμ' αὖθις πάλιν / αἴσχιον εἶδος ἔλαβον ἀντὶ τοῦ καλοῦ, 262–3), employing language that likens the marring of her beauty to the removal

---

[62] DK B 23, trans. Kirk, Raven, and Schofield 1983.

[63] cf. Grand-Clément 2011: 42–50.

[64] See, for instance, Pl. *Plt.* 277c1–3: 'For our talk, just like an image of a living creature, seems to have a sufficient outline, but has not yet achieved the vividness (ἐνάργειαν) that comes from pigments and the mixture of colours' (λόγος ἡμῖν ὥσπερ ζῷον τὴν ἔξωθεν μὲν περιγραφὴν ἔοικεν ἱκανῶς ἔχειν, τὴν δὲ οἷον τοῖς φαρμάκοις καὶ τῇ συγκράσει τῶν χρωμάτων ἐνάργειαν οὐκ ἀπειληφέναι πω). See also Skarsouli 2009: 165–76 and Pierre 2009: 179–87 on the relation between colour terminology and rhetoric.

of paint from a statue or votive offering.[65] Not only does this indicate the aesthetic value linked with the polychromy of artefacts like the korai, it is also significant that Helen identifies a particular tactile gesture ('rubbing off', ἐξαλειφθεῖσα) as the mode in which her beauty could be removed. This idea chimes with depictions of women's weaving that likewise suggest an intimate correlation between women's handiwork and the beauty of their textiles.[66] But whereas Helen imagines removing her beauty with a sweep of the hand, her creation of textiles and those of other women depict a much more intimate and prolonged engagement of women's hands with the colourful fabric they produce.

Descriptions of cloth and cloth-making in Homer frequently conceptualise weaving as an extension of women. Perhaps the clearest instance of this idea is the shroud Penelope weaves for Laertes. This textile, and Penelope's deployment of it in order to deceive her suitors, have long been treated as a physical manifestation of her cunning. Indeed, Penelope herself describes it as such when she says that she 'winds a skein of tricks' (δόλους τολυπεύω, Od. 19.137). On this formulation, Penelope's weaving is conceptualised not just as a *symbol* of her guile, but as a material, physical extension of it. The shroud, then, embodies Penelope's craftiness because it is through the weaving of it that she enacts her ruse.[67] Elsewhere, too, textiles are imagined as extensions of the minds and bodies who wove them.[68] In what follows, I want to suggest that Penelope's shroud and its embodiment of her cunning are just an especially marked instance of the form of extended cognition that defines women's textiles more generally.

The conception of weaving as an embodied cognitive process accords well with the enactive approach to perception that I have argued is encouraged by the representation of *poikilia* in painted and sculpted textiles. For if the perception of *poikilia* relies on dynamic, embodied interactions with material things, then conversely the pro-

---

[65] cf. LeVen 2013: 239.

[66] The argument advanced here is thus indebted to Mueller 2010, which examines how textiles work to perpetuate women's memory and *kleos* in the *Odyssey*. Of particular relevance here is Mueller's focus on the significance of allusions to Helen's hands, which are 'possessed of the skill to commemorate and to destroy' in a way that 'is reminiscent of the inherent ambiguity of weaving itself in the Homeric poems' (13). See also Whitley 2013 on 'material entanglements' in Homer as well as Grethlein 2008 on the relation between objects and memory in Homeric epic.

[67] Chapters 5 and 6 will focus on this enactive dimension of *poikilia* and its particular affinity with ruses and traps.

[68] This is very much in line with the conclusions of Mueller 2010, e.g. 'Women weave to be remembered. The finished products of their weaving, such as the *peplos* Helen gives to Telemachus, serve as *agents* of that memory – *mnēmata*' (8, emphasis added).

duction of *poikilia* in fabric likewise depends on a similarly dynamic process between human bodies and minds on the one hand and materials on the other. And this interactivity has been aptly termed 'material engagement' by Lambros Malafouris (2013). His work presents a version of the extended mind thesis (which, like the theory of enactive perception, emphasises the importance of embodiment in cognition) that not only contends that cognition operates through and even depends upon interaction with the material world, but makes the stronger claim that the materiality of things in fact plays an active and constitutive role in shaping cognitive processes.[69]

While Malafouris concentrates predominantly on prehistoric tool-making and cave painting in his work, his contentions are nonetheless applicable to the accounts of weaving adduced here. As we will see, Homer as well as the tragedians delineate textiles as extensions of the women that wove them by linking visual and tangible aspects of the fabric with the gestures and bodies of particular women. As Malafouris argues, Palaeolithic cave paintings should not be interpreted as the 'material residues of human consciousness' or as prehistoric man 'externalizing the contents of his or her mind'. Instead, the process of incising and painting these marks on cave walls is a way to 'construct external patterns for sensorimotor engagement' (Malafouris 2013: 202). As I will demonstrate, 'sensorimotor engagement' is precisely the feature of weaving that is underscored in these passages in their attention to the embodied, processual aspect of weaving.

Elsewhere in Homer, textiles are identified in terms of the feminine bodies that created them, as in Andromache's reference to the fine clothing stored in the Trojan palace that was 'wrought by the hands of women' (τετυγμένα χερσὶ γυναικῶν, *Il.* 22.511). The importance of this connection between women's hands and fabric is corroborated by a recurring description of Athena's weaving in the *Iliad*. Athena is said to wear an 'elaborate *peplos* that she made and fashioned herself with her own hands' (πέπλον μὲν κατέχευεν ἑανὸν πατρὸς ἐπ' οὔδει / ποικίλον, ὅν ῥ' αὐτὴ ποιήσατο καὶ κάμε χερσίν, *Il.* 5.735 = *Il.* 8.386). The association of *poikilia* with the patron goddess of weaving herself points up the superlative technical skill required for the creation of such a quality.[70] Moreover, the explicit reference in Homer to the *peplos* as the product of her own handiwork (αὐτὴ ποιήσατο καὶ κάμε χερσίν) – where her hands' labours receive extra attention in the hendiadys of ποιήσατο καὶ

---

[69] See especially Clark and Chalmers 1998 on the extended mind hypothesis, as well as Clark 1997.

[70] cf. n. 40 above, where I discussed the dedication of korai by craftsmen, *banausoi*, where *poikilia* would both delight the patron goddess of craft and reflect the manual skill embodied in the craftsmen's work.

κάμε χερσίν – emphasises how the *poikilia* wrought in textiles constitutes a visual and material testament to the physical workmanship involved.

From these allusions to the production of textiles in Homer, it becomes clear that the textiles classified by *poikilia* were valued not simply for their decorated aspect. Instead, the consistent attention given to the manual labour involved in the production of *poikilia* illustrates how these textiles were conceptualised as extensions of the individual(s) who made them.[71] And while the examples discussed so far highlight how textiles are emanations of the particular hands that wove them, elsewhere the term ἐμπάσσω captures a particular type of physical movement involved in the production of textiles. Its first appearance is in an oft-discussed passage at *Il.* 3.125–8, where Helen uses scenes from the Trojan War to pattern her diplax:

ἣ δὲ μέγαν ἱστὸν ὕφαινε
δίπλακα πορφυρέην, πολέας δ' ἐνέπασσεν ἀέθλους
Τρώων θ' ἱπποδάμων καὶ Ἀχαιῶν χαλκοχιτώνων,
οὓς ἔθεν εἵνεκ' ἔπασχον ὑπ' Ἄρηος παλαμάων.

And she was weaving a deep purple double-folded robe at her great loom, and she was working into it the many contests of the horse-taming Trojans and the bronze-clad Achaeans, which they were suffering at the hands of Ares on her account.

As many commentators both ancient and modern have discussed, this depiction of Helen's portrayal of the events of the Trojan War in her diplax parallels the activity of the poet.[72] What is equally significant, however, is that fact that Helen is not just weaving (ὕφαινε) but is simultaneously 'working in' (ἐνέπασσεν) scenes from the war, as this verb suggests a specific kind of tactile engagement with the fabric that could not be communicated by the verb ὑφαίνω alone. Moreover, the simultaneity of these actions, weaving and working, suggest a heightened degree of physical

---

[71] cf. Karanika 2014, who concentrates on the overlap between textile production and labour and female speech acts in ancient Greek thought.

[72] Gregory Nagy 2012 has elaborated the significance of this linkage between weaving and epic narration as follows: 'epic narration is visualized not only generally as the craft of weaving but also specifically as the specialized craft of pattern-weaving', 278. As he argues, the conceptualisation of epic storytelling as weaving is borne out in the two uses of the verb ἐμπάσσω that exclusively describe Helen's and Andromache's weaving: 'This story of war told by the pattern-weaving of Helen is linked to the overall story of war told by the pattern-weaving of Andromache. So the narrations woven into the *diplax* of Helen and into the *diplax* of Andromache are both linked with the overall narration of the Homeric *Iliad*' (2012: 277).

engagement involved in Helen's craft, one that reflects her familiarity with the events portrayed. Likewise does Andromache in *Iliad* 22 perform these same actions together: 'But she was weaving a double-folded purple robe at her loom in the inmost part of the house and was working into it <u>different-coloured</u> flowers' (ἀλλ' ἥ γ' ἱστὸν ὕφαινε μυχῷ δόμου ὑψηλοῖο / δίπλακα πορφυρέην, ἐν δὲ θρόνα <u>ποικίλ'</u> ἔπασσε, *Il.* 22.440–1).[73] Given that πάσσω is a verb used elsewhere in Homer to refer to the sprinkling or spreading of *pharmaka* – particularly those with healing powers used by the divine physician Paeëon (*Il.* 5.401, 900; also used of sprinkling salt at *Il.* 9.214) – the use of this term in the context of weaving seems likely to indicate a similarly technical kind of gesture. Moreover, Helen's and Andromache's adoption of this movement in association with imagery that is unparalleled in other Homeric allusions to weaving suggests that it involves a high degree of dexterity and know-how.[74]

The association of πάσσω with *pharmaka* in Homer in turn evokes comparison with Empedocles' description of painters' 'seizing pigments of many colours with their hands' (ἐπεὶ οὖν μάρψωσι πολύχροα φάρμακα χερσίν, DK B 23.3). As I argued above, Empedocles' account emphasises the embodied dimension of image-making with its focus on the physical manipulation of colour. Analogously, then, the use of ἐμπάσσω to describe the creation of decorated fabric implicates the embodied practices of Helen and Andromache in the very fabric they produce. Thus the inclusion of ἐμπάσσω in these passages highlights the way in which these textiles embody the dexterous physical gestures involved in their creation, and in turn function as extensions of the cognitive processes that enable each textile's creation. The word ἐμπάσσω, in other words, highlights the synergistic dynamic between the mental and the physical demanded by weaving.

In fact, research into ancient weaving technology has revealed a rationale for this persistent linkage between the bodies and movements of individual women and the textiles they produce. To weave even the most basic textile required constant movement and interaction with the warp and weft in 'a complex composition of woven and plaited parts integrated into a finished product by repeated gestures

---

[73] Scheid and Svenbro 1996: 53–8 provide a useful survey of the ancient testimonia on the meaning of the θρόνα referred to here; cf. Bolling 1958 and Lawler 1948. On this term see also Grand-Clément 2011: 461–2, who discusses in greater detail the connotations of magic associated with θρόνα.

[74] As Canevaro 2018: 64–7 discusses, an important difference between Andromache and Helen is that Andromache weaves within an inner chamber (μυχῷ), while Helen's location is underspecified (ἐν μεγάρῳ, *Il.* 3.125), a distinction that maps onto their choices of weaving imagery: Helen positions her work within the male, martial sphere, while Andromache sticks to floral motifs, the more appropriate choice for a woman.

of turning the piece around or upside down'.[75] Indeed, the ancient loom itself has been characterised by Susan Edmunds as 'more a method or process than a thing', a description that aptly captures the extent to which weaving occurred from the conjunction of persons and things. In other words, the creation of designs like Andromache's flowers or Helen's pictures of the Trojan War was not a product of what Tim Ingold calls a hylomorphic model of creation, in which artisans project a mental image onto material substrates. Instead, such textiles came into being from the interaction between persons and materials, in which the weaver is able to 'join with and follow the forces and flows of material that bring the form of the work into being' (Ingold 2010a: 97). And while the same could be said of the other handicrafts discussed here, like sculpting and painting, the point becomes especially clear in the case of weaving because of the literary examples that explicitly formulate a special relationship between weavers and their textiles.

Further, as Giovanni Fanfani and Ellen Harlizius-Klück have shown, the creation of patterns in cloth is contingent not only on physical dexterity, but also on no small degree of mathematical calculation.[76] This they characterise as a kind of 'visual algebra' (2016: 748), a term which well expresses the cognitive aspect of pattern-weaving: 'Knowledge of divisibility rules and of number features (such as odd, even, prime, relatively prime), as well as knowledge of common measures, least common multiples, and greatest common divisors was necessary to weave the elaborate patterns we see in the visual representations' (2016: 761).[77] This makes it clear that the production of the kind of textiles represented in vase painting and statuary would have involved as much manual as *mental* labour. Woven designs can thus be read as expressions not just of the weaver's manual dexterity, but of the continuous cognitive, mathematical engagement required for the weaving process.

There is another cognitive facet to Helen and Andromache's weaving that becomes salient in light of the narrative contexts for these portrayals. Helen's images implicate herself as the cause of the war and the soldiers' suffering (οὓς ἔθεν εἵνεκ' ἔπασχον ὑπ' Ἄρηος παλαμάων, *Il.* 3.128) and the fact that she already in book 3 can depict the 'many struggles' (πολέας δ' ἐνέπασσεν ἀέθλους, *Il.* 3.126) suffered speaks to her painful awareness of the devastation she has wrought and can now record in this textile. Significantly, Helen's work here is interrupted by Iris' arrival and sum-

---

[75] Harlizius-Klück and Fanfani 2016: 95. See also Barber 1991 for an exhaustive study of prehistoric and ancient weaving techniques in the Mediterranean and beyond.

[76] See too the study by Essinger 2007, which explores in fascinating detail how Jacquard's loom led to the development of the modern computer.

[77] See Harlizius-Klück and Fanfani 2016 (especially 74–8) and Barber 1991: 91–112 (on the technical constraints imposed by the warp-weighted loom) as well as Edmunds 2012.

mons to the walls of Troy to view the troops in real time. This creates two planes of perspective (not unlike the dual folds of Helen's diplax): Helen's mental vision of the Trojan War's events as transmitted on the textile and the real-life figures of that war that she views from Troy's battlements.[78] In this sense, Helen's diplax is also visibly incomplete in two ways, as it is both materially unfinished and incomplete in its record of the war's travails, which continue to play out before Helen's eyes.

While weaving provides a concrete form for Helen to delineate her particular perspective on the war, the same activity for Andromache is what occupies her during Hector's demise. Just as Iris interrupts Helen's work to bring her to the wall, when Andromache becomes aware of the lamentations from the wall she drops her shuttle to the floor (*Il.* 22.447–8). The two women, then, reveal different patterns of thought in these moments of textilic craftsmanship: Helen's perspective on her relationship to the war's travails and Andromache's realisation of the futility of her weaving in the face of Hector's death.

Nor is this conception of weaving as an extension of the feminine mind and body unique to Homer. In Aeschylus' *Libation Bearers*, for instance, Orestes presents Electra with a sample of her own workmanship as proof of his identity. And this token only works as such because, to Electra, it is recognisably unique to her: 'See this piece of weaving, the work of your own hand, the strikes of the batten and the animal design' (ἰδοῦ δ' ὕφασμα τοῦτο, σῆς ἔργον χερός, / σπάθης τε πληγὰς ἠδὲ θήρειον γραφήν, 232–3).[79] As in the depiction of Helen and Andromache 'working in' images, here too a specific gesture, the 'strikes of the batten', has become part of the fabric and remains visible there. That this aspect of the cloth is paired with the reference to its 'animal design' suggests that the two are equally perceptible and thus equally integral to defining the cloth as Electra's: both are tangible traces of her handiwork. Finally, that this is the last token Orestes presents before Electra recognises him testifies to the surety with which she recognises it as her own, since it is able to provide the definitive proof of Orestes' identity.

Likewise, in Euripides' *Ion* (1417–25), Creusa proves her identity to Ion by describing the unfinished piece of weaving she left in his basket.[80] Not only does she

---

[78] As Canevaro 2018: 181–2 rightly points out, though, Helen's knowledge of the war is decidedly incomplete: her work on the diplax is stalled by Iris before its completion, and when she surveys the battlefield from the wall she does not know yet that her brothers have already died (*Il.* 3.236–43).

[79] On the use of the batten as a tool for beating the weft into place see Barber 1991: 274.

[80] cf. Tuck 2009 on the relation between textile production and myth in Euripides' *Ion*, as well as Fletcher 2009, who offers an adroit interpretation of the fabric motif of this play and its relation to earlier poetic works: 'The fixed warp of the fabric, which includes not only the Hesiodic version but also several famous tragedies, now takes on an entirely different

name the images woven within it (a Gorgon's face, bordered by serpents, 1421–3), but she locates in it a temporal dimension by conceptualising it as an extension of her youth.[81] Thus as in Orestes' description of Electra's handiwork, the design on the cloth is only one way it is connected to Creusa. More important is the way it preserves her youthfulness, which becomes clear at once from the fact that she first names it as 'cloth which I once wove as a child' (σκέψασθ' · ὃ παῖς ποτ' οὖσ' ὕφασμ' ὕφην' ἐγώ, 1417). Moreover, that the fabric is 'unfinished, like a practice piece' (οὐ τέλεον, οἷον δ' ἐκδίδαγμα κερκίδος, 1419) indicates that the object offers tangible testament to Creusa's younger self by preserving a specific moment within the weaving process. Like Helen's and Andromache's, then, the incompleteness of Creusa's textile only adds to its meaningfulness. That Creusa concludes her description by addressing the fabric directly as 'a long-lost piece of my maidenhood' (ὦ χρόνιον ἱστῶν παρθένευμα τῶν ἐμῶν, 1425) makes explicit its significance as an extension of her (former) self: it is a παρθένευμα, a 'girlish pursuit', not an inanimate piece of fabric.

If we interpret the textiles represented in the literary sources as forms of material engagement, what becomes evident from these portrayals is how these objects are closely bound up with the physical and mental dimensions of their production. The weaving of patterns and images comprises a specific type of cognitive system, a form of technology that exhibits and preserves textures of thought and movement. And this provides an explanation for why the decoration encapsulated in the terminology of *poikilia* was desirable in textiles and served to mark such fabric as especially valuable: the elaborate patterns and images denoted by this term were not just ornamental, but visualised the intimate process between the fabric and the weaver's mind and body.

The cognitively extended creation of *poikilia* in fabric, then, complements the *perception* of this quality in other media like painting and statuary, which likewise involves the blurring of boundaries between humans and cloth. As I've argued in the second and third sections of this chapter, this is because the representation of *poikilos* cloth in statuary and painting is crucial to generating a particular kind of sensory engagement. Interpreting this imagery in light of Noë's version of enactive perception, Stafford's 'cognitive work of images' and Gell's 'technology of enchantment' – all of which identify different but compatible ways in which complicated stimuli

---

texture as it is shot through with the brilliance of a joyful reunion between mother and child. The new poetic fabric becomes a reweaving of the earlier texts which it incorporates' (129).

[81] On Homer's investiture of material objects with mnemonic functions, see especially Grethlein 2008.

affect visual experience – has made it possible to see how *poikilia* could attract, guide and entrance the gaze.

This last effect was especially pronounced in the case of the Acropolis korai and complements the literary portrayals of women's weaving, which likewise suggest how the creation of textiles preserved feminine agency in the form of their movements and thoughts. When these sets of evidence are taken together, we can imagine how the garments of the Acropolis korai may represent the kinds of cloth that skilled young women (or goddesses) could be expected to produce. If the scintillating quality of their textiles was conceived as the product of their own hands, this would add a further layer of complexity to these enigmatic figures, making their clothing not just a compelling decorative feature appropriate for an *agalma*, but a tangible assertion of their individual identities qua their work as weavers. The close association of *poikilos* cloth with women in particular that we have seen in this chapter in turn suggests a corresponding association between *poikilia*'s scintillating effects and the perception of female bodies writ large, and in Chapter 6 we will see this association resurface to devastating effect in the context of feminine seduction and deception. The next chapter, however, will delve deeper into the kind of force and vitality that *poikilia* could exercise by concentrating on its manifestations in metal armament.

2   Brazen Charm: The Vitality of Archaic Armour

HOMERIC BATTLE SCENES are brilliant with the flashing of metal. The *Iliad* in particular is filled with allusions to the radiance and glittering aspect of bronze armament, and the aim of this chapter is to show that the vivid phenomenology of Homeric bronze is not only a visual quality, but also functions as a symptom of a distinctive brazen vitality. By 'vitality' I am invoking the term used by Jane Bennett in her analysis of the lively qualities of metal (2010: 52–61) to refer to the dynamic properties that inhere in metallic microstructures.[1] The passages discussed here likewise challenge the conception of metal as a fixed, inert substance by disclosing how metal's sensuous properties – its sights and sounds, specifically – are expressions of a unique form of vitality that encompasses both human and nonhuman attributes.[2]

The agency associated with this vitality becomes especially apparent in the multifarious ways in which metal substances interact with human subjects. Possessed of

[1] See also Bennett 2010's formulation of material vitality as, 'the curious ability of inanimate things to animate, to act, to produce effects dramatic and subtle', 6. Her analysis of metallurgic vitality is much indebted to Deleuze and Guattari's 1987 account: 'what metal and metallurgy bring to light is a life proper to matter, a vital state of matter as such, a material vitalism that doubtless exists everywhere but is ordinarily hidden or covered, rendered unrecognizable, dissociated by the hylomorphic model. Metallurgy is the consciousness or thought of the matter-flow, and metal the correlate of this consciousness', 411.

[2] cf. Bennett 2010: 'metal is always metallurgical, always an alloy of the endeavors of many bodies, always something worked on by geological, biological, and often human agencies. And human metalworkers are themselves emergent effects of the vital materiality they work', 60. Webster 1954's observation about Homeric personifications is also strikingly apropos of the focus of the new materialisms: 'Homeric man, as I have said, was surrounded by things physical, animate, and invisible which were insufficiently understood. They all seemed to have some kind of life and so to be in some way human', 16.

the ability to entrance as well as terrify, metal also bears a special relationship to the humans who wear it by enhancing and even transfiguring their bodies. This intimate connection between armour and the male body is reflected in the fact that, as Nigel Spivey (1996: 71) notes, 'The art of the armourer is . . . very close to the art of the bronze sculptor.' The same technique of beating or hammering bronze (*sphyrelaton*) was employed for the fashioning of armour as well as early statuary, but even when this technique was not used, bronze retained a special link to the male body.[3] As Carol Mattusch (2014: 33) has summarised it, 'One of the most appealing features of bronze must have been the resemblance of its polished surface to the body of a nude athlete.' Thus if elaborately decorated and textured marble fabric defined the bodies of the Acropolis korai, bronze allowed for vivid materialisation of the male body. While in the previous chapter we saw how weaving could operate as a form of cognitive extension for women, here we will find a different kind of mind–material dynamic at work when we examine what happens when male bodies come into contact with metal armament, whether by perceiving it or wearing it themselves. As we will see, living bodies and pieces of armament together can form powerful new hybrids that align mortal men with the gods themselves.[4]

The figure of the Homeric aegis provides an apt segue between the last chapter and this one because the term αἰγίς, literally meaning 'goatskin', refers to both metallic and textile objects. While Athena's aegis is a tasselled garment that seems like a piece of fabric because of how she 'drapes it around her shoulders' (ἀμφὶ δ' ἄρ' ὤμοισιν βάλετ' αἰγίδα θυσσανόεσσαν / δεινήν, *Il.* 5.738–9), Zeus' aegis is said to have been forged by Hephaestus (*Il.* 15.309–10), is 'shining bright' (μαρμαρέην, *Il.* 17.594) as well as 'golden' (περὶ δ' αἰγίδι πάντα κάλυπτε χρυσείῃ, *Il.* 24.20–1), but is simultaneously also 'shaggy' (ἀμφιδάσειαν, *Il.* 15.309).[5] The divine aegis defies characterisation as one particular kind of material because it exhibits a seemingly paradoxical combination of metallic and fabric qualities, a fluidity that matches its capacity to both protect (*Il.* 24.20–1 of Hector's body) and terrify (*Il.* 15.230 of the Greeks; cf. *Il.* 17.596).[6] Moreover, the fact that the aegis terrifies specifically when

---

[3] On ancient bronzeworking techniques see especially Mattusch 2014: 55–95.

[4] This is a point also suggested in Vernant 1991: 27–49, who identifies Homeric gods as having a 'super-body': 'Living always in strength and beauty, the gods have a super-body: a body made entirely and forever of beauty and glory' (41). On human encounters with the divine in the *Iliad* in particular see also Turkeltaub 2007.

[5] On the etymology and mythology of the divine aegis, see Janko 1992 ad 308–11. See also Deacy and Villing 2009 on Athena's aegis in particular and its representations in text and art.

[6] See too the prominence of linen armour (and breastplates in particular) attested from Homer onwards. Aldrete, Bartell and Aldrete 2013: 11–20 provides a good survey of the

it is 'shaken' (τίναξε, 17.595, ἐπισσείων, 15.230) aligns its terrorising power with the divine body who wields it.[7] In these instances, the agency of the god and the aegis merge: the aegis with its 'dread' aspect (δεινήν, 15.309) and Apollo's 'shaking' of it are able to instantaneously strike fear into the Greeks. Taken together, these accounts of the aegis illuminate several features that will turn out to be consistently associated with armour's vitality: (1) the capacity to both terrorise and protect; (2) the varied and striking sensory effects that result from the conjunction of armour and flesh; and (3) the ontological instability that emerges from this conjunction, as armour variously endows warriors with the strength and appearance of nonhuman or even superhuman phenomena. And it is this feature of metal armament – that is, its ontological fluidity – that is responsible for its supernaturally powerful effects.

Affective Armour

It is clear that *poikilia* was equally at home in bronze and in fabric, given the formulaic use of the phrase 'elaborately wrought in bronze' (ποικίλα χαλκῷ) to describe armament of all types: breastplates (*Il.* 16.133–4), shields (*Il.* 10.149; cf. its designation of the shield in the Hesiodic *Shield of Heracles*, 423) and armour (ἔντεα, *Il.* 10.75; τεύχεα, *Il.* 3.327, 4.432, 6.504, 10.504, 12.396, 14.420) as well as chariots (*Il.* 4.226, 5.239, 10.322, 10.393, 10.501, 13.536, 14.431; *Od.* 3.492, 15.145).[8] As in the attribution of this quality to fabric, *poikilia* in this context not only confirms the finely crafted nature of armour, but designates the intersection of material and cognitive elements that accompany the perception of *poikilia* in this medium.

While *poikilia* characterises Hephaestus' construction of the last scene on Achilles' shield ('Εν δὲ χορὸν ποίκιλλε, 18.590), it also describes his former breastplate together with the epithet 'starry' (ἀστερόεις): 'He [Patroclus] situated the elaborate breastplate of starry aspect about his chest, the breastplate of swift-footed Achilles' (θώρηκα περὶ στήθεσσιν ἔδυνεν / ποικίλον ἀστερόεντα ποδώκεος Αἰακίδαο, 16.133–4). This epithet is elsewhere predominantly used to characterise the sky (οὐρανός, e.g. *Il.* 4.44, 15.371). Together, the combination of 'elaborate' and 'starry' may denote actual patterns of stars portrayed within the corselet, as Maria Rinaudo

---

literary and epigraphic evidence related to linen armament in the ancient Mediterranean world.

[7] See also Brouillet and Carastro 2018, who explore the sensorial and material dynamism of both Athena's aegis and the *kestos himas* given to Hera by Aphrodite in *Iliad* 14. Their approach, which focuses on the nexus of relationships activated by each object, thus has much in common with my own.

[8] See Mattusch 2014 for a good recent overview of the uses of bronze and the techniques involved in bronze workmanship in antiquity.

(2009) has argued, but may also simply refer to the glittering, luminous aspect that is repeatedly attributed to both fabric and metal in Homer with the terminology of *poikilia*.[9] On the other hand, in pursuing the analogy between metal and plumage or animal skins in her attempt to delineate more clearly the relationship between *poikilia* and colour, Adeline Grand-Clément (2011) has gone as far as to suggest that the play of light on bronze pieces may have caused them to *appear* to be multi-coloured.[10] On her interpretation, the visual impression of dappled light would have been phenomenologically similar to the perception of genuine variegation in colour, and thus she proposes that this justifies the designation of textiles as well as skin, plumage and metal with *poikilia*. While this interpretation of light's effects on colour perception is certainly possible, the more significant feature of *poikilia* in metal for my purposes is its association with what in English we could term a 'shimmer' or 'gleam'. This is because, as we will see, exceptional radiance is one way that the agency of Homeric armour is consistently manifested.[11]

As an attribute of metal workmanship, *poikilia* is but one of a constellation of terms invoked by Homer to encapsulate a uniquely metallic liveliness that imbues armour with a defensive as well as offensive capacity. The 'starry' (ἀστερόεις) aspect of Achilles' shield, for instance, is also used to describe Hephaestus' bronze house: '[Thetis arrived at] the undying, starry bronze house, pre-eminent among the immortals, which the lame-footed god had made himself' (ἄφθιτον ἀστερόεντα μεταπρεπέ' ἀθανάτοισι / χάλκεον, ὅν ῥ' αὐτὸς ποιήσατο κυλλοποδίων, *Il.* 18.370–1). This is the only other example in which ἀστερόεις is used as an epithet in Homer of anything except the sky, and here the combination of 'starry' together with 'undying' (ἄφθιτον) and 'pre-eminent' (μεταπρεπές) emphasises the house's visual distinctiveness as well as its durability. The bronze of the house is indestructible, just like the god who inhabits it (cf. the description at *Il.* 13.20–2 of Poseidon's underwater palace, which is made of gold and also 'imperishable', χρύσεα μαρμαίροντα τετεύχαται ἄφθιτα αἰεί).

---

[9] cf. Edwards 1991 ad 369–71. Rinaudo 2009, in an attempt to establish a closer semantic connection between archaic uses of *poikil/* and the origins of the term and its meaning of 'to prick' or 'to pierce', has proposed that ἀστερόεντα here denotes the inclusion of real images of stars within the surface of the bronze. On her interpretation, *poikil/* signifies the kind of image that results from the elaboration of metal in the form of embossing, inlaying or carving.

[10] cf. Grand-Clément 2011: 429: '*Poikilos* dénote la présence d'éléments de bronze *associés* à d'autres matériaux, créant ainsi un ensemble composite, un jeu de polychromie, un effet de bigarrure' (emphasis in original).

[11] cf. Hölscher 2018: 4–5 and passim on the agency imputed to objects when faced with human visual inspection.

Nor is this association of precious metal with divine accoutrements unique. As Richard Seaford (2004) has shown, the gods possess a number of metallurgic products that, in the human world, are not made of metal: for instance, golden sandals (*Il.* 24.341), golden cords (*Il.* 8.19, 25; 15.20) and golden reins (*Il.* 6.205).[12] While such implements make clear a special connection between gold and divinity, the value attached to gold encompasses bronze, as well, which is frequently cited in conjunction with gold in catalogues of high-value goods (e.g. bronze, silver, gold and ivory at *Od.* 4.70–5; bronze, gold and iron at *Il.* 6.48 and 10.379; bronze and gold at *Il.* 10.315 and 18.289, *Od.* 5.38). As we will see below, bronze has a particular significance for humans because of its capacity to endow mortal bodies with superhuman capabilities and characteristics.

It is in Hesiod's account of the 'golden race of men' (χρύσεον μὲν πρώτιστα γένος μερόπων ἀνθρώπων, *Op.* 109), however, that the confluence between gold and divinity is made explicit, since this group 'lived like gods' (ὥστε θεοὶ δ' ἔζωον, *Op.* 112).[13] It is also in this myth that the distinctively martial connotations of bronze are made apparent, since this generation's use of bronze goes hand in hand with their violent nature:[14]

Ζεὺς δὲ πατὴρ τρίτον ἄλλο γένος μερόπων ἀνθρώπων
χάλκειον ποίησ', οὐκ ἀργυρέῳ οὐδὲν ὁμοῖον,
ἐκ μελιᾶν, δεινόν τε καὶ ὄβριμον· οἷσιν Ἄρηος
ἔργ' ἔμελεν στονόεντα καὶ ὕβριες

And Zeus the father fashioned another race of mortal men, the third and brazen race, not like the silver race but from the ash tree, and they were terrible and mighty, for their concern was violence and the painful works of Ares. (*Op.* 143–6)

Unlike the gold and silver races, the bronze men are named as such because bronze is what they use, not what they are made of: 'Their arms were bronze, as were their houses, and their works were all in bronze' (ὧν δ' ἦν χάλκεα μὲν τεύχεα, χάλκεοι δέ

---

[12] See Seaford 2004: 30–3 for a full summary of the uses of and references to gold and silver in Homer. See also Lapatin 2015: 19–45 for a wide-ranging discussion of gold and silver in the ancient Greek and Roman worlds.

[13] On the association of precious metals with divine bodies, see especially Brouillet forthcoming.

[14] Comparable too is the figure of Talos as described by Apollonius Rhodes: 'His body and limbs were wrought in bronze unbreakable, but beneath the tendon by his ankle was a vein carrying blood' (δέμας καὶ γυῖα τέτυκτο / χάλκεος ἠδ' ἄρρηκτος, ὑπαὶ δέ οἱ ἔσκε τένοντος / σύριγξ αἱματόεσσα κατὰ σφυρόν, Ap. Rhod. 4.1645–7), discussed below at p. 80.

τε οἴκοι /χαλκῷ δ' εἰργάζοντο, 150–1). For this reason, as Glenn Most has observed, this group is the first in the myth to resemble contemporary humans.[15] Yet, as Helen Van Noorden has put it, 'There is a real question mark, I would argue, over the humanity of the Bronze race' (2014: 77). And this is because, as she argues, the description of the bronze men as having 'untouchable hands descending from their shoulders' (ἄπλαστοι· μεγάλη δὲ βίη καὶ χεῖρες ἄαπτοι ἐξ ὤμων, 148–9) and their origin from ash trees creates an affinity between this race and the *Theogony*'s depiction of the Titans (151–2) as well as primordial man (187, 563).[16] The bronze race is thus both recognisably like and unlike contemporary humans, and in this sense the Hesiodic account acknowledges an ambiguous ontological status of bronze that also plays out in Homeric battle scenes. For unlike gold, which is comparatively soft, copper alloys produce a bronze that is flexible as it is durable, resulting in surfaces as hard and impenetrable as the ferocious Bronze race.[17]

Bronze as Light

In Homer, bronze is most often described for its sensuous and aesthetic properties rather than its functional, practical ones. Brazen armament variously 'flashes' (στεροπῆς, *Il.* 19.363) and 'beams up to heaven' (οὐρανὸν εἴσω / λάμπ', *Il.* 11.44–5) as well as 'gleams like the moon' (τοῦ δ' ἀπάνευθε σέλας γένετ', *Il.* 19.374). The intense luminosity attributed to bronze is correlated with a particular kind of dazzling vibrancy that makes it akin to natural phenomena like the sun. This vibrancy can be expressed at the level of grammar, as when Homeric dressing scenes make pieces of armour the subject of verbs meaning 'to shine' or 'glow' (e.g. *Il.* 13.340–4, 19.362). Even the most provocative of such expressions, though, have much to reveal about the archaic conceptualisation of bronze. Lambros Malafouris (2013: 65) captures this relation between metaphorical expression and lived experience as follows, 'More specifically, material metaphors objectify sets of ontological correspondences, making possible the construction of powerful associative links among material things, bodies, and brains.' Throughout this chapter, we will see the Homeric poet attempt to capture bronze's vitality in a multitude of ways, from literal descriptions to personification to similes and metaphors. The vibrancy of bronze thus finds

[15] Most 1997: 110; cf. Currie 2012 on the structure of the myth and the interpretative difficulties posed by the order of races.

[16] Van Noorden 2014: 77–8.

[17] As Zorach and Phillips 2016: 97–8 note, apropos of Glaucus' exchange of gold for bronze armour with Diomedes at *Il.* 6.234–6, armour made of gold would have been far too heavy to wear, and so in spite of the Homeric poet's claim that Zeus had stolen Glaucus' wits in this instance, Glaucus in fact would have been better off with bronze armour!

expression in the poetic imaginary, as its variable inflections animate correspondingly vivid descriptions.[18]

In one exemplary instance of bronze's power, once Agamemnon has donned his whole panoply, the gleaming bronze of his armour is said to reach into the heavens in a show of strength that heralds the martial *aristeia* that is to come. This beam prompts Athena and Hera to thunder in response: 'The bronze from him gleamed far into heaven, and Athena and Hera raised a clamour in response' (τῆλε δὲ χαλκὸς ἀπ' αὐτόφιν οὐρανὸν εἴσω λάμπ' · / ἐπὶ δ' ἐγδούπησαν Ἀθηναίη τε καὶ Ἥρη, *Il.* 11.44–5). By making the bronze the subject of the verb, the sentence structure locates an active force in the gleam of the bronze. This reinforces its supernatural power, one that is manifested in its illumination of the heavens. The gleaming bronze is thus conceptualised as an animate as well as an animating force by virtue of its capacity to both light up the sky and, in doing so, prompt Athena and Hera to audibly respond.

Moreover, as the verses leading up to 11.44–5 emphasise, Agamemnon's arming for battle consists in the addition of a variety of metals to his body: the 'gleaming bronze' (νώροπα χαλκόν, 16), the silver ankle-pieces on his greaves (ἀργυρέοισιν ἐπισφυρίοις ἀραρυίας, 18), the gold, tin and cyanus of his breastplate (24–5), the gold and silver of his sword (29–31) and the bronze, tin and cyanus of his shield (33–5). One effect of this kind of detail in Homeric arming scenes is to convey how the Homeric warrior becomes something else when he dresses for battle and so embodies a mix of human and nonhuman entities – a transformation that in this scene is marked by the thunderous approbation of Athena and Hera.[19] As Melissa Mueller has articulated this phenomenon in her study of the dynamic between Ajax and his shield,

[18] Although some examples that I will adduce here are clearly metaphorical (e.g. the 'brazen voice' of Achilles at *Il.* 18.222, discussed below), as the cognitive metaphor theory of Lakoff and Johnson 1980 first emphasised and explored in detail, the intelligibility of such expressions develops from and relies on familiarity with the lived, sensuous experience of particular materials like that of bronze (cf. Gibbs 2017, which offers a robust overview of the scholarship as well as the criticism born out of Lakoff and Johnson's work). See also Nicole Boivin 2008: 47–64's thorough dissection of the role that metaphor has played in anthropology and material culture studies, and in particular her discussion of how changes in technology lead to new metaphors and therefore, to new concepts. Thus metaphorical constructions like those I discuss here, ones that attribute animate qualities to matter, need not be treated as purely linguistic entities or poetic flourishes, but can offer insight into how the experience of certain materials impacted archaic conceptions of the human body and its faculties.

[19] That the warrior's dressing effects a change or transformation of sorts in the man is of a piece with another feature that unites arming scenes in the *Iliad*: namely, that they precede moments and events of great significance for the warrior.

we can appreciate that within the Homeric duel there is a leveling of human and non-human participants. The fighting hero is a perfectly blended person-weapon, the boundaries of his autonomous self vanishing into those of the panoply he has donned. (2016a: 139)

Nor, however, is the 'perfectly blended person-weapon' a monolithic category: different persons, different armour and different groups of armoured men will exhibit distinctive features and capacities, even within the same battle scene.

The *Iliad* 11 passage's attention to the distinctive material elements of the warrior's unique panoply (a defining feature of the arming type-scene) construes the relation between Agamemnon and his armour as a form of assemblage. This is a term that came to prominence with the work of Deleuze and Guattari (1987) (followed and expanded by the more recent work of DeLanda 2006 and 2016), and Yannis Hamilakis (2013) provides a particularly clear definition of the concept as it is used by these authors: 'Assemblages are not bounded wholes; they are non-hierarchical, heterogeneous, contingent rather than permanent and stable, and rhizomatic rather than dendritic, that is, they do not follow a linear and hierarchical order' (126). In his own study of Bronze Age Crete, Hamilakis elaborates on the notion of assemblage to include sensory experience. Noting that the bodies, things and ideas that together form an assemblage are also always accompanied by sensory stimuli, he argues that 'Sensorial assemblages can be brought together and constituted for specific performative events. They can be temporarily territorialized in specific locales, and later dispersed, de-territorialized, and re-assembled ... elsewhere' (2013: 127). Agamemnon's dressing scene and the profound visual and audible effects that accompany it thus seem to exemplify this kind of sensorial assemblage, not only because the sensuous features of his armour's materiality become most exigent at this particular moment before battle (i.e. before Agamemnon's *aristeia*), but because the text also communicates the transience of the armour's effects: once Athena and Hera have signalled their response and 'honoured the king of Mycenae' (τιμῶσαι βασιλῆα πολυχρύσοιο Μυκήνης, 46), the narrative swiftly shifts (μὲν ἔπειτα, 47) to focus on the line of charioteers. As subsequent examples will attest, the sensorial field generated from armour's materiality constitutes a crucial element of its vitality, as the sights and sounds it generates powerfully affect the humans in its vicinity.

Homeric arming scenes also illustrate well the heterogeneity and non-hierarchical nature of the assemblage because they stress the individuality of each piece of armour as well as the entanglement between living beings and materials embedded within: Agamemnon's corselet, for example, was a gift from Cinyras (11.20–3), his shield bears the glaring face of the Gorgon (11.36–7), and his baldric is crowned with a three-headed serpent (11.38–40). Further, that these scenes typologically depict the warrior in the act of dressing (rather than describing the armour alone, for instance) means that the various parts of the warrior's body are also on display as he fits each piece to the appropriate part of his body. Even Agamemnon's shield, which he carries and does not wear against his skin, is characterised with an epithet that identifies it in terms of its relation to human bodies, 'man-covering', ἀμφιβρότην (32). Conversely, the shield is also 'fierce' (θοῦριν), an adjective that imputes an offensive capability to the shield in addition to its obvious defensive function.[20]

The gorgoneion on Agamemnon's shield contributes in no small part to the shield's offensive force because of how this visage 'glares fiercely' from its surface (δεινὸν δερκομένη, *Il.* 11.37). Similarly, Athena's aegis contains 'the head of the awful monster, the Gorgon, terrible and terrifying' (ἐν δέ τε Γοργείη κεφαλὴ δεινοῖο πελώρου / δεινή τε σμερδνή τε, *Il.* 5.741–2).[21] It is the pseudo-Hesiodic *Shield of Heracles*, however, which develops the idea of glaring shields to an extreme by locating multiple terrifying sets of gazes therein. The first figure described is Fear, who 'glares back with eyes burning like fire' (ἔμπαλιν ὄσσοισιν πυρὶ λαμπομένοισι δεδορκώς, 145), where the adverb ἔμπαλιν emphasises the reciprocity between the gaze of viewer and figure.[22] Elsewhere in the *Shield* the serpents worn by the Gorgons display a ferocious gaze (ἄγρια δερκομένω, 236), and so too does Fate 'glare terribly and bellow with a clanging sound' (δεινὸν δερκομένη καναχῇσί τε βεβρυχυῖα, 160) in a combination of awesome sound and sight that parallels the thunder and dazzling radiance of Agamemnon's dressing scene.

As Rainer Mack has suggested, the presence of the gorgoneion on shields recalls Perseus' defeat of the monster by staging 'an opposition of the "petrifying" gaze of Medusa and the objectifying gaze of the viewer' (2002: 592). The apparition of glaring eyes on shields can thus terrorise opponents because such figures are designed to force a confrontation between the 'gaze' of a shield and that of a spectator.[23] In this way, the delineation of frontal gazes animates the surface of the shield by imparting

---

[20] cf. Hainsworth 1993 ad 32: 'θοῦριν . . . is unexpected as epithet of something naturally to be thought of as defensive equipment'.

[21] On Homeric armour see especially Snodgrass 1967. Chase 1902 remains the most comprehensive account of shield devices attested in the literary and archaeological record, while Lissarrague 1990, 2008a, 2008b and 2018 represent the authoritative studies of armour's representation in vase painting.

[22] On the iconography of personifications like that of Fear in Greek art, see especially Shapiro 1993.

[23] See also the important and recent discussion by Grethlein 2016, which explores how representations of the Gorgon in archaic and classical vase painting demonstrate that 'sight was an object of pictorial representation that appealed to a broader fascination with reflexivity – as both the object and subject of visual inquiry'.

to it the apparition of a human sensory faculty.[24] And even in the absence of such designs, descriptions of Homeric shields and armour more generally reveal a congruity between the gleam of metal and that of eyes that gives both the capacity to terrorise opponents. For by portraying metal armament, especially bronze, as a material that can emanate blinding light, armour is depicted similarly to how both the sun and the human gaze itself were thought to work: that is, by emitting beams of light.[25]

For instance, at *Iliad* 19.16–17 Achilles' eyes 'blazed, as if a fire had been kindled there' (ἐν δέ οἱ ὄσσε / δεινὸν ὑπὸ βλεφάρων ὡς εἰ σέλας ἐξεφάανθεν); likewise do Agamemnon's eyes 'blaze' at *Iliad* 1.104 (ὄσσε δέ οἱ πυρὶ λαμπετόωντι ἐΐκτην); while at *Odyssey* 4.150 Menelaus refers to the 'missiles' of Telemachus' eyes (ὀφθαλμῶν τε βολαί).[26] While these examples well illustrate the aggressive force of the gaze, they also conform with other, later descriptions that draw an explicit connection between light, the sun and sight. The *Homeric Hymn to Demeter* offers an exemplary summation of this link by relating that Helios is one who 'looks down on the earth with your beams' (καταδέρκεαι ἀκτίνεσσι, 70).[27] On this 'extramissionist' approach to vision, the human eye operates by casting out beams of light that, by making physical contact with the objects in the field of vision, generate visual experience. And the depictions of the Greek army in *Iliad* 2 and 19 indicate that armour may not only reflect but also seem to *emit* light in a manner akin to the human eye.[28] Moreover, these examples also make it clear that it is not only the extraordinarily valuable armour of figures like Achilles and Agamemnon that is capable of extreme visual effects. Descriptions of the army en masse also testify to the supernaturally powerful effects of armour's luminosity. As we will see, bronze is the material of war par excellence because of the unique auditory and visual components that make this substance akin to a force of nature like lightning.

So intense is the gleam of the Greek army's armour in *Iliad* 19 that it 'reaches

---

[24] For a rich study of representations of frontal faces and gazes in archaic and classical art and literature, see especially Frontisi-Ducroux 1995.

[25] Prier 1989 was one of the earliest studies to explore the significance of this 'extramissionist' account of vision as it is embedded in the Homeric vocabulary of sight and appearance. More recently, see Squire 2016 for a compilation of essays that explore different conceptualisations of sight and viewing in the ancient world. On the relationship between sun and sight see especially Bielfeldt 2016, as well as Rudolph 2016 on Presocratic accounts of sight.

[26] cf. also *Od.* 19.446, where a boar is said literally to flash fire from its eyes, πῦρ δ᾽ ὀφθαλμοῖσι δεδορκώς.

[27] See also Pindar's ninth paean (Pind. fr. 52), which designates the sun's beam as 'the mother of eyes' (ἀκτὶς ἀελίου . . . μᾶτερ ὀμμάτων, 1–2) as well as the *Homeric Hymn to Helios* 9–11.

[28] cf. Shirazi 2018 in her study of the materiality and phenomenology of bronze mirrors in Euripides: 'Bronze has always been an important metal for thinking about light, but before bronze reflected light, it emitted it', 102.

heaven' (οὐρανὸν ἷκε) and the earth itself is said to 'beam', apparently in delight: 'The gleam reached up to heaven, and all the earth around beamed beneath the flash of bronze' (αἴγλη δ᾽ οὐρανὸν ἷκε, γέλασσε δὲ πᾶσα περὶ χθὼν / χαλκοῦ ὑπὸ στεροπῆς, 362–3).[29] Significantly, the verb used here to describe the earth, γελάω, itself connotes brightness and gleaming and for this reason also frequently means 'to smile'.[30] This creates a mirroring effect between the gleam of bronze and the corresponding beam emitted from the earth. In doing so, this description captures the dynamic and affective quality of metal, as a material that both moves by itself (οὐρανὸν ἷκε) by virtue of its gleam, and as a catalyst that can generate reactions from other substances – in this case, the earth beneath the warriors' feet. Like the thunder elicited by Agamemnon's panoply, so too is the gleam of bronze here envisaged as an animating force in its capacity to provoke a vivid affective response across an expanse of land. Here, however, this capacity is even more pronounced because the bronze provokes a 'beam' not from the gods, but from the earth – another non-human substance. Likewise, as the following section will reveal, the audible qualities of metal are as fundamental to armour's martial efficacy as its visual attributes.

Heavy Metal: The Sound of Battle

Made from a material that emits the vibrancy of fire, metal armour also possesses a terrifying sonority.[31] As Mark Edwards has observed (1991 ad 19.362–3), since the phrase οὐρανὸν ἷκε is elsewhere used in the *Iliad* to denote the movement of sound (12.338, 17.425), its appearance in *Iliad* 19 is suggestive of the noise that inevitably accompanies the advancing army. And the quality of this sound is intimated by the phrase 'bronze lightning' (χαλκοῦ ὑπὸ στεροπῆς, 19.363), which is of a piece with the simile in *Iliad* 2 that likens the advancing Greek army to thunder and lightning: 'And then they went, as if all the land was consumed with flame, and the earth groaned beneath them, as it does beneath Zeus in his wrath, delighting in thunder'

---

[29] On such 'animistic' portrayals in Homer see also Kokolakis 1980, who argues that such figurations in Homer are not unique to him, but reflect an old and widespread animistic worldview. See also the treatment of personification by Webster 1954, who argues instead that personifications aided in the formulation of abstract thoughts and concepts.

[30] cf. Clarke 2005 on the link between smiling and brightness conveyed by γελάω and see also the earlier work by Stanford 1936: 115–16, who emphasises that, 'there was no Pathetic Fallacy of a laughing Mother Earth or a smiling homestead, but only the more obvious image of *brightness in general*', 116, emphasis in original.

[31] On the sonority of metal, see also Brouillet forthcoming, who notes how metallic luminosity and its striking sonorous qualities together strengthen this material's association with divinity.

(οἳ δ' ἄρ' ἴσαν ὡς εἴ τε πυρὶ χθὼν πᾶσα νέμοιτο· / γαῖα δ' ὑπεστενάχιζε Διὶ ὣς τερπικεραύνῳ / χωομένῳ, 2.781–3). The use of this simile focuses attention on the blending of auditory and visual elements comprised by the army's movement by envisioning it as a confluence of natural phenomena: the fiery gleam of the army (πυρὶ χθὼν πᾶσα) seems to set the earth ablaze, while the thundering of their feet (γαῖα δ' ὑπεστενάχιζε) evokes Zeus' celestial powers. The armour on the warriors becomes akin to lightning and thunder by simultaneously lighting up the land and causing the earth to 'groan' (in *Iliad* 2) rather than 'beam' (as in *Iliad* 19).

Moreover, since lightning descends from heaven to earth, the fact that the bronze gleam of the army goes in the other direction, from earth to heaven, frames it as a counterpart to the celestial phenomenon. This offers an explanation, too, for the use of the adjective 'brazen' as an epithet of the sky at *Il.* 5.504, 17.425 and *Od.* 3.2. In the *Odyssey* passage, 'the heaven full of bronze' is where the sun ascends 'in order to shed light on immortals and mortals' (οὐρανὸν ἐς πολύχαλκον, ἵν' ἀθανάτοισι φαείνοι / καὶ θνητοῖσι βροτοῖσιν, *Od.* 3.2–3). The sky is aptly described as brazen here because the sun's beams refract light against the 'bronze' of the sky, analogous to the way that the gleam of the bronze of the Greek army reaches heaven because of the dazzling light that emanates from bronze in sunlight.

Similarly, in both *Iliad* 5 and 17 the sky is conceptualised as brazen during battle, as clouds of dust (*Il.* 5.504) and noise (*Il.* 17.425) rise through the air. The latter passage is the most similar to the depiction from *Iliad* 19 discussed above, since here it is the 'iron din' rather than the gleam of bronze that reaches skyward: 'the iron din reached bronze heaven through the empty aether' (σιδήρειος δ' ὀρυμαγδὸς / χάλκεον οὐρανὸν ἷκε δι' αἰθέρος ἀτρυγέτοιο, 17. 424–5). This description envisions an auditory response between the din of battle and the sky above, one in which the metallic clang of armour seems to clash against the surface of the sky. Thus in this instance the allusion to 'bronze heaven' may refer to the way that the sounds of battle seem to echo from the sky. Just as the clash of weapons creates an 'iron din', a correspondingly metallic clanging obtains when the sound of battle 'reaches heaven'.[32] As Sean Gurd (2016: 31) has observed, 'the *Iliad* is a soundful poem that strongly associates sound with war, destruction, terror, and death'. The martial cacophonies of the *Iliad* are the first in a trend of associating loud, discordant noise with human

---

[32] See Gurd 2016 on the figuration of discordant sounds in Greek thought, especially pp. 27–32 on the significance of auditory imagery and onomatopoeia in Homeric battle scenes. On the mixing of bronze and iron in early epic, see West 1978 ad 150, who notes that 'bronze continued to be the standard metal' in epic in spite of the introduction of iron in the eleventh century. On Homeric armour more generally see also Snodgrass 1967: 36–8 and Lorimer 1950.

upheaval and discord, a trend that Gurd traces from Homer and Hesiod down through Aristophanes. Seen in this light, bronze armament – even as it is crafted by human hands and in service to humans – both reflects and perpetuates human chaos.

The affective character of the sight and sound of armour is well articulated at *Iliad* 13.340–4, which makes explicit how the flash of armour blinds onlookers and causes anguish:

> ὄσσε δ' ἄμερδεν
> αὐγὴ χαλκείη κορύθων ἄπο λαμπομενάων
> θωρήκων τε νεοσμήκτων σακέων τε φαεινῶν
> ἐρχομένων ἄμυδις· μάλα κεν θρασυκάρδιος εἴη
> ὃς τότε γηθήσειεν ἰδὼν πόνον οὐδ' ἀκάχοιτο.

And the brazen shine from the glittering helmets, the polished corselets, and the gleaming shields dazzled their eyes as the troops thronged: whoever could, at such a time, feel glad in seeing the struggle, and not anguished, would be bold-hearted indeed. (*Il.* 13.340–4)

Here the rhyme between each piece of armour and its epithet, combined with the proliferation of harsh consonants (both highlighted by Janko 1992 ad 339–44), makes the striking sound of this description consonant with the piercing quality of the brazen sounds discussed above.[33] Further, that the 'brazen shine' (αὐγὴ χαλκείη) is imagined to possess a blinding force makes it akin to the sun and, analogously, to the human eye. This association between sight, sound and light beams is succinctly captured at the end of book 13, where the sound of the clashing armies rises through the sky and 'reaches the eyes of Zeus' (ἠχὴ δ' ἀμφοτέρων ἵκετ' αἰθέρα καὶ Διὸς αὐγάς, 13.837). The term αὐγή that at 13.340 designated the 'gleam' of bronze here denotes Zeus' gaze and the rays emitted from it. Not only does this suggest how bronze's gleam imparts to it a sense of vision,[34] but the same synaesthetic combination of sight and sound that we have seen in the examples above emerges from this battle scene as well, since it is a 'din' (ἠχή), an audible phenomenon, that reaches Zeus' *eyes*.[35]

From these examples, a vitality to metal and particularly to bronze becomes

---

[33] Stanford 1967 and 1981 remain the most robust studies on this kind of linkage between sound and sense in early Greek poetry.

[34] cf. *Od.* 19.18, where smoke is said to 'blind' (ἀμέρδω) armour, using the same term used in *Iliad* 13.340 to describe the way that armour, conversely, can blind onlookers; cf. Janko 1992 ad 339–44.

[35] See Porter 2013 on the phenomenon of seeing sound in a variety of classical Greek sources, as well as Weiss 2018 on the conflation of sound and sight in Aeschylus.

apparent from armour's depictions as an animate material interface, covering the flesh underneath while simultaneously having its own agency in the form of its glare as well as the piercing sound it creates upon impact. In this way, the Homeric panoply obtains both offensive and defensive properties from its material components. While the examples adduced in this section portray the effects of metallic vitality on onlookers, in the following section we will re-examine the significance of the human–armour assemblage by focusing on the relationship between armour and the body of its wearer.[36] These passages will indicate how the visual and auditory properties of armour were thought to be able to enhance and even transfigure the human body by endowing it with superhuman and/or nonhuman attributes.[37]

Bodies Nonhuman and Superhuman

One of the most pervasive ways in which armour interacts with its wearer is through affect, which in turn can manifest in visible changes to the warrior's appearance and physical abilities.[38] In *Iliad* 13.340–4, for instance, the narrator's account of the blinding onslaught of the clashing armies includes a reckoning of the dual affects associated with brightly shining objects: on the one hand, such appearances can evoke joy (γηθήσειεν) in spectators, but on the other hand, they may equally cause grief (ἀκάχοιτο): 'whoever could, at such a time, feel glad in seeing the struggle, and not anguished, would be bold-hearted indeed' (μάλα κεν θρασυκάρδιος εἴη / ὅς τότε γηθήσειεν ἰδὼν πόνον οὐδ' ἀκάχοιτο, 343–4). Bronze is here articulated as a material that can evoke opposing ends of the spectrum of human emotions, from extreme gladness to grief. By calling attention in these verses to the radically different potential reactions associated with bronze, the narrator captures the multidimensionality of bronze's affect. In one sense, the objects constructed from bronze may evoke responses of delight and gladness just like other, similarly well-crafted objects. As we saw above, bronze frequently appears alongside gold in catalogues of prestige

---

[36] On the construction of the body and its relation to mental states in Homer, see especially Clarke 1999 and Holmes 2010, especially pp. 41–83.

[37] See also the discussion by Spiegel 2020, which focuses on instances in which man–weapon entanglements fail or malfunction.

[38] cf. Vernant 1991: 37: 'The hero's accoutrements, the prestigious arms that represent his career, his exploits, and his personal value, are a direct extension of his body. They adhere to him, form an alliance with him, are integrated into his remarkable figure like every other trait of his bodily armor.' See too the discussion by Lissarrague 2008a, who argues that archaic and classical vase paintings display an equal interest in the armour and the bodies of warriors: 'Dans ce register, la representation des arms fait l'object d'une attention graphique aussi riche que celle portée aux corps.'

goods, and descriptions of heroic armour likewise stress the beauty of bronze. For example, Sarpedon's shield is of 'beautiful bronze' (καλὴν χαλκείην, *Il.* 12.295), the armour of Achilles that was stripped from Patroclus is 'of beautiful, shining bronze' (ἔντεα καλὰ μετὰ Τρώεσσιν ἔχονται χάλκεα μαρμαίροντα, *Il.* 18.130–1), and Agamemnon's shield, with its combination of bronze, tin and cyanus, is characterised as a 'highly wrought' (πολυδαίδαλον) and 'beautiful' (καλήν) object.[39]

But the *Iliad* 13 passage's reference to the 'boldness of heart' (θρασυκάρδιος εἴη, 13.343) that would allow an onlooker to take pleasure in the army's appearance also recalls Hesiod's picture of the race of bronze, who are defined not only by their preference for bronze but also by their 'hard hearts': 'But they possessed dauntless spirits of adamant, being rough men' (ἀλλ' ἀδάμαντος ἔχον κρατερόφρονα θυμόν, ἄπλαστοι, *Op.* 147–8). This race thus has precisely the constitution envisaged by *Iliad* 13's reference to 'boldness of heart' (θρασυκάρδιος, 343): their temperament and strength are as unyielding as the bronze that permeates their world. Similarly, that Ares, the god of war, is named several times with the epithet 'brazen' (χαλκέος) in Homer provides further support for this confluence between the materiality of bronze and a martial character. As I will suggest, this congruity is more than a metaphorical one. The following examples intimate a mutually reinforcing effect between the terrible strength of the bronze men and the temperament of this material.

In a striking image, Iphidamas' death at the hands of Agamemnon is imagined as a 'sleep of bronze': 'Thus he fell, and slept a sleep of bronze' (ὣς ὃ μὲν αὖθι πεσὼν κοιμήσατο χάλκεον ὕπνον, *Il.* 11.241). 'Bronze sleep' as a metaphor for death blends two ideas: that of Sleep as the brother of Death (cf. *Il.* 16.672 and Hes. *Theog.* 212) and the conception of bronze as the material of war and therefore of destruction.[40] The uniqueness of this image is apt for the unusual pathos that pervades this scene: this is the only instance in the Homeric epics where the narrator refers to an individual as 'pitiful' (οἰκτρός, 242), a remark that corroborates the picture to follow of the youth's life cut short. As the poet goes on to recount, there is a bride left behind by the youth, from whom he had not yet 'known joy' (ἧς οὔ τι χάριν ἴδε, 11.243). Thus the image of 'brazen sleep' sets the tone for the heightened pathos of the verses

---

[39] ἂν δ' ἕλετ' ἀμφιβρότην πολυδαίδαλον ἀσπίδα θοῦριν / καλήν, ἣν πέρι μὲν κύκλοι δέκα χάλκεοι ἦσαν, / ἐν δέ οἱ ὀμφαλοὶ ἦσαν ἐείκοσι κασσιτέροιο / λευκοί, ἐν δὲ μέσοισιν ἔην μέλανος κυάνοιο, *Il.* 11.32–5. The aesthetic value attached to armour is also clear from the fact that such pieces were offered up as dedications in sanctuaries; see e.g. Lissarrague 2008b for discussion of some of the dedicated shields found in the Olympic sanctuary.

[40] See Budelmann and LeVen 2014 for a thorough examination of this kind of blending in Timotheus, using the conceptual integration theory as formulated by Fauconnier and Turner 2002.

following the description of Iphidamas' death by offering us a poignant encapsulation of the permanence and harshness of his demise.

Moreover, a supernatural ferocity to bronze becomes apparent from the fact that not even divine flesh is impervious to bronze weaponry. Diomedes' blow with his spear to Aphrodite's hand in *Iliad* 5 provides vivid testimony of this (335–40). Here the bronze tip of his spear is personified as being 'pitiless' (νηλέϊ χαλκῷ, 330) to highlight its destructiveness as it rends Aphrodite's flesh (δόρυ χροὸς ἀντετόρησεν, 337).[41] This in spite of the fact that Aphrodite is not only immortal, but also has 'golden' as one of her epithets (e.g. *Il.* 3.64, 5.427, 9.389, etc.). While this is clearly not a literal reference to her material constitution, it does associate the goddess with the radiance of the metal and underscores the immortality of her beauty. For gold and silver, unlike bronze, are not subject to decay and thus share with the gods an immortal disposition. This is an association explicitly rendered in the *Odyssey*'s account of the gold and silver dogs that guard Alcinous' palace (χρύσειοι δ᾽ ἑκάτερθε καὶ ἀργύρεοι κύνες ἦσαν, 7.91), which are 'undying and unageing for all time' (ἀθανάτους ὄντας καὶ ἀγήρως ἤματα πάντα, 7.94). Moreover, the dazzling radiance associated with gold as well as bronze is also a typical feature of divine epiphanies, which suggests that gods and precious metals have visual splendour in common as a token of their immortality.[42] This confluence of precious metals with the strength and vitality of the gods thus intimates how armour can endow human bodies with superhuman qualities.

The personification of Diomedes' spear-point as 'pitiless' is a clear instance of what Aristotle dubbed Homer's habit of 'speaking of inanimate things as though they were animate through the use of metaphor' (κέχρηται Ὅμηρος πολλαχοῦ τῷ τὰ ἄψυχα ἔμψυχα λέγειν διὰ τῆς μεταφορᾶς, *Rh.* 1411b31-1412a8).[43] Rather than interpreting Homeric personifications as indicative of a genuinely animistic world-

---

[41] cf. *Il.* 11.574, 15.317, 21.168, where bronze-tipped spears are 'eager to pierce flesh' (λιλαιόμενα χροὸς ἆσαι), and 15.542, where a flying spear is 'eager' (μαιμώωσα).

[42] See especially Petridou 2015 for a detailed and wide-ranging study of epiphany in ancient Greek thought. For the radiance accompanying epiphanies see e.g. *Od.* 19.40, *Hom. Hymn Dem.* 188–9, *Hymn. Hom. Ven.* 173–5, *Hymn. Hom. Ap.* 442, 444. On the luminous aspect of divine epiphanies and its reification in art, see especially Steiner 2001: 95–104, Neer 2010: 112–14, and Platt 2011: 86–91. See also Brouillet forthcoming on how literary portrayals of the consonance between precious metals and divine bodies construe divine beings as themselves forms of *agalmata*.

[43] On Homeric 'animism' and personification see the useful overviews of Webster 1954 and Kokolakis 1980, as well as the more recent work of Holmes 2010: 75–6, Bielfeldt 2014, Grethlein 2020 for varying interpretations of the significance of Homer's attribution of human emotions and capabilities to inanimate objects.

view, both ancient and modern exegeses focus on their impact at the level of narrative. For Aristotle and other ancient commentators, the effect of such figures is to enhance the vividness of the narrative through 'the appearance of actuality (*energeia*)' effected through this kind of language (ἐν πᾶσι γὰρ τούτοις διὰ τὸ ἔμψυχα εἶναι ἐνεργοῦντα φαίνεται· τὸ ἀναισχυντεῖν γὰρ καὶ μαιμᾶν καὶ τἆλλα ἐνέργεια, *Rh.* 1412a3-4). In other words, the attribution of feelings and desires to objects vivifies the story by intensifying the actions and events taking place within it. A different, but not incompatible, view articulates how such figures may not be purely linguistic expressions, but relate the idea that humans can transfer agency and emotions to the objects they use. Brooke Holmes nicely puts it as follows, 'By assuming the force of desire, weapons extend agency beyond the embodied agent' (2010: 75). On this view, the pitilessness of Diomedes' spear does not exist independent of the warrior and his own feeling. However, what both interpretations address, albeit in different ways, is how objects can become animating (in the context of narrative) as well as animate (in their entanglements with human agents). And the relations between humans and bronze that I will explore next in this section intimate the conception of a mutual interactivity between human and inhuman qualities, not just the embodiment of human agency in objects.

Like the 'pitiless bronze' that rends Aphrodite, another epithet used for bronze, ἀτειρής, 'unyielding', characterises Diomedes' spearhead precisely at the moment when it penetrates flesh and slices off Pandarus' tongue (τοῦ δ᾽ ἀπὸ μὲν γλῶσσαν πρυμνὴν τάμε χαλκὸς ἀτειρής, 5.292).[44] In both Aphrodite's and Pandarus' wounds, these characterisations of bronze emphasise the disparity between metal and skin by highlighting the former's invulnerability and the latter's penetrability. In what follows, however, we will see Homeric warriors depicted in their armour as being more akin to the giant Talos, whose body of bronze renders him indestructible except at the ankle, where he has a fleshy tendon.[45] Analogously, the following examples will reveal the capacity for metal to conjoin with and so enhance the workings of the body.[46] This is because the same unyielding quality that enables the bronze spear tip to pierce flesh is also what can render the human body equally impenetrable.

---

[44] See also the comments of Purves 2015: 87: 'So too . . . do words for metal and flesh align at the moment of death.'

[45] 'His body and limbs were wrought in bronze unbreakable, but beneath the tendon by his ankle was a vein carrying blood' (δέμας καὶ γυῖα τέτυκτο / χάλκεος ἠδ᾽ ἄρρηκτος, ὑπαὶ δέ οἱ ἔσκε τένοντος / σύριγξ αἱματόεσσα κατὰ σφυρόν, Ap. Rhod. 4.1645–7).

[46] See Lissarrague 2008a and 2018 on the portrayal of armour in painting as a 'second skin' and 'second body'.

A Wall of Armour, a Human Boulder and Brazen Voices

The thickness and weight of bronze are the focus of a scene in *Iliad* 13, where the Achaeans are arrayed so tightly that their armour overlaps to form one impenetrable layer:

φράξαντες δόρυ δουρί, σάκος σάκεϊ προθελύμνῳ·
ἀσπὶς ἄρ᾽ ἀσπίδ᾽ ἔρειδε, κόρυς κόρυν, ἀνέρα δ᾽ ἀνήρ·
ψαῦον δ᾽ ἱππόκομοι κόρυθες λαμπροῖσι φάλοισι
νευόντων, ὡς πυκνοὶ ἐφέστασαν ἀλλήλοισιν·
ἔγχεα δ᾽ ἐπτύσσοντο θρασειάων ἀπὸ χειρῶν
σειόμεν᾽ ·

locking spear by spear, shield against layered shield, so one shield leaned on another, helmet on helmet, and man against man, and the crests of horsehair on their shining helmets touched as their heads bent, so close-packed were they standing amongst each other, and the spears shaken from their bold hands formed overlapping folds. (13.130–5, Lattimore 1951)

In this description the compactness of the formation is vividly expressed in the language itself with its profusion of polyptoton, asyndeton and chiasmus, a combination that compresses the words as closely as the ranks they describe.[47] Further, as Hector observes upon witnessing this phenomenon, the visual effect is to make the army seem not like a group of men, but like a wall or bastion, 'making themselves so like a tower' (μάλα πυργηδὸν σφέας αὐτοὺς ἀρτύναντες, 13.152). This description thus forms the converse to the examples of this chapter's first section, where the dynamism of bronze's gleam and sound was what terrified opponents. Instead, here the strength of the Achaean force derives not just from their numbers, formation or arms, but from how the combination of all of these gives them the fixity and impenetrability of an inanimate structure.

A similar juxtaposition of inanimate and animate as well as fixity and movement occurs in the portrait of Hector's attack that follows the description of the Achaean army. Hector is said to be like a boulder that, once dislodged from its position by flooding, goes speeding down a cliff:

[47] cf. Purves 2015: 87: 'It is not just that helmet leans against helmet, shield against shield, or man against man, but that the careful organization of these words in the line suggests a certain material compatibility between the three.'

Τρῶες δὲ προὔτυψαν ἀολλέες, ἦρχε δ' ἄρ' Ἕκτωρ
ἀντικρὺ μεμαώς, ὀλοοίτροχος ὣς ἀπὸ πέτρης,
ὅν τε κατὰ στεφάνης ποταμὸς χειμάρροος ὤσῃ
ῥήξας ἀσπέτῳ ὄμβρῳ ἀναιδέος ἔχματα πέτρης·
ὕψι δ' ἀναθρῴσκων πέτεται, κτυπέει δέ θ' ὑπ' αὐτοῦ
ὕλη· ὃ δ' ἀσφαλέως θέει ἔμπεδον, εἷος ἵκηται
ἰσόπεδον, τότε δ' οὔ τι κυλίνδεται ἐσσύμενός περ

And the Trojans pressed forward en masse, and Hector led them eagerly ahead,
like a great rolling stone from a rock face that a river swollen with winter rain has
wrenched from its socket and with immense washing broken the hold of the unwilling rock face; the springing bolder flies on, and the forest thunders beneath it; and
the stone runs unwavering on a strong course, till it reaches the flat land, then rolls
no longer for all its onrush. (13.136–42, translation adapted from Lattimore 1951)

This simile is remarkable for the entanglement it portrays not only between humans
and things, but between things themselves. First, this image depicts not the transfer
of agency (as in cases where armour is personified) but the activation of vitality
in and by different forces. This is clear from the fact that the simile details the
interaction between the boulder and its environment: the water 'breaks' (ῥήξας,
139) the rock, which is 'unwilling' or 'ruthless' (ἀναιδέος, 139), and the forest
'thunders' (κτυπέει, 140) beneath the onslaught of the stone. The cascade of water
that dislodges the stone is classified with an adjective literally meaning 'unspeakable' (ἀσπέτῳ ὄμβρῳ, 139), an epithet which in Homer often conveys the immense
magnitude of natural phenomena (e.g. the sea at *Od.* 5.101, the air at *Il.* 8.558). And
as Hector testifies, he has also been spurred on by a supernaturally powerful outside
force like the rain, since it is Zeus himself who urged him onward (εἰ ἐτεόν με /
ὦρσε θεῶν ὤριστος, ἐρίγδουπος πόσις Ἥρης, 153–4). Thus Hector is like a boulder
and so possesses its power and speed, but more particularly, he is like one that has
effectively been brought to life by the supernaturally strong floodwater that sets the
stone in motion.[48]

The lifelike aspect of the stone is indicated by the repeated attribution of human
characteristics to it: it 'leaps', 'flies', 'runs' and 'is eager'. This choice of language
emphasises the speed and lightness with which the boulder traverses the forest, and
thus its motion appears at odds with its magnitude and solidity, a seemingly paradoxical union of weight and motion that we will see again below in Achilles' testing

---

[48] For a discussion of such speed and the leaping performed by Homeric warriors that focuses
on this gesture's relevance to the narrative writ large, see Purves 2019: 93–116.

of his new armour. Both the stone and Hector, then, are extraordinary figures to behold. Both seem to exhibit a hybrid ontology that endows them with supernatural speed and strength.[49]

As we saw in the 'Heavy Metal' section above, Homer correlates with armour a unique sonority, and this too can manifest itself in human form and serve to make the latter a more formidable opponent. As in the Hector simile discussed above, a hybridity between humans and materials occurs in the description of Achilles' war cry that consists of a 'brazen voice' that is as 'clear as a trumpet's sound':

ὡς δ᾽ ὅτ᾽ ἀριζήλη φωνή, ὅτε τ᾽ ἴαχε σάλπιγξ
ἄστυ περιπλομένων δηΐων ὕπο θυμοραϊστέων,
ὣς τότ᾽ ἀριζήλη φωνὴ γένετ᾽ Αἰακίδαο.
οἳ δ᾽ ὡς οὖν ἄϊον ὄπα χάλκεον Αἰακίδαο,
πᾶσιν ὀρίνθη θυμός·

Like a clear voice, like that of a trumpet when it peals under the force of the murderous enemies attacking the city, so piercing too was the voice of the son of Aeacus. And when they heard the brazen voice of the son of Aeacus, the spirits in everyone were stricken. (*Il.* 18.219–23)

The choice of 'brazen' to characterise Achilles' voice reinforces its similarity to the trumpet, which was itself probably made of bronze.[50] This phrasing thus works to depict sound in materialist, sensuous terms that nonetheless can issue forth from human mouths as well as from the instruments played by humans.[51] The simile also suggests a continuity between the structures of human bodies and the trumpet, as both produce sound through hollow cavities. And what gives rise to this comparison is the striking timbre of both, as denoted by 'piercing' (ἀριζήλη), 'peals' (ἴαχε) and the response it elicits ('the spirits in everyone were stricken', πᾶσιν ὀρίνθη θυμός).

This portrayal also accords with the passages discussed in the first section of this

---

[49] Mueller 2016a observes the same endowment of supernatural strength at work in the *Iliad*'s portrayal of Ajax: 'The *sakos* almost supernaturally extends Ajax's human agency, allowing him to enact the role – and to assume the identity – of the *herkos Achaiōn* (something he would not be able to do without his shield)', 139.

[50] See Krentz 1993 for a good survey of the evidence for the material composition and uses of the ancient Greek trumpet.

[51] On the dominating sound of the war-trumpet see especially Nooter 2019, who suggests that the instrument's sound appropriates 'the disembodied invulnerability of the gods to enhance the imagined powers of certain men over others' (248). My focus on bronze's unique ontology thus harmonises nicely with this analysis.

chapter that identified a confluence between the sound of clashing bronze and the sky (e.g. σιδήρειος δ' ὀρυμαγδὸς / χάλκεον οὐρανὸν ἷκε δι' αἰθέρος ἀτρυγέτοιο, 17.424–5).[52] Here too brazen sound is afforded a similarly affective quality, as the sound not only strikes fear into the hearts of the Trojans, but sends them into 'unspeakable panic' (ἀτὰρ Τρώεσσιν ἐν ἄσπετον ὦρσε κυδοιμόν, *Il.* 18.218). That the same adjective, 'unspeakable' (ἄσπετον) – one that described the force of rushing water (ἀσπέτῳ ὄμβρῳ, 139) in the simile likening Hector to a rolling boulder – occurs here too, emphasising the supernatural effect of Achilles' voice by literally suggesting that its impact is beyond human description. And in both examples, the use of similes that assimilate Achilles' and Hector's bodies to material things mirrors the conjunction of metal armour and flesh that helps to endow each figure with such extraordinary ferocity.

Further, the fact that 'brazen' is applied to a human voice indicates a blurring between the sounds of human and object rather than between object and environment (as in the example from *Il.* 17.424–5). As John Heath puts it, 'The adjective [sc. 'brazen'] here more likely emphasizes Achilles' inhumanity: his voice is not that of a man, but of a weapon' (2005: 125).[53] And this blurring is underscored by the use of 'voice' (φωνή) in connection with both the trumpet and Achilles, since elsewhere this word in Homer applies almost exclusively to human voices.[54] Conversely, as Heath notes, the adjective 'piercing' (ἀριζήλη) only here applies to a human voice in Homer, as opposed to Zeus' lightning (*Il.* 13.244) and the picture of Ares and Athena on Achilles' shield (*Il.* 18.519). Likewise, Achilles' 'brazen voice' here is also linked with Athena, since she is said to 'utter her voice' from afar (ἔνθα στὰς ἤϋσ', ἀπάτερθε δὲ Παλλὰς Ἀθήνη / φθέγξατ',18.217–18). Thus this depiction of Achilles' voice as both 'brazen' and 'piercing' seems designed to span multiple ontological registers: divinity, human, object, sound.[55]

[52] In this passage, as in those discussed in the first section of this chapter, the phenomenon of brazen sound is also accompanied by blinding light: Athena kindles a 'fearsome blaze' (δεινὸν . . . δαιόμενον) of 'unwearying fire' (ἀκάματον πῦρ) around Achilles' head to further his terrifying effect on the Trojans: ἡνίοχοι δ' ἔκπληγεν, ἐπεὶ ἴδον ἀκάματον πῦρ / δεινὸν ὑπὲρ κεφαλῆς μεγαθύμου Πηλεΐωνος / δαιόμενον· τὸ δὲ δαῖε θεὰ γλαυκῶπις Ἀθήνη, *Il.* 18.225–7.

[53] See also the analysis by Ford 1992: 194: 'These brazen voices are unusually strong, but essentially in their massy solidity; the metaphor of a bronze voice evokes the dynamic sublime of sheer power rather than the mathematical sublime of totality.'

[54] *Od.* 10.239, which relates how Odysseus' men have the 'heads and voices and hair of pigs' (οἱ δὲ συῶν μὲν ἔχον κεφαλὰς φωνήν τε τρίχας τε), is the notable exception, but here, as in the comparison of Achilles to a trumpet, there is still a distinctively human connotation to φωνή because this verse relates the transformation of humans into animals.

[55] On this description of Achilles' battle cry see also Nooter 2017: 23: 'His voice combines

Stentor is similarly possessed of a brazen voice in these lines where Hera takes on his likeness:

ἔνθα στᾶσ' ἤϋσε θεὰ λευκώλενος Ἥρη
Στέντορι εἰσαμένη μεγαλήτορι χαλκεοφώνῳ,
ὃς τόσον αὐδήσασχ' ὅσον ἄλλοι πεντήκοντα·

There the white-armed goddess Hera stood and gave voice in the likeness of great-hearted, brazen-voiced Stentor, whose voice was as great as that of fifty men. (*Il.* 5.784–6)

Here, the 'brazen' quality of a human voice is explicitly connected with its volume, and it is significant that the epithet occurs not in a simile, but in another form of likeness. This consists in the fact that it is not Stentor who is described here, but Hera's adoption of Stentor's vocal prowess. For as in the simile likening Achilles' voice to the trumpet, the implication here is that a 'brazen voice' is ontologically indeterminate, as something occupying no fixed medium and so something that can be manifested in gods, humans and instruments alike.

Elsewhere the propensity for bronze to endow human figures with superhuman qualities (whether in voice or physical strength) is even more pronounced. For example, before the Catalogue of Ships in *Iliad* 2, the poet declares that even if he had an 'unbreakable voice and a heart of bronze' (φωνὴ δ' ἄρρηκτος, χάλκεον δέ μοι ἦτορ ἐνείη, 490) he would not be able to recount the Greek forces without the help of the Muses. The implication, therefore, as in the image of a 'brazen voice', is that a 'brazen heart' would be tantamount to having otherworldly power because of the strength and ferocity associated with a brazen materiality.

The Armour of Achilles and Blazing Weaponry

When Achilles dons his new armour in book 19, the description of this event brings together all of the vital aspects of armour discussed so far: its embodiment of characteristics of natural phenomena, its terrifying sound, and its transformative effect on the human body. In so doing, these passages emphasise the supernaturalising effect of divinely fashioned bronze.[56] The transformative impact of the armour is clear

---

human embodiment with qualities of the divine, even as it is combined literally here with the divine voice of Athena.'

[56] cf. Brouillet forthcoming, who argues that descriptions of divine bodies in Homer 'make ineffective a distinction between body, clothing, and adornment' ('qui rend inopérante la distinction entre corps, vêtement et parure').

from the moment that Achilles first dons it. First, since it is new, Achilles tests out his movements in it, and the verb used to describe this activity is an unusual one, ἐντρέχω:

πειρήθη δ᾽ ἕο αὐτοῦ ἐν ἔντεσι δῖος Ἀχιλλεύς,
εἰ οἷ ἐφαρμόσσειε καὶ ἐντρέχοι ἀγλαὰ γυῖα·
τῷ δ᾽ εὖτε πτερὰ γίγνετ᾽, ἄειρε δὲ ποιμένα λαῶν

And godlike Achilles tested himself in his armour, to see if it fitted his frame, and to see how his shining limbs ran within it, and the armour became his wings and lifted up the shepherd of the people. (19.384–6)

The verb ἐντρέχω, used here in its only appearance in the Homeric corpus, articulates a specific relation between Achilles' limbs and his new armour: he needs to be able to move freely in it, as though it were a second skin.[57] And Achilles' motion of 'testing out' the armour recalls a similar motion described in the ekphrasis depicting the creation of his shield, where the nimble dancing of the figures portrayed on the shield is compared to the dexterity of a potter at his wheel. Like Achilles, who couples his body with the armour in the dexterous motion captured in ἐντρέχω, the potter of *Iliad* 18 likewise merges body and material in testing out the 'run' of his wheel:[58]

οἳ δ᾽ ὁτὲ μὲν θρέξασκον ἐπισταμένοισι πόδεσσι
ῥεῖα μάλ᾽, ὡς ὅτε τις τροχὸν ἄρμενον ἐν παλάμῃσιν
ἑζόμενος κεραμεὺς πειρήσεται, αἴ κε θέῃσιν·

And they were running in circles very nimbly with their cunning feet, as when a potter sits with a wheel fitted in his hands and tests it to see if it will run. (18.599–601, translation adapted from Lattimore 1951)

All three figures – Achilles, the potter, and the dancers to whom the potter is compared – move with effortless dexterity: the dancers with their 'cunning feet' (ἐπισταμένοισι πόδεσσι), Achilles with his 'shining limbs' (ἀγλαὰ γυῖα) and the potter with his hands (ἐν παλάμῃσιν). The affinity that emerges between Achilles' testing of the armour and the description of the armour's creation suggests that the

---

[57] On the portrayal of archaic armour as a second skin in vase painting see especially Lissarrague 2008a.

[58] cf. my discussion of this passage in the Introduction, pp. 6–16.

coupling of his armour together with his body creates something distinct from either his body or the armour: a form of artefact like Hephaestus' image of the dancers. And it may also explain why this is the only time in Homer that the adjective ἀγλαός is applied to a human body. For the appearance of this adjective in this context further underscores the merging between Achilles' armour and his flesh by attributing a divine gleam to both.

The metals of his shield (wrought of bronze and tin as well as gold and silver, *Il.* 18.474–5) are the source of his radiance, as 'its gleam went forth from afar like that of the moon' (αὐτὰρ ἔπειτα σάκος μέγα τε στιβαρόν τε / εἵλετο, τοῦ δ' ἀπάνευθε σέλας γένετ' ἠΰτε μήνης, 19.373–4). This apparition in turn is likened to a fire burning high in the mountains that appears to sailors caught in a storm at sea (375–8). The simile communicates the affective quality of the shield by indicating how it appears to Achilles' men as a lone beacon of hope, forming a marked contrast to the Myrmidons' first reaction to Achilles' new armour.[59]

When Thetis first presents Hephaestus' creation, the armour 'rings out' (τὰ δ' ἀνέβραχε δαίδαλα πάντα, 19.13) as Thetis sets it down, with the result that 'trembling seized the Myrmidons' and they cannot even look upon the arms (Μυρμιδόνας δ' ἄρα πάντας ἕλε τρόμος, οὐδέ τις ἔτλη / ἄντην εἰσιδέειν, ἀλλ' ἔτρεσαν, 19.14–15). Achilles, however, is filled with wrath and his eyes 'blaze terribly': 'When he saw it, rage entered him even more, and his eyes blazed, as if a fire had been kindled there' (ὡς εἶδ', ὥς μιν μᾶλλον ἔδυ χόλος, ἐν δέ οἱ ὄσσε / δεινὸν ὑπὸ βλεφάρων ὡς εἰ σέλας ἐξεφάανθεν, 19.16–17). The emphasis on Achilles 'blazing' aspect presages his fiery appearance during his attack on Hector, but at the same time, he is also filled with gladness. Twice the narrator remarks on the pleasure Achilles takes in regarding his new armament: 'He felt pleasure holding the glorious gifts of the god in his hands. And when he had taken his fill of pleasure in regarding the cunningly wrought arms' (τέρπετο δ' ἐν χείρεσσιν ἔχων θεοῦ ἀγλαὰ δῶρα. / αὐτὰρ ἐπεὶ φρεσὶν ᾗσι τετάρπετο δαίδαλα λεύσσων, 19.18–19). The divine and extraordinary quality of the armour becomes manifest in the multivalence of its affects, as it delights as profoundly as it frightens depending on the individual's perspective (i.e. as onlooker or as wearer). Bronze is thus correlated with radically different extremes, an aspect that mirrors its presentation of a paradoxical combination of dynamism (in the form of its glare and sound) and fixity (in its structural solidity).

The trepidation that lays hold of the Myrmidons at first sight of Achilles' armour is the same that overcomes Hector as Achilles attacks: 'the bronze flashed around him like a beam of blazing fire or the rising sun' (ἀμφὶ δὲ χαλκὸς ἐλάμπετο εἴκελος αὐγῇ

---

[59] cf. Edwards 1991 ad 372–80: 'the illustration also brings out the longing with which the defeated Greeks . . . are looking towards this sign of safety'.

/ ἢ πυρὸς αἰθομένου ἢ ἠελίου ἀνιόντος, 22.134–5), causing Hector to tremble in fear (ἕλε τρόμος, 136). Here the active force of the armour's gleaming metal becomes particularly clear with the juxtaposition of χαλκὸς as the subject of ἐλάμπετο and τρόμος as the subject of ἕλε. The armour thus seems to take on a life of its own, with Hector as the passive recipient of its effects, in a manner consonant with the passages discussed in the 'Bronze as Light' section above. And in a simile that more fully develops the destructive agency of bronze in *Iliad* 2, the numberless bronze of the Greek army is compared to a forest fire:

ἠΰτε πῦρ ἀΐδηλον ἐπιφλέγει ἄσπετον ὕλην
οὔρεος ἐν κορυφῇς, ἕκαθεν δέ τε φαίνεται αὐγή,
ὣς τῶν ἐρχομένων ἀπὸ χαλκοῦ θεσπεσίοιο
αἴγλη παμφανόωσα δι' αἰθέρος οὐρανὸν ἷκε.

As when annihilating fire sets ablaze a vast woodland on the crest of a mountain, and the light is visible from a distance, so they moved, and the dazzling gleam of the heavenly bronze reached through the aether and reached the heavens. (2.455–8)

Not only does the simile convey the extraordinary luminosity of the army on the move, it also communicates the terrible destructiveness (ἀΐδηλον) associated with such blazes. Similarly, Hector 'blazes with fire' as he attacks the Greek ships (αὐτὰρ ὃ λαμπόμενος πυρὶ πάντοθεν ἔνθορ' ὁμίλῳ, 15.623), as does Diomedes in book 5 when Athena 'kindles an inexhaustible fire' from his helmet and shoulders (δαῖέ οἱ ἐκ κόρυθός τε καὶ ἀσπίδος ἀκάματον πῦρ, *Il.* 5.4). In each of these examples, the ferocity of the attacking force finds vivid expression in the apparition of flames that emerge from their armour during their onslaught. Not only, then, does the sight of their armour in rapid motion inspire fear because of its resemblance to fire, this appearance also communicates the ferocity of the figures wearing the armour.

In this sense, the intensity of feeling in each warrior is imagined to literally radiate outwards from his armour. For in each of the cases cited above, each figure has been influenced by divine forces: Athena is literally said to 'kindle' flame from Diomedes' armour (and does the same for Achilles at *Il.* 18.225–7, discussed above) in addition to endowing him with strength (5.1–2), Zeus 'rouses' Hector in *Iliad* 15 (603, cf. 594), and Athena flies among the Greeks and rouses them to fight (2.450–2). The metal of armour in this way becomes a conduit for affect, since when it is conjoined to the human body, it both reflects and radiates the rancour and energy of the wearer.[60]

---

[60] This interpretation also accords with the analysis of Purves 2015: 'for Homeric heroes, and for Ajax in particular, there is a special sense in which arms and body can merge, allow-

Achilles' armour, once it has been stripped from Patroclus' body, has a comparable impact on Hector, where the transformative power of divine armour is made explicit:

Ἕκτορι δ᾽ ἥρμοσε τεύχε᾽ ἐπὶ χροΐ, δῦ δέ μιν Ἄρης
δεινὸς ἐνυάλιος, πλῆσθεν δ᾽ ἄρα οἱ μέλε᾽ ἐντὸς
ἀλκῆς καὶ σθένεος· μετὰ δὲ κλειτοὺς ἐπικούρους
βῆ ῥα μέγα ἰάχων· ἰνδάλλετο δέ σφισι πᾶσι
τεύχεσι λαμπόμενος μεγαθύμου Πηλεΐωνος.

The armour clung to Hector's skin, and Ares the terrible war god entered him, so that from the inside he was filled with force and strength. He went forward bellowing loudly to his celebrated companions, and appeared before them all radiant in the arms of great-hearted Peleion. (17.210–14)

The conjoining of the armour with Hector's body has the instantaneous effect of allowing Ares to 'enter' him and so fill him with might and strength, which manifest both in his battle cry and in his shining appearance. The armour is thus imagined to possess a force that actually penetrates and permeates Hector's body (πλῆσθεν δ᾽ ἄρα οἱ μέλε᾽ ἐντὸς / ἀλκῆς καὶ σθένεος). Further, the phrase ἰνδάλλετο δέ σφισι πᾶσι / τεύχεσι λαμπόμενος ('appeared before them all radiant in the arms') makes it clear that the physically enhancing effects were visible to all in the form of the armour's sheen.

The destructiveness of the figures that is communicated in their comparison to fire derives in part from the speed with which fire moves and spreads. As Elaine Scarry has observed, Homer describes the 'radiant ignition' emanating from warriors' armour in order to communicate the swift movements of these heavily armed figures: 'what he [Homer] moves are images that have weight (Achilles spins on his heels), images that, because they have become radiant, seem to rise on buoyant wings' (1999: 83). The connection between flashing light and rapid movement identified by Scarry is consonant with the use of the adjective αἰόλος to describe armour (e.g. *Il.* 7.222, 5.295, 4.489) as well as wriggling, swift-moving creatures like serpents (*Il.* 12.208), worms (*Il.* 22.509) and wasps (*Il.* 12.167) in addition to the appearance of horses' running feet (*Il.* 19.404). As Eleanor Irwin notes, 'Αἰόλος is "gleaming" whether that gleam is caused by a bright surface reflecting light (like armour) or a swiftly moving object' (1974: 214). Thus the Homeric narrator's emphasis on the

ing for a moving boundary between inner and outer self, as well as between human and nonhuman materials', 82–3.

radiance of armour, especially when comparing it to fire, locates a rapidity to the warriors' movements that seems at odds with the weight of the metallic panoply. Rather than weighing down the body, the flashing of metal armament instead has the uncanny effect of seeming to lighten and quicken the wearer's movements. This idea finds explicit formulation at the end of Achilles' arming scene, where the armour becomes 'as wings' to him and lifts him up (τῷ δ᾽ εὖτε πτερὰ γίγνετ᾽, ἄειρε δὲ ποιμένα λαῶν, 19.386) in addition to giving him a terrifying aspect.

Paris, on the other hand, presents a different but no less extraordinary picture when arrayed in his armour:

οὐδὲ Πάρις δήθυνεν ἐν ὑψηλοῖσι δόμοισιν,
ἀλλ᾽ ὅ γ᾽, ἐπεὶ κατέδυ κλυτὰ τεύχεα <u>ποικίλα</u> χαλκῷ,
σεύατ᾽ ἔπειτ᾽ ἀνὰ ἄστυ ποσὶ κραιπνοῖσι πεποιθώς.
ὡς δ᾽ ὅτε τις στατὸς ἵππος ἀκοστήσας ἐπὶ φάτνῃ
δεσμὸν ἀπορρήξας θείῃ πεδίοιο κροαίνων
εἰωθὼς λούεσθαι ἐϋρρεῖος ποταμοῖο
κυδιόων· ὑψοῦ δὲ κάρη ἔχει, ἀμφὶ δὲ χαῖται
ὤμοις ἀΐσσονται· ὁ δ᾽ ἀγλαΐηφι πεποιθὼς
ῥίμφά ἑ γοῦνα φέρει μετά τ᾽ ἤθεα καὶ νομὸν ἵππων·
ὣς υἱὸς Πριάμοιο Πάρις κατὰ Περγάμου ἄκρης
τεύχεσι παμφαίνων ὥς τ᾽ ἠλέκτωρ ἐβεβήκει
καγχαλόων, ταχέες δὲ πόδες φέρον·

'But Paris did not stay long in his lofty house, but when he had put on his renowned armour <u>shimmering</u> with bronze, he ran through the city, trusting in his swift feet, as when some stalled horse who has been well fed at his manger breaks free from his tether and runs galloping, bearing himself proudly, over a field to the fair-flowing river where he is accustomed to bathe. And he holds his head high, and his mane flutters over his shoulders; sure of his splendour, his knees carry him lightly to his customary places and the horse pasture. Thus from the peak of Pergamon went Paris, son of Priam, resplendent in his armour like a sunbeam, and exultant, and his swift feet carried him. (*Il.* 6.503–14)

That Paris is here likened to a prancing racehorse rather than a blazing fire underscores the physical beauty and allure of his armoured body rather than its terrorising aspect.[61] Moreover, while it is a common feature of armour descriptions to empha-

---

[61] Lovatt 2013: 265: 'Horse images, beginning with Paris at *Il.* 6.506–11, place a particular focus on the physical beauty of the warrior in motion.' See ibid. 268–71 for more on the erotic aspects of this scene and on epic descriptions of male beauty in general.

sise the swift movements even of the heavily armed figure, the horse simile conveys a remarkably different kinetic quality, expressive of pride and joy as well as rapidity: so delighted is Paris in his own radiance that he is 'exultant' (καγχαλόων, 514). This example presents a corollary to the passages discussed above, where the martial rage instilled in warriors becomes manifest in the fearsome glint of their armour. An analogous interaction between the warrior's body, emotions and armour is observable in this description, but to markedly different effect. For here the radiance of Paris' armour is instead a reflection of the exuberance that makes him akin to a horse running free. In this way, Paris embodies explicitly how armour can function as a kind of *agalma*: an object of delight whose pleasing effect is often, as it is here, tied to the radiance of materials.

Life in/of Metal

The portrayal of Paris in his armour is in line with Alcaeus' picture of a house 'shimmering' with armament, where warriors' helmets with their 'nodding white plumes' are explicitly referred to as 'adornments for men's heads' (τὰν λεῦκοι κατέπερθεν ἵππιοι λόφοι / νεύοισιν, κεφάλαισιν ἄν-/ δρων ἀγάλματα, 140.6–7).[62] While the reference to plumes 'nodding' is a Homeric formula, what is absent from the wording here is an adverb that typically accompanies this phrase in the *Iliad*: δεινόν (e.g. at *Il.* 3.337, 11.42, 16.138; cf. 6.470). When this phrase appears, it is always the horsehair plume that is said to do the nodding, suggesting that at least part of what makes this a frightening apparition is the confusion of human, animal and object embodied in the crest: it was once a part of an animal, now divorced from the animal and affixed to metal, and seems to move of its own accord, adopting a humanlike gesture.

In a paradigmatic illustration of the helmet's fearful aspect, in book 6 of the *Iliad* the baby Astyanax recoils from the sight of his father's helmet, and it is specifically the bronze and the nodding of the plume that scare him (ταρβήσας χαλκόν τε ἰδὲ λόφον ἱπποχαίτην, / δεινὸν ἀπ' ἀκροτάτης κόρυθος νεύοντα νοήσας, 6.469–70). What terrifies Astyanax, then, is precisely the defamiliarising effect of the bronze and horsehair plume on his father's visage.

Alcaeus instead focuses on the aesthetic effects of metal armament outside the sphere of battle by referring to how the interior of a house 'shimmers with bronze, the whole ceiling adorned for Ares with shining helmets' (μαρμαίρει δὲ μέγας δόμος / χάλκῳ, παῖσα δ' Ἄρη κεκόσμηται στέγα / λάμπραισιν κυνίαισι, 140.3–5). Alcaeus here envisions the panoply as a form of decoration (κεκόσμηται) that

---

[62] See Lissarrague 2018 on armour as a form of *kosmēsis* for warriors. For a recent reappraisal of the view that interprets Alcaeus here to be glorifying war, see Spelman 2015.

infuses the house's interior with a brazen shine. In this way, Alcaeus harks back to the Homeric arming scenes discussed above, which, especially in the case of Paris, alluded to the simultaneously beautiful and terrifying aspect of armour. When it is the interior of a house arrayed with armour, though, the glimmer of bronze becomes a source of pleasure rather than a tactical manoeuvre designed to strike fear into the enemy.

As the poem continues, however, the hall begins to be depicted as though it were a human body wearing each piece of equipment: the plumes of helmets 'nod' as though worn by a moving figure, and bronze greaves 'hide' the pegs on which they are hung, analogous to the way they cover the wearer's flesh:

> κὰτ
> τὰν λεῦκοι κατέπερθεν ἴππιοι λόφοι
> νεύοισιν, κεφάλαισιν ἄν-
> δρων ἀγάλματα· χάλκιαι δὲ πασσάλοις
> κρύπτοισιν περικείμεναι
> λάμπραι κνάμιδες, ἔρκος ἰσχύρω βέλεος

Down from the ceiling white helmets with horsehair crests nod, adornments for men's heads. And shining bronze greaves, the defence against a strong arrow, hide the pegs they're hanging on. (140.5–10)

While the initial focus was on the spectacular quality of armament, at this point Alcaeus reminds his listeners of the primary, martial function of these items.[63] That he does so by attributing to the hanging helmets and greaves the same activities they fulfil in battle (crests nodding, the greaves as a defence against arrows) identifies the humanity in these objects. Even when these accoutrements are removed from the battlefield, they retain their connection to human bodies.[64] And while in Homer the waving of plumes on a warrior's helmet is a fearsome sight because of the way the crest seems to come to life, in Alcaeus this same spectacle is classified as an *agalma* (κεφάλαισιν ἄν- / δρων ἀγάλματα, 8–9): an object of delight. In this sense, Alcaeus' characterisation of the helmets' nodding plumes as *agalmata* assimilates the helmets

[63] cf. Swift 2015: 99, who also notes that 'Behind the immediate sight of the armour in storage lies a ghostly spectacle of the armed conflict for which it is meant.'

[64] cf. Spelman 2015: 357: 'The static beauty that pervades the tableau . . . implicitly contrasts with the hectic work of war for which these objects were created, and in which speaker and addressee are now entangled.' See also Burnett 1983: 125: 'The poet has changed magnificent but lifeless things into a vivid apprehension of their potential, his music working to transform their beauty into aggressive energy.'

to other metallic objects that also incite wonder and delight because of the dynamic aspect of the images contained within.

In such descriptions, the tension between the apparition of movement and the materiality of the object is precisely what renders them extraordinary.[65] It is often *thauma* that attends the experience of such artefacts. Richard Neer has described this effect as resulting from 'the uncanny way in which images are *twofold*: in the perception of, say, a painted lion, one sees both the image and its material support, both the lion and the mere facture of the painting' (2010: 113).[66] In the same way as representations in metal invite wonder because they make apparently inanimate material seem animate, likewise the extraordinary visual and acoustic effects attributed to armoured figures are generated by the seemingly paradoxical union of living bodies with metal substances.

One of the best literary examples of the tension between (inanimate) material and a lifelike aspect is in the ekphrasis devoted to Achilles' shield in *Iliad* 18. As the discussion of this passage in the Introduction explained, this description is marked by its oscillation between the animate quality of the figures portrayed therein and the reminders of their material qualities: figures seem to move and produce sound even as the poet remarks on Hephaestus' craftsmanship and the materials he uses to forge each image.[67] Of particular relevance to this chapter is the allusion to the 'golden' aspect of the depiction of Athena and Ares:

ἦρχε δ᾿ ἄρά σφιν Ἄρης καὶ Παλλὰς Ἀθήνη
ἄμφω χρυσείω, χρύσεια δὲ εἵματα ἕσθην,

---

[65] cf. Becker 1995: 85: 'Defamiliarization, attention to the medium, increases the admiration of the audience for the mimetic capabilities of the work of art.'

[66] cf. Hunzinger 2015: 427, who describes the relation between *thauma* and representational imagery as arising from, 'the coexistence of the inanimate and the animate: inert material supports depictions endowed with life, as mobile, vocal, and noisy as living creatures'. See also Grethlein 2017: 158–90, who fruitfully uses Richard Wollheim's 1980 theory of 'seeing-in' (which involves attending to represented objects as much as the material medium in which they are represented) in application to a variety of ancient and modern images. Neer 2002: 48–9 similarly demonstrates the applicability of Wollheim to archaic vase painting.

[67] The Foundry Cup (c. 480 BCE), whose tondo displays Thetis visiting Hephaestus at his forge, offers a comparably rich meditation on representation and represented. This vase, whose exterior portrays of the process of statue making, repeatedly blurs the distinction between the depiction of a living person and that of a sculpted one by making it difficult to distinguish 'real' bodies from fashioned ones. Neer 2002: 77–85 offers a fascinating discussion of this issue, demonstrating that 'The most immediate and lifelike renderings collapse into themselves, while seemingly inanimate objects acquire a miraculous vitality' (83). See also Mattusch 1980 on what this cup can reveal about bronzeworking techniques.

καλὼ καὶ μεγάλω σὺν τεύχεσιν, ὥς τε θεώ περ
ἀμφὶς ἀριζήλω· λαοὶ δ᾽ ὑπολίζονες ἦσαν.

And Ares and Pallas Athena were leading them, both in gold, and clad in golden clothes, beautiful and tall in their arms, both being divine and conspicuous, and the mortals were smaller. (18.516–19)

Numerous critics have highlighted the interpretative crux posed by this description: does the 'golden' refer only to the medium of Athena and Ares' representation in the shield or to their physical reality in this scene?[68] For as we saw above, the gods themselves are frequently characterised as exhibiting the splendour and radiance of metal. Thus what the characterisation of these gods as 'golden' betokens is the possibility of a shared corporeality between divine bodies and metals, one that makes it impossible to distinguish between the gold of the representation and the gold of the gods' bodies. And taken together with the Homeric depictions of bronze-clad warriors and their supernatural powers, this chapter has revealed the conception of a continuity between life and life*like*ness that derives from the conjunction of metal with living bodies, whether human or divine: bronze armour serves as both an aggressive and a defensive force to protect the flesh underneath, and figures wrought in metal seem to bring this material to life by making it seem as supple as human flesh.

As the example of Athena and Ares encapsulates and as the next chapter will explore in detail, the lifelikeness of crafted images – like the depictions of armoured bodies discussed here – interrogate the boundaries between humans and materials as well as life and lifelikeness. For if artefacts can seem alive and living beings seem to appropriate qualities of the material, then the distinction between person and artefact appears permeable and unstable. And in subsequent chapters, we will see how this fluidity between humans and objects continuously and variously manifests itself in the realm of *poikilia* in particular.

[68] See, most recently, Squire 2013: 160 for a succinct characterisation of the question posed by this description: 'Within this poetic replication of a forged artistic object, then, exactly where are the boundaries between reality and replication?'

3 Mind Tools: Art, Artifice and Animation

WE HAVE SEEN in previous chapters a persistent correlation between *poikilia* and the beguiling effects of material objects.[1] But in this chapter my focus will be on the phenomena that are explicitly said to confuse ontological categories between human and nonhuman to form unique combinations that can equally delight or destroy.[2] Take, for instance, Herodotus' account of the Egyptian labyrinth at Lake Moeris (II.148.6), where he relates how the scale and complexity of the structure's 'most intricate winding passages' (οἱ εἰλιγμοὶ ποικιλώτατοι) furnish 'an immense wonder' (θῶμα μυρίον) and that it is so magnificent as to seem beyond human capabilities (τὰ δὲ ἄνω μέζονα ἀνθρωπηίων ἔργων). Among the other curiosities adduced here will be artefacts that are genuine automata in addition to life*like* images and similar feats of superhuman construction.[3] The reason for grouping such objects

---

[1] cf. Grand-Clément 2015: 412–16 on the 'poikilic agency' that consists in *poikilia*'s ability to ensnare and beguile the senses, as well as Grand-Clément 2011: 419–88 for a discussion of *poikilia* in relation to other ancient Greek colour concepts. See too Neer 2002: 14–54 on the scintillating effects of *poikilia* in Attic vase painting.

[2] A comparable approach to materiality and corporeality defines the special issue of *Art History* 2018 edited by Milette Gaifman and Verity Platt. In their introduction to this collection of essays, Gaifman and Platt identify the following issues as central to investigations of body–object relationships in antiquity, issues that will likewise surface prominently in this chapter: 'the mutually constitutive relationship between bodies and their physical environments; the nature of the human body as itself a material object; and the extension of corporeality to the world of artefacts, both in the cultural imagination and through embodied practices that challenge conventional subject–object distinctions' (2018: 416).

[3] On ancient accounts of automata and automation see, for instance, Liveley 2006, which fruitfully applies Donna Haraway's 1991 reading of the cyborg figure to ancient myths, while Devecka 2013 focuses on the concept of the robot in the Athenian cultural imaginary,

as Hephaestus' self-moving tripods and robotic handmaidens alongside things like labyrinths and riddles is because all of these examples confront, in one way or another, the boundaries and contours of the human body and mind.[4] By traversing poetry and prose and criss-crossing between the archaic and classical periods, it will become clear how the same questions circulate throughout a variety of genres and periods. And through a concentration specifically on instances in which human attributes (such as voice or movement) seem to attach to nonhuman entities – or conversely, where divine or otherwise nonhuman characteristics manifest themselves in manmade products – we will acquire clearer insight into the ontological planes whose muddling gives rise to these apparent paradoxes.

While in earlier chapters I have sought primarily to illuminate the porousness of materials in their interactions with human agents, in this chapter we will confront the opacity of things as much as the propensity for humans to 'couple' with objects in their environment. Thus this chapter will examine two facets of human cognition and will probe the conditions under which objects veer towards one or the other of these categories: (1) the intractability or inscrutability of the material entity and the wonder that this evokes; (2) 'intelligent objects', or the means and mechanisms by which material objects function as extensions of the human mind. These two interpretative lenses will therefore impart a guiding structure to this chapter.

The first, which inflects the varying strands of new materialist thought adumbrated in the Introduction, emphasises the opacity and intractability of material objects: this is what Bill Brown has termed the 'thingness' of things. By this he refers to the way in which material things are both vividly and sensuously perceptible while remaining metaphysically elusive. The term 'thing', for Brown, aptly expresses this vagueness, in contrast to 'object', which implies a hierarchical relationship to a (human) subject. As he sums it up, '[Things] lie both at hand and somewhere

and Berryman 2003 considers how such early accounts of automata fit into a history of Greek technology and argues that the presence of automata in Homer does not imply the conception of a mechanical (i.e. non-magical) way to create such objects. See also Cuomo 2007 for a broader perspective on the role of technology in both Greek and Roman cultures. On the mythology surrounding Hephaestus and his craftsmanship see especially Delcourt 1982.

[4] For similar investigations into human and material interactions in a variety of literary and archaeological contexts see Gaifman and Platt 2018, Canevaro 2018, Telò and Mueller 2018, Mueller 2016a, Purves 2015, Holmes 2015 and Bielfeldt 2018 and 2014. The comments of Telò and Mueller 2018: 2 best summarise the type of human–nonhuman interactivity that is at stake for this chapter in their description of how tragic objects compel readers 'to interrogate how these exchanges problematize the relationship between human and nonhuman; the connectivity (or lack thereof) they project; and the continuity or discontinuity of personhood and thingness that emerges from them'.

outside the theoretical field . . . Things lie beyond the grid of intelligibility the way mere things lie outside the grid of museal exhibition, outside the order of objects' (2001: 5).[5] Other new materialist critics also attend to the 'excess' that inheres in material substances. Diana Coole and Samantha Frost frame this excessiveness as follows: 'For materiality is always something more than "mere" matter: an excess, force, vitality, relationality, or difference that renders matter active, self-creative, productive, unpredictable' (2010: 9). It is therefore with an eye to material presence *and* excess that in the first three sections of this chapter I will examine a selection of objects that all inspire wonder, *thauma*, precisely because of the different ways in which each of them takes on the 'active' and 'unpredictable' qualities alluded to by Coole and Frost.

The second portion of this chapter –'Intelligent Things,' 'Hephaestus' Tools' and 'The Ships of the Phaeacians and Other "Smart" Objects' – is indebted to theories of embodied and extended cognition, which emphasise a cooperative and dynamic relationship between the human mind and body and external, material 'props'. The particular account of extended cognition formulated by Andy Clark (discussed in further detail below) is especially attentive to the permeability between brains, bodies and things, and will attune us to similarly porous aspects of user–tool and user–object interactions. We will encounter visions of objects functioning as seamless extensions of mind by means of the mysterious currents of vitality that inspired wonder and bewilderment as well as dread in the first section. However, these case studies will in turn cast humans into a different light since they, like humanlike automata, also can be viewed as bundles of animated matter.[6]

---

[5] In this respect, Brown's approach has important commonalities with object-oriented ontology as well as with correlationism, which both (albeit in very distinctive ways) grapple with the unknowability of objects and things in the world. See e.g. Morton 2012: 208, who defines his object-oriented ontology as one that recognises 'everything as a weird entity withdrawn from access, yet somehow manifest', as well as Bennett 2012's response to the object-oriented ontology (OOO) of Graham Harman and Timothy Morton, in which she emphasises that 'objects are always *coy*, always leaving hints of a secret other world, "alluding" to an "inscrutable" reality "behind the accessible theoretical, practical, or perceptual qualities"' (225). Quentin Meillassoux 2008 is the leading figure in the correlationism debate (centred on the extent to which human thought and the phenomenal world are co-constituted), which likewise recognises an epistemological intractability to nonhuman things, but nevertheless aspires to overcome this impasse through confrontation with the 'radical contingency' of nature. See too Harman 2011's lucid exploration of Meillassoux's philosophy.

[6] Kenneth Gross, in his study of the trope of the living statue in Western thought, comes to a similar conclusion: 'Our imaginary identification with so alien a creature as a moving statue or an automaton can be profoundly satisfying, partly because that identification may

Finally, the conclusion will return us to the *poikilia* that surfaced so prominently in the first three sections and examine its relation specifically to speech that seems nonhuman in origin. Not only will this pave the way for the next chapter's concentration on *poikilia* and lyric language, but we will also see how, in the realm of language, *poikilia* falls in between the two categories that shaped the preceding sections, as it names the beguiling effect of speech as well as the unique type of cognition that has produced this effect.

Paradoxical *Poikilia*: Labyrinthine Passageways

Herodotus' description of the Egyptian labyrinth at Lake Moeris is a good place to begin because of the explicit connections it draws between *poikilia*, materiality and the limits of human endeavours.[7] So wondrous is this labyrinth that all of Greece's marvels put together cannot compare to it:

τῶν ἐγὼ ἤδη εἶδον λόγου μέζω ἐόντα. εἰ γάρ τις τὰ ἐξ Ἑλλήνων τείχεά τε καὶ ἔργων ἀπόδεξιν συλλογίσαιτο, ἐλάσσονος πόνου τε ἂν καὶ δαπάνης φανείη ἐόντα τοῦ λαβυρίνθου τούτου. καίτοι ἀξιόλογός γε καὶ ὁ ἐν Ἐφέσῳ ἐστὶ νηὸς καὶ ὁ ἐν Σάμῳ.

Of all the wonders I have seen, this labyrinth truly is beyond words. If someone were to reckon up all the walls and splendid architecture of Hellas, all these would still clearly fall short of this labyrinth in labor and expense, although the temples in Ephesus and Samos are certainly remarkable. (II.148.1–2, translation adapted from Purvis in Strassler 2009)

The labyrinth exceeds the capacities of human speech: it is 'beyond words' (λόγου μέζω).[8] The pyramids, too, are 'beyond words', but the labyrinth exceeds even the pyramids in its marvellousness (ὁ δὲ δὴ λαβύρινθος καὶ τὰς πυραμίδας ὑπερβάλλει, II.148.3). Herodotus thus implicitly sets himself the task of describing what he explicitly conceives as falling outside the realm of human description. As we will see,

spare us diverse anxieties about our place in the world, in our own bodies, about the proper location of the human' (1992: 135). See, more recently, Riskin 2016 for a wide-ranging survey of the intellectual history of scientific approaches to the study of life and mind.

[7] On Herodotus' use of the terminology of θωμ- ('wonder') throughout the *Histories* see especially Munson 2001: 232–65.

[8] Indeed, whether or not the structure as described by Herodotus actually existed remains a matter of debate; see West 1987 for a good summary of the issues at stake in the veracity of Herodotus' account of the labyrinth and Lake Moeris.

however, the syntax with which he characterises the twists and turns of the labyrinth goes some way towards mirroring the complexity of the structure.[9] But the fact that he stipulates that the marvel of the labyrinth is 'beyond words' is a concession to the way that nonhuman matter, especially on such a scale, can resist and defy human intelligibility in the manner described by Bill Brown in the quotation cited above. In this sense, this description is of a piece with the Homeric usages of the term 'unspeakable' (ἄσπετος) discussed in the previous chapter, which likewise located an 'inexpressible' quality in the immensity of forces of nature. What sets the labyrinth apart, however, is the fact that it is manmade, as Herodotus goes on to emphasise. But this idea – that wondrous objects can be somehow 'inexpressible' or 'unspeakable' – will prove to be a recurrent feature of the objects adduced in this section, as will the task that Herodotus takes on here: of trying to put the first-hand experience of the inexpressible into words.

Equally striking is his insistence that all the 'walls and the splendid architecture' (τείχεά τε καὶ ἔργων ἀπόδεξιν) of Greece put together could not surpass this structure for its 'labor and expense' (πόνου τε ἂν καὶ δαπάνης). With this phrasing, Herodotus suggests that the wonder of architecture consists in the sheer physical effort involved in the construction of monuments and the costliness of its materials. This is a significant pair of criteria with which he gauges Greek and Egyptian monuments because it makes clear that he finds human labour and expense plainly visible in the material dimensions of the labyrinth: this building, in other words, is viewed as an index of human labours and economic value. Of note too is his use of the term συλλόγισαιτο in his hypothetical comparison between Greek and Egyptian buildings, given that he has just classified the labyrinth as beyond speech or reckoning, *logos*. There is a paradox to Herodotus' project here, for at the same time as he insists on the incommunicable marvel of the labyrinth he also conceives of the products and expense of human labour as something that can be 'reckoned up' (συλλόγισαιτο). Manmade structures thus seem to have the capacity to both embody and exceed the bounds of the human: reflecting economic value and manual labour while simultaneously standing aloof from such calculation attempts.[10] This is neatly conveyed by the less vivid conditional force of συλλόγισαιτο . . . φανείη, which

---

[9] cf. Munson 2001: 241: 'From a narratological perspective, we should notice how conspicuously the persona of the narrator has invaded his subject. He celebrates, groups, excepts, compares, compares again, and ranks.'

[10] On this relationship between materialism and labour see especially Hall 2018, who argues that the non-anthropocentric focus of the new materialisms should not exclude socioeconomic factors: 'If we are fully to appreciate the role of materials and objects in a play written in the fifth century BCE in Athens, then we would surely be well advised to ask how those materials were thought about in that society as well as their vitality or thing-power' (207).

intimates that such a task (of tallying up the totality of Greece's material labours) lies beyond human capabilities.

'Beyond words' notwithstanding, Herodotus goes on to give a remarkably lucid description of the parts of the labyrinth he was able to experience first-hand in traversing the structure. In this narrative, *poikilia* achieves its superlative form specifically in the labyrinth's complex of winding passages:

οὕτω τῶν μὲν κάτω περὶ οἰκημάτων ἀκοῇ παραλαβόντες λέγομεν, τὰ δὲ ἄνω μέζονα ἀνθρωπηίων ἔργων αὐτοὶ ὡρῶμεν· αἵ τε γὰρ διέξοδοι διὰ τῶν στεγέων καὶ οἱ εἱλιγμοὶ διὰ τῶν αὐλέων ἐόντες <u>ποικιλώτατοι</u> θῶμα μυρίον παρείχοντο ἐξ αὐλῆς τε ἐς τὰ οἰκήματα διεξιοῦσι καὶ ἐκ τῶν οἰκημάτων ἐς παστάδας, ἐς στέγας τε ἄλλας ἐκ τῶν παστάδων καὶ ἐς αὐλὰς ἄλλας ἐκ τῶν οἰκημάτων.

Thus what I relate about the underground chambers comes from hearsay. But I saw the upper chambers myself, and they are superhuman feats of construction. I was struck with awe and wonder by the <u>most intricate</u> passageways that lead through vestibules and the paths that zigzag through the courtyards; I passed from courtyards to chambers and from chambers to corridors of columns, and then from the corridors of columns into other vestibules leading to other chambers and out again to other courtyards. (II.148.6, trans. Purvis in Strassler 2009, slightly modified)

When Herodotus turns from his description of the overall structure of the labyrinth to its interior dimensions, he asserts that they are not just beyond Greek buildings, but in excess of human accomplishment altogether (τὰ δὲ ἄνω μέζονα ἀνθρωπηίων ἔργων). This is borne out by the '<u>most intricate</u> passageways' (οἱ εἱλιγμοὶ <u>ποικιλώτατοι</u>), which together with the maze of entryways (αἵ τε γὰρ διέξοδοι διὰ τῶν στεγέων) constitute an immense source of wonder (θῶμα μυρίον παρείχοντο). Herodotus' language here, as in his preface to this description, invokes the language of calculation (μυρίον) only to undermine it, since it is the feeling of wonder, *thauma*, that is countless in its immensity. The *poikilia* of the labyrinth consists in the enormity of its scale (on a par with the immense wonder it evokes) as well as the complexity of its design, for as the description relates, the passages wind in every conceivable direction and into every conceivable type of space.[11] And the dizzying effect of this construction finds expression in the extended parallelism of the syntax. This oscillates from ἐκ to ἐς and back again in a layering of prepositional phrases that seems designed to mirror the contorted trajectory of the labyrinthine passageways.

---

[11] cf. Hunzinger 2015: 426–7, who classes Herodotus' description of the labyrinth with other examples that associate *poikilia* with protean, shifting phenomena.

In this way, Herodotus imparts to his account the *poikilia* of the labyrinth in the very attempt to convey how it in fact exceeds human capacity for description.

To sum up: the labyrinth seems to occupy a plane beyond the confines of human reason and speech, but still manifests the labour and expense that brought it into being. Structures like the labyrinth thus appear to be fundamentally paradoxical because part of what makes them wondrous is that they are manmade in spite of the fact their scale and complexity suggest otherwise. The *poikilia* of the labyrinth in particular is treated as tangible evidence of its wondrousness as well as a cause of it: it is both a feature of the material organisation of the labyrinth and a quality that emerges from Herodotus' first-hand experience of the structure's confines and his subsequent description of it. In this sense, it is little wonder that he locates a super-lative form of *poikilia* in the labyrinth. Since Herodotus has to traverse the structure in order to describe it, this structure exhibits on a vast scale the kind of embodied, dynamic engagement depicted in the first chapter and evokes a similar sense of awe to what we saw in the second chapter's discussion of metallic vitality.

Poikilia in Miniature

If the labyrinth's monumental scale accounts for its dizzying effect, the *poikilia* wrought in miniature is no less able to elicit amazement. Odysseus' brooch as described in *Odyssey* 19 is also a source of wonder, but because of the level of detailed craftsmanship captured within its small surface:

> πάροιθε δὲ δαίδαλον ἦεν·
> ἐν προτέροισι πόδεσσι κύων ἔχε ποικίλον ἐλλόν,
> ἀσπαίροντα λάων· τὸ δὲ θαυμάζεσκον ἅπαντες,
> ὡς οἱ χρύσεοι ἐόντες ὁ μὲν λάε νεβρὸν ἀπάγχων,
> αὐτὰρ ὁ ἐκφυγέειν μεμαὼς ἤσπαιρε πόδεσσι.

> And in front was a crafted image. A hound was holding a <u>dappled</u> fawn in its forepaws, pinning it as it struggled. And everybody wondered at how, although it was made of gold, the dog was holding the fawn, strangling it, while the fawn was writhing with its feet, trying to escape. (*Od.* 19.227–31)

This brooch has no archaeological parallel and is philologically unique, as well.[12] Its conception and description, like the labyrinth, strain the bounds of human

---

[12] cf. Morris 1992: 28 on the attempts to match archaeological parallels to the brooch and the philological anomalies of its description.

imagination and language. And as in the depiction of the ploughed field in Achilles' shield that was discussed in the Introduction, wherein the likeness of the field appeared freshly ploughed 'although it was rendered in gold' (ἡ δὲ μελαίν' ὄπισθεν, ἀρηρομένη δὲ ἐῴκει, / χρυσείη περ ἐοῦσα· τὸ δὴ θαῦμα τέτυκτο, *Il.* 18.549–50), Odysseus relates how his brooch exhibited movement within although the figures were wrought in gold (ὡς οἱ χρύσεοι ἐόντες).

As *poikilia* described the intricacy and multitude of the labyrinth, here it char-acterises the dappled aspect of the fawn that 'was writhing with its feet, trying to escape' (αὐτὰρ ὁ ἐκφυγέειν μεμαὼς ἤσπαιρε πόδεσσι). The brooch, then, com-mands wonder as much as the labyrinth (τὸ δὲ θαυμάζεσκον ἅπαντες) because they both seem to exceed the capacities of human craftsmanship by mobilising metal and stone into dynamic designs: the monumental convolutions of the labyrinth and the minute detail portraying the kicking and struggling of the fawn. *Poikilia* thus marks the verisimilitude of the image (an aspect already connoted by the brooch's characterisation as a *daidalon*) in its representation of the fawn's dappled hide, as well as the finely wrought aspect of the brooch itself.[13] And based on the previous chapter's exploration of the liveliness of Homeric armour, the concessive participle in this description (ὡς οἱ χρύσεοι ἐόντες) can be read slightly differently: the fawn and the dog resemble their living counterparts, even though the latter share nothing in common with gold. To put it another way, the participle does not concede that gold is inert and so at odds with the dynamic aspect of the image. Instead, it is a concession to the unusual materiality in which the vitality of the dog and deer finds expression. At the same time, by portraying a scene of destruction and death, the brooch gestures towards the terror that can accompany *thauma* (as a response to objects that seem to come alive).

If the liveliness of artefacts can cause wonder and delight, the same apparition can equally inspire dread. This is precisely the idea formulated by Deianeira in Sophocles' *Trachiniae* when she describes what happened when she saw the destruc-tive effects of Nessus' deadly tincture on the tuft of wool with which she had anointed Heracles' robe. This is also described as a marvel, a *thauma*, albeit a disastrous and 'unforeseen' one (θαῦμ' ἀνέλπιστον, 673). While Herodotus focuses on the monu-mental scale of human labour and materials that have gone into the labyrinth's con-

---

[13] cf. Steiner 2001: 21: 'The "dappled" quality of the fawn spans the two dimensions: most immediately referring to the appearance of the animal's variegated or spotted hide, it also calls attention to the quality of *poikilia*, the element of adornment and embellishment that all fine works of art should display. It is the meeting of these two facets that prompts the wonder that the audience experiences.' See also Neer 2010: 57–69 on the centrality of 'twofoldness' ('the depiction and its material at once', 59) to the archaic Greek concept of wonder.

struction, the 'marvel' of the wool consists in its utter destruction, which Deianeira characterises as follows: 'I see an unutterable pronouncement, impossible for human understanding' (δέρκομαι φάτιν / ἄφραστον, ἀξύμβλητον ἀνθρώπῳ μαθεῖν, 693–4). She here uses the language of sight (δέρκομαι) to describe the apparition of the wool disintegrating, but defines this apparition as a kind of utterance (φάτιν). The paradox presented by the wool's destruction thus finds expression in Deianeira's synaesthetic combination of sight and sound, a figure that in turn is emphasised by the term ἄφραστον, 'unutterable', which situates the terrible effects of the potion outside the limits of human expression and comprehension, as she goes on to make explicit with 'impossible for human understanding' (ἀξύμβλητον ἀνθρώπῳ μαθεῖν). Like Herodotus, who set out to describe the experience of a structure that seemed to him to be beyond human capabilities, Deianeira recruits unusual language in the attempt to convey the extraordinariness of her experience.

More specifically, this event is beyond human comprehension because the incredible transformation exhibited by the wool gives it an uncanny and terrible vitality. Unlike the wondrously lifelike figures on Odysseus' brooch, the wool really does become, in a sense, alive: it 'devoured itself' (ἀλλ' ἐδεστὸν ἐξ αὑτοῦ φθίνει, 677). In the heat and light, it melts into nothing and crumbles into the earth (ὡς δ' ἐθάλπετο, / ῥεῖ πᾶν ἄδηλον καὶ κατέψηκται χθονί, 697–8), transforming into a 'clot of bubbling foam' (θρομβώδεις ἀφροί, 702). In the same way that the words to describe this phenomenon elude Deianeira, so too does the wool itself become chemically unstable and physically elusive by crumbling into tiny bits.

Each of the scenarios we have considered features objects that seem to 'lie beyond the grid of intelligibility', as Brown (2001: 5) characterised it. At the same time, the intractability of these objects is by no means passive, as is clear from the *thauma* that grips human spectators in the presence of each of these objects.[14] The labyrinth, the brooch and the tuft of wool, in other words, are *forces* and not just sources of marvel.[15] And the final example to consider in the context of these mysterious and awe-inspiring objects is the figure of Pandora, who, as described in Hesiod's *Theogony*, is deliberately crafted to be both a marvel and a snare and whose description offers a view into the process of fabricating lifelike objects.

---

[14] cf. Bennett 2010: 4–5: 'I realized that the capacity of these bodies was not restricted to a passive "intractability" but also included the ability to make things happen, to produce effects.'

[15] It is worth drawing attention again here to Prier 1989's interpretation of Homeric *thauma*, which Neer 2010: 67 neatly summarises: 'The word *thauma*, "wonder", is itself intermediate . . . It does not simply name a class of objects, but also a state of mind.'

A Wonder to Behold: Pandora in the *Theogony*

Unlike her instantiation in the *Works and Days*, this Pandora is not endowed with a voice or mind of her own and so is therefore a kind of 'dummy', as Martin West (1978: 158 ad 61–2) has distinguished her.[16] Nonetheless, she is an awe-inspiring marvel like those discussed above, and it is for this reason she represents a 'sheer trap, irresistible to men' (δόλον αἰπύν, ἀμήχανον ἀνθρώποισιν, 589):

αὐτίκα δ' ἀντὶ πυρὸς τεῦξεν κακὸν ἀνθρώποισι·	(570)
γαίης γὰρ σύμπλασσε περικλυτὸς Ἀμφιγυήεις	
παρθένῳ αἰδοίῃ ἴκελον Κρονίδεω διὰ βουλάς·	
ζῶσε δὲ καὶ κόσμησε θεὰ γλαυκῶπις Ἀθήνη	
ἀργυφέῃ ἐσθῆτι· κατὰ κρῆθεν δὲ καλύπτρην	
δαιδαλέην χείρεσσι κατέσχεθε, θαῦμα ἰδέσθαι·	(575)
ἀμφὶ δέ οἱ στεφάνους νεοθηλέας, ἄνθεα ποίης,	
ἱμερτοὺς περίθηκε καρήατι Παλλὰς Ἀθήνη·	
ἀμφὶ δέ οἱ στεφάνην χρυσέην κεφαλῆφιν ἔθηκε,	
τὴν αὐτὸς ποίησε περικλυτὸς Ἀμφιγυήεις	
ἀσκήσας παλάμῃσι, χαριζόμενος Διὶ πατρί.	(580)
τῇ δ' ἔνι δαίδαλα πολλὰ τετεύχατο, θαῦμα ἰδέσθαι,	
κνώδαλ' ὅσ' ἤπειρος δεινὰ τρέφει ἠδὲ θάλασσα·	
τῶν ὅ γε πόλλ' ἐνέθηκε, χάρις δ' ἐπὶ πᾶσιν ἄητο	
θαυμάσια, ζωοῖσιν ἐοικότα φωνήεσσιν.	
αὐτὰρ ἐπεὶ δὴ τεῦξε καλὸν κακὸν ἀντ' ἀγαθοῖο,	(585)
ἐξάγαγ' ἔνθά περ ἄλλοι ἔσαν θεοὶ ἠδ' ἄνθρωποι,	
κόσμῳ ἀγαλλομένην γλαυκώπιδος Ὀβριμοπάτρης·	
θαῦμα δ' ἔχ' ἀθανάτους τε θεοὺς θνητούς τ' ἀνθρώπους,	
ὡς εἶδον δόλον αἰπύν, ἀμήχανον ἀνθρώποισιν.	
ἐκ τῆς γὰρ γένος ἐστὶ γυναικῶν θηλυτεράων,	

Right away he fashioned an evil for humankind in exchange for fire. For the much-renowned Crooked-Footed god moulded from earth a likeness of a shy maiden according to the plans of Cronus' son; and the goddess bright-eyed Athena

---

[16] See also Vernant 2011 on Pandora as analogue for images and craftsmanship in archaic thought, Francis 2009 on the Hesiodic descriptions of Pandora in the context of archaic ekphrasis, Steiner 2001 (especially pp. 24–6 on the *Theogony*'s rendering of Pandora) on statues in Greek thought, and Spivey 1995 for a survey of examples of 'bionic statues' in Greek literature and art.

girdled and adorned her with silvery clothing, and with her hands she hung a highly wrought veil from her head, a wonder to see; and around her head Pallas Athena placed freshly budding garlands that arouse desire, the flowers of the meadow; and around her head she placed a golden headband, which the much-renowned Crooked-Footed god made himself, working it with his own skilled hands, to do a favour to Zeus the father. On it there were contrived many designs, highly wrought, a wonder to see, as many terrible creatures that the earth and sea produce; he put many of these into it, wondrous, similar to living animals endowed with speech, and gracefulness breathed upon them all. Then, when he had contrived this beautiful evil thing in exchange for that good one, he led her out to where the other gods and the human beings were, while she exulted in the adornment of the mighty father's bright-eyed daughter; and wonder gripped the immortal gods and the mortal human beings when they saw the sheer trap, irresistible to men. For from her comes the race of female women. (*Theog.* 570–90, translation adapted from Most 2006)

Pandora has much in common with the Acropolis korai discussed in Chapter 1: she takes the form of a young maiden, is elaborately clothed and decorated, and so is imbued with the *charis* that marked those statues as votive objects.[17] But unlike the korai, the figure of Pandora is defined by a paradoxical union of goodness and evil (καλὸν κακὸν, 585): the beauty that belies the wickedness she is designed to bring to mankind. Furthermore, that she is fashioned in the likeness of a youthful woman (παρθένῳ αἰδοίῃ ἴκελον, 572), when both women and the likenesses thereof do not yet exist in the mortal world, creates an equally perplexing impasse since she resembles an absent prototype. It is in this sense, too, that we can understand why she is characterised as 'irresistible' or 'impossible' (ἀμήχανος, 589) for humans, since Pandora embodies something totally alien to human craft and experience.[18] In this respect, the *Theogony*'s Pandora has an important commonality with the automata that are the focus of the next section: like those imaginary objects, she 'resembles' an entity that does not yet exist in the real world. There are, however, similar portrayals of divine feminine adornment in early epic (the focus of Chapter 6).[19] These too describe the process of beautification as one akin to the construction and adornment

---

[17] On the artefactual nature of the *Theogony*'s Pandora see especially Wickkiser 2010 as well as Chesi and Sclavi 2020.

[18] cf. Plato's use of this term at *Phaedrus* 229d–e in connection with creatures like centaurs, chimeras and gorgons, creatures who he says are of an 'impossible nature' (ἄλλων ἀμηχάνων . . . φυσέων) because they are impossible to explain.

[19] See especially pp. 196–209 below.

of a statue. And as we will see, superlative feminine beauty is conventionally one that assimilates living flesh to artificial surfaces.[20]

Not only is Pandora cited here as the progenitor of all women (ἐκ τῆς γὰρ γένος ἐστὶ γυναικῶν θηλυτεράων, 590), but she also represents the first instance of craftsmanship in the *Theogony*'s narrative.[21] Her descendants thus represent a version of human life in which life imitates craft, rather than the other way around.[22] And this is what undergirds her function as a 'trap' (δόλος) since the spectacle she presents causes gods and humans alike to be 'gripped' by 'wonder' (θαῦμα δ' ἔχ' ἀθανάτους τε θεοὺς θνητούς τ' ἀνθρώπους, 588).[23] Zeus has designed Pandora with an eye to the beguiling and stupefying effects that can be generated from marvellous material objects: the very kinds of effects adumbrated in the passages discussed above.[24] But unlike these examples, Hesiod's narration of her construction explicitly offers a view into the dynamism of matter.[25] Pandora's coming-into-being literally unfolds before the reader's eyes as each bit of her takes shape, in an amplification of the similar

---

[20] As Hunzinger 2015: 427 has observed, the presentation of Pandora as an artefact is also stressed in her characterisation with forms of the neuter gender up until she is presented to the gaze of gods and men, where she suddenly becomes feminine (ἀγαλλομένην, 587). See also Hunzinger's remark on the transition from Pandora's description to that of her headband, whose description 'suddenly and meaningfully substitutes for that of the creature herself' (429).

[21] cf. Kenaan 2008: 36: 'As already noticed by numerous readers, Pandora is the first work of art, the first product of manufacture, and the first manifestation of *technē* as opposed to *phusis*. Even more importantly, *Theogony* introduces through the making of Pandora the very experience of objectification. The presentation of Pandora as an object of art results in an ekphrasis, which, by virtue of its rhetorical quality, creates two portraits: that of the object (the creation of Pandora), and that of the act of gazing at the object (the responses to Pandora).'

[22] See also the comments of Vernant 2011: 405 on the significance of the *Theogony*'s Pandora for humanity writ large: 'From the moment that woman is *produced*, humans must *reproduce* in order to exist.'

[23] cf. Hunzinger 2015: 430 on this passage: 'Here the wonder's beauty is a snare: sign of defeat, mark of ignorance and lack of mental acuity.'

[24] Suggestive in the context of Pandora's function as a snare are the comments of Gross 1992: 37 in his (psychoanalytically informed) discussion of the figure of the animated statue in Western thought: 'external statues may become the places onto which we project our most intimate opacities . . . Yet if statues are a place from which aspects of our internal lives are thrown back to us, it is not always in a form we can recognize.'

[25] cf. Vernant 2011: 410–11: 'In effect she [Pandora] can be considered either as a living maiden, the first one, but one created in the manner of an *agalma*, a fabricated precious object. Or one can regard her as an *agalma*, one of the masterpieces of grace achieved by the art of the demiurge, but an *agalma* too into which life has been breathed.'

dynamism that attended the experience of the labyrinth, brooch and wool. These, too, commanded wonder because each strained beyond its material confines into the realm of living, moving beings: the labyrinth through the endless windings of its passageways, the brooch with its apparition of animals engaged in a struggle for life, and the wool with its spontaneous self-destruction and transformation. If Pandora represents the first instance of craftsmanship as well as the prototype of women, then her description and the wonder she evokes suggest that subsequent products of craftsmanship and their descriptions will likewise have the power to captivate their spectators.[26]

That Pandora's efficacy as a snare relies on human responses to her (rather than active participation on her part) is clear from the fact that the only indication of her vitality comes in the phrase 'exulting in the adornment' (κόσμῳ ἀγαλλομένην, 587). This discloses how Pandora herself (and by extension, the race of women that descend from her) finds delight in her beauty, a beauty that consists in the *charis* that 'is breathed' over her crowned head (χάρις δ' ἐπὶ πᾶσιν ἄητο, 583).[27] Pandora thus possesses the same animating radiance that emits from her finery, underscoring how she is as much a product of handicraft as are these objects. This continuity between woman and material is strengthened by the fact that her headband contains figures that are ontologically similar to her: fashioned by the hands of Hephaestus, elaborately and skilfully wrought, and made in resemblance of living creatures.[28] Significantly, though, Pandora is fashioned from earth, while the headband is golden. While the latter is forged from material as incorruptible as divinity itself, Pandora's 'likeness' to mortal women derives in part from the relative fragility of her body's substance. And this contrast throws into high relief the different degrees to which humans and material things can persist through time. Seen in this way, the temporal scale of material things has more in common with divinities than with humans, a fact that may account for the supernatural qualities afforded to the material exempla in this chapter.[29]

---

[26] cf. Canevaro 2018: 222, who notes that 'the archaic epic tradition questions the potentiality of a progression from inanimate object to animate being, and problematizes the blurring of the boundary between person and thing'. See further Canevaro 2018: 248–55 on the relationship between Pandora and her objects (especially her *pithos*) and Hesiod's vision of Iron Age human life.

[27] On the figuration of *charis* in archaic Greek thought see especially MacLachlan 1993.

[28] cf. Canevaro 2018: 252, who notes that 'the thing [the headband] is more vital than is the person'. Vernant 2011: 411 goes so far as to call Pandora's accoutrements 'extensions of her body, and they work in the same way as she'.

[29] cf. the gold and silver guard dogs that Hephaestus crafts to guard the palace of Alcinous (*Od.* 7.91–4), which are explicitly characterised as 'immortal and unageing' (ἀθανάτους

The description of Pandora's crown, and in particular its representation of 'similar to living animals endowed with speech', look ahead to the next section and its concentration on nonhuman objects.[30] So far, we have looked at a collection of wondrous objects that are beyond words and human understanding. But as Pandora's crown has already intimated, the idea of genuinely animate objects is a remarkably ductile one. For if the passages in this section have depicted humans confronting and trying to make sense of perplexing and paradoxical phenomena, the next section will explore this dynamic from the opposite side by investigating the circumstances and mechanisms that were imagined to allow nonhuman substances to become animate and so resemble humans.[31]

Intelligent Things

While some material phenomena compel a sense of wonder in human observers because of their inscrutability, others, conversely, incite wonder because of how integrated they are with human or divine minds. This is true even in the case of the *Theogony*'s Pandora, who represents the manifestation of Zeus' will. Even as she is designed as a 'sheer trap' (δόλον αἰπύν, 589) for mankind, this is nevertheless in keeping with her status as a contrived 'evil' (τεῦξεν κακὸν, 570) of Zeus, as emphasised by the above description's references to his will (Κρονίδεω διὰ βουλάς, 572; χαριζόμενος Διὶ πατρί, 580). And this correlation between divine will and fabulous artefacts is especially true of the automated beings that populate Hephaestus' workshop, which are, to borrow Aristotle's terminology, 'living tools' in every sense: obedient and attuned to their master's will, these are objects 'ensouled' to the extent that they display, to different degrees, animate features.[32] Indeed, Aristotle even

---

ὄντας καὶ ἀγήρως ἥματα πάντα, 94). Although the fact that the dogs are designed to serve as guards suggests that they are animate in some way, I exclude them from my discussion here since they, unlike Hephaestus' bellows, tripods and handmaidens, are not explicitly said to be engaged in any activity. On their function as magical talismans see especially Faraone 1987.

[30] For an interpretation of Pandora (and her crown in particular) that focuses on its relation to ancient Greek philosophical accounts of nature, craft and representation, see Summers 1999.

[31] On the animacy of amber and ivory in particular see also Neer 2018b, who notes that 'the combination of causal efficacy and inert equipment produces wonder' (475).

[32] 'A slave is a kind of ensouled tool', ὁ δοῦλος κτῆμά τι ἔμψυχον, Arist. *Pol.* 1253b33. On the similarities between Hephaestus' automata and Pandora see Canevaro 2018: 220–2 and Berryman 2009: 25, who notes of Hephaestus' automata that 'they seem to be conscious and to respond directly to their master's will'. See also Gaifman and Platt 2018: 414–15, who

cites the craftsman god's self-moving tripods as an example of the kind of technology that would render human slaves obsolete:

Εἰ γὰρ ἠδύνατο ἕκαστον τῶν ὀργάνων κελευσθὲν ἢ προαισθανόμενον ἀποτελεῖν τὸ αὑτοῦ ἔργον, καὶ ὥσπερ τὰ Δαιδάλου φασὶν ἢ τοὺς τοῦ Ἡφαίστου τρίποδας, οὕς φησιν ὁ ποιητὴς αὐτομάτους θεῖον δύεσθαι ἀγῶνα, οὕτως αἱ κερκίδες ἐκέρκιζον αὐταὶ καὶ τὰ πλῆκτρα ἐκιθάριζεν, οὐδὲν ἂν ἔδει οὔτε τοῖς ἀρχιτέκτοσιν ὑπηρετῶν οὔτε τοῖς δεσπόταις δούλων

For if every tool could perform its own work when ordered, or by seeing what to do in advance, like the statues of Daedalus in the story, or the tripods of Hephaestus which the poets say 'enter self-moved the company divine', – if thus shuttles wove and quills played harps of themselves, master-craftsmen would have no need of assistants and masters no need of slaves. (Arist. *Pol.* 1253b33–1254a2, trans. Rackham 1932)

The world Aristotle imagines here, where automation can fully replace human labour, is one that would require tools to heed commands as well as 'seeing what to do in advance' (προαισθανόμενον).[33] While Daedalus and Hephaestus are an obvious pair to cite in this context, since the former was also credited in antiquity with the creation of automata in the form of living statues, what differentiates Hephaestus is the fact that his automata are fashioned as *tools* designed to fulfil specific purposes. And while the vocabulary of their descriptions shares much in common with portrayals of artefacts, Hephaestus' automata have specific functions aligned with his metallurgy as well as with his physical handicaps.[34] If Daedalus was popularly associated with statues that moved and spoke of their own accord with such a degree of autonomy that they needed to be tied down (cf. Pl. *Menex.* 97d), the examples I dwell on here all depict animated artefacts working in close connection with humans.[35]

likewise identify in Hephaestus' automata and Aristotle's concept of the 'living tool' fertile terrain for unpacking the notion(s) of 'embodied objects' in ancient thought.

[33] On the significance of automata in the classical imaginary see Devecka 2013, who concludes that 'So for Aristotle, a motivating element in the construction of imaginary robots was precisely that fact of Greek social life that they were meant to elucidate and explain – chattel slavery' (63).

[34] On the relationship between Hephaestus' disability and his automata see especially Liveley 2006. More recently, see Noel 2018 on the ancient Greek 'prosthetic imagination', whose origins she detects in the body–weapon relationship depicted in Homer.

[35] Morris 1992: 215–37 offers a comprehensive overview of the emergence of a specifically Athenian trope (especially in drama) connecting Daedalus with animated statues.

Aristotle's invocation of the self-moving shuttle in the *Politics* passage bears comparison with Plato's discussion of language's functionality. Indeed, Plato relies on the same object as analogue: words are like the weaver's shuttle because each is a 'tool' (ὄργανον) used to differentiate things, 'A word is, then, a tool for teaching and for separating out reality, as a shuttle is to the web' (ὄνομα ἄρα διδασκαλικόν τί ἐστιν ὄργανον καὶ διακριτικὸν τῆς οὐσίας ὥσπερ κερκὶς ὑφάσματος, *Cra.* 388b–c). If language operates as Plato imagines, then it would seem to align with Aristotle's picture of automated instruments, since even ordinary language users employ words as naturally and easily as a weaver wields the shuttle. Indeed, as Aristotle puts it elsewhere, the faculty of speech is the hallmark of any creature that is 'ensouled', and therefore it belongs only to humans (ἡ δὲ φωνὴ ψόφος τίς ἐστιν ἐμψύχου, *De an.* 420b5–6).

This set of passages draws attention to two points that will prove central to this section: (1) that intelligible language is a natural and uniquely human tool; and (2) that the most efficacious tools are those that, like language, can be put to work in concert with the human will. In this sense, these examples share an important commonality with contemporary theories of mind that likewise stress the close integration between human cognition and the body, including its physical environs. First formulated in a 1998 paper by Andy Clark and David Chalmers, the theory of extended mind claims that cognition is not necessarily brain-bound, but can operate in a 'coupled system' with physical environs. This relationship is defined as follows: 'the human organism is linked with an external entity in a two-way interaction . . . if we remove the external component the system's behavioral competence will drop, just as it would if we removed part of its brain' (Clark 2008: 222). The paradigmatic example to illustrate this kind of coupled system comes in the figure of Otto, who has Alzheimer's disease and so always carries with him a notebook in which he continually writes down new information. When Otto decides to visit the Museum of Modern Art in New York City, he accesses the relevant page in his notebook where the address is written and so makes his way there. Inga, by contrast, also decides to visit an exhibit at the same museum, but manages to recall the address of the museum and navigate to it without the aid of a notebook and simply by remembering that it was on 53rd Street. Given that both Otto and Inga achieve their goals, albeit by different routes, what this comparison illustrates is that there is nothing substantively different about Inga's recollection and Otto's consultation of his notebook. The only distinction is that one takes place in the head (Inga) and one relies on an external prop (Otto's notebook). This suggests that Otto's notebook forms as much a part of his cognitive processing as Inga's memory does for hers, even though one is external, while the other is not.

Andy Clark has expanded on this theory in numerous subsequent works and has argued that language can be viewed as a tool similar to Otto's notebook: in other words, language, too, is a kind of external 'prop' not unlike the shuttle that Plato introduces in the *Cratylus*. As Clark (2008: 58–60) has argued, language is technological to the extent that it provides an external and material set of symbols that enable us to formulate thoughts and thereby put those thoughts into a form accessible to both ourselves and others. It is for this reason that language can function as 'a key cognitive tool by means of which we are able to objectify, reflect upon, and hence knowingly engage with our own thoughts, trains of reasoning, and cognitive and personal characters' (2008: 59). In fact, so naturally do humans make use of this faculty that Clark has characterised language as 'a kind of magic trick by which to go beyond the bounds of our animal natures' (2003: 81). That he has elsewhere discussed language as 'the ultimate artifact' in a chapter of this title (1997: 193–218) brings us back to Hephaestus and his magical artefacts, since the god's reliance on his automata well illustrates the kind of 'coupled system' envisaged by Clark. And as we will see in the following examples, language and voice are conceived as faculties that can be implanted from without and serve to animate nonhuman substances, enabling them to 'couple' with users in a manner akin to Hephaestus' interactions with his workshop tools.[36] And it is also, of course, by means of the language deployed to describe these wondrous objects that the nature of the human mind and body can become an object of contemplation in these passages.

Hephaestus' Tools

Among Hephaestus' tools, the bellows play the most central role in the construction of Achilles' shield in book 18 as an integral component of the god's metalworking:

τὰς δ' ἐς πῦρ ἔτρεψε κέλευσέ τε ἐργάζεσθαι.
φῦσαι δ' ἐν χοάνοισιν ἐείκοσι πᾶσαι ἐφύσων
παντοίην εὔπρηστον ἀϋτμὴν ἐξανιεῖσαι,
ἄλλοτε μὲν σπεύδοντι παρέμμεναι, ἄλλοτε δ' αὖτε,
ὅπως Ἥφαιστός τ' ἐθέλοι καὶ ἔργον ἄνοιτο.

---

[36] On the significance of Hephaestus' automata for interpreting the liveliness of Homeric objects writ large, see especially Bielfeldt 2014, who illuminates the reciprocal interactivity that inheres between material things and mortals as well as between objects and gods. On the hybridity of bodies see also Uhlig 2018 on the construction of the satyr body, figures who 'incorporate new elements into their own bodies, new skins to create ever more complex forms of composite nudity' (167).

He turned these into the fire and ordered them to get to work. And all twenty got to blowing into the melting-pots, emitting every kind of strong-blowing blast, and were ready to hand at one time then another, in whatever way he desired, as he bustled about and his task was carried out. (*Il.* 18.469–73)

Not only are the bellows 'self-moving' in the literal sense of 'automaton', they are presented as working in conjunction with Hephaestus' will.[37] They heed his orders (κέλευσέ τε ἐργάζεσθαι) and remain poised to assist the god whenever (ἄλλοτε . . . ἄλλοτε δ' αὖτε) and in whatever way he needs (ὅππως Ἥφαιστός τ' ἐθέλοι).[38] The bellows, in short, are physically ready to hand as well as ready to adapt to the crafts-man's process. And their ability to do so is not just a convenience for Hephaestus, but allows him to focus on using his other tools: the tongs and hammer that he takes up a few verses later (γέντο δὲ χειρὶ / ῥαιστῆρα κρατερήν, ἑτέρηφιδὲ γέντο πυράγην, 476–7).

Similarly, when Thetis first approaches Hephaestus in his workshop he is at work on another set of automata: the tripods that can move by themselves between his home and the assembly of the gods:

τὸν δ' εὗρ' ἱδρώοντα ἑλισσόμενον περὶ φύσας
σπεύδοντα· τρίποδας γὰρ ἐείκοσι πάντας ἔτευχεν
ἑστάμεναι περὶ τοῖχον ἐϋσταθέος μεγάροιο,
χρύσεα δέ σφ' ὑπὸ κύκλα ἑκάστῳ πυθμένι θῆκεν,
ὄφρά οἱ αὐτόματοι θεῖον δυσαίατ' ἀγῶνα
ἠδ' αὖτις πρὸς δῶμα νεοίατο θαῦμα ἰδέσθαι.
οἳ δ' ἤτοι τόσσον μὲν ἔχον τέλος, οὔατα δ' οὔ πω
δαιδάλεα προσέκειτο· τά ῥ' ἤρτυε, κόπτε δὲ δεσμούς.
ὄφρ' ὅ γε ταῦτ' ἐπονεῖτο ἰδυίῃσι πραπίδεσσι.

[And Thetis] found him sweating and bustling to and fro about his bellows in haste, for he was crafting tripods, twenty altogether, to stand around the wall of his well-built hall, and he placed golden wheels beneath the base of each, so that they might enter the assembly of the gods of their own accord and come back home again, a marvel to see. And these were completed so far but their cunningly

---

[37] However, as Bielfeldt 2014: 39 observes, Homeric objects do exhibit their own will and willingness to act, as well.

[38] cf. the gates of Olympus as described at *Il.* 5.749–51 (= *Il.* 8.393–5), which are also charac-terised as αὐτόμαται because they open and close themselves in accordance with the will of the Horae.

wrought handles were not yet attached: Hephaestus was preparing these and was forging their bonds. While he was labouring over these things in his visionary mind . . . (*Il.* 18.372–80)

This description makes clear that the automatic capacity of the tripods derives from the wheels attached to their bases (κύκλα . . . ὄφρά). However, they still, like the bellows, perform a vital part of Hephaestus' mental and physical labour. That the tripods are not yet complete is significant because their description therefore opens a window into Hephaestus' mind and his purpose in crafting them. Unlike the bellows, which are depicted already engaged in their task, the tripods are still part putative: Hephaestus is still 'labouring over' them in his 'visionary mind' (ὅ γε ταῦτ' ἐπονεῖτο ἰδυίῃσι πραπίδεσσι). Three words here reveal how Hephaestus' creation here consists in a close cooperation between his body and mind. His physical work (ἐπονεῖτο) coincides with the workings of the mysterious πραπίδες, a term that Ruth Padel has analysed as having 'an uncertain physiological meaning, but nevertheless connect[ing] intuitive, mental, and emotional experience to the body' (1992: 19–20).[39] That its dative form here could indicate either an instrumental or locative use of the case drives home the intimacy of the connection between the god's mental and physical activity by conveying how his labours operate in his mind as much as they extend out into the visible world. The latter point is sharpened by the use of the adjective ἰδυίῃσι, which can refer to 'knowing' as well as physical 'seeing'. As Françoise Frontisi-Ducroux has argued, this term in conjunction with πραπίδεσσι paints Hephaestus' work as a task of bringing to life the images in his mind (2002: 479).

Furthermore, the visual connotations of ἰδυίῃσι conform with the striking spectacle that the tripods are designed to create. Whereas the bellows are presented as utilitarian in appearance, the tripods are clearly crafted for aesthetic impact as well as functionality. They, like the shield itself, will inspire wonder (θαῦμα ἰδέσθαι) in their automation, and their handles (literally, their 'ears') are 'cunningly wrought' (οὔατα . . . δαιδάλεα). While the characterisation of handles as 'ears' is not unusual, this term becomes more salient here in light of the animated aspect of the tripods: the tripods are not only self-moving, like real living beings, but seem to have body parts. And given that the bellows were said to respond to Hephaestus' commands (κέλευσέ τε ἐργάζεσθαι, *Il.* 18.469), that the tripods are still lacking the part that may enable them to 'hear' Hephaestus' orders makes it clear why they are still unfinished in spite of the wheels that grant them mobility.

---

[39] cf. Clarke 1999: 72 in his study of the Homeric terms for cognition and cognitive faculties: 'Knowledge and cognitive activity take place in the same way, in or by means of the apparatus.'

If the tripods and bellows enable us to glimpse extensions of Hephaestus' mind into his handiwork, his golden handmaids have the clearest connection to his physical disability in that they use their automatic capacities to help him move:[40]

δῦ δὲ χιτῶν', ἕλε δὲ σκῆπτρον παχύ, βῆ δὲ θύραζε
χωλεύων· ὑπὸ δ' ἀμφίπολοι ῥώοντο ἄνακτι
χρύσειαι ζωῇσι νεήνισιν εἰοικυῖαι.
τῇς ἐν μὲν νόος ἐστὶ μετὰ φρεσίν, ἐν δὲ καὶ αὐδὴ
καὶ σθένος, ἀθανάτων δὲ θεῶν ἄπο ἔργα ἴσασιν.
αἳ μὲν ὕπαιθα ἄνακτος ἐποίπνυον· αὐτὰρ ὃ ἔρρων.

He put on a tunic, and took up a stout staff, and went haltingly to the door. And the golden servants, looking just like young living maids, hastened to support their master. In them was mind together with understanding, and in them was also voice and strength, and they have knowledge of handiwork, endowed by the immortal gods. And these were busying about around their master as he limped. (*Il.* 18.416–21)

In this description, Hephaestus' halting movements are emphasised almost as much as the handmaids' lifelike features. Not only are these figures able to move dexterously and spring unbidden to their master's aid, they are endowed with the key ingredients of human cognition: mind, understanding, voice, strength and practical skills, albeit with no indication of how this implantation was achieved.[41] But as Aristotle recognised in his account of automation in the *Politics*, it is not enough for tools to be automatic: their optimal utility will rely on their being able to 'see what to do in advance' for their user. That these humanlike faculties are located within the handmaids' bodies and so are belied by the gold that makes up their flesh rehearses a strategy of concealment that will also be operative in Pandora's description in the *Works and Days*. But in their combination of cognitive faculties and obedience, the handmaids typify Aristotle's definition of the slave as a 'living tool'. Crucially, though, unlike the human slave, the handmaids, by virtue of being golden automata, seem to be as

[40] See also the comments of Bielfeldt 2018: 424, which draw attention to the 'inner life' afforded to the maidens: 'What truly animates the maiden crutches, however, is the inner impulse of tools to be of service – a drive towards helpful action.'

[41] cf. Berryman 2009: 25: 'Nothing is said about internal mechanisms in the handmaidens or the bellows. Rather, they seem to be conscious and to respond directly to their master's will.' See also Clay 1974 on the differentiation between Homeric humans and gods in terms of voice vocabulary, and Pelliccia 1995 on the relationship between words for cognitive faculties, voice/speech organs and body parts in archaic and classical Greek thought.

immortal as their maker. In this sense, Hephaestus' handmaids imagine how such artefacts could improve upon their human counterparts as well as supplant them.

The Ships of the Phaeacians and Other 'Smart' Objects

It is not only Hephaestus who interacts in a kind of coupled system with the tools in his workshop. The ships of the Phaeacians, for instance, 'understand the thoughts and minds of men' and therefore have no need of captains or steering oars, as Alcinous explains to Odysseus:

> εἰπὲ δέ μοι γαῖάν τε: τεὴν δῆμόν τε πόλιν τε·
> ὄφρα σε τῇ πέμπωσι τιτυσκόμεναι φρεσὶ νῆες·
> οὐ γὰρ Φαιήκεσσι κυβερνητῆρες ἔασιν,
> οὐδέ τι πηδάλι᾽ ἔστι, τά τ᾽ ἄλλαι νῆες ἔχουσιν·
> ἀλλ᾽ αὐταὶ ἴσασι νοήματα καὶ φρένας ἀνδρῶν

> Tell me your country, your people, and your city, so that our ships can send you there, preparing the way by their wits. For there are no pilots among the Phaeacians, nor is there need for rudders such as other ships have: rather our ships themselves understand the thoughts and minds of men. (*Od.* 8.555–9)

Just as Hephaestus developed his tripods 'in' or 'with' his mind (ἐπονεῖτο ἰδυίῃσι πραπίδεσσι, *Il.* 18.380), the ships likewise can rely on their own cognitive faculties in order to discern the course of their passengers. That Alcinous makes explicit what the ships do *not* need throws into sharp relief how much normal seafaring relies on a nexus of human and nonhuman forms: the ships themselves together with pilots (κυβερνητῆρες) and rudders (πηδάλια), which also require human operators.[42] Instead, the Phaeacian ships function in a different kind of hybrid system in which they simply 'understand' (ἴσασι) what their passengers want and can act accordingly without need of even the kind of instruction that Hephaestus gives his bellows. Moreover, this is not the only thing that makes these ships supernatural: they operate perfectly and are impervious to destruction (οὐδέ ποτέ σφιν / οὔτε τι πημανθῆναι ἔπι δέος οὔτ᾽ ἀπολέσθαι, 8.562–3). Indeed, so flawlessly do the ships complete their voyages that they incur the wrath of Poseidon, which is directed against them as well as at the land itself of the Phaeacians (8.564–9).

---

[42] cf. Canevaro 2018: 159–63, who illuminates how this passage contributes to the *Odyssey*'s unique penchant for object-oriented similes: 'It is only in the *Odyssey* that there are a number of scenes in which objects in the main narrative are "animated" by simile' (162).

While the Phaeacian ships represent an idealised version of seafaring, one that removes the need for human intervention (and thus, the potential for human error), the idea that material and nonhuman things could helpfully penetrate human life is not confined to epic, but also circulates in Athenian tragedy. In these instances, inanimate objects are imagined to be able to audibly profess truths that are invisible or otherwise unknown to human actors. This idea in turn reflects an intuition that material things are somehow attuned to human activity. And this trope is uniquely poignant in the context of tragedy, where the very objects that are called upon to speak are physical props that are integral to the drama in addition to being the kind of external cognitive 'props' typified in the example of Otto's notebook. By wishing for things to 'take on' voice, these passages testify to a desire for an exceptionally close bond between humans and objects.[43] In so doing, these instances in turn cast human actors in a different light, as the speakers in each example are 'voicing' prescribed words in exactly the manner that the characters desire for objects to do.[44]

For instance, in Aeschylus' *Libation Bearers* Electra wishes that the lock of hair left at her father's tomb had a 'voice and mind' like a messenger so that its source could be confirmed: 'Would that it had a voice and mind like that of a messenger, so that I would not be tossed about in two minds' (εἴθ' εἶχε φωνὴν ἔμφρον' ἀγγέλου δίκην, ὅπως δίφροντις οὖσα μὴ 'κινυσσόμην, 195).[45] First, by relating how the hair's unconfirmed identity as Orestes' causes her to be 'tossed about in two minds' (δίφροντις ... 'κινυσσόμην), Electra's confusion echoes the effects of objects' intractability that was explored in the section 'Paradoxical *Poikilia*: Labyrinthine Passageways'. Further, by wishing for the lock to acquire 'voice and a mind' (φωνὴν ἔμφρον'), Electra reveals her belief that the presence of these faculties would necessarily lead her to the truth.[46] And this idea finds a parallel at the very opening of

---

[43] Although these examples are not consistent in the terminology used for 'voice' (employing φθογγή, φωνή, as well as φθέγμα, all of which can refer to human as well as nonhuman sounds), each of them imagines the voice (and not necessarily a specifically human language) as a conduit for communicating with humans. On the ancient voice and auditory aesthetics see especially Gurd 2016 (focused on Greek sources) as well as Butler 2015 and Lachenaud 2013 for more wide-ranging surveys of ancient conceptions of voice and sound. On nonhuman sounds in particular see Bettini 2008.

[44] cf. Hall 2006: 288: 'When the ancient actor opened his mouth, beneath his sculptured, painted mask, and forced the air from his lungs through his larynx, teeth and lips, it was his voice that allowed matter to become mind, art, and emotion, and the carnal, biological body to meet the metaphorical body politic.' On Aeschylus' construction of voice and vocality see especially Nooter 2017.

[45] I here follow the reading adopted by Denniston and Page 1957, which prints ἔμφρον' at 195 instead of the variant εὔφρον'.

[46] Differently, see Billings 2018 on the deceptiveness of the urn and its figuration through

the trilogy, where the Watchman declares that 'if the house of Atreus could take on a voice, it would speak very clearly' (in contrast to his own silence) (οἶκος δ᾽ αὐτός, εἰ φθογγὴν λάβοι, / σαφέστατ᾽ ἂν λέξειεν, 37–8). Here, too, the implication is that inanimate objects could speak truthfully and communicate important information if only they could be endowed with voice in the manner of Hephaestus' handmaids.

In Euripides' *Hippolytus*, the idea of speaking objects is more specifically expressed as a conception of objects functioning as witnesses.[47] First, Phaedra articulates concern that the house could betray a woman's illicit secrets: 'How are they not afraid that darkness, their helpmeet, and the chambers of the house might break into speech?' (οὐδὲ σκότον φρίσσουσι τὸν ξυνεργάτην / τέραμνά τ᾽ οἴκων μή ποτε φθογγὴν ἀφῇ;, 417–18). On this formulation, while darkness conspires to conceal illicit deeds, such obscurity would not prevent the physical setting of those deeds from testifying. To Phaedra, then, a house's rooms could function as an impartial and immovable witness to what has taken place within its walls.

In a strikingly similar vein, Hippolytus wishes for the house to be able to speak and so attest to his innocence: 'O house, would that you could voice aloud a sound and bear witness as to whether I am innately wicked' (ὦ δώματ᾽, εἴθε φθέγμα γηρύσαισθέ μοι / καὶ μαρτυρήσαιτ᾽ εἰ κακὸς πέφυκ᾽ ἀνήρ, 1074–5). Hippolytus is explicit here about the formal testimony the house could provide through his use of the word μαρτυρήσαιτε, 'bear witness', with its forensic connotations. For both Phaedra and Hippolytus, then, the private domicile would be the ultimate character witness, 'if only' (εἴθε) it could acquire a means of communicating. The remoteness of this possibility, however, is one that Theseus mocks in his response to Hippolytus' address to the house: 'You are devising escape cleverly in calling to voiceless witnesses: but the deed silently reveals you as evil' (ἐς τοὺς ἀφώνους

---

language in Sophocles' *Electra* (although this object, unlike those discussed here, is not called upon to speak aloud).

The connection between truthful speech and nonhuman, speaking things is prominently associated with the oracle at Dodona, where rocks and trees were traditionally the medium of prophecy, as reported in Plato's *Phaedrus* ('[the consultants of the oracle,] for whom it was sufficient to listen to an oak or rock, if only it spoke the truth', ἅτε οὐκ οὖσι σοφοῖς ὥσπερ ὑμεῖς οἱ νέοι, ἀπέχρη δρυὸς καὶ πέτρας ἀκούειν ὑπ᾽ εὐηθείας, εἰ μόνον ἀληθῆ λέγοιεν, 275b–c).

[47] Space does not permit me to address the important question of the relationship between written language and materiality, but on this topic see, most recently, Petrovic, Petrovic and Thomas 2018.

On the significance of the writing tablet, *deltos*, as a central prop of the *Hippolytus* (particularly in relation to Phaedra's revenge) see especially Mueller 2016a: 163–78. See also Torrance 2013: 147–52 on Phaedra's suicide note, as well as Segal 1992 on the *Hippolytus*' treatment of language and communication.

μάρτυρας φεύγεις σοφῶς· / τὸ δ' ἔργον οὐ λέγον σε μηνύει κακόν, 1076–7).[48] Theseus here zeroes in on the paradox of summoning a 'voiceless witness' and, in so doing, underscores the fact that objects could only acquire human voice by means of a divine power like that of Hephaestus. Even there, as we have seen, this is a distinctly opaque process: 'voice' and 'mind' are simply implanted in the handmaids as easily as the ears are affixed onto his tripods.

This connection between the endowment of voice and divine craftsmanship is made explicit in Euripides' *Hecuba*, when the beleaguered Trojan queen wishes for extra voices to emerge from her limbs and hair and so aid her in her plea to Agamemnon:

εἴ μοι γένοιτο φθόγγος ἐν βραχίοσι
καὶ χερσὶ καὶ κόμαισι καὶ ποδῶν βάσει
ἢ Δαιδάλου τέχναισιν ἢ θεῶν τινος,
ὡς πάνθ' ὁμαρτῇ σῶν ἔχοιντο γουνάτων
κλαίοντ', ἐπισκήπτοντα παντοίους λόγους.[49]

If only there was a voice in my arms and hands and my locks of hair and the step of my feet, as by the craftsmanship of Daedalus or some one of the gods, so that all of them together could lay hold of your knees, clamouring, beseeching you with every kind of word. (836–40)

Here, Hecuba imagines her arms, hands, hair and feet as discrete physical entities that could be mustered as a chorus of clamouring voices in a feat that would be characteristic of divine craftsmanship.[50] And in her conceptualisation of parts of

---

[48] This creates a stark contrast with Theseus' reaction to Phaedra's suicide note, an object to which he repeatedly ascribes voice (e.g. at 865, 877–80). The difference, of course, is that the tablet contained written testimony, whereas Hippolytus simply wishes for the house to speak. Whereas the tablet is conceived by Theseus as an extension of Phaedra's voice, its message proves deceptive. On the schematics of this tablet's agency see especially Mueller 2016a: 169: 'Simultaneously speechless and, at least to Theseus's ear, shouting out accursed things (877), the tablet also embodies the paradox of voiceless voice. Despite being fashioned out of seemingly inert substance, it is possessed of a performative kind of *logos* . . . It forces one speaker to release from his mouth a deadly curse, while in turn preventing another from speaking up in his own self-defense.'

[49] cf. Euripides' Electra, who likewise states that her 'hands, tongue, beleaguered spirit and shorn hair' are 'imploring' Orestes to return (πολλοὶ δ' ἐπιστέλλουσιν, ἑρμηνεὺς δ' ἐγώ, / αἱ χεῖρες ἡ γλῶσσ' ἡ ταλαίπωρός τε φρήν, /κάρα τ' ἐμὸν ξυρῆκες, ὅ τ' ἐκεῖνον τεκών, 333–5).

[50] cf. Morris 1992: 220, who notes of this description, 'Such a feat can only be performed

the human body becoming animate with the help of a god, Hecuba's image calls to mind the *Works and Days*' description of Pandora. For the very faculties that bring Pandora to life, seemingly by magic, are also those that animate 'real' humans. Her description, therefore, makes the relationship between human cognition and the human body appear as a source of wonder not unlike the automata discussed above.

In each of the previous cases, we have seen authors imagine how objects, once endowed with human qualities – movement, thought and/or voice – could work in concert with human agents. There is not always a seamless integration, as Iphigenia's misinterpretation of the 'speaking column' (50–2) of her dream portends in Euripides' *Iphigenia in Tauris*. The *Works and Days*' vision of Pandora, however, goes the furthest in depicting how human qualities attached to nonhuman substances could be marshalled as a 'sheer, intractable deception' for humans:

Ἥφαιστον δ' ἐκέλευσε περικλυτὸν ὅττι τάχιστα (60)
γαῖαν ὕδει φύρειν, ἐν δ' ἀνθρώπου θέμεν αὐδὴν
καὶ σθένος, ἀθανάτης δὲ θεῇς εἰς ὦπα ἐίσκειν
παρθενικῆς καλὸν εἶδος ἐπήρατον· αὐτὰρ Ἀθήνην
ἔργα διδασκῆσαι, πολυδαίδαλον ἱστὸν ὑφαίνειν·
καὶ χάριν ἀμφιχέαι κεφαλῇ χρυσέην Ἀφροδίτην (65)
καὶ πόθον ἀργαλέον καὶ γυιοβόρους μελεδώνας·
ἐν δὲ θέμεν κύνεόν τε νόον καὶ ἐπίκλοπον ἦθος
Ἑρμείην ἤνωγε, διάκτορον Ἀργεϊφόντην.
Ὣς ἔφαθ', οἳ δ' ἐπίθοντο Διὶ Κρονίωνι ἄνακτι . . .
[αὐτίκα δ' ἐκ γαίης πλάσσε κλυτὸς Ἀμφιγυήεις (70)
παρθένῳ αἰδοίῃ ἴκελον Κρονίδεω διὰ βουλάς·
ζῶσε δὲ καὶ κόσμησε θεὰ γλαυκῶπις Ἀθήνη·
ἀμφὶ δέ οἱ Χάριτές τε θεαὶ καὶ πότνια Πειθὼ
ὅρμους χρυσείους ἔθεσαν χροΐ· ἀμφὶ δὲ τήν γε
Ὧραι καλλίκομοι στέφον ἄνθεσι εἰαρινοῖσιν· (75)
πάντα δέ οἱ χροΐ κόσμον ἐφήρμοσε Παλλὰς Ἀθήνη·]
ἐν δ' ἄρα οἱ στήθεσσι διάκτορος Ἀργεϊφόντης
ψεύδεά θ' αἱμυλίους τε λόγους καὶ ἐπίκλοπον ἦθος
τεῦξε Διὸς βουλῇσι βαρυκτύπου· ἐν δ' ἄρα φωνὴν
θῆκε θεῶν κῆρυξ, ὀνόμηνε δὲ τήνδε γυναῖκα (80)
Πανδώρην, ὅτι πάντες Ὀλύμπια δώματ' ἔχοντες

through "the arts of Daidalos or one of the gods", that is, through magical powers bestowed on inanimate objects by the gods or divine craftsmen, in particular by Daidalos. This plea elaborates a figure of speech where an inanimate object comes alive by speaking.'

δῶρον ἐδώρησαν, πῆμ' ἀνδράσιν ἀλφηστῇσιν.
αὐτὰρ ἐπεὶ δόλον αἰπὺν ἀμήχανον ἐξετέλεσσεν . . .

He commanded renowned Hephaestus to mix earth with water as quickly as possible, and to put the voice and strength of a human into it, and to make a beautiful,
lovely form of a maiden similar in her face to the immortal goddesses. He told
Athena to teach her crafts, to weave richly worked cloth, and golden Aphrodite to
shed grace and painful desire and limb-devouring cares around her head; and he
ordered Hermes, the intermediary, the killer of Argus, to put a dog's mind and a
thievish character into her. So he spoke, and they obeyed Zeus, the lord, Cronus'
son. Immediately the famous Lame One fabricated out of earth a likeness of a
modest maiden, by the plans of Cronus' son; the goddess, bright-eyed Athena, gave
her a girdle and ornaments; the goddesses Graces and queenly Persuasion placed
golden jewellery all around on her body; the beautiful-haired Seasons crowned her
all around with spring flowers; and Pallas Athena fitted the whole ornamentation
to her body. Then into her breast the intermediary, the killer of Argus, set lies and
guileful words and a thievish character, by the plans of deep-thundering Zeus; and
the messenger of the gods placed a voice in her and named this woman Pandora
(All-Gift), since all those who have their mansions on Olympus had given her a gift
– a woe for men who live on bread. When he had completed the sheer, intractable
deception . . . (*Op.* 60–83, trans. Most 2006, slightly modified)

If the Pandora of the *Theogony* presents a danger to men because she is a dazzling
artefact, this Pandora physically reifies a duplicitousness common to actual humans
in her combination of a human form that serves as a vessel to conceal her cognitive
profile: her 'dog's mind and thievish character' (κύνεόν τε νόον καὶ ἐπίκλοπον ἦθος,
67).[51] Whereas the *Theogony*'s description dwelled on the marvel evoked by Pandora's
appearance, this version of Pandora presents her as a kind of black box because of the
faculties hidden within her. And in spite of her cognitive similarities to humans, the
main feature that sets Pandora apart is that her entire being is designed as a 'sheer,
intractable deception' (δόλον αἰπὺν ἀμήχανον, 83), a 'woe' (πῆμ' ἀνδράσιν, 82). For
in her endowment with voice, lying words and character, as well as strength, Pandora
illustrates how these essential and distinguishing features of human intelligence can

---

[51] See Brockliss 2018 for a reading of the *Works and Days* that is informed by Timothy
Morton's concept of 'dark ecology', which delineates the interpenetration between humans
and their environs. Of Pandora, Brockliss suggests that ancient audiences might have found
in her 'a representative of humanity in general and her "canine mind" as an indication of
what all humans, rather than women in particular, are like' (2018: 8).

function in opposition to the very humans she is designed to replicate. Thus she is explicitly designed to exist in a coupled system with men, albeit a destructive one.[52] It is fitting, then, that Pandora herself also releases into the world evils that are themselves characterised as *automatoi* ('By themselves evils wander about in silence, bringing evils for mortals', αὐτόματοι φοιτῶσι κακὰ θνητοῖσι φέρουσαι / σιγῇ, *Op.* 103–4) and can traverse the world at will. One of the criteria used to distinguish such cognitive props as Otto's notebook, after all, is the extent to which the absence of the tool would affect the user's ability to function. And insofar as Pandora's absence would have made a profound difference to human life, it would appear that she is as essential to the version of human life ordained by Zeus as Otto's notebook is to his memory.[53]

Moreover, Pandora's figuration in terms of the same substances and capacities that define humans raises a troubling question: exactly how human is she?[54] Conversely, are humans themselves examples of the kind of animatron embodied by Pandora: that is, a kind of 'black box' consisting of a physical body animated mysteriously from within?[55] There was a continuity between objects and humans in the case of the 'speaking objects' invoked in tragedy, where the desire for objects to take on voice invited reflection on the status of the human. But this is to prefigure the next chapter's focus on the poet's voice and its capacity to animate.

Given the aura of the divine and fantastical that pervades the examples discussed

---

[52] Brockliss 2018: 9–10 reaches a similar conclusion, noting that Pandora's mere resemblance to a maiden 'calls into question her identity and that of humans more generally'. See also Pucci 1977: 103, who focuses on the closeness between Pandora and Zeus: 'Zeus and Pandora, however, act together, simultaneously and complementarily: the "original" and the "copy" collaborate in one action, creating a new figure of difference.'

Apposite too for characterising Pandora's duplicity are the comments of Clark 2003: 48 on the potential danger of seamless integration between humans and technology: 'The danger is one of loss of control. Opaque technologies were, of course, hard to use and control; that's what made them opaque. But truly invisible, seamless, constantly running technologies resist control in a subtler, perhaps even more dangerous, manner. How then can we alter and control that of which we are barely aware?'

[53] cf. Canevaro 2018: 250: 'Pandora is crucial in defining the Iron Age human condition.'

[54] Again, this conclusion aligns with that of Gross 1992: 135: 'the fiction of animation is also likely to remind us of how alien and how disruptive of what we think of as the human are our vital energies, how catastrophic, petrifying, or mechanistic a form the entry into life can assume'. See too the conclusions of Chesi and Sclavi 2020, who note that 'the cyborg Pandora represents the intimate union of the human and the technical' (307).

[55] cf. Francis 2009: 16: 'As Hephaestus' metallic maids demonstrate, there is no clear line between an image of life and life itself. What keeps an image in human form, endowed with power, ability, and speech, from being alive?'

in this section with their depictions of objects that speak and move as if by magic, the figure of the *Works and Days'* Pandora and the trap that she poses for humans (a trap that works precisely because of her likeness to them) centres attention on the opacity of the human body itself and the mechanisms that allow it to move, speak and think. We turn, then, by way of conclusion, to speech and the means by which this faculty in particular informs and inflects what it means to be human.

Conclusion: *Poikilia* and the Riddle of Speech

Conspicuously absent from the preceding section was the quality of *poikilia* that loomed large in the awe-inspiring objects of the first three sections of this chapter. However, we have also seen in these descriptions of living objects the prominence of voice and speech as the means by which objects become animate and intervene (for better or worse) in human affairs. Therefore, here and in the following chapter, we will explore language as the medium in which *poikilia* makes its presence felt. In the particular set of examples discussed here, we will find that *poikilia* across different genres and time periods consistently manifests itself in a form of language that suggests a not-quite-human origin and therefore requires a correspondingly distinctive mode of interpretation.

One connection between *poikilia*, language and the automata discussed already emerges from the consonance between the beguiling effects afforded to each due to their supernatural qualities. The effects of *poikilia* in language come to the fore in Plato's *Menexenus*, where Socrates ironically expounds upon the magical effects of funeral orations.[56] He reports how such performances 'bewitch the souls of those listening' because of how beautifully the speakers ornament (ποικίλλοντες) their speeches with their diction (κάλλιστά πως τοῖς ὀνόμασι ποικίλλοντες, γοητεύουσιν ἡμῶν τὰς ψυχάς, 234c7–235a2). As a result of hearing such speech, Socrates imagines himself to have become 'better, taller and more beautiful' (ἡγούμενος ἐν τῷ παραχρῆμα μείζων καὶ γενναιότερος καὶ καλλίων γεγονέναι, 235a9–235b1) and remarks that the state itself appears 'more marvellous than before' (θαυμασιωτέραν αὐτὴν ἡγεῖσθαι εἶναι ἢ πρότερον, 235b6–7).[57] As Socrates portrays it here, the style

---

[56] It is also ironic that the *Menexenus* itself has been characterised by modern scholars as a 'riddle' because of its anomalous status among Plato's dialogues and the numerous interpretative difficulties posed within, on which problems see especially Kahn 1963 and Collins and Stauffer 1999.

[57] As Kerch 2008: 110 notes, this description of the 'bewitching' and 'astounding' effects of rhetoric chimes with several other passages (*Prt.* 328d3, *Phdr.* 234d1, 242d7 and 242e1) in which Socrates describes the mind-altering impact of speech. See also Walsh 1984 on the relation between enchantment and poetic language in Greek thought more generally.

in which the orators praise belongs to the realm of *poikilia* because their language generates a tantalising but illusory effect. And here too, *poikilia* is correlated with wonder (θαυμασιωτέραν). In this case, however, *poikilia* is not confined to the medium in which it is manifested, but has a transitive effect: it makes *something else* appear more wondrous. In attributing this supernaturally powerful effect to speech, Socrates' conception of verbal *poikilia* is in line with the perplexing character of those wondrous objects we examined first in this chapter.

The *poikilia* Herodotus identified in the labyrinth is similar to that which he attributes to oracular speech.[58] Speaking of the oracle of Dionysus in Thrace, he comments that the prophetess here pronounces oracles 'no more convoluted' (οὐδὲν ποικιλώτερον) than the ones given in Delphi (πρόμαντις δὲ ἡ χρέωσα κατά περ ἐν Δελφοῖσι, καὶ οὐδὲν ποικιλώτερον, 7.111.2). The notoriously riddling speech of the Pythia thus shares in common with the labyrinth a bewildering effect which is closely associated with its nonhuman (i.e. divine) origins.[59] Similarly, in Aristophanes' *Knights* Demosthenes relays an oracle to the Sausage-Seller and characterises it as 'cleverly and enigmatically worked together' (καὶ ποικίλως πως καὶ σοφῶς ἡνιγμένος, 196). As the complexity of the labyrinth's structure demanded careful navigation, the *poikilia* that belongs to the Pythia's speech similarly relies on interpretation in order to become meaningful.

But the destructive potential latent in the *poikilia* of the Pythia's obscurity (and the potential misinterpretation thereof) is made explicit in *poikilia*'s application to another riddling speaker, the Sphinx 'of riddling song' (ἡ ποικιλῳδὸς Σφὶγξ, Soph. *OT* 130). While the Pythia is part nonhuman insofar as she is the mouthpiece for the god in human form, the Sphinx is physically a hybrid creature comprised of human and animal features.[60] And like the Pythia, the Sphinx deploys her riddles in lyrical form, as the hapax compound ποικιλῳδός emphasises. As we will see in the following chapter, this combination of *poikilia* and lyricism has implications not only for the relationship between nonhuman entities (like the Sphinx) and language, but also for the relationship between poetic language and the material items it conjures. For now, though, the salience of the Sphinx's *poikilia* is that it names both a formal

---

[58] On oracular obscurity and its connection with divinity see especially Kindt 2006, Maurizio 1995 and 1993 and Manetti 1993: 14–35. See especially the summation by Kindt 2006: 37: 'oracular obscurity represents the very dichotomy between the gods and mortal men'.

[59] cf. Maurizio 1993: 82: 'At the moment when the distance between the human world and divine seems obliterated, linguistic obfuscation, however it is achieved, indicates that that distance is not to be crossed; human language becomes strange and untranslatable and as such it becomes the god's language.'

[60] cf. Neer 2002: 45: '[the Sphinx] is the very form of an enigma, joining real things and impossibilities in three dimensions'.

quality of her language (as riddling and lyrical) and the perplexing impact it has on human listeners.

Sophocles' *Trachiniae* is equally emphatic about the distinctive mode of inter-pretation required for the *poikilia* of language. *Poikilia* here names speech that seems riddling because it is unbelievable and even nonsensical. Hyllus has just told Heracles that he should not seek vengeance on Deianeira, and that he grieves in vain (ἐν οἷς / χαίρειν προθυμεῖ κἂν ὅτοις ἀλγεῖς μάτην, 1118–19). Because Heracles cannot fathom Hyllus' meaning, since he believes that his wife murdered him, he responds by characterising his perplexity as a result of Hyllus' 'riddling': 'Stop once you've said what you desire: in my sickness I understand nothing of what you've just now been <u>riddling</u>' (εἰπὼν ὃ χρῄζεις λῆξον. ὡς ἐγὼ νοσῶν / οὐδὲν ξυνίημ' ὧν σὺ <u>ποικίλλεις</u> πάλαι, 1120–1). Just as Theseus mocked Hippolytus for calling on the house to testify, 'a voiceless witness' (ἀφώνους μάρτυρας, Eur. *Hipp.* 1076), Heracles finds Hyllus' words similarly intractable. And by citing his compromised physical state (ὡς ἐγὼ νοσῶν) as the reason why he cannot understand Hyllus, Heracles makes clear that such apparently contradictory language requires a level of cognitive effort rendered impossible by the deteriorating condition of his body. The *poikilia* of Hyllus' language, in other words, requires its interpreter to be operating at full capacity, with both body and mind intact.

All of the forms of *poikilia* discussed so far in this section – funerary orations, oracular speech, the Sphinx's riddling song and Hyllus' own 'riddle' – attract a rigorous process of decoding like the one Polynices identifies in his explicit reference to hermeneutics in Euripides' *Phoenissae*. Here Polynices asserts that truthful speech is simple (ἁπλός), not 'riddling' (ποίκιλος):

> ἁπλοῦς ὁ μῦθος τῆς ἀληθείας ἔφυ,
> κοὐ <u>ποικίλων</u> δεῖ τἄνδιχ' ἑρμηνευμάτων·
> ἔχει γὰρ αὐτὰ καιρόν· ὁ δ' ἄδικος λόγος
> νοσῶν ἐν αὑτῷ φαρμάκων δεῖται σοφῶν.

> Truthful speech is simple by nature, and has no need for <u>subtle</u> interpretations: it itself contains the proper measure. But unjust speech, being diseased in itself, requires clever treatments. (469–72)

For Polynices, *poikilia* is symptomatic of the 'sickness' not of the interlocutor, but of unjust speech (ὁ δ' ἄδικος λόγος / νοσῶν ἐν αὑτῷ). Such language requires 'clever treatments' in the form of '<u>subtle</u> interpretations' (<u>ποικίλων</u> ἑρμηνευμάτων). In contrast to truthful speech, which is 'by nature' (ἔφυ) simple, false speech is *un*natural to the extent that it both reflects and requires human manipulation. The contrast forged here between truth and falsehood juxtaposes simplicity:natural versus complexity:interpretation, and this is significant, given that the terminology of ἑρμήνευμα can refer to the translation of foreign languages (e.g. at Hdt. II.125.6, Aesch. *Ag.* 1062) as well as interpretation more generally (Aesch. *Ag.* 616), including the work of poets. Pindar's claim that he 'has many swift arrows that speak to those who understand, but for the whole (subject) there is need for interpreters (ἑρμηνέων)' expresses a similar idea (πολλά μοι ὑπ' ἀγκῶνος ὠκέα βέλη / ἔνδον ἐντι φαρέτρας / φωνᾶντα συνετοῖσιν· ἐς δὲ τὸ πὰν ἑρμηνέων / χατίζει, *Ol.* 2.83–6, trans. Race 1997b).

In Plato's *Ion* the conception of poets as interpreters becomes even more pronounced, as Socrates proposes that 'poets are nothing but the interpreters of the gods' (οἱ δὲ ποιηταὶ οὐδὲν ἀλλ' ἢ ἑρμηνῆς εἰσιν τῶν θεῶν, 534e). Leaving aside the vexed question of how much agency Socrates means to impute to poets with the terminology of ἑρμηνεύς here, the important point to note is that both Pindar and Plato style poets as intermediaries whose task is to mediate between human and non-human realms, analogous to the work of the *hermeneus* who translates one language into another.[61] And what it means to act as a *hermeneus* specifically in the realm of song will form the subject of the next chapter.

From this wide-ranging set of examples two overarching themes emerge as recurrent features of thought across a variety of literary contexts: (1) that the terminology of *poikilia* can denote both a formal aspect of language and the beguiling or bewildering effects of that language's style on human listeners; (2) an association of *poikilia* in language with nonhuman origins or capabilities as a result of its potential for misinterpretation and bewilderment. These passages thus bring us back to the awe-inspiring objects that opened this chapter, which inspired wonder precisely because of the way their dynamic, lively qualities seemed to defy human explanation and, therefore, human origins. Likewise, as a quality that reflects something of its speaker and as one that draws attention to human fallibility (both cognitive and bodily, as in the case of Heracles), the *poikilia* in language examined here has allowed us to probe the boundaries and continuities between living bodies and the tools with which these bodies engage.

In short, then, we have gained a clearer picture of the issues at stake in the kinds of mind–material interactions subsumed by the concept of *poikilia*. As Plato observed in the *Republic*, *poikilia* is a correlate of 'that which is never the same' (οὐδέποτε ταὐτόν, 568d5), and it is precisely this shiftiness, this quality of 'never being the same', that has come to the fore here. First, the objects examined in this chapter

---

[61] On Presocratic and early Socratic theorisations of poetry and poetic inspiration, see especially Ledbetter 2003.

have delineated with particular clarity how material things are neither wholly opaque nor wholly reflections of the human. Instead, the tension between these poles – how material forms seem to recede from intelligibility at the same time as they reveal their origins from the human mind – form the axes around which many experiences of wonder, *thauma*, tend to cluster. And correspondingly, we have seen that wonder, and its relation to perplexing phenomena (including the operations of the human mind and body), is itself fundamental to human experience.[62] As Aristotle put it, echoing Plato's sentiment in the *Theatetus* (155d3), wonder, *thauma*, is the origin of philosophy, because it was puzzling over perplexities that led humankind to broader speculations about the nature of the universe, including the place of humans in it.[63] As we will see in the next chapter, the realm of lyric song provides a forum no less fertile than philosophy in which to grapple with the relationship between human bodies and minds and their physical, material environs.

---

[62] cf. Plato's use of *thauma* at *Laws* 644d7–8 to characterise humans as 'puppets' (θαῦμα μὲν ἕκαστον ἡμῶν ἡγησώμεθα τῶν ζῴων θεῖον) of the gods, an image he deploys precisely because the inner life of human is characterised by a bewildering variety of conflicting desires and impulses that suggest an affinity with the strings that tug a puppet this way and that.

[63] 'For it is because of wonder that men both now and at the beginning began to philosophise', διὰ γὰρ τὸ θαυμάζειν οἱ ἄνθρωποι καὶ νῦν καὶ τὸ πρῶτον ἤρξαντο φιλοσοφεῖν, Arist. *Metaph.* 982b12–13.

4   The Protean Shape of Lyric *Poikilia*

IN THIS CHAPTER, I turn to the lyric genres to investigate why *poikilia* looms so large in this relatively small extant corpus.[1] Not only does the terminology of *poikilia* recur across this diverse array of poets and genres (and often in novel compound words), but modern commentators, too, have often singled out *poikilia* as peculiarly suited to lyric. As Barbara Hughes Fowler (1984: 119) has put it, 'their [the early lyricists'] passion, one might in fact say, was for τὰ ποικίλα'.[2] 'Passion' is a key word here, since *poikilia* in the context of this chapter refers to objects that are not only precious but also highly desirable: whether for their own sake or by their association with another target of desire. *Poikilia*, in short, is a quality that seems to have fascinated ancient poets and their audiences as well as a feature that, to modern scholars, has seemed apposite for lyric language writ large.[3]

Emblematic of *poikilia*'s significance is the fact that it is the first word preserved in the extant corpus of Sappho, who invokes Aphrodite with the epithet ποικιλόθρονα: 'Ornate-throned immortal Aphrodite, wile-weaving daughter of

[1] I use the term 'lyric' in its capacious sense, although 'melic' would equally apply to the examples at stake here, since they do not include elegiac or iambic genres. On the vagaries in defining 'lyric' see especially Budelmann 2009.

[2] In a similar vein, LeVen 2013 explores the evolution of *poikilia*'s connotations across the archaic and classical periods: 'This is, I believe, what ποικίλος encapsulates in the archaic and classical period: it captures, in the description of an animal, an artifact or a sound, the notion that the luscious patterns in a bird's feathers, the wrought motives of a shield, or the many-voiced and swift-moving notes of a lyre cause an aesthetic reaction of rapt pleasure through the senses' (238).

[3] cf. Freeman 1995, who explores how the prominent metaphor schemas in Shakespeare's *Macbeth* have in turn resurfaced again and again in critics' discussions of the play.

Zeus', πο]ικιλόθρο[ν' ἀθανάτ' Ἀφρόδιτα, / παῖ] Δ[ί]ος δολ[όπλοκε (1.1–2, trans. Campbell 1982).[4] This single compound has attracted intense scrutiny.[5] If θρόνα is kept, commentators have suggested that it refers to a throne (as indicated in David Campbell's translation), while more recent scholars have debated whether it refers to a woven floral motif, actual flowers or love charms.[6] The last interpretation relies in no small part on the apparition of the phrase ποικίλα θρόνα in the description of Andromache's weaving (ἐν δὲ θρόνα ποικίλ' ἔπασσε, *Il.* 22.440–1) and the implication of love charms therein evoked by the verb ἐμπάσσω in that description.[7] But if -φρον is preferred, the translation of ποικιλ/ would change dramatically and liken it to 'wile-weaving' (δολόπλοκε) by making it an attribute of mind, a domain in which *poikilia* is equally at home. In sum, the understanding and translation of this epithet are as shifting and variable as the 'wile-weaving' goddess it purports to describe, and the divergent interpretations of this compound reflect *poikilia*'s prominence in both

[4] The text of Sappho used throughout is that of Lobel and Page 1955 (LP). As Budelmann 2018: 116 notes, that this probably formed the first poem in the first book of the Alexandrian edition of Sappho is striking since the rest of the poems in this book were arranged in alphabetical order according to the first word of each poem.

[5] The manuscript tradition records both ποικιλόθρονα and ποικιλόφρον as the first word of Sappho 1.1, but the meaning of θρόνα is still a subject of debate. Jouanna 1999: 101–5 provides an excellent and detailed summary of this epithet's various interpretations, whereas I only highlight the main issues here. Bolling 1958, following Lawler's 1948 discussion of θρόνος in Homer, argues that in both Homer and Sappho the epithet should be understood to refer not to a throne, but to flowers, an interpretation followed closely by Putnam 1960, who proposes that the epithet denotes Aphrodite's floral-patterned robe. More recently, Scheid and Svenbro 1996: 53–8 have addressed this issue at length and provide a useful survey of the ancient testimonia on θρόνα. They have also shown that ποικιλόθρονα could have been understood as referring to a woven floral motif. However, see also Budelmann 2018: 117, who points out that 'There is . . . no instance of a -θρονος compound that is evidently derived from θρόνα, whereas formation from θρόνος is manifest in several cases', as well as Jouanna 1999, who argues forcefully for the epithet's derivation from θρόνος and suggests that it is a conscious adaptation of Homeric diction on Sappho's part.

[6] See further Grand-Clément 2011: 461–2, who discusses in greater detail the connotations of magic associated with this term and has fruitfully used the description of Aphrodite's clothing in the *Cypria* to elucidate the meaning of ποικιλόθρονα (462–3). In that text, the narrator describes how the Graces and Hours prepared garments for Aphrodite by dyeing them with all different kinds of flowers, which in turn lent them a beautiful fragrance (fr. 4 1–6) (Ath. xv. 682 D, F). ποικιλόθρονα, on this view, thus could be taken to refer to the colourful as well as fragrant aspect of Aphrodite's garments.

[7] On the significance of the choice of the verb ἐμπάσσω and its association with drugs (*pharmaka*; cf. *Il.* 5.401, 900), see my earlier discussion at pp. 55–9 as well as Grand-Clément 2011: 460–1. On the possible magical connotations of θρόνα see especially Petropoulos 1993.

the material and cognitive spheres. In this sense, the *poikilia* of this epithet presages the oscillations in perspective and voice that characterise the remainder of the song. As Jennifer Stager (2016: 113–14) has summed it up, the whole poem can be read as an expression of *poikilia* in its protean shifts between speakers, perspectives and attitudes.[8] And even with a secure referent for the adjective (e.g. -θρον/, the most widely accepted reading), the meaning of *poikilos* remains ambiguous.[9] The variety of readings and interpretations that has clustered around this single word is a testament to the indeterminacy and liveliness of *poikilia* as a *word*.[10]

The *poikilia* of Sappho 1, in the congruity between the vagaries of the term's meaning and the correspondingly scintillating quality of the goddess it denotes, well illustrates the perspective that I will develop throughout this chapter. In what follows, we will see how the complexity of the word's meaning (and in turn, the complexities of the phenomena it denotes) makes *poikilia* a phenomenon that is pleasurable not only to experience first-hand, but also to imagine.[11] And in each example, we will see how the word aids in the construction of highly vivid and highly particular imaginative scenarios because of the variety of sensory features that the terminology of *poikilia* can encapsulate simultaneously.[12] Or, to employ the terminology of ancient literary criticism, this chapter will illuminate the *enargeia* or 'vividness' of *poikilia* as a descriptive term and the kinds of mental images, *phantasiai*, it promotes.[13]

---

[8] See also Schlesier 2011, who interprets Sappho's depiction of Aphrodite as an analogue for the poet's own voice and persona.

[9] On the ambiguities of this epithet see also Burnett 1983: 249–51, who proposes that 'there is likewise an instant when both meanings [of *throna*] operate together to give us a throned and floriate divinity' (250).

[10] In attending to the variety of possible meanings evoked by *poikilia*'s word forms rather than trying to pin down a precise meaning for each instance, my approach here is similar to that of Foley 1999 in his analysis of Homer's *sēmata* (which he defines as something that 'both names and is the tangible, concrete part that stands by contractual agreement for a larger, immanent whole, and as such it mimics a central expressive strategy of Homeric poetry: traditional referentiality', 13), but departs from his work insofar as I do not posit a 'traditional' sense to *poikilia*. See too the discussion of Stanford 1936: 106–17 on the problems involved in affixing singular meanings to Greek descriptive terms.

[11] cf. Peponi 2016: 2: 'lyric poetry created, within its verbal fabric, a visual world to be accessed and enjoyed through intense imaginative activity'.

[12] See also Schmitz 2013 for a reading of Sappho 1 focused on the construction of an imaginary 'possible world' therein.

[13] In using these terms, I am not claiming that ancient readers and critics would have applied or understood these terms in the framework I construct here, but their existence as terms of literary criticism spotlights precisely the kind of imaginative vividness that I think forms of *poikilia* help to generate in these examples. For an overview of imagination and mental

The readings that follow will rely on several distinct but related ways of approaching language and verbal imagery. First, in attending to *poikilia* as a linguistic object as well as an attribute of (imagined) material objects, I am primarily approaching it as an example of the kind of 'mind-transforming cognitive scaffolding' that Andy Clark (2008: 44) attributes to all language: 'As soon as we formulate a thought in words or on paper, it becomes an object for both ourselves and for others' (2008: 58).[14] And there is a cognitive payoff to this objectification, which he characterises in broad strokes as follows: it is through language that 'we are able to objectify, reflect upon, and hence knowingly engage with our own thoughts, trains of reasoning, and cognitive and personal characters' (2008: 59). Clark thus emphasises how language enables humans to 'think about thinking', and this point will gain special significance in the context of Pindar in particular, who frequently uses *poikilia* as a way to conceptualise his own 'thinking' in using it to characterise his own poetic activity and craftsmanship.[15]

Elaine Scarry's influential *Dreaming by the Book* is aligned with Clark's account of linguistic scaffolding insofar as she likewise discerns in language distinctive models for 'thinking about thinking' in her theory of perceptual mimesis.[16] However, her account is more deeply indebted to the theory of enactive perception discussed in Chapter 1, as her focus in this book is on how literary language in particular manages to succeed in replicating 'the deep structure of perception' (1999: 38).[17] This

imagery in ancient thought, see Sheppard 2015, while Webb 2009 has become a standard work on the relationship between ekphrasis and *enargeia/energeia* in ancient criticism. Zanker 1981 focuses specifically on ancient testimony connecting *enargeia* with poetry, and Manieri 1998 is a rigorous investigation of the origins and evolutions of the concepts of *enargeia* and *phantasia*.

[14] Similar to the notion of 'scaffolding' is the Gibsonian account of the 'affordance', on which see especially Cave 2016: 46–62 on the application of this concept to language and literary conventions.

[15] The fact that *poikilia* frequently appears in hapax compounds in the examples at issue in this chapter provides a very literal form of this kind of 'scaffolding'; cf. Sigelman 2016: 15 on Pindar's coinage of unusual compounds: 'Compound adjectives, by virtue of their very complexity, testify to a poet's conscious reflection on the nature of the adjective.'

[16] Similarly, Dimitrios Yatromanolakis 2009 has argued that Sappho's interest in highly specific attributes of the beloved illustrates Scarry 1999: 18's claim that beauty 'always takes place in the particular, and if there are no particulars, the chances of seeing it go down', and articulates the significance of this focus as follows: 'By focusing on details of female beauty and on specific snapshots of past and present experiences of the narrating voice, a number of Sappho's songs articulate intricate discourses about desire and female companionship' (215).

[17] See also the cognitive literary criticism developed in Cave 2016, which is indebted in part to Scarry 1999's work.

structure is one predicated on a dynamic engagement with the world rather than the pictorialist model of perception that locates detail-rich internal representations in the mind's eye.[18] As such, Scarry identifies several modes by which writers encode aspects of perception in order to reproduce the experience of physical perception in language, what she calls 'the felt experience of image-making' (1999: 48).[19] One of these is especially relevant to *poikilia*, and that is the notion of 'imaginability'. Like Sappho summoning Aphrodite via her floriate *throna*, Scarry likewise zeroes in on the figure of the flower and queries why 'flowers so often push themselves forward as primary candidates for our sense of what imagining is' (1999: 44). Similarly, my question in this chapter centres on why *poikilia* surfaces so prominently in lyric contexts, and what effect(s) are created by its presence.[20]

Taken together, the distinctive approaches to language and imagery applied to the examples in this chapter offer a way to account for *poikilia*'s place in the lyric imagination. As we have seen in the example from Sappho 1, the kind of linguistic 'scaffolding' created by ποικιλόθρονα seems decidedly more complicated than Clark's account would allow. But I will contend that this complexity is key to the imagery this term helps to create because the word's many shades of meaning help to convey something of the phenomenal quality *of* glamour and desirability: the complex tex-

---

[18] See too the important recent work of Grethlein and Huitink 2017, who convincingly demonstrate how Homer's characteristic vividness can best be explained by an enactive understanding of perception. My approach here is very similar to theirs in its focus on accounting for how vivid imagery can be created from language even in the absence of the kind of exhaustive detail that characterises our phenomenal experience of vision, a phenomenology that they articulate as follows: 'an inescapable impression that what we "see" is a detailed and extended display that truthfully corresponds to the scene before our eyes' (69).

[19] Thus while I use the terminology standardly involved in describing imaginative processes (i.e. 'image', 'picture' etc.), I use these in an enactivist sense to mean, as Thompson 2007: 143 has summed it up, that 'Visualizing is rather the activity of mentally representing an object or scene *by way of mentally enacting or entertaining a possible perceptual experience of that object or scene*' (emphasis added).

[20] My concentration on the possible effects generated solely by the language of lyric aligns with the 'intrapoetic' approach taken by Sigelman 2016, who notes how the recent scholarly focus on the function and social context(s) of lyric poetry has entailed neglecting to attend to these works as poetry (8). See too the formulation of Budelmann and Phillips 2018: 4: 'The important point here is that poems do not just communicate precepts, narratives, and attitudes that align with normative ideologies, knowledge, and beliefs, but that they can also be exploratory, opening up new ways of encountering realities and of understanding emotions and ideas.' See too Wells 2009 for an 'inside out' (10) approach to Pindaric language, although his focus is on the linguistic pragmatics of epinician.

tures of thought and feeling that attend real-life encounters with beautiful objects.[21] For this reason, in using the term 'vividness' I mean not simply the clarity or detail of the mental image evoked by poetic language, but also the clarity and distinctness of the phenomenal experience *of* that imagining.[22]

In the first section, passages from Sappho, Alcman and Anacreon will place *poikilia* in the context of erotic and sensuous allure, where we will find this word recurring in conjunction with desirable objects and people. In these settings, the multifariousness of the word *poikilia* maps onto the rich and varied sensory experiences conveyed by each poet. As the following sections will show, however, Pindar presses the conceptual richness of *poikilia* to an extreme by deploying this term in unusual and novel ways that heighten attention both to the imaginative process itself and to the poet's role in generating such projections. In short, this chapter will illuminate how *poikilia* is a word as scintillating and lively as the objects and phenomena it purports to describe.[23] The word group comprised by *poikilia* will thus emerge as a kind of vibrant matter in its own right in how it operates as 'both object and idea, both artifact and symbol' (Zeitlin 1996: 29).[24]

The Imaginative Matter of *Poikilia*: Scintillating Objects in Sappho, Alcman and Anacreon

If it is at least clear that the *poikilia* of Sappho 1 correlates with both the beauty and variability of Aphrodite, the *poikilia* that Sappho attributes to the Lydian *mitra* in

---

[21] This is very much in line with the conclusion drawn by LeVen 2013: 238: 'Ποικίλος is not exactly synonymous with "beautiful" either: it is not simply a judgment on beauty, but a self-conscious expression of the sensual nature of its experience.'

[22] Because my focus is on the possible effects associated with evocations of *poikilia* in Pindar (whether or not they are metaphorical), I am less interested in how the word functions as a metaphor (i.e. in the domains it links) and what such metaphorical constructions represent than in the complexities involved in conceptualising this quality at all.

[23] In this respect, these forms of *poikilia* are also akin to what the philosopher Susanne Langer termed 'virtual objects' in her 1953 study of art and aesthetics. In the context of poetry, words create virtual experiences 'not by recalling objects that would elicit the feeling itself, but by weaving a pattern of words – words charged with meaning and colored by literary associations – akin to the dynamic pattern of the feeling' (230).

[24] Here I borrow Froma Zeitlin 1996's phrase to capture the multivalence of the image of the ancient Greek marriage bed. In this sense, the multivalences of both literal and figurative forms of *poikilia* discussed here highlight one of the criticisms that has been levelled at the classic model of conceptual metaphor theory formulated by Lakoff and Johnson 1980: namely, that the links between concept and direct experience may be more complex than the one-to-one correspondences adumbrated in their account.

two papyri fragments that probably formed part of the same poem offers a different perspective on the desirability of this attribute:

ἀλλα ξανθοτέρα<ι>ς ἔχη[
[_]τα<ὶ>ς κόμα<ι>ς δάιδος προ[
σ]τεφάνοισιν ἐπαρτια[
ἀνθέων ἐριθαλέων· [
[_]μ]ιτράναν δ' ἀρτίως κλ[(10)
ποικίλαν ἀπὺ Σαρδίω[ν
. . .].αονιασπολεις [

. . .

(98b) σοὶ δ' ἔγω Κλέι ποικίλαν [
οὐκ ἔχω πόθεν ἔσσεται [25

But for the girl who has hair yellower than a torch (it is better to decorate it) with wreaths of flowers in bloom. Recently . . . a <u>decorated</u> headband from Sardis . . . (Ionian?) cities.

. . .

But for you, Cleis, I have no way of obtaining a <u>decorated</u> headband. (trans. Campbell 1982)

Whereas in Sappho 1 the poet invoked Aphrodite's presence by way of *poikilia*, here the focus is on the *absence* of this quality.[26] The audience is asked to imagine the *poikilia* of the *mitra* as well as its lack, given Sappho's pronouncement that she cannot provide one for Cleis. That Sappho expresses regret at not being able to proffer the *mitra*, coupled with the fact that it is said to be a recently arrived import, intimates the desirability of the garment and makes its absence all the more poignant. Yet the adjective *poikilos*, as we have seen, does not have a fixed material denotation, hence its possible translation with various English words like 'scintillating', 'decorated, 'finely wrought', 'shimmering', 'colourful' etc.[27] Sappho's *mitra*, in other

---

[25] Although *poikilia* appears in line 6 of fr. 98b (ποικιλασκ . . .) I exclude it from my analysis here since these verses are too fragmentary to determine the context for this term with any certainty.

[26] cf. Ferrari 2010: 13: 'In this perspective the headband becomes a *deixis* of absence.'

[27] The argument for a translation of 'colourful' in the context of the *mitra* finds support from the comments of the scholiast on Aristophanes' *Peace* 1174 (p. 205 Dübner), who records that Lydian dyes were of superior quality, citing as illustration Sappho fr. 39 and its reference to a ποίκιλος μάσλης from Lydia, which suggests that the Lydian *mitra* may also have been variegated in colour.

words, can be visualised and translated in a variety of ways that correspond to the sense of complexity or variegation innate to the word family. As in Sappho 1, in this context the multiplicities of *poikilia*'s meaning reify the elusiveness of the *mitra*: endowed with a vivid imaginative presence by this adjective, its precise physical attributes remain out of focus.[28]

That *poikilia* is the only quality attributed to the *mitra* apart from its country of origin indicates that this is the aesthetic feature of the *mitra* that makes it alluring, even if its status as a (presumably) luxe import would also boost its material value. And if the *mitra*'s Lydian origins suggest that it is a tangible marker of the 'luxury' (*habrosunē*) that Sappho elsewhere claims to covet (ἔγω δὲ φίλημμ' ἀβροσύναν, 'I am a lover of luxury', fr. 58.25), the attribution of *poikilia* to this garment suggests that this quality is a material corollary of *habrosunē*.[29] With this in mind, Sappho's picture of the *mitra*, and its apparent desirability and connection with luxury, can be interpreted as an example of the glamorous phenomena that are Virginia Postrel's focus in her 2013 study (*The Power of Glamour: Longing and the Art of Visual Persuasion*). Her theorisation of the glamour attached to glitter and sparkle is especially appropriate to a term like *poikilia*, which describes many of the same qualities she discusses:

> Glitter, sparkle, and shine not only grab the eye. Like the shifting colors of iridescence, they also confuse it. We cannot quite focus on the light's source, and when we try to, it seems to move elsewhere. Like shadows, glittering objects distort perception. (2013: 120)

For Postrel, shining, decorated materials invite a protean form of perception because their appearances are dynamic, never appearing twice in the same way, and it is the mysteriousness of this phenomenology that accounts for the pull that such materials exert on human spectators. Sappho's verbal image of the *mitra*, with its atten-

---

As will become clear, I lean on the translation of 'scintillating' in this chapter, as this well captures the convergence between material and phenomenal qualities operative in the examples discussed here.

[28] By this I mean not that there is no material evidence visualising the *mitra* (see, for instance, the figures on an Attic red-figure cup collected in Kurke 1992: 115 with discussion), but that its quality of *poikilia* is nonspecific; cf. the formulation of Stehle 1996: 220: 'Description in her poetry is often both very sensuous and very unspecific.'

[29] The standard study devoted to *habrosunē* in archaic and classical thought remains Kurke 1992, who delineates the political implications of this word family and its connection to aristocratic elites, but see also Burnett 1983: 214 n. 13 for a survey of the possible historical contexts that have been proposed for these verses.

dant variety of possible translations, thus behaves like the glittering material objects Postrel describes in the quote referenced above, objects which also cannot quite be pinned down and, for that reason, incite a longing akin to what Sappho implicitly attributes to Cleis.

By channelling the glamour of the Lydian *mitra* specifically through its *poikilos* quality, Sappho homes in on its scintillating aspect: both its sensuous allure and the cognitive effect of that allure. A similar effect is achieved when the *poikilia* of a garment is combined with a human figure, as in fragment 39 LP, which recounts a 'decorated strap covering the feet, a fine piece of Lydian handiwork' (πόδας δὲ / ποίκιλος μάσλης ἐκάλυπτε, Λύδιον κάλον ἔργον). Again, the quality of *poikilia* is affiliated with exotic origin, and its conjunction with the feet highlights how this *poikilos* aspect means that the garment is both decorated and decora*tive* when it is actually worn. Elsewhere, the term μάσλης (μάσθλης) seems to refer to leather material, and is twice used metaphorically by Aristophanes to denote someone deceptive or conniving, a conception presumably based on the flexible, metamorphic quality of leather (as a material for human garments fashioned from animal skins).[30] If Sappho also refers to a leather medium in fr. 39, then the Aristophanic uses of μάσθλης are illuminating because of the close association that also exists between *poikilia* and cunning or deceit (one that is attested as early as *poikilia*'s connection to the materially decorated or various).[31] With this in mind, the physical composition of Sappho's μάσλης and its *poikilos* aspect come into closer alignment as mutually enforcing qualities: the vivid aspect of the garment finding form in a material (leather) that is as smooth and protean as the tricksters that *poikilia* elsewhere characterises. Seen in this way, the apposition 'a fine piece of Lydian handiwork' gains clearer significance as a commentary on how the accessory refracts multiple modes of *poikilia* simultaneously.

Sappho's collocation of *poikilia* and *athurmata* makes more explicit this link between pleasure and *poikilia* by locating this quality in objects that exist only to delight: 'baubles' or 'trinkets':[32]

πόλλα δ' [ἐλί]γματα χρύσια κάμματα
πορφύρ[α] καταύτ[..]να, ποίκιλ᾽ ἀθύρματα,
ἀργύρα τ' ἀνάρ[ι]θμα [ποτή]ρ[ια] κάλέφαις.

---

[30] 'What a charlatan! What a knave!' (ὡς δ' ἀλαζών, ὡς δὲ μάσθλης, Ar. *Eq.* 269); 'Conniving, dissembler, slippery, impostor' (μάσθλης, εἴρων, γλοιός, ἀλαζών, Ar. *Nub.* 449).

[31] On the associations of this term with leather see e.g. Ferrari 2010: 6 n. 10.

[32] See Kidd 2019: 99–102 on the semantics of *athurma*, especially his summation at p. 101, that *athurmata* are 'objects of immediate pleasure'.

And (there are) many golden bracelets and (perfumed?) purple robes, <u>ornate</u> trinkets and countless silver drinking-cups and ivory. (fr. 44 8–10, trans. Campbell 1982)

Appearing within a catalogue of precious objects, *poikilia* is afforded the same status as gold, purple dye, silver and ivory.[33] And as the naming of those materials specifies the value of these objects, the adjective *poikil'* likewise confirms the desirability of the jewellery and clothing as 'trinkets'.[34] It is also significant that this catalogue appears as a form of direct speech attributed to the messenger, since this creates a double layer of representation: Sappho imagining the sort of gifts that would accompany Andromache and her imagining how a messenger would experience and describe those objects. This segment of Idaeus' speech that is preserved thus articulates the luxurious accoutrements of the wedding as well as dramatising the experience of perceiving these objects *and* recounting their splendour. And by relaying the gifts simply in the form of a list, this recitation of their material attributes serves to recreate in language the experience of witnessing this profusion of delightful objects. Here, then, we see a literal form of the kind of twofold perspective that has been operative throughout the examples seen so far, one in which the terminology of *poikilia* denotes the glamour and desirability of material things as much as it works to conjure something of the phenomenal quality of an encounter with such objects.[35]

Further, the etymology of *athurmata* suggests its relation to the verb *athurō*, 'to whirl', and Stephen Kidd has perceptively interpreted this as a reflection of the giddiness induced by the toys and baubles denoted by *athurmata*, 'as if the soul whirled when it feels delight, or expressed delight through "whirling", or alternatively, perhaps the act of whirling itself was felt to produce certain giddy sensations' (2019: 100). If this is correct, then we have in fr. 44 a possible candidate for a more precise phenomenological character for *poikilia* in the connection Idaeus draws between *poikilia* and objects that induce or are suggestive of a kind of 'whirling', a dynamic consonant with the 'distortion of perception' noted by Postrel in her analysis of glitter's allure.

---

[33] On the persistent connection drawn between purple and gold in Greek thought, see especially Grand-Clément 2016.

[34] I thus follow Budelmann 2018: 143 ad loc. in interpreting ποίκιλ᾽ ἀθύρματα in apposition to ἐλίγματα . . . κάμματα.

[35] Although Snell's 1953 account of the 'discovery of the mind' and the 'rise of the individual' in Greek literary history is outdated, his analysis of this poem nonetheless captures the aesthetic effect of this catalogue of precious objects: 'Even the wedding gifts are more important than the action, precisely because they are so precious in appearance. Thus the tale leaps from one bright station to the next, and the climaxes glow with the brightness whose lustre survives the day' (63).

In Alcman's *Partheneion* 1, we again see *poikilia* appearing within a catalogue of precious objects as well as a consonance between *poikilia* and a certain type of material in its attribution to a snake forged in metal.[36] This is a material that, as we have seen in Chapter 2, is especially hospitable to refracting light to produce a shimmering effect not unlike an actual snakeskin. Here the chorus of maidens declare that 'neither is an abundance of purple enough for protection, nor a <u>scintillating</u> serpent, made entirely of gold, nor a Lydian headband, the delight of dark-eyed young women' (οὔτε γάρ τι πορφύρας / τόσσος κόρος ὥστ' ἀμύναι, /οὔτε <u>ποικίλος</u> δράκων /παγχρύσιος, οὐδὲ μίτρα / Λυδία, νεανίδων / ἰανογ[λ]εφάρων ἄγαλμα, 1.64–9). While it has been proposed that the chorus here refers to aspects of their costuming, that they say that it is 'not enough' nonetheless creates a disjunct between two objects of perception: the chorus leaders and a chorus' accoutrements. Whether or not the chorus is referring to real objects that would have been visible to their audience, the effect of deictically summoning each item in turn focuses attention on the most salient aspects of each: those qualities that rival Hagesichora and Agido, but do not surpass them. And these qualities are specifically those that are most visible physically as well as mentally: the rich hue of purple, the shimmering gold of a snake ornament, and the Lydian *mitra* beloved by 'dark-eyed' girls.[37]

As Anastasia-Erasmia Peponi observes, this 'intentionally literal' catalogue, in contrast to the metaphorical imagery invoked for the description of the chorus leaders, 'sounds inadequate and deficient' (2004: 313). But its focus on the discrete visual details of adornment is a good example of the kind of perceptual mimesis discussed by Scarry. For in the same way that not every aspect of a painting can be taken in at a single glance, so too does the recounting of each detail of a scene like this mimic actual visual perception, at least insofar as the limitations of the foveal field require the eye to actively traverse its target in the kind of dynamic engagement described in Chapter 1.[38] Thus in naming each item, whether or not these things

[36] The bibliography on this work is vast and in recent years (following the general trend in scholarship on Greek lyric) has focused predominantly on performance scenarios. See Budelmann 2018: 64–5 for a comprehensive overview of the seminal discussions and commentaries devoted to this poem.

[37] See also the comments of Swift 2016: 259 on the heightened visuality of this catalogue: 'Each item is listed and described quickly, before the girls move on to the next: again the implication is that the chorus are drawing the audience's attention to what they can already see, and encouraging them to focus their gaze on these details.' Her article illuminates the centrality of self-referential visual imagery to parthenaic song in particular and interprets it as a way for the chorus members to 'actively attempt to control and direct the gaze of their audience' (282).

[38] cf. the succinct description by Noë 2004: 103: 'Another way to put this is that when we see,

were actually visible to the audience, these verses (like Sappho's account via Idaeus of Andromache's wedding gifts) offer an explicit 'viewing guide' for how the viewer is to visually or imaginatively perceive each segment of the spectacle.

However, the phrase ποικίλος δράκων offers a significant variation within this catalogue of putatively deictic references. This is because the animal is effectively assimilated to its representation, one that is 'entirely of gold' (παγχρύσιος).[39] The fact that the serpent is named before the specification παγχρύσιος means that the living animal is evoked only to immediately be reified in (what is assumed to be) a bracelet or bangle. Similarly, that the term 'delight' (ἄγαλμα, 69) forms the hinge between the chorus's recitation of material goods and their subsequent allusions to individual people (Ναννῶς, Ἀρέτα, Σύλακις, Κλεησισήρα etc., 70–2) establishes an affinity between things and persons by positioning them together as equally lovely and desirable.[40] As the recitation of accessories engages the audience in a mental (re) construction of these elements, that the naming of individual women forms part of the same strophe brings these figures into the same visual frame. This profusion of proper names – like Idaeus' catalogue of the wedding gifts – is thus as literal as the references to their finery and achieves a similar effect by temporarily dissolving the choral body into its individual members (whether or not they refer here to actual participants in the performance). This blurring between the perceptual (the concrete referents of the catalogue) and conceptual (the mental images conjured by their naming) dramatises the audience's (enactive) experience of perceiving the chorus and, in doing so, draws attention to the fact that in this context, bodies and material things are mutually supportive actors in performance.

So far I have argued that *poikilia* contributes to the effect of perceptual mimesis in each example because of its capacity to evoke an array of vivid and pleasurable sensory qualities simultaneously. But perhaps the most provocative example of the kind of imaginative work to which *poikilia* can contribute comes in Anacreon *PMG* 358:[41]

σφαίρῃ δηὖτέ με πορφυρῇ
βάλλων χρυσοκόμης Ἔρως
νήνι ποικιλοσαμβάλῳ
συμπαίζειν προκαλεῖται·

we experience the way the environment structures sensorimotor contingency.'

[39] cf. Hutchinson 2001: 95: 'ποικίλος conflicts, as a description of the object, with παγχρύσιος. The word is designed to suggest at first, with a touch of humour, a real snake.'

[40] cf. Rosenmeyer 1966: 347: 'They [the young women] are mentioned because along with crimson garments and gold brooches, they share the quality of desirability.'

[41] For an exhaustive overview and discussion of the scholarship devoted to this poem see especially Gellar-Goad 2017.

Golden-haired Eros once again rouses me, casting the <u>richly hued</u> ball, to sport with the young girl, the one with the fancy sandals.

Whereas Sappho's focus in fr. 39 was on the craftsmanship of the footgear, the speaker here emphatically situates this aspect of the woman's dress in an erotically charged context. These brief verses offer a vividly colourful vignette: the multiple compounds that appear in quick succession propel the construction of this tableau, matching each object or figure named with one sensuous attribute. This emphasis on the sensuous finds expression even in the form of ποικιλοσαμβάλῳ, a compound which, unlike χρυσοκόμης, has no parallel before Anacreon and which may self-consciously employ an Aeolic instead of Ionic form.[42] This miniature catalogue of attributes thus culminates in an epithet that is as 'fancy' in its composition as the sandals it describes. Moreover, its proximity to συμπαίζειν, with its connotations of quick or light movement (whether in play or in sex), suggests that the *poikilos* aspect of her sandals may derive in part from the apparition of her feet in motion.[43]

Much of the attention focused on this poem has been devoted to interpretation of the second stanza and the young woman's apparent rejection of the speaker, but the setting depicted in this first stanza has also been variously interpreted according to whether the ball game is real or metaphorical. Thus in spite of its highly visual language, 'the first stanza paints a vivid and yet simultaneously vague picture', in T. H. M. Gellar-Goad (2017: 51)'s words.[44] In this sense, the first stanza generates an effect similar to the uses of *poikilia* discussed already, where the word's denotation is of a quality simultaneously vivid but diffuse in its potential referential range.

Nevertheless, what is uncontested is that this stanza manages to convey a lucid impression of the speaker's thoughts and perceptions. As Felix Budelmann (2018: 193) has put it, 'In a stylized manner the two stanzas *mimic the speaker's consciousness*' (emphasis added). Similarly, Woodbury (1979: 280) has argued that the description of Eros as 'golden haired' 'describes the object of the *frisson* of recognition felt by the speaker', and Davison (1959: 42) contends that the characterisation of the woman in terms of her sandals indicates that the speaker was lying down until roused by the ball, at which point the first glimpse he catches of the woman is of her shoes.

---

[42] As Hutchinson 2001: 275 points out, while the compound appears Aeolic, 'one can have no confidence that it was not an East Ionic form too'.

[43] On the varying connotations of this verb see e.g. Budelmann 2018: 194 ad loc.

[44] cf. Hutchinson 2001: 276, who notes in reference to ποικιλοσαμβάλῳ that, 'However fetching the item, it is striking that a word is not chosen to convey the girl's beauty more directly. This increases our detachment.' By contrast, I would contend that focusing in on one particular and particularly vivid aspect compels a deeper engagement by prompting the listener to imagine the rest of the girl for themselves.

I rehearse this set of comments because implicit in each is the recognition that, in spite of the vagueness of the setting, this first stanza illustrates how phenomenal experience can be vividly conveyed, whether it was real or imaginary. To put it another way: what Anacreon does here, as the commentators cited above intuit, is to communicate the *impression* of a scene and its attendant feelings in a manner consistent with the similarly impressionistic kind of data that would be communicated by actual perception. The effect Anacreon cultivates here is thus much in line with what Emily Troscianko (2014a: 19) has suggested in the context of Kafka's imaginative scenarios: that the vividness that can be experienced even in the absence of much detail testifies to how 'reducing imaginable detail' can nonetheless 'intensify experiential richness'.

To return to the notion of linguistic scaffolding: what kind of 'material reality' does *poikilia* constitute in the context of lyric? On the one hand, we have seen that there is a clear correlation between this word and coveted or pleasurable items. In this sense, the term connotes the alluring pull exerted by such objects. Indeed, this is a force that extends even into contemporary scholarship, where *poikilia* has not infrequently been adopted as a byword for the complexities of lyric language and imagery. On the other hand, the word's intrinsic semantic complexity also helps to convey something of the scintillating quality *of* glamour and desirability that makes certain objects or figures appear in manifold and ever-shifting ways. From Sappho's Lydian *mitra* to Alcman's *drakōn* to Anacreon's fancy-sandalled love interest, *poikilia* has repeatedly surfaced as something that is fanciful in two senses of the word: as a delightful quality to experience first-hand and as a word that invites vivid imaginative projections. It is significant too that there is a distinctive gendered dimension to these forms of *poikilia*, which are all coveted by women and/or worn by desirable women. For in Chapter 6, we will see female characters portrayed as capitalising on this association by deploying *poikilia* as a mode of deception.[45]

I want to conclude this section with the opening of the *Philebus*, where Plato links *poikilia* to the vagaries of pleasure as a concept, since this well encapsulates what we have seen in this section:

τὴν δὲ ἡδονὴν οἶδα ὡς ἔστι <u>ποικίλον</u>, καὶ ὅπερ εἶπον, ἀπ' ἐκείνης ἡμᾶς ἀρχομένους ἐνθυμεῖσθαι δεῖ καὶ σκοπεῖν ἥντινα φύσιν ἔχει. ἔστι γάρ, ἀκούειν μὲν οὕτως ἁπλῶς, ἕν τι μορφᾶς δὲ δήπου παντοίας εἴληφε καί τινα τρόπον ἀνομοίους ἀλλήλαις

---

[45] See also Canevaro 2018 for a full-length study devoted to how Homeric women appropriate or repurpose objects to express forms of their own agency.

I know that pleasure is a <u>complex</u> thing, and since, as I said, we are to begin with her, we must consider and examine what her nature is. For, when you just simply hear her name, she is only one thing, but surely she takes on all sorts of shapes which are even, in a way, unlike each other. (12c5–9, trans. Fowler 1925, slightly modified)

Plato's use of *poikilia* here to characterise the protean character of pleasure is a summation that could be applied to the concept of *poikilia* across the lyric corpus, since the forms to which the same term is attached are as distinctive and alluring as the modulations of pleasure that Plato identifies here.

Similarly, Pindar's characterisation of the changing months with the same adjective (νῦν δ᾽ αὖ μετὰ χειμέριον <u>ποικίλων</u> μηνῶν ζόφον, *Isthm.* 3/4.36) links this quality with another eternally changing phenomenon. This use of the adjective thus presages the diverse ways in which Pindar deploys *poikilia*. In the following sections, we will consider Pindar's provocative and novel figurations of *poikilia*, many of which inspire imaginative scenarios even more complex than those we have seen already and which work to focus attention on the mental processes underpinning their own manifestation.

Pindaric *Poikilia* and the Victorious Imagination

It is in Pindar that *poikilia* has garnered the greatest scrutiny and it is here that it becomes a term of reference for lyric composition.[46] This, together with the fact that Pindar's language is itself notoriously complex (and so not unlike the perplexing phenomena discussed in the previous chapter), makes *poikilia* a central component

[46] The nature and identity of the Pindaric speaker have been a perennial point of interest for ancient and modern critics alike. For a thorough survey of the issues related to this question see especially Miller 1993: 245–8 and D'Alessio 1994, who fruitfully challenges Mary Lefkowitz 1991's influential distinction between the poet and the chorus as speaker. For the sake of convenience, I will use 'Pindar' to refer to the Pindaric *persona loquens* without assuming that this is identical to the biographical person of Pindar. Nor do I assume that the speaking 'I' of the poems is necessarily always equivalent to Pindar the poet, since it is well known that Pindar also adopts the persona of the chorus (cf. Lefkowitz 1991 10–11) as well as the victor (cf. Currie 2013). It does, however, seem incontestable that the speaking 'I' of the poems must be identical to the entity that is engaged in the enunciation of praise (cf. Miller 1993, Wells 2009), whether this occurs in choral or monodic performance, and whether that speaker is Pindar the poet, the chorus or the victor himself. My interest here is in how *poikilia* relates to the task of constructing and perceiving Pindar's lyrics, and so my argument does not depend on the identity of the *persona loquens*, only on how, specifically, that speaker articulates the relationship between *poikilia* and the language of song.

of his poetics. As is reflected in numerous modern appraisals of Pindar's style, which take their cue from the poet's explicit comments on his own craft, *poikilia* crops up again and again as a byword for the complexity, intricacy and/or obscurity of his verses. For instance, W. H. Race (1983) has identified the use of negative expressions in Pindar as an exemplar of his stylistic *poikilia*, which Race conceptualises as 'variety'. For Ilja Pfeijffer (1999: 22), 'The kind of ποικιλία Pindar is aiming at is structural diversity that results from the use of different kinds of material', while for John Hamilton (2003), *poikilia* is a quintessential component of Pindar's obscurity.[47] And as recently as 2017, Rana Saadi Liebert has argued for the fundamentality of *poikilia* to what she terms an 'apian poetic program. From the sweetness of honey and the artistry of *poikilia* Pindar constructs a model for skillful poetic composition based on the bee's productive activity' (69). Like Liebert, I am interested in the pleasurable qualities of Pindar's imagery, and the readings offered here will complement her analysis of the sensuous and somatic dimensions of Pindar's figurations of *poikilia*.[48]

Pindar's evocations of *poikilia* are often interpreted in relation to the similar analogies with craftsmanship that recur throughout his verses.[49] Critics have detected therein a sense of competition between the verbal and plastic arts,[50] but more recent work has delineated the extent to which these are mutually reinforcing sets of images that work in tandem to foster a unique mode of praise.[51] These interventions have also instructively refocused attention on the unique aesthetics of Pindar's verses

---

[47] See also Wells 2009: 129–84, who defines Pindar's *poikilia* as a process of 'orchestration', one that reflects the 'novelistic' style that he attributes to the poet.

[48] Given that my interest is not to explicate Pindar or propose a unitary meaning to his usages of *poikilia*, but instead to illuminate the variable shades of meaning attached to his evocations of *poikilia*, in treating Pindar's metaphors for song I focus on the sensuous and material denotations of the language he uses rather than delving into the source and target domains mapped by such usages (cf. Lakoff and Johnson 1980, with excellent discussion and bibliography of applications of conceptual metaphor theory to ancient Graeco-Roman texts in Zanker 2019: 1–29).

[49] The most comprehensive overview of these metaphors remains Steiner 1986: 52–65.

[50] See e.g. Ford 2002: 113–30, who observes how this use of craft metaphor has often been treated as evidence for the emergence, in the fifth century, of a perceived rivalry between the plastic arts and poetry (and epinicia in particular) because of their shared commemorative function. See also Steiner 1986: 52–65, and especially p. 60: 'It [*poikilos*] evokes all the embellishment and adornment which makes the Pindaric ode a thing of remarkable beauty and craftsmanship.' See also e.g. Finkelberg 1998: 100–30, Scheid and Svenbro 1996, and Nagy 1996 on earlier uses of craft metaphors in Homer and Hesiod.

[51] See e.g. Kurke and Neer 2019, Spelman 2018, Fearn 2017, Kirichenko 2016, Kurke 2015, Athanassaki 2012, Pavlou 2010, Steiner 1993.

rather than concentrating solely on the sociopolitical contexts to which his figures allude. But while Pindar's metaphors underscoring the sweetness and pleasure-giving aspects of his song have by no means gone unnoticed, the intensity of interest devoted to the unity and functionality of his verses has meant that comparatively less attention has been paid to those aspects of Pindar's language that must have contributed to his audiences' enjoyment of his poetry.[52]

Critics of an older generation, however, were unabashed in noting the peculiar pleasures afforded by Pindar. As Asya Sigelman has discussed (2016: 19), Gilbert Norwood (1945: 97) found in Pindar a 'vivid, electrical effect . . . the sentence must be a living creature (surely!), for its members heave and quiver'. In what follows, I will suggest that one way that Pindar achieves this effect of heightened vitality is by inspiring complex imaginative projections in his figurations of *poikilia*.[53] And rather than seeking unity across these instantiations of *poikilia*, what will emerge is a kaleidoscopic miscellany of different effects, as was the case with the lyric examples discussed already.[54]

Pythian 8, Pythian 10 and Olympian 1

In the previous chapter we saw a variety of objects imagined as having human voices, and a similar example from Pindar conjures such a 'speaking object' in order to place song and material artefacts on the same continuum.[55] It is fitting that this fragment depicts the combination specifically of a 'foundation' (κρηπίς) with human voice, since its imaginative construction will likewise be foundational for the interpretations of Pindaric *poikilia* formulated here:

[52] cf. the observation made by Fitzgerald 2016: 203 n. 8: 'Few ancient poets have set so much store by variety (or *poikilia*) as Pindar . . . and yet it is the unity of the Pindaric ode that has engaged the attention of scholars far more than its *poikilia*.'

[53] In this respect, my attempt to illuminate the imaginative range of Pindaric images of *poikilia* is similar to the approach adopted by Budelmann and LeVen 2014, although their focus is specifically on how Timotheus employs blended metaphors: '[Timotheus] does not simply *draw on* our minds' capacity for blending, but he *stimulates* it to the highest degree' (198, emphasis in original).

[54] See also Briand 2013 and 2016 for analyses of the visual effects created by Pindar, especially his notion of the 'spectacular efficiency' (2016: 247) that makes vivid imagery not only an aesthetic device, but also instrumental for epinician specifically.

[55] The generic context of this poem is unknown, but Aristides, who quotes these lines, says that it was composed for the citizens of Thebes (*Or.* 28.57). Like Pindar's epinicia, then (where *poikilia* predominantly appears), this poem was also probably intended for a civic, public setting (even if it was performed by young women as a *partheneion*, as Power 2011: 110 suggests).

κεκρότηται χρυσέα κρηπὶς ἱεραῖσιν ἀοιδαῖς·
εἶα τειχίζωμεν ἤδη <u>ποικίλον</u>
κόσμον αὐδάεντα λόγων

A golden foundation has been hammered out for our holy songs. Come now, let us build already an <u>elaborate</u> ornament, one that speaks with human voice. (Pind. fr. 194)

From the outset, the material and the audible are imagined in harmony. The first three words (κεκρότηται χρυσέα κρηπὶς) suggest the physical 'hammering out' of a golden substance, but the shift in focus to song immediately following (ἱεραῖσιν ἀοιδαῖς) in turn casts the verb κεκρότηται in a fresh light, since this verb can refer to rattling or knocking sounds (e.g. *Il.* 15.453, *Hymn. Hom. Ap.* 234) as well as to the kinds of manual craftsmanship that produce such sounds, like the hammering or forging intimated by the inclusion of the 'golden foundation'. As Timothy Power (2011: 11) has noted, this verb can also apply to the sound of dancing feet, as exemplified in *Paean* 6.17–18 Maehler: 'As they sing they stamp the ground with a swift foot' (μελπ[ό]μεναι / ποδὶ κροτέο[ντι γᾶν θο]ῷ). Thus the dative ἱεραῖσιν ἀοιδαῖς could be construed as instrumental, that the 'golden foundation' is forged *by* holy songs: physically (by means of dancing feet) as well as audibly.

The reference to 'build[ing]' (τειχίζωμεν) likewise suggests a manual process, but the fact that it is an 'elaborate ornament' being built complicates this picture, since the object of this verb, κόσμον, can designate both material and immaterial forms of 'orderliness' or 'ornamentation'. And its conjunction with the adjective ποικίλον puts us in similarly ambiguous territory between the tangible and the audible, an ambiguity further heightened by 'one that speaks with human voice' (αὐδάεντα λόγων). The adjective used here, αὐδήεις, is significant because, as a word that characterises specifically *human* speech, it communicates how the *kosmos* being 'built' (τειχίζωμεν) is envisioned both as a living, speaking artefact and as a speaking, human presence that is *like* an artefact in its orderliness and *poikilia*.[56]

By merging the domains of the material and the audible in this way, these verses forge a fabulous object whose existence is obviously impossible outside the realm of the imagination.[57] Nonetheless, its description manages to give it a vivid presence

[56] On αὐδήεις as denotative of human voice in particular see LSJ s.v., but especially *Il.* 19.407 (where it characterises the speech of Achilles' horse).
[57] In this sense, Pindar deploys images of *poikilia* in a manner that aligns with Clark's account of 'surrogate material structures', which work to facilitate understanding of things that are 'absent, counterfactual, or even impossible' (2010: 24). While Clark's focus in this particu-

not unlike ekphrastic depictions of putatively 'real' objects like Achilles' shield in *Iliad* 18. In so doing, this passage provides a particularly illustrative example of a state of attention in which the effect is not to co-opt the realness of the material world by pointing to objects outside the text, but to highlight the imaginative processes that make it possible for such fantastical phenomena to be pictured at all.[58] The consistent thread linking Pindaric figures of *poikilia* is that they point not to extrapoetic things, but to the surface of the imagination and its capacity to combine multifarious sensory registers and word meanings in new and unusual ways.[59]

Pindar's forms of *poikilia* thus foster what Gabrielle Starr (2015: 257) has termed a 'bidirectionally-focused state of attention' in her essay on aesthetic engagement and vivid imagery. We have seen already in this chapter how earlier lyric poets could exploit the capaciousness of *poikilia* as a descriptive term in order to create an effect similar to what Elaine Scarry called perceptual mimesis. Starr's 2013 study of neuroaesthetics (*Feeling Beauty: The Neuroscience of Aesthetic Experience*) elaborates more fully than Scarry on the kinds of perceptual processes (including, but not limited to, vision) that can be replicated in and activated by language (although she acknowledges her affinity with and debt to Scarry's work). A point that is fundamental to Starr's work is the fact that imagination and perception are closely linked: reading or hearing about sensory experience activates the same areas of the brain that are involved in lived experience.[60] On this account,

lar work is on the role of physical props (like models, drawings, and the like), elsewhere he attributes a very similar function to language in saying that, 'language enables us to exploit our basic cognitive capacities of pattern recognition and transformation in ways that reach out to *new behavioral and intellectual horizons*' (1997: 194, emphasis added).

[58] Interpretations of ekphrasis tend to rely on the language of 'coopting' to characterise the depiction of objects; cf. Cunningham 2007: 61: 'It [the ekphrastic encounter] lays claim to the absolute *thereness* of an aesthetic object, the thereness writing is (rightly) so doubtful about.'

[59] In this respect, my conclusions align with those of Bonifazi 2004 in her study of the cognitive effects of the different kinds of deixis employed by Pindar, where she notes that 'Pindar's style does not seek univocal indications, either/or indexicals; rather, it privileges hybrid, ambiguous, and polysemantic deictic features' (401). Her analysis of the inferential activity on the part of the audience prompted by the 'imbalance between linguistic and extralinguistic text processing' effected in deictic expressions supports my reading of the bidirectional focus of Pindar's figurations of *poikilia*. See too, in the same issue of *Arethusa*, Calame 2004, who delineates the simultaneous operation of intra- and extra-discursive modes of reference in a variety of lyric poets, including Pindar.

[60] cf. Troscianko 2014a: 20, although her focus is on vision, whereas the examples adduced here do not by any means appeal exclusively to this sense. For a good summary of the scholarship that uncovered this continuum between perception and imagination, see Troscianko 2014b: 86–92.

'perceptual activity is both self-generated and sparked by external presentation – for example the words that carry rhythm and rhyme, or the textual details that drive description' (2015: 257). This is a helpful lens to apply to the terminology of *poikilia* in Pindar in particular, since we will find here that *poikilia*'s apparition likewise consistently inspires a bidirectional focus: on the (imagined) manifestation of this aspect in the phenomenon so described and on the imaginative process itself.[61] And given that many of these figures appear explicitly in connection with song or poetic language (unlike in the lyric poets already discussed), the capacity to evoke this dual form of perception becomes a part of the poet's distinctive self-fashioning.

The vision related by Amphiarus in *Pythian* 8 illustrates well how Pindar constructs and manipulates a bidirectional focus. As Amphiarus surveys the Epigonoi at the gates of Thebes, he observes that their lineage is conspicuous among them (φυᾷ τὸ γενναῖον ἐπιπρέπει, 44) and goes on to remark, 'I clearly see Alcmaeon, the first at the gates of Cadmus, wielding a <u>gleaming</u> dragon upon his blazing shield' (θαέομαι σαφὲς / δράκοντα <u>ποικίλον</u> αἴθας Ἀλκμᾶν' ἐπ' ἀσπίδος / νωμῶντα πρῶτον ἐν Κάδμου πύλαις, 45–7). As the scholiast notes of this shield device, the snake symbolises Amphiarus' prophetic powers and so this spectacle is not only Amphiarus seeing his son, but Amphiarus seeing a reflection of himself.[62] In other words, what the scholiast detects at work in the seer's vision is the kind of dual focus fundamental to Starr's theory, where perception is both internal and external. This is evident from the fact that it is the serpent that Amphiarus sees first, as conveyed by the anastrophe of the two accusatives, δράκοντα and Ἀλκμᾶνα. And it is the same strategy we saw in Alcman's allusion to a similar *poikilos drakōn*, where the deferral of the adjectival 'made of gold' left the form of the snake ambiguous for an instant. Likewise, the intimation here is that Amphiarus perceives the shield's image as though it were the real creature that in turn is a reflection of his own prophetic powers. And here, as with the golden snake of Alcman, we are made to understand that the animal's representation renders its *poikilia* all the more visually striking, as here it forms part of the 'blazing' aspect of Alcmaeon's shield. Likewise, in narrating Amphiarus' perception of this bi-focused apparition, Pindar asks his audience to imagine both the shield and the seer's particular mode of perceiving it.

---

[61] Thus in referring to 'imagination' I mean what Grethlein and Huitink 2017: 69 n. 16 succinctly designate as an 'imaginative *experience* of perception' (emphasis in original) and not mental pictures.

[62] Schol. *P.* 8.66a: 'Why does Alcmaeon have a serpent on his shield? Because the animal is appropriate for omens, and Amphiarus is a seer. His child preserved a sign of his father's art' (διατί ὁ Ἀλκμαίων εἶχεν ἐπὶ τῆς ἀσπίδος δράκοντα; ὅτι ἐπιτήδειον πρὸς οἰωνοὺς τὸ ζῷον, μάντις δὲ καὶ ὁ Ἀμφιάραος·).

In *Pythian* 10, *poikilia* is also correlated with serpents as well as with a certain mode of vision, this time the 'stony death' caused by the Gorgon's stare:

ἔπεφνέν τε Γοργόνα, καὶ <u>ποικίλον</u> κάρα
δρακόντων φόβαισιν ἤλυθε νασιώταις
λίθινον θάνατον φέρων. ἐμοὶ δὲ θαυμάσαι
θεῶν τελεσάντων οὐδέν ποτε φαίνεται
ἔμμεν ἄπιστον

He slew the Gorgon, and, bearing her head <u>shimmering</u> with locks of serpents, came to the islanders, bringing them stony death. But to me, no marvel, if the gods bring it about, ever seems beyond belief. (46–50, trans. Race 1997b, slightly modified)

While it is not unusual that *poikilia* should characterise the Gorgon's head of snakes, given the common attribution of the adjective to this animal, the word order here toys with this association by delaying specification that this quality consists in her hair. Syntactically, then, *poikilia* is the most prominent feature of the monster's head; its positioning in the sentence, moreover, seems designed to replicate the very act of perception, even suggesting perhaps that the shimmering of the Gorgon's head would be discernible before the observation could be made that this was because her hair was formed of snakes. There are also two levels of seeing at work here: while the Gorgon's gaze brings 'stony death', her distinctive appearance itself becomes a vivid focus of the imaginative gaze through its naming with *poikilia*. In the poet's hands, then, the transformative gaze of even the Gorgon's gruesome visage is itself transformed into an aesthetic object that can form part of the similarly varied quality of the poem's language. For in the juxtaposition of myth and gnomic statement effected here, the shimmering, snaky head of the Gorgon is implicitly cast as the sort of fantastical, barely believable feat that only gods can accomplish, and so establishes *poikilia* as a characteristic of such phenomena.

Poikilia's appearance in *Pythian* 10 in conjunction with this statement on wonder, divinity and believability recalls the much-discussed example of Pelops' shoulder in *Olympian* 1, where *poikilia* is similarly implicated within a narrative about a hybrid form. *Olympian* 1 also models the dual perspective on lyric *poikilia* discussed above (whereby it is a prominent quality *within* this corpus as well as a feature *of* lyric language), as here *poikilia* describes the fanciful or deceptive embellishment of tales:

τοῦ μεγασθενὴς ἐράσσατο Γαιάοχος   (25)
Ποσειδάν, ἐπεί νιν καθαροῦ λέβητος ἔξελε Κλωθώ,

ἐλέφαντι φαίδιμον ὦμον κεκαδμένον.
ἦ θαύματα πολλά, καί πού τι καὶ βροτῶν φάτις ὑπὲρ τὸν ἀλαθῆ λόγον
δεδαιδαλμένοι ψεύδεσι ποικίλοις ἐξαπατῶντι μῦθοι.
Χάρις δ᾽, ἅπερ ἅπαντα τεύχει τὰ μείλιχα θνατοῖς,   (30)
ἐπιφέροισα τιμὰν καὶ ἄπιστον ἐμήσατο πιστόν
ἔμμεναι τὸ πολλάκις·

[Lydian Pelops], whom Poseidon, holder of the earth, loved, when Clotho removed him from the pure cauldron, distinguished by his gleaming ivory shoulder. Truly there are many marvels, and yet I suppose the words of mortal beings that are beyond the true account can deceive, stories adorned with titillating lies; and Grace, who fashions all things sweet for mortals, furnishes dignity and often contrives to make believable the unbelievable. (25–32)

The figure of the hybrid creature has followed us into this chapter from the previous one, but here it raises questions about the nature of poetic language and representation. This passage has proven to be something of an interpretive crux for modern readers, since Pindar here seems to be denouncing the very kind of lyrical adornment (daidal/, poikil/, charis, meilicha) he elsewhere professes to be his specialism.[63] Moreover, his allusion to the deceitfulness of poetry recalls Hesiod's narration of his encounter with the Muses, who claim to be able to speak truths as well as 'lies that are like the truth' (ἴδμεν ψεύδεα πολλὰ λέγειν ἐτύμοισιν ὁμοῖα, Theog. 27).[64] In Olympian 1, too, the pleasure of poetry is bound up with deception, as Pindar makes explicit in saying that 'charis . . . contrives to make believable the unbelievable' (ἄπιστον ἐμήσατο πιστόν / ἔμμεναι τὸ πολλάκις, 31–2). That he does this in the context of narrating the tale of Pelops' consumption by the gods, a narrative that he then explicitly rejects within the same poem as untrue (σὲ δ᾽, ἀντία προτέρων, φθέγξομαι, 36; ἔννεπε κρυφᾷ τις αὐτίκα φθονερῶν γειτόνων, 47; ἀφίσταμαι, 52), is equally perplexing. The image of Pelops' reconstruction with an ivory shoulder

---

[63] Elsewhere, Pindar is explicit about the charis that inheres in his poetry; see e.g. Pyth. 6.2, Pyth. 9.3–4, 89–90, Nem. 9.54. On the 'honey' of Pindar's praise see Ol. 10.98; for his attribution of daidal/ see Ol. 1.105, Ol. 5.21, Nem. 11.18.

[64] See Walsh 1984: 37–61, who focuses on the relationship between the pleasure of poetry and different kinds of forgetfulness. On the concept of 'poetic fictions' in Pindar see especially Pratt 1993: 115–29, who argues that 'the epinician poets leave room for an appreciation of poetic invention as long as that invention does not interfere with the encomiastic function of their poetry', and also Finkelberg 1998: 170–2 on this passage from Olympian 1, who analyses Pindar's revision of the myth of Pelops as 'one more in the series of poetic replacements of reality which he so sharply disapproves of in others' (170).

thus is construed as one of the 'titillating lies' (ψεύδεσι ποικίλοις) that 'deceive' (ἐξαπατῶντι).[65]

But by entwining specifically the image of a prosthetic device – Pelops' 'gleaming ivory shoulder' – within a meditation on how language can also be manipulated and beautifully crafted, Pindar highlights the fact that words are also a kind of prosthesis. This is clear from the fact that they can serve to turn objects into images (including deceptive ones like that of Pelops' reconstruction) and that the stories comprised by these images are likewise a form of object to the extent that they can be embellished and imbued with *charis*.[66] Together with the fact that Pindar evokes the prosthetic shoulder (whose gleaming aspect and precious material resonate with other, similarly luxurious objects that Pindar incorporates as analogues for his own songs) precisely in order to reject the version of the tale to which it belongs thus draws attention to the malleable and prosthetic-like relationship that exists between individual speaker and language.[67] In this materialistic picture of language and its (mis)uses, Pindar's account here is remarkably in line with Andy Clark's notion of linguistic scaffolding discussed above. But whereas Clark dwells on the cognitive benefits afforded by language, Pindar's point here is to highlight how its flexibility and user dependence render it as dynamic and potentially misleading as perception itself.

The dynamism of *poikilia*'s significance for Pindar becomes apparent when we contrast *Olympian* 1's picture of 'titillating lies' with *Pythian* 9's appropriation of the same term to describe the encomiast's task: 'To elaborate a few deeds among great ones is for wise men to hear' (βαιὰ δ᾽ ἐν μακροῖσι ποικίλλειν ἀκοὰ σοφοῖς, 77–8).[68]

---

[65] cf. Noel 2018: 161–2, who discusses in detail how Pindar's description of the shoulder piece 'seems to suggest that this exceptional prosthesis enhances Pelops' beauty and seductive power' (161). For a summary of the difficulties in interpretation involved in Pindar's inclusion of the ivory shoulder, see especially Most 2012: 269–71.

[66] See also on this passage Noel 2018, who links the 'prosthetic imagination' expressed in Pelops' ivory shoulder to the similarly intimate continuities depicted in Homer between bodies and pieces of armour.

[67] I use 'prosthetic-like' rather than 'prosthetic' because I am not claiming an identical relationship between physical prostheses and language, but instead proposing to look at language as operating the kind of integrated and 'coupled' system I discussed in the preceding chapter in relation to Hephaestus and his animated tools.

[68] On the interpretative difficulties of this verse and its ramifications for scholarly understanding of Pindar's stylistics see especially Young 1983, who notes that, 'Pindar does not commend choosing a few items and then merely embellishing them in fancy dress, but, rather, taking a few items or just a small portion to develop, to "elaborate" in full inherent detail' (169). For a critique of Young's reading see also Hamilton 2003: 84–93, who interprets Pindar's *poikilia* instead as the 'poetic practice of tempering the light of praise by means of the darkness [sc. envy of the gods] that opposes it' (80).

This statement has occasioned a host of interpretations centred on the meaning of ἐν μακροῖσι and the implications of ἀκοὰ σοφοῖς. But whether the former phrase refers to 'embroidering small things at length' (as Wilamowitz 1922: 263 would have it) or 'elaboration of a few themes amid lengthy ones' (as Race 1997b translates it), the verbal form of *poikilia* here names a compositional practice predicated on selection and compression.[69] In this sense, Pindar seems here to allude to a process similar to what we saw most prominently in Anacreon fr. 358 *PMG*: the selection and organisation of a few richly salient details that together create a vivid but nonspecific image. Further, that the object of the infinitive *poikillein* in this verse is a vexing phrase (βαιὰ δ᾽ ἐν μακροῖσι) that defies straightforward interpretation encapsulates the complexity of interpreting *poikilia* that we have seen throughout this chapter: although it putatively assumes fixed, material dimensions (as connoted here by βαιὰ and ἐν μακροῖσι), *poikilia* resists being pinned to a single mode of interpretation – perhaps because of the variety of ways in which this process of *poikillein*, 'elaboration', could conceivably be carried out.[70]

The consistent thread linking these disparate examples of Pindaric *poikilia* is the bidirectional mode of attention they inspire. On the one hand, their function as descriptive terms prompts reflection on the specific qualities they may pick out in each instance. On the other hand, they also evoke a second kind of 'seeing': seeing how the poet's language compels us to mentally conjure images in particular ways. In doing so, Pindar exploits the plasticity of language and his audience's imagination to showcase his own form of craftsmanship. And in what follows, we will see even more explicit and elaborate figures linking *poikilia* with Pindar's own poetic vision.

Olympian 6, Nemean 5 and Nemean 4

So far, we have seen Pindar associate *poikilia* with poetic or narrative processes as well as with fantastical objects, and *Olympian* 6 offers an example of how these can be connected. Here, Pindar lays claims to another form of *poikilia*, this time a process of 'weaving': 'I will drink, while I weave my <u>decorated</u> song for heroic spearmen' (πίομαι, ἀνδράσιν αἰχματαῖσι πλέκων / <u>ποικίλον</u> ὕμνον, 86–7).[71] While the linkage between weaving and song has a long lineage and is by no means unique to Pindar,

---

[69] cf. Grethlein 2011: 395 n. 41.

[70] cf. Maslov 2015: 163, who notes in his discussion of Pindaric metaphor and simile that, 'The paradoxical quality of Pindaric images, their apparent resistance to conventionalization, directly contributes to the conceptual work they perform.' See also Young 1983: 159 on the quantitative force of βαιός.

[71] On the future form of πίομαι see most recently D'Alessio 2004: 289–90, who argues that 'we have here a case of production projected into the future' (290).

this is the earliest extant and most explicit proclamation of the potential for *poikilia* to belong both to the medium of textiles and to that of song, a connection made all the more emphatic by the use of the first person and the placement of the adjective ποικίλον squarely between 'weaving' and 'song'.[72] In so doing, this figuration draws attention to how the speaker is capitalising on the variable shades of the term's meaning that allow for its intelligible application to song. The metapoetic implications of this brief phrase thus run deeper than a claim that the song in question is as skilfully crafted as a textile. As in *Olympian* 1, this phrasing conveys the speaker's awareness of the user–artefact relationship that obtains for language as much as for tools like the weaver's shuttle.[73]

While we have already seen in the first section how the word *poikilia* can function as a form of linguistic 'scaffolding' to convey the experiential quality of desirable things, here Pindar is explicit about how he is deploying this word as a form of scaffolding to characterise his own poetics. And as we have seen throughout these examples from Pindar, this user–artefact relationship is one that affords its user the ability to combine words in novel ways that in turn propel its audience to attend to their experiences of familiar phenomena (textiles and song) in unfamiliar ways.

Further, that this proclamation of 'weaving a decorated song' occurs within an ode especially replete with similarly novel composites – such as the 'golden pillars' and 'far-shining front' that open the poem (χρυσέας κίονας, 1–2; πρόσωπον τηλαυγές, 3–4), the 'message stick of the Muses' (σκυτάλα Μοισᾶν, 91), the 'mixing bowl of loud-resounding songs' (γλυκὺς κρατὴρ ἀγαφθέγκτων ἀοιδᾶν, 91), the 'flower' of song that concludes the poem (ἐμῶν δ᾽ ὕμνων ἄεξ᾽ εὐτερπὲς ἄνθος, 105) – fixes attention on the vitality of this *poikilos humnos*. For in spite of their fantastical quality, these figures are vividly conveyed in their sensuality and appeal to multiple senses simultaneously (particularly in the case of the 'sweet mixing bowl of loud-resounding songs'). While we saw in *Olympian* 1 how Pindar seemed to disdain the pleasures such fantasies can offer, it was there too that we saw a sustained recognition on the poet's part of the capacity for words and stories to be as alluring as material things.[74] And here in *Olympian* 6, the application of *poikilia* to his own song

---

[72] On the persistent correlation between weaving and song in archaic and classical terminology see, most recently, Fanfani 2017. See also Nagy 2002: 70–98, who proposes that the word family of ὕμνος is derived from the verb 'to weave' (ὑφαίνειν) and thus that the uses of this term always convey the sense of a song as a 'woven' creation.

[73] Prior to the 2008 discussion of language cited above, Clark 1997: 217 presented the concept of linguistic scaffolding in terms of 'a special kind of user/artifact relationship – one in which the artifact is reliably present, frequently used, personally "tailored", and deeply trusted'.

[74] My conclusion here thus aligns closely with that of Fearn 2017: 127: 'Pindar's subtle evocations of and attitudes to art and the monuments of contemporary material culture . . .

(πλέκων / <u>ποικίλον</u> ὕμνον, 86–7) can be read as an encapsulation of the similarly imaginative figures that define many of this poem's other depictions of song, which likewise manipulate familiar terms and objects in order to reimagine these in new and fantastical ways.

Nemean 5, by contrast, incorporates *poikilia* in a way that focuses on the gendered differences in this quality. For while the victor Pytheas' uncle Euthymenes 'twice fell into the lap of Victory and grasped <u>scintillating</u> songs' (Νίκας ἐν ἀγκώνεσσι πίτνων <u>ποικίλων</u> ἔψαυσας ὕμνων, 42), the mythic section of the second strophe recounts how a chorus of Muses sang at Peleus' and Thetis' wedding about Hippolyta's failed attempt to seduce Peleus:

Πηλέα θ᾽ ὥς τέ νιν ἁβρὰ Κρηθεῖς Ἱππολύτα δόλῳ πεδᾶσαι
ἤθελε ξυνᾶνα Μαγνήτων σκοπόν
πείσαισ᾽ ἀκοίταν <u>ποικίλοις</u> βουλεύμασιν,
ψεύσταν δὲ ποιητὸν συνέπαξε λόγον,
ὡς ἦρα νυμφείας ἐπείρα κεῖνος ἐν λέκτροις Ἀκάστου
εὐνᾶς. τὸ δ᾽ ἐναντίον ἔσκεν· πολλὰ γάρ νιν παντὶ θυμῷ
παρφαμένα λιτάνευεν.

[And they sang of] Peleus, and how refined Hippolyta, Cretheus' daughter, wanted to ensnare him with a ruse, once she persuaded her husband, overseer of the Magnesians, to be a partner in crime through her <u>shifty</u> designs: she fashioned a false and fabricated tale, alleging that in Acastus' own marriage bed that man tried to get her wifely love. But the opposite was the case, for she many times and with all her heart entreated him beguilingly. (26–32)

In its linkage between *poikilia* and feminine deception and eroticism, this passage resonates with themes discussed in the last chapter, but it has relevance here too because of the connection it posits between *poikilia* and Pindar's version of the song of the Muses. On the one hand, it presents in common a quality of Euthymenes' victory songs and Hippolyta's machinations. On the other hand, in the same way that the Muses sing of this episode in order to highlight Peleus' virtue in rebuffing Hippolyta, so too does the evocation of her wiles make this form of *poikilia* a foil to that of Euthymenes' approbations.[75] The contrast between these amounts to its own

are part of the same general way that Pindaric victory odes are precisely *about* the extent to which the world of things can be accessed through performance/reperformance/song/text. Victory odes are thematizers of enactment' (emphasis in original).

[75] cf. Segal 1998: 174, who similarly notes how the contrast developed by this ring composition has the effect of juxtaposing the Muses' praise with the rhetoric of Hippolyta, as well

instantiation of *poikilia* in what Hamilton (2003: 77) has dubbed the poet's 'chiaro-scuro': that is, a juxtaposition that highlights Pytheas' and his family's superiority, just as the Muses did with Peleus' wedding song. It also highlights the different functions of each form of *poikilia*. While Hippolyta aimed to persuade, Euthymenes' songs are ones that he actively and successfully 'grasped' (ἔψαυσας, 42) through his own endeavours. But by drawing attention to these distinctive inflections of the same concept in close succession, Pindar capitalises on the multivalences of the word and the distinctive sensuous pleasures it can encompass (feminine seduction as well as acclaim and celebration) as a way of structuring the relation between his mythic and encomiastic material.[76]

Pleasure is also a motivating force in *Nemean* 4's depiction of song, where Pindar relates how the young victor's father, had he been alive to see this victory, 'would have celebrated the victory, playing <u>animatedly</u> and often on the kithara, and leaning on this melody' (<u>ποικίλον</u> κιθαρίζων θαμά κε, τῷδε μέλει κλιθείς, / υἱὸν κελάδησε καλλίνικον, 14–16). Here too, *poikilia* features in an imagined scenario like Pindar's envisioning of the Muses' wedding song in *Nemean* 5, and notably it is one that features a monodic, rather than choral, performance. By locating *poikilia* in the song the victor's father *would have* sung, this description poses *poikilia* as a natural, familiar mode in which to celebrate athletic victory, a claim that also comports well with Pindar's claims elsewhere that his songs are the product not solely of *technē*, but of inspiration.[77] This idea finds support in the verb used here, κελαδέω, which, as I have argued elsewhere, channels the resonance of natural phenomena like flowing water into the medium of Pindar's song.[78] And the presence of *poikilia* as an adverb alongside 'often' (θαμά) makes clear that this quality belongs not only to the song itself but to the particular energy and disposition that produces it: the paternal pride and gladness that would motivate repeat performances of his son's victory song.

The public, communal reach of praise's pleasure is instead what is made explicit in *Nemean* 8, where Pindar also envisions a different and specifically masculine function for the Lydian *mitra*:[79]

---

as Burnett 2005: 63 n. 12 on the different kinds of speech depicted in this poem; Burnett also points out how the 'ornate hymns' of Victory are juxtaposed with the 'elaborate blan-dishments' of Hippolyta.

[76] cf. Fearn 2017: 38 on this ode: 'The diversity of scholars' responses to the interpretative difficulty gives greater credence to the possibility that the original reception of Pindaric poetics was similarly complex, and that the poem is not only anticipating interpretative scrutiny, but also provoking it.'

[77] cf. Steiner 1986: 40–51.

[78] See Lather 2019 for fuller discussion of the significance of the *kelados* to Pindaric poetics.

[79] cf. too Pindar fr. 179, where the speaker declares that 'I am weaving an <u>elaborate</u> headband

ἱκέτας Αἰακοῦ σεμνῶν γονάτων πόλιός θ' ὑπὲρ φίλας
ἀστῶν θ' ὑπὲρ τῶνδ' ἅπτομαι φέρων
Λυδίαν μίτραν καναχηδὰ <u>πεποικιλμέναν</u>,
Δείνιος δισσῶν σταδίων καὶ πατρὸς Μέγα Νεμεαῖον ἄγαλμα

As a suppliant, I am clasping the revered knees of Aeacus on behalf of his beloved
city and these citizens, bearing a Lydian fillet resoundingly <u>ornamented</u>, a Nemean
offering for the double stadion races of Deinias and his father Megas. (13–16)

Instead of a coveted item in the feminine wardrobe (as we saw in Sappho and Alcman)
Pindar presents the athlete's fillet as a public dedication, an *agalma* presented 'on behalf
of his beloved city and these citizens' to commemorate Deinias' victory. Moreover,
the materiality imputed to the song is also expressed in the tactile language of these
verses: the 'bearing' (φέρων) of the *mitra* as well as the 'clasping' (ἅπτομαι) of knees.
This palpability also becomes evident in the particular mode of sound (καναχηδά)
afforded to the *mitra*, as this is one that emphasises sound's origins in the contact
between different bodies.[80] Thus, as we saw in Pind. fr. 194, here *poikilia*'s reification
explicitly takes the form of an object imbued with sound, the 'resounding' conveyed by
καναχηδά. As this adverb and its cognate noun encompass loud, reverberating sounds
in particular, including that of the *aulos* itself (cf. *Pyth.* 10.39, Bacchyl. 2.12 and Soph.
Trach. 212), the perfective aspect of πεποικιλμέναν furthers this notion of resounding
by suggesting the *mitra*'s continued resonance through the song's performance. And
while, as we have seen, *poikilia* is perfectly at home in the context of the *mitra* and its
material allure, the term gains additional force here. For it self-reflexively denotes the
kind of complexity effected in this verse in the use of the participle to conceptually and
grammatically intertwine a material object with a resounding quality.

While it is clear that Pindar takes pains to distinguish his work from the deceptive, seductive pleasures in *poikilia*'s province, he nonetheless cultivates a scintillating effect in his language and imagery. For as this survey makes clear, *poikilia*
performs different roles in each context: its meaning and salience have to be individ-

---

for the sons of Amythaon' (ὑφαίνω δ' Ἀμυθαονίδαισιν <u>ποικίλον</u> ἄνδημα) in a poem of
uncertain genre. Nevertheless, this image combines the weaving of *Olympian* 6 (discussed
below) with the figure of the decorated headband in a way that makes explicit how the
speaker is crafting a new form from these elements to endow it with a commemorative or
encomiastic function.

[80] The adverb appears in Hesiod's *Theogony* to describe the sound of rivers (ποταμοὶ
καναχηδὰ ῥέοντες, 367), and in Homer the noun καναχή refers to heavy 'clangs' that occur
when armour is struck or to the gnashing of teeth. See Lather 2017: 133–4 for further
discussion of this term's significance as an attribute of music.

ually construed. Each figuration, as we have seen, prompts a bidirectionally focused state of attention that is devoted, on the one hand, to conceptualising the object or phenomenon so described and, on the other hand, to the imaginative process itself in its ability to conjure multiple senses and/or meanings simultaneously. From this dual perspective, we gain a clearer sense of why Pindar frequently marshals *poikilia* as a trademark of different facets of his own style: the word broadly captures the kind of imaginative complexity that defines such figures as the 'elaborate, speaking ornament' addressed earlier.[81] And as noted in the section 'Pindaric *Poikilia* and the Victorious Imagination', such images were part of what prompted modern readers to find a higher vitality or 'electricity' in Pindar's verses. By taking these observations seriously and as a crucial component of Pindaric poetics, my aim here has been to expand these readings by exploring the varied spectrum of imaginative effects contained in these examples of Pindaric *poikilia*.

A focus on just one of Pindar's descriptors of his poetry also draws attention to a different aspect of *poikilia*'s vitality, one that becomes apparent from the philological approach that treats Pindar as a corpus: a fixed, relatively stable collection that allows for easy tracking of a single word and its variant shades of meaning.[82] Further, we have seen conceptual fluidity of *poikilia* from the brief summary of scholarly interpretations of Pindaric *poikilia* offered above, where each commentator offered a distinctive definition of this quality. The word family of *poikilia* thus emerges as a reified entity that is nonetheless as dynamic and evocative as the things it describes. In the next and concluding section, I explore how this dynamism is literally embodied in the unique compounds that Pindar employs to describe the distinctive voices within his poetic worlds.

Visible and Audible Movement: *Poikilia*'s Scintillating Shape

The example of the wryneck or iynx ties together several dominant features of the Pindaric *poikilia* seen so far and, in its avian focus, provides a good entry point to this

---

[81] cf. the conclusion of Kirichenko 2016: 23: 'Pindar's epinicians point to the inextricably dialectical relationship between the two media [sc. text and image], with words always conjuring up mental images and images always tied to (either engendered by or conducive to) verbal utterances, written or oral, spelled out or implied.'

[82] In this respect, my conclusion here accords with that of Kurke 1991: 262, although her focus is much different from mine in its groundbreaking exploration of the various social contexts in which epinician is embedded: 'Indeed, much of the notorious difficulty of Pindar's poetry is attributable to the constant flux, overlap, and shift of the symbolic systems that inform his language and imagery. The text shimmers with multiple patterns of meaning which operate simultaneously, each pointing to a different segment of the poet's social world.'

section's interest in *poikilia* and sound. More specifically, here we will see *poikilia* construed as a quality that is simultaneously visual, auditory and kinetic. In *Pythian* 4, Jason's seduction of Medea is attributed to Aphrodite's gift of the *poikilos iynx*:

πότνια δ᾿ ὀξυτάτων βελέων
<u>ποικίλαν</u> ἴυγγα τετράκναμον Οὐλυμπόθεν
ἐν ἀλύτῳ ζεύξαισα κύκλῳ
μαινάδ᾿ ὄρνιν Κυπρογένεια φέρεν
πρῶτον ἀνθρώποισι, λιτάς τ᾿ ἐπαοιδὰς ἐκδιδάσκησεν σοφὸν Αἰσονίδαν

But the Cyprus-born queen of sharpest arrows bound the <u>dappled</u> wryneck to the four spokes of the inescapable wheel and brought from Olympus that bird of madness. (213–17)

Poikilia is a common attribute of birds, describing both the appearance of their undulating feathers and the sound of their songs. Here, however, the adjective also has an obvious erotic connotation because Aphrodite is its source: a goddess who, as we will see in the next chapter, features *poikilia* prominently among her tools of seduction. But as Sarah Iles Johnston (1995: 180) has noted, the image of the wryneck tied to a wheel appears to be practically unique to the Pindaric imagination.[83] This figuration of the iynx thus situates *poikilia* within the realm of song and seduction as well as with the 'whirling' or wheeling motion that was also connoted by Sappho's *poikila athurmata* and that, as we will see, is a dynamic correlated with birdsong itself.[84] In its innovative combination of whirling movements, sensuous pleasure, seductive sound and magical, divine gifts, then, Pindar's description of the wryneck seems to encapsulate many of the same features of *poikilia* that the poet cultivates in his use of this term to characterise his own art.

While we have seen great variation in the word *poikilia*'s significance across the lyric corpus, this variability acquires a certain materiality in the voices it also characterises. In *Olympian* 3, for instance, *poikilia* describes the 'voice' of the phorminx and, by extension, the sound of the song to which it contributes:

ὕμνον ὀρθώσαις, ἀκαμαντοπόδων   (3)
ἵππων ἄωτον. Μοῖσα δ᾿ οὕτω ποι παρέ στα μοι νεοσίγαλον εὑρόντι τρόπον
Δωρίῳ φωνὰν ἐναρμόξαι πεδίλῳ

[83] As Johnston 1995 notes, the three other references to this image (which occur significantly later than Pindar's composition) may well have drawn from Pindar as their source.

[84] See further Johnston 1995 for a robust examination of the implications of Pindar's figure of the *iynx* here and the commentary that it offers on the role and effects of the voice.

ἀγλαόκωμον· ἐπεὶ χαίταισι μὲν ζευχθέντες ἔπι στέφανοι   (6)
πράσσοντί με τοῦτο θεόδματον χρέος,
φόρμιγγά τε <u>ποικιλόγαρυν</u> καὶ βοὰν αὐλῶν ἐπέων τε θέσιν
Αἰνησιδάμου παιδὶ συμμεῖξαι πρεπόντως, ἅ τε Πίσα με γεγωνεῖν·   (9)

Having set up a victory song, a flower for the untiring feet of horses. And the Muse thus stood beside me as I found a sparkling new way to join the glorious sound of the revel to the Dorian sandal. Since the garlands that have been yoked upon my head enjoin upon me this god-given responsibility, to fittingly mix together the <u>scintillating</u> voice of the lyre and the shout of flutes and the arrangement of words for the child of Ainesidamos, that which Pisa bids me to celebrate aloud. (3–9)

The epithet ποικιλόγαρυν speaks at the most general level to this excerpt's interest in the harmonious and innovative blending of distinct elements. On the one hand, ποικιλόγαρυς certainly refers to an auditory element in the variable tones of the instrument, but it is also of a piece with the visual and kinetic details that pervade this description: the 'setting up' (ὀρθώσαις) of a victory song, 'the sparkling new way' (νεοσίγαλον τρόπον), 'the glorious sound of the revel' (ἀγλαόκωμον). In this sense, the *poikilia* of the phorminx registers the *poikilia* of musical performance itself and the multiple sensory fields it encompasses.

On the other hand, given the term's prominence as an attribute of finely wrought artefacts, the *poikilia* evoked here also bears affinity with the forms of manual craftsmanship – 'setting up' (ὀρθώσαις), 'joining' (ἐναρμόξαι), 'mixing together' (συμμεῖξαι) – that metaphorically represent the construction of song. Seen in this way, the *poikilia* of the phorminx may refer not only to a quality of its sound, but also to the dexterity and expertise with which this sound is articulated. Thus the epithet could equally be understood as denotative of a 'many-toned voice' and of a 'skilfully wrought voice', meanings which align with the allusion to both the *aulos*' 'shout' (βοὰν αὐλῶν) and the 'arrangement of words' (ἐπέων τε θέσιν).[85]

Not only is song here cast as a form of skilful blending (of sound with metre and, correspondingly, dance; of phorminx, *aulos* and lyrics), the compulsion to mixture (συμμεῖξαι) extends to ontological registers: the song becomes a material object that can be 'erected', sound becomes something that can be 'joined to' the 'Dorian

---

[85] Regrettably, space does not permit me here to address Pratinas' use of *poikilia* (*TrGF* 3 = Ath. *Deipnosophistae* 14.617b–f) to characterise song (ποικιλόπτερον μέλος, 5) as well as the sound of the *aulos* (τὸν φρυνεοῦ <u>ποικίλου</u> πνοὰν ἔχοντα, 10), but I discuss this important passage as well as the portrayal of avian *poikilia* in Aristophanes' *Birds* in Lather 2016: 162–79.

sandal', garlands as well as Pisa 'bids' the speaker to create, and the phorminx and *aulos* are afforded 'voices' of their own. Not only is this dense layering of metaphor characteristic of Pindaric 'obscurity', but its quick succession of imagery also dramatises the scintillating aspect of *poikilia* that is equally visible in the smooth and rapid movements of two animals *poikilia* frequently describes: birds and serpents.[86]

The *poikilia* of the phorminx's sound bears comparison with the similar compound ποικιλόδειρος that Hesiod uses as an attribute of the nightingale, a bird which, like the lyre, is a vehicle of song:

ὧδ' ἴρηξ προσέειπεν ἀηδόνα <u>ποικιλόδειρον</u>
ὕψι μάλ' ἐν νεφέεσσι φέρων, ὀνύχεσσι μεμαρπώς·
ἣ δ' ἐλέον, γναμπτοῖσι πεπαρμένη ἀμφ' ὀνύχεσσι,
μύρετο· τὴν ὅγ' ἐπικρατέως πρὸς μῦθον ἔειπεν·
'δαιμονίη, τί λέληκας; ἔχει νύ σε πολλὸν ἀρείων·
τῇ δ' εἶς, ᾗ σ' ἂν ἐγώ περ ἄγω καὶ ἀοιδὸν ἐοῦσαν'

Thus the hawk addressed the nightingale with the <u>undulating</u> throat, bearing her up high among the clouds, gripping her with his talons. And she was weeping pitifully, being pierced with his sharp claws. But he addressed her sharply, 'Lady, why do you cry? One much stronger than you now holds you, and you will go wherever I take you, even though you are a songstress.' (*Op.* 203–8)

Unlike the other birds that the term *poikilia* describes elsewhere in the archaic corpus, the nightingale is not known for its distinctive coloration.[87] For this reason, the epithet ποικιλόδειρος has prompted speculation about its meaning in connection with the drab colouring of the nightingale if it does not denote the bright and multiple colours that occurs in its designation of other kinds of plumage.[88] Given its designation here as a 'songstress' (ἀοιδός), ποικιλόδειρος is typically read as a reference to the elaborate quality of the bird's song, since the nightingale is often depicted

---

[86] See also the observation of Basil Gildersleeve that captures this effect: 'And so Pindar's metaphors are slides that come out in such quick succession that the figures seem to blend because the untrained eye cannot follow the rapid movement of the artist' (1885: xliv).

[87] Elsewhere, the same epithet describes birds distinctive for their elaborately coloured plumage, like the mallard (πανέλοπες ποικιλόδειροι τανυσίπτεροι, Alcaeus fr. 345, ποικίλαι αἰολόδειροι πανέλοπες, Ibycus fr. 36a), while the epithet πτεροποίκιλος designates the black partridge (ἀτταγᾶς) at Ar. *Av.* 248–9.

[88] West 1978 ad loc. dismisses the term as 'not very appropriate to the nightingale', given its dull colouring, and theorises that Hesiod may have had in mind an earlier version of the fable in which a thrush or dove featured instead of the nightingale.

as a pre-eminent singer.[89] But this does not exhaust the potential semantic range of *poikilos*. Eleanor Irwin, in her study of poetic uses of χλωρός and χλωρηίς, observes that, 'the neck or throat is only noteworthy as the source of the music the nightingale sings. If one observes a song-bird, one can see the throbbing of the throat as he pours forth his song' (1974: 72–3), and she thus proposes translating the nightingale's χλωρηίς as 'throbbing' or 'trembling'.[90] In other words, what is visually distinctive about the nightingale's body is the particular kinetic quality of its throat that occurs concomitant with its production of sound.

Having established this connection between movement and the epithet χλωρηίς, Irwin further suggests that the term denotes an appearance akin to that which she observes in Pindar's use of ὑγρός to characterise the back of Zeus' eagle (*Pyth.* 1.9). Both, she argues, are suggestive of a visible 'fluid continuity' (74) that consists in the apparition of rapid movement beneath a smooth surface.[91] It is in this context that ποικιλόδειρος gains clearer signification: as the visible articulation of movement in the nightingale's throat that appears in tandem with the sonorous movements of its song. For this reason, I offer instead a translation of 'undulating throat' for ποικιλόδειρος (as distinct from the 'throbbing' or 'trembling' conveyed by χλωρηίς), for this communicates both the movements of its voice and the frequent 'turning' or 'twisting' that becomes visibly apparent in the bird's throat.

The audiovisual phenomena discussed so far in this chapter thus have something

---

[89] Democritus B 154 DK is explicit about the paradigmatic function of birdsong when he says that it is by imitating the nightingale and swan that humans create song (καὶ τῶν λιγυρῶν, κύκνου καὶ ἀηδόνος, ἐν ᾠδῆι κατὰ μίμησιν); cf. Bacchylides' allusion to the 'honey-voiced Cean nightingale' (καὶ μελιγλώσσου τις ὑμνήσει χάριν / Κηΐας ἀηδόνος, 3. 97–8). cf. Nagy 1996: 39–41 and Steiner 2007: 180.

[90] Irwin 1974 remains the most comprehensive and authoritative source on colour terminology in Greek poetry, and see especially pp. 68–75 for a summary of the different ways that scholars, ancient and modern, have tried to understand the relationship between χλωρηίς and the nightingale. See more recently Clarke 2004 for a somewhat different interpretation of χλωρός that explains the word's wide semantic range as a reflection of a 'prototypical concept' that encompasses multiple experiential characteristics of the phenomena described with this word. On this view, greenness of hue is only one of the qualities that χλωρός can denote, which explains its application to objects and beings that do not exhibit this colour.

[91] See Arist. [*Col.*] 793b9–12, where plumage is cited along with water and clouds as a material that manifests different shades in different lights because of the 'smoothness' (λειότητα) of their texture: ὥσπερ τὸ ὕδωρ καὶ τὰ νέφη καὶ τὰ πτερώματα τῶν ὀρνίθων· καὶ γὰρ ταῦτα διά τε τὴν λειότητα καὶ τὰς προσπιπτούσας αὐγάς, ἄλλοτε ἄλλως κεραννυμένας, ποιεῖ διαφόρους τὰς χρόας. Thus, feathers provided a particularly viable surface in which to observe movement and change.

significant in common with certain types of animals named with the same adjective. This is so because, in these instances, *poikilia* describes a particular aspect that arises from both the texture and movements of these creatures in order to signify both physical and kinetic dimensions. For instance, the adjective appears as an epithet of live snakes (e.g. Pind. *Pyth.* 10.46, 4.249; Thgn. 1.602; Eur. *Heracl.* 376, *IT* 1245) as well as worms (Alc. fr. 93.1), and in these contexts it captures the convergence between the animal's fluid movement and the iridescence of its skin. And as Aristotle observed of feathers as well as water and clouds, the apparition of a continuous variation in colour arises because of the smoothness of each medium.[92] Thus the word's dual application to plumage and scales is suggestive of the way that the fluttering or undulation of each animal enhances the appearance of variegation in each, a convergence that is captured in the epithet Hesiod uses to describe the nightingale.

With this in mind, we can gain a better understanding of the 'whirling' dynamics portrayed in *Olympian* 4: 'The Horae, whirling to the song of the <u>scintillating</u> lyre, sent me as a witness to the most lofty contests' (ὦραι ὑπὸ <u>ποικιλοφόρμιγγός</u> ἀοιδᾶς ἑλισσόμεναί μ' ἔπεμψαν / ὑψηλοτάτων μάρτυρ' ἀέθλων, 2–3). Here the *poikilia* of the lyre effects a whirling of the Horae that in turn propels the speaker as a 'witness' to the athletic competitions. Whereas in *Olympian* 3 it was the voice of the lyre that exhibited *poikilia*, the fact that here the instrument itself bears this attribute suggests that *poikilia* assumes a material form as well as an audible one. This is reflected in the variety of ways that the compound can be understood: whether 'lyre of embroidered notes' or 'of varying tones'. Where the latter emphasises an auditory aspect, the former draws attention to the overlap between craftsmanship and music effected in this compound. And by exhibiting specifically the 'whirling' motion denoted by ἑλισσόμεναί, the Horae's dynamism thus corresponds to the kind of swift, fluid movement visible in *poikilia*'s application to birds and serpents. In relating this sense of whirling to his compulsion to praise, Pindar identifies how song can be both animated (by virtue of the sonic complexities afforded by the lyre) and animat*ing* in its capacity to set the Horae, poet and lyre 'whirling'.

I conclude with these examples because in their visualisations of whirling or undulating sounds, they reify the protean shape of lyric *poikilia* that we have been tracing throughout this chapter. The kind of 'scaffolding' *poikilia* creates turns out to be rather more fluid than Clark's account envisaged, but meaningfully so. Rather

---

[92] Incidentally, 'smoothness' (λειότης) is one of the qualities that Dionysius of Halicarnassus identifies in Sappho 1 as a contributing factor in the pleasure (*charis*) these verses afford (ταύτης τῆς λέξεως ἡ εὐέπεια καὶ ἡ χάρις ἐν τῇ συνεχείᾳ καὶ λειότητι γέγονε τῶν ἁρμονιῶν, *Comp.* 23), an observation that conforms with the continuity between the material and sonic textures of the nightingale's song that I propose here.

than seeking unity in this term's significance, I have sought to press its complexity of meaning in order to illuminate the different kinds of imaginative work it asks of its interlocutors. In the first section, we saw a correspondence between the shiftiness of the term's meaning and the scintillating materials it describes in a form of perceptual mimesis that in turn enacted the glamorous, elusive allure of the figures depicted in Sappho, Alcman and Anacreon. In the second section, I argued that Pindar employs this terminology in describing song for the similar purpose of inciting a bidirectional mode of perception, in which both the phenomenon described and the process of envisioning it were made vivid (thanks to the poet's craftsmanship in generating such imagery). The final section and its exploration of the shimmering quality of sound has returned us to the observation from which we began, namely the prominence of *poikilia* as a figure within lyric as well as a way to characterise lyric as a genre. By treating the word family as a kind of vital material in its own right, the complexities of lyric figurations of *poikilia* have been brought into sharper focus.[93]

---

[93] This chapter's interest in the vitality of *poikilia* as a literary concept has thus drawn inspiration from the injunction of Felski 2011 to consider texts as 'nonhuman actors' that are not reducible solely to the particular sociopolitical circumstances in which they were produced.

5   *Mētis* and the Mechanics of the Mind

THE MATERIALS UNDER discussion in this chapter are decidedly more mundane than those focused on in previous chapters, featuring twigs and leaves and animal fat rather than precious metals and fabrics. The everyday character of these materials, however, will prove a crucial feature of these objects' significance.[1] For in examining the relationship between *poikilia* and the specific brand of cunning termed *mētis*, 'cunning intelligence', we will find therein a special relationship between this form of cognition and ordinary objects, including the most familiar material of all: the human body.

Like the shimmering aspect of birds' plumage and song discussed at the end of the last chapter, the cast of characters featured in this chapter can exhibit *poikilia* in multiple modalities simultaneously. In this respect, Theognis' description of the octopus will prove paradigmatic for the readings offered here:[2]

> θυμέ, φίλους κατὰ πάντας ἐπίστρεφε ποικίλον ἦθος,
>   ὀργὴν συμμίσγων ἥντιν' ἕκαστος ἔχει.
> πουλύπου ὀργὴν ἴσχε πολυπλόκου, ὃς ποτὶ πέτρῃ,
>   τῇ προσομιλήσῃ, τοῖος ἰδεῖν ἐφάνη.
> νῦν μὲν τῇδ' ἐφέπου, τότε δ' ἀλλοῖος χρόα γίνου.
>   κρέσσων τοι σοφίη γίνεται ἀτροπίης.

---

[1] See also Miller 2010 and Harvey et al. 2013 for a variety of studies on the agency and vitality of 'everyday' objects and technologies.

[2] See too, on the relevance of this passage for archaic sympotic poetry and art, the now-classic discussion of Neer 2002: 14–18, who notes that 'the cuttlefish's transformation is, in theory at least, a complete identification with the environment' (17). For him, the *poikilia* of this passage is one of the defining terms of archaic sympotic aesthetics.

My spirit, turn out an <u>adaptable</u> disposition to match with all your friends, combining together in whatever mood each one has. Maintain the temperament of the
crafty octopus, which clings to a rock and takes on its appearance. Now follow
along in this way, at another time take on a different complexion. Cleverness is in
truth greater than rigidity (I. 213–18)

Here, Theognis draws on the frequent association of *poikilia* with colourful appearances in order to visualise the 'disposition', *ēthos*, as a visible, physical entity that can
be 'turned out' (ἐπίστρεφε) at will.[3] The analogy with the octopus, which physically
changes its colour in order to blend in with its surroundings (ὃς ποτὶ πέτρῃ, / τῇ
προσομιλήσῃ), emphasises the superficial character of the *ēthos*, which likewise
will consist in adopting 'a different complexion' (ἀλλοῖος χρόα γίνου) according to
whichever 'mood' it seeks to 'combine together with' (ὀργὴν συμμίσγων). Further,
that the octopus does so specifically by 'clinging to' (προσομιλήσῃ) a rock indicates
that its capacity for blending in depends upon its ability to cunningly engage with
its environment. The tactilic component of the octopus' blending thus makes it
clear that Theognis has in mind a process remarkably in tune with Empedocles'
description of the way painters create their lifelike images. This consists in artists
'seizing pigments of many colours with their hands' (μάρψωσι πολύχροα φάρμακα
χερσίν, DK B 23.3) in order to mix them in due proportion (ἁρμονίῃ μείξαντε, DK
B 23.4) and create 'forms resembling all things' (ἐκ τῶν εἴδεα πᾶσιν ἀλίγκια, DK B
23.5), a process that is itself described in terms of *poikilia* (ποικίλλωσιν, DK B 23.1).
This parallelism between the *poikilia* of the *ēthos* and that of painting highlights
what is only implicit in Theognis' characterisation of the *poikilon ēthos*: namely, that
one's comportment is as flexible and fluid as paint, since the former can also produce
incalculably many different forms at will.

But unlike the *poikilia* of textiles or paintings, which can contain many colours
within a single surface, the *poikilia* of the *ēthos* consists in the individual's capacity to
assume single 'colours' at different times (νῦν μὲν . . . τότε δ') in whatever environment in which it is immersed. Given that its defining characteristic is the ability to
change over time, the *poikilia* of the *ēthos* is thus revealed to be even more dynamic
than a multicoloured material. Moreover, Theognis' advice – by assimilating human
demeanour to the octopus's appearance and its ability to physically blend in with its
surroundings – presupposes a seamless integration between body, mind and world
that will be operative throughout the examples discussed in this chapter.

---

[3] I use 'Theognis' to refer simply to the Theognidean speaker or 'I' and in so doing am not
making claims about the historical figure of Theognis and his identification (or not) with
the 'I' within these poems.

In the Theognis example, *poikilia* is equated not only with the variegated, shifting appearances we have seen in previous examples, but more specifically with the conscious manipulation of those appearances. The octopus provides the ideal visualisation of this idea because of the ease and exactitude with which it alters itself. In this respect, the octopus is aligned with a creature like the fox, whose quality of *poikilia* is more specifically cast as a form of 'cleverness'. For instance, Alcaeus compares a political figure's attempt at prediction to the cunning of a fox (ὁ δ' ὡς ἀλώπα [/ ποικ[ι]λόφρων εὐμάρεα προλέξα[ις / ἤλπ[ε]το λάσην, fr. 69.6–8LP).[4] And Alcaeus' characterisation pinpoints a facility common to three figures who share the epithet of *poikilomētis*: the ability not only to forecast the thoughts and actions of others, but also to adapt accordingly. More precisely, the characters we will meet in this chapter and the next are exceptionally fluent at creating, reading and manipulating the kinds of relationships between people and objects that I have drawn out in previous chapters.[5]

The particular sort of intelligence that excels at this kind of manipulation falls within the lexical sphere of *mētis*, 'cunning intelligence', and one of its epithets, *poikilomētis*, 'of cunning mind'. The terrain of this epithet is dominated by three male figures: Prometheus, Odysseus and Hermes. Like the other adjectives that also characterise *mētis* (e.g. *poly-*, *aiolo-*), *poikil/* refers to the multiplicity and versatility that define *mētis*. Each of the figures named with this epithet, as we will see, are like Theognis' octopus in that they are able to assume different forms and dispositions to achieve their own ends. Detienne and Vernant (1978) have already illuminated a great deal about the semantic and conceptual range covered by *mētis*'s instantiations across Greek literature. While they have drawn attention to how *poikilia* signifies the shifting, multiple nature of *mētis*, my goal is to complement and expand their study by illuminating the precise and idiosyncratic ways in which *mētis* and its quality of *poikilia* were thought to extend into the physical world. I will demonstrate that the *poikilia* of *mētis* (and of cunning and deception more generally) has a decidedly concrete basis. For what we will find in this chapter is that the figures who rely on *mētis* consistently enact and extend this mode of thinking into their material environs, like Theognis' octopus in its 'clinging to a rock' (ποτὶ πέτρῃ, 215). In short, these portrayals of *mētis* suggest that this faculty could not exist as such without the presence and support of things outside the brain.[6]

---

[4] Similarly, in the fable of the fox and leopard, Aesop equates the fox's proverbial cunning with *poikilia*: 'How much greater is the beauty that belongs to me, since it is not something I have in my body, but is in my <u>cunningly wrought</u> spirit' (πόσον ἐγὼ καλλίων ὑπάρχω, ἥτις οὐ τὸ σῶμα, τὴν δὲ ψυχὴν πεποικιλμένην ἔχω, *Fable* 12 (Hausrath and Hunger 1970)).

[5] cf. Minchin 2019, who focuses specifically on Odysseus' mastery of emotional intelligence.

[6] This is a conclusion hinted at by Detienne and Vernant 1978: 20 in characterising *mētis* as an intelligence that 'must adapt itself constantly to events as they succeed each other and be pliable enough to accommodate the unexpected so as to implement the plan in mind more

Prometheus, Hermes and Odysseus excel at developing and exploiting the kinds of material props and scaffolding that Andy Clark and Lambros Malafouris have discussed in their respective studies of extended cognition and material engagement. Accordingly, I propose to put these figures alongside those like Otto and his notebook and prehistoric man with his stone knapping.[7] For as we will see, the purveyors of the *poikilomētis* epithet are adept at 'supersizing' the mind (to use Clark's 2008 term) and do so in order to achieve very specific (albeit morally ambiguous) ends: disguising, stealing and hoodwinking.[8] As Detienne and Vernant (1978: 21) have put it, '*Mētis* is itself a power of cunning and deceit. It operates through disguise. In order to dupe its victim it assumes a form which masks, instead of revealing, its true being.' All of the figures dubbed *poikilomētis* are masterful at crafting traps, *doloi*, and the figure of the trap or snare is accordingly what ties together the material of this chapter.[9] This is so because of the literal and figurative levels of entanglement involved in *mētis* and captured in its epithet *poikilomētis*. For not only do *doloi* 'entangle' by deceiving others, they are also profoundly entangled with their makers.[10]

successfully. It is thus that the helmsman pits his cunning against the wind so as to bring the ship safely to harbor despite it.' See also their discussion of Athena's brand of *mētis* (1978: 215–58) and its decidedly practical applications.

[7] On Otto and his notebook see Clark 2008: 230: 'Otto's internal processes and his notebook constitute a single cognitive system . . . for Otto, notebook entries play just the sort of role that beliefs play in guiding most people's lives'. On knapping, see the summary of Malafouris 2013: 19, which contends that knapping (the process of flaking stone off of a core) is 'an *act of thought* – that is, a cognitive process that criss-crosses the boundaries of skin and skull, since its effective implementation involves elements that extend beyond the purely "mental" or "neural"' (emphasis in original).

[8] Pratt 1993 remains, to my knowledge, the only full-length study devoted to lying and deception in archaic and classical Greek thought.

[9] cf. Detienne and Vernant 1978: 299, who likewise recognise in the image of a net the confluence between *mētis* and its material expressions: 'If the shifting net is the most perfect of images for *mētis*, the combination of the circle and the bond also appears in a whole series of actions and objects of an equally technical nature which are both the products and the instruments of the intelligence of cunning.'

[10] See also the provocative recent study on the anthropological significance of traps and entrapment by Corsín Jiménez and Nahum-Claudel 2019, who draw attention to how 'traps are bridges between meaning and materiality, human and thing, predator and prey, technology and ecology, ontology and epistemology. Traps assemble bodies, knowledge practices, materials and environments in transformative encounters and consequential infrastructures' (384–5). Their summation is also remarkably in tune with the comments of Detienne and Vernant 1978: 294–5 on the significance of the figure of the net to *mētis*: 'the net is a composition of woven or plaited links and its structure marks it out as the epitome of the bond for it is both bound together and, at the same time, its effect is to bind'.

Prometheus is an illustrative example of what I mean by this kind of 'entanglement'. In the first section I examine how the Titan cognitively extends his *mētis* into his *doloi* through his dexterity with material things.[11] While Ian Hodder's (2012) concept of 'entanglement' has surfaced in previous chapters to capture the shifting and heterogeneous mutual dependencies that exist between humans and things, here it comes to the fore because these dependencies become exceptionally clear in the context of ruses and inventions. The second section will then turn to Hermes and Odysseus and their richly inventive forms of *mētis*.[12] Like Prometheus, both of these characters engage adroitly with their material environs, but do so not exclusively in order to craft *doloi*. Instead, their facility with craft enables them to fashion objects that in turn become unique extensions of their identities. But as we will see in the third section's focus on how Hermes and Odysseus exploit speech and body language in attempts to deceive, the recognition of such attempts by their would-be targets is tantamount to a re-cognising of the boundaries between minds, bodies and things. For it is the recognition of the heightened level of entanglement effected in ruses that lays bare the artificial character of deception and its reliance on material media.

Crafting Cognition with Prometheus

In Chapter 3, I discussed the example of material scaffolding most often cited in reference to Clark's extended mind thesis: the notebook Otto uses to remember the address of the Museum of Modern Art, a 'prop' that is as critical to his trip to the museum as Inga's (internal) memory is to hers. While in that chapter the example served to highlight the continuities between Hephaestus' mind and his craftsmanship, the salience of the example to this chapter is what the absence of Otto's notebook would do to his functioning: without it, and the collection of information it stores, he wouldn't be able to find his way to the museum on his own.[13] To put

---

[11] Hodder's summation of entanglement provides a clear framework in which to place the mind–material interactions portrayed in this chapter: 'The distinctive aspect of entanglement derives from the attention given to the term "depend" in the relationships between things and between humans and things' (2012: 112). As Malafouris 2013: 33–4 details, his material engagement theory (and my own approach here) has much in common with Hodder's theory of entanglement, but focuses less on social processes and more on the 'process and making of the human mind' (2013: 34).

[12] On the relationship between Hermes and Odysseus and their respective statuses as trickster figures, see especially Van Nortwick 2009: 83–97. See also Bergren 2008: ch. 8 on how *mētis* links together Odysseus and Penelope.

[13] Clark 2008: 222 subsequently defined this coupling between user and artefact as follows: 'the human organism is linked with an external entity in a two-way interaction . . . if we

it another way, Otto's notebook plays an active role in the construction of Otto's thoughts and so too in his decision-making and actions. The tools and props used and constructed by exemplars of *mētis* play a comparably constitutive role: without them, *mētis*, and its favourite mode of action, deception, couldn't succeed. This in turn will render even more significant Zeus' ultimate punishment of Prometheus: binding the Titan to a rock disables his *mētis* because it makes him unable to engage with anything in his environment. This dependence of *mētis* on material environs, then, represents one strand of the 'entanglement' I discussed above, and this is a concept that can be illuminated more clearly through closer attention to how, specifically, users of *mētis* interact with things.

While Clark focuses on the generation and exploitation of feedback loops between cognitive processes and external media, we have seen that Malafouris pursues a complementary approach by exploring how particular material properties actively shape, enhance and/or constrain thought.[14] This is what he has termed material engagement theory, and which he explores most fully in his 2013 book. However, a more recent publication builds on this work to offer an articulation of this theory that best encapsulates a recurrent trait of *mētis*. Malafouris refers to hand-crafted clay vases as 'mind traps' because of how they 'presuppose the blending of various creative intelligences and agencies (both human and nonhuman)' (2018: 765). And the language of trapping that Malafouris uses here is apt for the kinds of foils and disguises fashioned by Prometheus, Hermes and Odysseus. Further, the 'hylonoetic field' Malafouris identifies in the interactivity between the potter and his clay is what justifies his description of clay vases in this way: 'In this *hylonoetic* field the material properties of clay are also important (maybe as important as the neural properties of the potter's brain)' (ibid., emphasis in original). It is in this spirit that we can best appreciate *mētis*'s particular affinity with fashioning disguises and traps. For all of the figures discussed here do not simply impose their cunning on passive, inert materials, but think through and with things. They are portrayed as engaging in active processes of making not unlike a potter at his wheel.[15] And it is for this reason

remove the external component the system's behavioral competence will drop, just as it would if we removed part of its brain'.

[14] In fact, Chalmers 2019 has recently offered a slightly revised version of the original extended mind thesis that brings it more in line both with Malafouris's material engagement theory and with the enactivist approach championed by Noë 2004: 'A subject's cognitive processes and mental states can be partly constituted by entities that are external to the subject, in virtue of the subject's sensorimotor interaction with these entities' (2019: 15).

[15] Note too the tradition that Prometheus fashioned the first humans out of clay (Apollod. *Bibl.* 1.45.2–3), which further underscores Prometheus' special connection to the kind of extended cognition involved in human craftsmanship.

that the materials exploited in aid of *mētis* function analogously to Otto's notebook (that is, as forms of extended cognition).[16]

While Zeus is the literal, physical embodiment of *mētis* (having swallowed the eponymous goddess), Prometheus is traditionally credited with the introduction of technology to humans through his theft of fire.[17] On this account, Prometheus could be said to be the father of extended intelligence writ large: Prometheus' theft allows for the proliferation of the very things that not only allow for human survival, but guarantee its evolution. While my focus here will be on the accounts of Prometheus' thefts recounted in Hesiod's *Theogony* and the *Works and Days*, the Aeschylean *Prometheus Bound* offers a succinct characterisation of fire's centrality to human intelligence in calling it a 'teacher of every skill and a great resource' (διδάσκαλος τέχνης πάσης βροτοῖς πέφηνε καὶ μέγας πόρος, 110–11; cf. πᾶσαι τέχναι βροτοῖσιν ἐκ Προμηθέως, 506). Given the conceptual proximity of *poikilia* to superlative forms of craftsmanship, *poikilia* thus is poised to characterise Prometheus' intelligence as well as his deceptiveness (ποικίλον and αἰολόμητιν at *Theog.* 511 and ποικιλόβουλος at *Theog.* 521; ποικίλῳ at *PV* 308). And in the same way that Prometheus' cunning offers a template for human craftsmanship, so too will his particular manifestations of *mētis* prove paradigmatic for the lengthier accounts of the operations of *mētis* attributed to Hermes and Odysseus.

Prometheus' theft of fire is possible because of his ability to recognise and then capitalise on the hollowness of the fennel stalk as a means for concealing fire (ἐν κοίλῳ νάρθηκι, *Op.* 50, *Theog.* 567). The same adjective, 'hollow', *koilos*, is also a crucial feature of another well-known *dolos*: the Trojan horse, the product of Odysseus' cunning (κοῖλον δόρυ, *Od.* 8.507; κοῖλον λόχον, *Od.* 8.515 = *Od.* 4.277). In both ruses, an innocuous exterior belies the more salient features concealed within the hollow space: the 'far-seeing gleam of unwearying fire' on the one hand (ἀκαμάτοιο πυρὸς τηλέσκοπον αὐγήν, *Theog.* 566) and the 'best of the Argives' on the other (πάντες ἄριστοι Ἀργείων, *Od.* 8.512–13). In these infamous ruses we thus

---

[16] cf. Malafouris 2018: 764 on the need for theories of 4E cognition to attend more closely to the material manifestations of cognition: 'The challenge for the 4E approach demands reconnecting the brain with the body and beyond, with proper attention to *specific activities and varieties of material practices in specific contexts*' (emphasis added). His point is that the very phrase 'extended cognition' already implies an ontological distinction between (inner) brain and (outer) world, and thus seeks to displace this dichotomy through attention to the interstices between thought and material practices. The passages discussed in this chapter, I suggest, offer a step forward in this regard by portraying the particular ways in which each figure's cunning operates through their distinctive material practices.

[17] For a wide-ranging survey of the history of the Prometheus myth narrated in the *Theogony* and discussion of its relationship to *Works and Days*, see especially West 1966 ad 507–616.

see a reversal of a phenomenon that arises from incredibly lifelike artefacts. Whereas we have seen that such likenesses seem to belie their own materiality, in the cases of the theft of fire and the Trojan horse, each trickster (Prometheus and Odysseus) relies on the apparently innocuous and inert aspects of fennel and wood in order to fashion them into objects that are much more than they appear.[18]

But whereas the Trojan horse was crafted specifically for this purpose, what Prometheus exemplifies with the fennel is a canny ability to identify and engage with material affordances by re-envisioning and repurposing the fennel as a cover for fire.[19] In Prometheus' use of the fennel stalk as a conveyance for fire, he typifies a process Malafouris (2013: 169–77) describes in relation to the practice of stone knapping:

> in this case intention no longer comes before action but is *in the action*; the activity and the intentional state are now inseparable. Thus, the boundary between the mental and the physical collapses. The line between intention and material affordance becomes all the more difficult to draw. (2013: 176, emphasis in original)

In the case of Prometheus, his intention to steal fire is inseparable from his ability to capitalise on the hollow space of the fennel stalk. Prometheus' *mētis* thus finds realisation in the merging of the mental and material that allows his ruse to take form and succeed.

While the endowment of humanity with fire allows human life and craft to flourish, the innovative ways in which Prometheus deploys new materials (like the fennel stalk and the animal fat discussed below) is also a template for the relationship between human craftsmanship and the props and tools that allow craftsmen to work and, in so doing, to craft ever more sophisticated objects. Or, on the more pessimistic view offered in the *Works and Days*, fire is an essential component of the dreary, unending labour that defines human life (κρύψαντες γὰρ ἔχουσι θεοὶ βίον ἀνθρώποισιν, 42). And Pandora, as we saw in Chapter 3, is a central player in this misery.[20] That Zeus makes explicit that Pandora is the price humanity has to pay for fire (καλὸν κακὸν ἀντ' ἀγαθοῖο, *Theog.* 585; ἀντὶ πυρὸς δώσω κακόν, *Op.* 57)

---

[18] Interestingly, Plutarch explicitly locates a peculiar vitality in fire itself in saying that 'For there is nothing more like an ensouled being than fire' (οὐδὲν γὰρ ἄλλο μᾶλλον ἐμψύχῳ προσέοικεν ἢ πῦρ, *Quaest. conv.* 703a).

[19] On the notion of affordance see Hodder 2012: 49, which derives in part from Gibson 1986's theorisation of affordances, one that Hodder neatly summarises as follows: 'He [Gibson] defined the affordances of an object as its potentialities for a particular set of actions.'

[20] See Mueller 2016b on how the *Theogony* and *Works and Days* present mortality writ large as a form of disease.

establishes an equivalence between the specificities of Prometheus' fennel stalk ruse and the crafting of Pandora. For in the *Works and Days*' account of her creation, Pandora's glittering exterior belies the unsavoury qualities embedded within (ἐν δ' ἄρα οἱ στήθεσσι διάκτορος Ἀργεϊφόντης / ψεύδεά θ' αἱμυλίους τε λόγους καὶ ἐπίκλοπον ἦθος, 77–8), making her an analogue for the *pithos* that accompanies her, which is also a container for evils (*Op.* 94–8).[21] For these reasons, Pandora operates as a living *dolos*, a 'sheer, intractable deception' (δόλον αἰπὺν ἀμήχανον, 83). By crafting Pandora in this way – as a bundle of evils contained within an alluring, highly wrought exterior – Zeus ensures that she will be resistant to the very canniness and cunning that allowed Prometheus to steal fire. In this sense, as I argued in Chapter 3, Pandora is designed to operate in a tightly coupled system with mankind, albeit one that perpetuates evil rather than progress. For if fire aids and abets human livelihood, Pandora is the means by which mankind can 'feel pleasure at heart while embracing its own destruction' (ᾧ κεν ἅπαντες / τέρπωνται κατὰ θυμὸν ἑὸν κακὸν ἀμφαγαπῶντες, 57–8).

What precipitates the exchange of fire and Pandora is another trick of Prometheus': his offering to Zeus of a choice between bones concealed beneath a layer of fat or meat hidden within an ox's stomach.[22] And while we are told that Prometheus merely hides away meat in the ox's stomach (καλύψας γαστρὶ βοείη, *Theog.* 539), the description of the bones and fat highlights the cunning he makes this offering embody: 'But for Zeus Prometheus put out the white bones of the ox, having dressed them up with cunning skill and covering them with shining fat' (τῷ δ' αὖτ' ὀστέα λευκὰ βοὸς δολίη ἐπὶ τέχνη / εὐθετίσας κατέθηκε καλύψας ἀργέτι δημῷ, *Theog.* 540–1). In other words, Prometheus' cunning allows him to find an innovative use for the fat and make it into a functional material.

In so doing, he acts in a way not unlike Hephaestus, who likewise excels at 'overlaying', but with more traditional media for craft: gold and silver (ὡς δ' ὅτε τις χρυσὸν περιχεύεται ἀργύρῳ ἀνὴρ / ἴδρις, ὃν Ἥφαιστος δέδαεν καὶ Παλλὰς Ἀθήνη / τέχνην παντοίην, *Od.* 6.232–4). The context for this image of melding materials is also significant because it appears as an analogy for Athena's beautification of Odysseus (ὡς ἄρα τῷ κατέχευε χάριν κεφαλῇ τε καὶ ὤμοις, *Od.* 6.235). In each instance, Prometheus, Hephaestus and Athena deploy their craftsmanship in order

---

[21] On the significance of Pandora's *pithos* and its relationship to other storage containers in early epic, see especially Canevaro 2018: 245–59, who concludes that 'she [Pandora] is so inextricably linked with her object that in some instances she actually combines with it, becoming all but indistinguishable from its expected contents' (259).

[22] For readings of this episode that situate it within the wider context of ancient Greek conceptualisations of sacrifice, see Stocking 2017.

to artificially enhance a material surface. And the fact that Zeus chooses the portion gleaming with fat testifies to how this shining aspect makes it more appealing, as was Athena's goal in Odysseus' makeover. But in the case of Prometheus, this outcome is all the more remarkable because of the unlikely substance with which he carries out this change. He sees the shining, flexible character of the fat and refashions it to do the work of a more conventional substance like silver or gold or their corollary, *charis*.[23]

When Zeus selects the bones, he is enraged and becomes intent on punishing humanity (κακὰ δ᾽ ὄσσετο θυμῷ / θνητοῖς ἀνθρώποισι, τὰ καὶ τελέεσθαι ἔμελλε, *Theog.* 551–2). In spite of deception being Prometheus' explicit intent (e.g. ἐξαπαφίσκων, *Theog.* 537; δολοφρονέων, 550), the narrative is equally insistent that Zeus was *not* deceived: 'Zeus recognised and was not unaware of the deceit' (Ζεὺς δ᾽ ἄφθιτα μήδεα εἰδὼς / γνῶ ῥ᾽ οὐδ᾽ ἠγνοίησε δόλον, *Theog.* 550–1).[24] Nonetheless, Zeus selects the offering that he knows to be a trap. This is clear from the fact that he is able to see the offering as a product of craftsmanship, *technē*: 'And when he saw the white bones craftily tricked out' (ὡς ἴδεν ὀστέα λευκὰ βοὸς δολίῃ ἐπὶ τέχνῃ, *Theog.* 555). That Zeus is not just aware of the trick (γνῶ ῥ᾽ οὐδ᾽ ἠγνοίησε, *Theog.* 551) but also able to *see* (ἴδεν) Prometheus' *doliē technē* therein indicates a shift in the perception of the sacrifice. What Zeus spies, in short, is the extension of Prometheus' cunning in the deceptive version of sacrifice placed before him.

It is unsurprising that Zeus should be able to do so, given that he is himself called *poikilomētis* by Hera in the *Homeric Hymn to (Delian) Apollo* in her outrage at his production of Athena (322). As we will see later in this chapter, the use of the epithet *poikilomētis* tends to occur precisely when a deception has been uncovered. This makes such instances good illustrations of how this form of intelligence invites a distinctive mode of perceiving and evaluating the world and the objects in it. In the sacrifice episode in particular, Zeus puts his own wiles into action (Ζεὺς δ᾽ ἄφθιτα μήδεα εἰδὼς, 550) by demonstrating his ability to see an object (the deceptive sacrifice) as an agent of Prometheus in its function as a trap. Within a brief time, the 'shining fat' (ἀργέτι δημῷ, 541) of the ox goes from (newly) lifeless organic matter to a craft material (τῷ δ᾽ αὖτ᾽ ὀστέα λευκὰ βοὸς δολίῃ ἐπὶ τέχνῃ / εὐθετίσας κατέθηκε καλύψας ἀργέτι δημῷ, 540–1) and finally, to a trap (γνῶ ῥ᾽ οὐδ᾽ ἠγνοίησε δόλον, 550–1). The description of the sacrifice's construction, which succinctly compresses the language of craft (δολίῃ ἐπὶ τέχνῃ, εὐθετίσας) with the raw materials of the ox

---

[23] On the conceptual link between *charis* and shining, glittering materials like gold see especially MacLachlan 1993: 31–40 and Steiner 2001: 194–8.

[24] For an interpretation of this apparent inconsistency that finds therein evidence of distinctive narratives concerning Prometheus' exchange with Zeus, see Loney 2014.

(ὀστέα λευκὰ, ἀργέτι δημῷ), makes it clear how this construction provides a physical instantiation of Prometheus' *mētis* and its ability to manipulate and repurpose its environs in novel, unexpected ways. And this episode, by so explicitly contrasting Prometheus' and Zeus' interactions with the sacrifice, thus shows how even the most mundane material substance can refract multiple modes of intelligence and perception.

Prometheus' *doloi* are inextricably tangled up with his particular form of *mētis* and are equally entangled with their intended target, Zeus. The relative simplicity of Prometheus' ruses (hiding one thing inside another) belies the complexity of cognitive and bodily engagement they involve.[25] More generally, Prometheus offers a particularly illustrative example of how *mētis* finds extension not just in the *use* of materials, but in the canny manipulation of them. If Prometheus existed as a 'brain in a vat', deprived of his body and material environs, it is unclear that he could still be said to embody *mētis*, given his affinity for the crafting of *doloi* from the items in his immediate environment.[26] In the next sections, however, we will see Hermes and Odysseus exercise their *mētis* both in forms of manual craftsmanship and in their own speech and appearances. For they, too, are possessed of a *doliē technē* like that which Zeus identified in Prometheus' deceptive offering, but this skill is not confined (at least in archaic sources) to *doloi*. Nevertheless, the works crafted by Hermes and Odysseus are no less entangled than the *doloi* of Prometheus, as the inventions of each of these are fundamental to his individual identity.

Mētis, the Mother of Invention

We have seen how Prometheus cannily exploits the affordances of at-hand organic materials in order to effect his ruses. The mutual importance of mind and material in these endeavours emerges as a fundamental component of his *mētis*. The Hermes of the eponymous *Homeric Hymn* (4), however, takes this aptitude a step further

---

[25] The basic schema of Prometheus' ruses with Zeus (i.e. hiding one thing within another) could also be interpreted as an extreme and literal version of the intractability that proponents of object-oriented ontologies (OOO) locate in all things, e.g. Hodder 2012: 208: 'OOO goes for the ontological jugular and thinks of everything as a weird entity withdrawn from access, yet somehow manifest.' See too Brown 2001: 5's articulation of this idea, i.e. 'Things lie beyond the grid of intelligibility', which could describe Prometheus' *doloi* because they are designed precisely in order to be unknowable (by virtue of their hidden contents).

[26] For bibliography relevant to and discussion of the 'brain in a vat' thought experiment (where a brain is isolated from all other parts of the body and world but is still alive and neurologically active), see Clark 2009: 980–1.

by inventing entirely new objects and technologies. The *Homeric Hymn to Hermes* narrates at some length the fantastical creations forged by the god when he is still a baby: the tortoise into a lyre and myrtle and tamarisk into sandals, and sticks into fire-starters (as well as the pan pipes, referred to briefly at 511–12). Hermes, like Prometheus, relies heavily on the at-hand, organic materials in his vicinity, which he then repurposes into craft forms. And while Prometheus dissembled by means of skilful concealment, Hermes' *mētis* extends even more prominently out into the world within his inventions, inventions which in turn reshape the divine hierarchy. For as this *Hymn* relates, Hermes is a newcomer to the Olympian pantheon, and so his initial existence is marked by newness and revelation in the form of such marvellous creations.[27]

Moreover, these creations are bound up with his identity: so inventive and mischievous is the god that, even as a baby, he cannot but help to devise material expressions for his ideas. The main narrative of the hymn places Hermes' mischievousness centre stage by relating his theft of Apollo's cattle and the subsequent face-off between the deities. But this theft, together with Hermes' sacrifice of two of the cattle and the eventual reconciliation between the gods, relies on Hermes' dexterity with material engagement: he invents sandals to conceal his tracks, develops firesticks to roast the cattle meat, and uses the lyre as a peace offering to placate Apollo. If Prometheus' *mētis* couldn't exist without his material ingenuity, so too Hermes' characteristic *mētis* and mischievousness are constituted by his ability to invent new things from the materials available to him.

While Prometheus brings fire wholesale to humans, the *Hymn* celebrates Hermes as the inventor of the technique of kindling fire using two pieces of wood. In this sense, he represents an evolution of sorts from the blaze of fire stolen by Prometheus, as Hermes demonstrates how the skilful adaptation of materials allows for more efficient usage of heat and light:

σὺν δ' ἐφόρει ξύλα πολλά, πυρὸς δ' ἐπεμαίετο τέχνην.
δάφνης ἀγλαὸν ὄζον ἑλὼν ἐπέλεψε σιδήρῳ
ἄρμενον ἐν παλάμῃ, ἄμπνυτο δὲ θερμὸς ἀϋτμή·
Ἑρμῆς τοι πρώτιστα πυρήϊα πῦρ τ' ἀνέδωκε.
πολλὰ δὲ κάγκανα κᾶλα κατουδαίῳ ἐνὶ βόθρῳ
οὖλα λαβὼν ἐπέθηκεν ἐπηετανά· λάμπετο δὲ φλὸξ
τηλόσε φῦσαν ἱεῖσα πυρὸς μέγα δαιομένοιο.

---

[27] See too the discussion by Thomas 2018, who explores how this *Hymn* and its presentation of lyre song provocatively combine lyric genres.

he brought together a great quantity of wood and tried his hand at the craft of fire. He took a beautiful bay branch and trimmed it with a knife, grasped closely in his hand, and the breath of heat blew up. It was Hermes who first imparted the fire-sticks and fire. He took and laid many dry close-grained logs in abundance within a sunken pit, and the flame beamed out far, radiating the blast of the fire as it blazed powerfully. (108–14)

Like Theognis' octopus reaching out to the rock with which it will blend in, Hermes' process here is purposefully tactile, as the verb ἐπιμαίομαι can refer to 'striving' as well as to 'grasp'. The fact that fire is here classed as a *technē* that Hermes 'tries at' (ἐπεμαίετο) also highlights the fact that he is inventing both a new tool and a new process.[28] First, Hermes illustrates a close engagement between thought and material in his work with the wood (cutting, whittling and twirling). This demonstrates how continuous adaptation of the wood leads to further, more sophisticated possibilities that in turn allow for him to generate not just fire, but the particular mode of generating fire using objects he has designed for this purpose, πυρήια.[29] While the description is condensed, the process is nonetheless clear. Hermes selects a particular type of wood (bay), strips and whittles it (ἐπέλεψε σιδήρῳ) so that he is then able to use it to drill into another piece of wood and thus create a breath of fire. The closeness between Hermes' idea and activity is typified in the physical gesture required for this technique, as he has to keep one stick 'grasped closely in his hand' in a phrase that parallels those used for other forms of manual craftsmanship (cf. *Il.* 18.600 of a wheel and *Od.* 5.234 of an axe). Indeed, as Detienne and Vernant (1978: 318 n. 8) observe, the word for hand or palm, *palamē*, is elsewhere used as shorthand to refer to cunning or know-how.[30] Hermes' employment of the fire-sticks here thus provides a clear illustration of the knowledge and manual dexterity that he synthesises even as a baby.

While the economy of this description has led some editors to posit a lacuna between lines 109 and 110, in fact this passage's compression can be read as a reflection of the speed and dexterity with which Hermes devises the technique, which is

---

[28] Vergados 2013 ad 108 notes that this verb communicates how 'Hermes thought of and desired fire, whereupon he immediately created it by grasping the πυρήια.'

[29] cf. Ihde and Malafouris 2019: 206–9 on the prehistoric Acheulean hand-axe and the process of stone knapping that brought it into existence: 'The act of knapping does not simply execute the knapper's intent already formed in the knapper's head before the act but rather *brings forth* the knapper's intention. The flaking intention is constituted, at least partially, by the stone itself . . . Every stroke prepares and carves the platform for the next. Every stroke can also reveal something new about the stone's qualities and affordances' (207–8).

[30] e.g. Thgn. 624, Hdt. VIII.19, Pind. *Ol.* 13.52, Ar. *Vesp.* 645.

itself a testament to the symbiotic union illustrated here between his mind, hands and tools.[31] Further, the fact that a knife (σιδήρῳ, 109) is referred to metonymically in terms of its materiality (iron) emphasises how Hermes' *technē* depends upon the specific material properties of the tools at hand (wood and iron). And while Hermes fashions the fire-sticks himself, equally important to this process is his method of selecting and piling on wood to create the resulting 'blast' of fire (φῦσαν ἱεῖσα πυρὸς μέγα δαιομένοιο).[32] The word used to describe the strength of the fire, φῦσαν, is significant because of its denotation in Homer of Hephaestus' bellows (*Il.* 18.372, 409, 412, 468, 470).[33] Its use here thus underscores Hermes' inventiveness by suggesting how he has succeeded in devising another kind of fire generator with the fire-sticks rather than the bellows.

Hermes' invention of the fire-sticks rehearses and expands upon several aspects of *mētis* that we have seen so far in this chapter. First, although his mind works quickly in generating his ideas, this description nevertheless takes pains to show how his thoughts gradually find realisation in the god's skilful handling of the materials available to him. Second, this exploitation of his material environs testifies to his superlative ability to identify the affordances therein. Hermes, like Prometheus, embodies a particular mode of perceiving the world, one in which he is especially attuned to the potentialities of material and to his own body in manipulating that material. Third, not only do the *Hymn*'s descriptions of Hermes' inventions illustrate a close mind–material engagement, but these passages draw attention to the reciprocal interaction between these domains. In the invention of the fire-sticks, for instance, we saw how the shaping of bay wood with a blade provides the crucial component of the fire-sticks, and how Hermes' handling of this material ('grasping it closely in his hand') allows for the drilling gesture that generates the spark. This portrayal thus highlights how different combinations and interactions between ideas, bodies and things yield new and hitherto unnoticed possibilities.

An even closer mind–body relationship is forged from Hermes' invention of prosthetic 'feet'. When Hermes steals Apollo's cattle, he tries to conceal his guilt by fashioning sandals from foliage that are 'beyond description or imagination' (ἄφραστ' ἠδ' ἀνόητα):

σάνδαλα δ' αὐτίκ' ῥιψὶν ἐπὶ ψαμάθοις ἁλίῃσιν
ἄφραστ' ἠδ' ἀνόητα διέπλεκε, θαυματὰ ἔργα,

---

[31] See Vergados 2013 ad 109–14 on how this description relates the speed of Hermes' work.

[32] I follow the text of West 2003 here in printing φῦσαν rather than the φύζαν favoured in Allen, Halliday and Sikes's 1936 edition.

[33] cf. my earlier discussion of Hephaestus' connection to his bellows at pp. 111–12.

συμμίσγων μυρίκας καὶ μυρσινοειδέας ὄζους.
τῶν τότε συνδήσας νεοθηλέαν ἀγκαλὸν ὥρην
ἀβλαβέως ὑπὸ ποσσὶν ἐδήσατο σάνδαλα κοῦφα
αὐτοῖσιν πετάλοισι, τὰ κύδιμος Ἀργειφόντης
ἔσπασε Πιερίηθεν ὁδοιπορίην ἀλεγύνων,
οἷά τ᾽ ἐπειγόμενος δολιχὴν ὁδόν, αὐτοτροπήσας

At the sands of the seashore he immediately plaited with wickerwork sandals beyond description or imagination, marvellous works, combining tamarisk and myrtle shoots. Then, binding together their fresh growth in an armful, he tied the light sandals securely under his feet, including their foliage, which the glorious slayer of Argus carried away from Pieria in preparing for his travel. Tying together an armful of their fresh growth, he bound the light sandals securely on his feet, foliage and all, which the glorious Argus-slayer had plucked from Pieria as he prepared his journeying, improvising as one does when hastening on a long journey. (79–86, translation adapted from West 2003)

As with the fire-sticks, where Hermes adapted the wood with a blade, here too the god deploys an existing technique, weaving, to fashion the sticks into footwear that he can 'securely' (ἀβλαβέως) attach to his feet. While αὐτοτροπήσας conveys the impression of improvisation, Hermes is nonetheless intentional in his work, since he not only gathered the twigs in advance (ἔσπασε Πιερίηθεν ὁδοιπορίην ἀλεείνων) but also selected specifically those he could combine and plait.[34] The sandals are 'marvellous works' not only because of the unconventional material with which Hermes has crafted them, but because of their efficacy in disguising his tracks. But unlike Prometheus' trick with the fat and the fennel, the sandals themselves are tangential to Hermes' plan: in fact, he ultimately throws them into the river Alpheios (139). Instead, it is the tracks they leave behind that form the linchpin of Hermes' ruse, since these prints belie the materials he improvised with to effect their construction. Not only, then, can Hermes anticipate Apollo's consternation at the sight of the tracks, but he reveals himself to know exactly how the components of his sandals will interact with the earth to leave behind baffling marks.

The 'beyond description or imagination' and 'marvellous' aspect of the sandals attributed to them during their construction finds confirmation in Apollo's reaction to their tracks:

---

[34] On Hermes' intentions with the sandals and their relationship to his divinity see also Cursaru 2012.

ὦ πόποι, ἦ μέγα θαῦμα τόδ᾽ ὀφθαλμοῖσιν ὁρῶμαι·
ἴχνια μὲν τάδε γ᾽ ἐστὶ βοῶν ὀρθοκραιράων,
ἀλλὰ πάλιν τέτραπται ἐς ἀσφοδελὸν λειμῶνα·
βήματα δ᾽ οὔτ᾽ ἀνδρὸς τάδε γίνεται οὔτε γυναικός
οὔτε λύκων πολιῶν οὔτ᾽ ἄρκτων οὔτε λεόντων
οὔτέ τι κενταύρου λασιαύχενος ἔλπομαι εἶναι,
ὅς τις τοῖα πέλωρα βιβᾶι ποσὶ καρπαλίμοισιν.
αἰνὰ μὲν ἔνθεν ὁδοῖο, τὰ δ᾽ αἰνότερ᾽ ἔνθεν ὁδοῖο.

Oh wow, this is truly a wondrous marvel that I'm looking at. These are certainly the tracks of straight-horned cows, but then again, they are facing backwards towards the asphodel meadow. And these, on the other hand, are footprints of neither man nor woman, nor of grey wolves or bears or lions, nor of a shaggy-necked centaur do I expect that they are, whoever makes such monstrous strides with their swift feet. Bizarre stuff on one side of the road, and weirder still on the other! (219–26)

The wondrous character of the sandals thus literally leaves its mark in the form of prints that are as strange as the shoes themselves. They comprise a 'wondrous marvel' (μέγα θαῦμα) that leads Apollo to assume that the maker of the prints must be some fantastical being due to their size and inscrutable shape.[35] Hermes thus (temporarily) conceals his identity in the form of what is 'bizarre' and new (αἰνά). As Apollo tells it later, he relates that the prints looked as though Hermes was not using his feet, but 'walking on slender oak trunks': 'He had some other device and was rubbing such monstrous tracks as if someone were walking on slender oak trunks' (ἀλλ᾽ ἄλλην τινὰ μῆτιν ἔχων διέτριβε κέλευθα / τοῖα πέλωρ᾽ ὡς εἴ τις ἀραιῇσι δρυσὶ βαίνοι, 348–9). In this formulation, Apollo makes explicit the material character of Hermes' *mētis* by equating Hermes' prints with his *mētis*. However, Hermes' attempt proves ultimately unsuccessful. As we will see in the next section, while Hermes exploits his infantile appearance to protest his innocence, Apollo as well as Hermes' own mother recognise that Hermes' carefully crafted attempts to deflect suspicion are in fact tokens of his characteristic wiliness.[36]

While the sandals are conceived specifically with an eye to the perplexity their

---

[35] cf. Vergados 2013 ad 223, who notes that in Apollo's catalogue of animals, 'The poet thus places standard combinations of animals in a sequence leading from humans and common creatures to an imaginary one.'

[36] On Hermes' deceptiveness see also the study by Heiden 2010, who finds in this text an alternative model of truth and truthfulness based on personal relationships and cooperation rather than objective truth.

tracks will evoke, Hermes invents the lyre for his own benefit and pleasure. In the construction of the lyre – the invention that will eventually effect accord between Apollo and Hermes – the swift congruity of thought and action is made explicit as Hermes 'devised his work as quick as his thought': 'And as when a sudden notion passes through the breast of a man who is constantly visited by thoughts, or when sparkling glances spin from someone's eyes, so glorious Hermes made his action as quick as his word' (ἀνέρος ὅν τε θαμειναὶ ἐπιστρωφῶσι μέριμναι, / ἠ᾿ ὅτε δινηθῶσιν ἀπ᾿ ὀφθαλμῶν ἀμαρυγαί, / ὡς ἅμ᾿ ἔπος τε καὶ ἔργον ἐμήδετο κύδιμος Ἑρμῆς, 43–6). But while Hermes devises the idea for the lyre as soon as he spies the tortoise (saying that it will 'sing very beautifully', μάλα καλὸν ἀείδοις, 38), he starts only by hollowing out the animal's shell with a chisel (41–2). It is then that action and word meet as Hermes fashions and adds the stalks, arms, cross-bar, oxhide and finally the strings from sheep's guts (47–51). As Athanassios Vergados (2013) notes of lines 39–51, this description is not technically correct or comprehensive, but what it does is to describe the lyre's composition in a way that would be intelligible to a non-expert audience. In so doing, this description indicates that Hermes consciously planned to fashion the same instrument that would be known to the *Hymn*'s audience.[37] By detailing the construction of the prototypical lyre in this way, the narrator focuses attention on how the instrument came into being from the god's uniquely canny resourcefulness.

While Hermes is swift and improvisatory in his work, the lyre is also emphatically a product of craftsmanship: it is something that Hermes 'constructs' (τεῦξε, 52), doing so with a faculty elsewhere associated with Hephaestus' metallurgy (πραπίδεσσιν ἑῇσι, 49).[38] Thus, like Prometheus with the fat and fennel, Hermes reforms the organic materials around him (tortoise shell, sheep's innards, oxhide, reed stalks) into technical components of a creation infused with his own ingenuity. And the improvisatory construction of the lyre from the materials at hand is matched by the song that he 'rattles off' upon its completion (ἐξ αὐτοσχεδίης, 55). While Hermes is instantly able to coax music from the newly fashioned lyre, when he bequeaths it to Apollo he explains that it will only produce such music from a skilful cooperation between player and instrument.[39] This relationship finds clear expression in Hermes' description of the lyre's playing in terms of 'asking' (ἐξερεείνειν,

---

[37] See Vergados 2013 ad 42, who notes that the description of Hermes' scooping out the tortoise's flesh is 'an image inspired from the construction of the *aulos*'.

[38] See Richardson 2010 and Vergados 2013 ad loc.

[39] See also Peponi 2012: 98–114 for detailed analysis of this *Hymn*'s presentation of Apollo's aesthetic response to Hermes' music, which focuses on the intense and erotic pleasure Hermes' music elicits.

483; 487), which establishes song as what emerges from a reciprocal interaction between player and instrument.[40] Only with 'skill and expertise' (τέχνη καὶ σοφίη) will the lyre sound out pleasingly; with rough or unskilled handling it will produce discordant noise (μετήορά τε θρυλλίζοι, 488). Just as the lyre's construction was successfully executed by Hermes' cunning, its music likewise depends on close and skilful bodily engagement.[41]

This *Hymn*, by detailing at such length the relationship between Hermes' cunning and his manual skilfulness, makes it clear that his inventiveness relies on much more than ideation. Instead, his ploys only achieve realisation because of his attentiveness to existing materials and technologies and a skilful, sensitive engagement with these. And as we will see in the next section, Hermes' interlocutors recognise this facility as a fundamental aspect of his wily character.

Similarly, Odysseus makes the crafting of bespoke objects a part of his identity.[42] While analysis of Odysseus' cunning has tended to focus on his powers of speech and persuasion, he is, as Helen claims, skilled in 'all manner' of 'deceits and wiles' and not just rhetoric alone (εἰδὼς παντοίους τε δόλους καὶ μήδεα πυκνά, *Il.* 3.202). And while the inventiveness of Prometheus and Hermes is undoubtedly enhanced by their divinity, Odysseus too time and again proves himself dexterous with objects.[43] For example, at *Odyssey* 5.241–61, Odysseus builds his own raft from the ground up, chopping down trees on Calypso's island and fashioning a seaworthy vessel with only the tools provided by the nymph.[44] While Calypso furnishes the means by which Odysseus can put his technical expertise to work, Circe also teaches him another medium in which to deploy this skill.[45] *Mētis*'s tendency to bring together minds and

---

[40] cf. Vergados 2013 ad 483: 'The song is conceived of as a process of question-and-answer between the bard and the lyre.'

[41] cf. Heiden 2010: 410, who notes, 'Not the inanimate equipment that meets the eye, Hermes' lyre is a personal agent, feminine in gender, with sensitive feelings of pleasure and aversion.'

[42] This section drew much inspiration from Canevaro 2018: 109–65 on Odysseus' relationships to objects and their centrality to his selfhood. The analysis I offer here is thus intended as a complement to this study by focusing specifically on the relationship between objects, materials and *mētis*.

[43] cf. Canevaro 2018: 143–4: 'As well as creating objects, Odysseus also repurposes them: expressing, exploring, *enacting* his own changing identity by changing the nature of things' (emphasis in original).

[44] cf. on this passage Dougherty 2001: 32–7, who develops a metapoetic reading that finds in Odysseus' construction of the raft a parallel for oral composition.

[45] See also Odysseus' treatment of the Cyclops' olive-wood club at *Od.* 9.325–8 and 382–6, and Canevaro 2018: 146–50's discussion of the Cyclops episode and its implications for Odysseus' identity as one that is uniquely 'object-oriented'.

materials finds succinct expression in the characterisation of a special knot taught to Odysseus by Circe, one that he uses to fasten the gifts of precious clothing given to him by Arete: 'an elaborate (ποικίλος) knot, which queenly Circe had once taught him' (θοῶς δ' ἐπὶ δεσμὸν ἴηλε / ποικίλον, ὅν ποτέ μιν δέδαε φρεσὶ πότνια Κίρκη, 8.447–8). First, knowledge of how to tie the complex knot has come to Odysseus directly 'in his thoughts' (μιν φρεσί), a phrasing that, as Lilah Grace Canevaro has interpreted it, 'suggests something that becomes habitual or dispositional, something making its way into one's mental processes' (2018: 119). Presented in this way, the complexity of the knot and its construction is embedded in Odysseus' memory and so enables him to replicate it 'swiftly', even some time after having learned it. Moreover, it is this connection that allows the knot to be an adequate source of protection and keep his gifts safe even while he sleeps (*Od.* 8.443–5). This is because its physical complexity, its *poikilia*, will prove inscrutable to anyone without the kind of mental map provided to Odysseus by Circe. In this sense, the knot is both material and immaterial, both bodily and mental, as its existence depends on a precise and unique harmony between knowledge, bodily action and material.

Indeed, Odysseus stakes his own identity on this kind of harmony. This is most prominent in the descriptions of his wedding bed, one of the tokens by which he proves his identity to Penelope:[46]

τίς δέ μοι ἄλλοσε θῆκε λέχος; χαλεπὸν δέ κεν εἴη
καὶ μάλ' ἐπισταμένῳ, ὅτε μὴ θεὸς αὐτὸς ἐπελθὼν   (185)
ῥηϊδίως ἐθέλων θείη ἄλλῃ ἐνὶ χώρῃ.
ἀνδρῶν δ' οὔ κέν τις ζωὸς βροτός, οὐδὲ μάλ' ἡβῶν,
ῥεῖα μετοχλίσσειεν, ἐπεὶ μέγα σῆμα τέτυκται
ἐν λέχει ἀσκητῷ· τὸ δ' ἐγὼ κάμον οὐδέ τις ἄλλος.
θάμνος ἔφυ τανύφυλλος ἐλαίης ἕρκεος ἐντός,   (190)
ἀκμηνὸς θαλέθων· πάχετος δ' ἦν ἠΰτε κίων.
τῷ δ' ἐγὼ ἀμφιβαλὼν θάλαμον δέμον, ὄφρ' ἐτέλεσσα,
πυκνῇσιν λιθάδεσσι, καὶ εὖ καθύπερθεν ἔρεψα,

---

[46] On the significance of this bed as a symbol of Odysseus' and Penelope's marriage see the now classic study of Zeitlin 1996: 19–52. More recently, Grethlein 2020, Webb 2018 and Canevaro 2018: 98–107 have developed new readings of Odysseus' bed from a variety of perspectives. While Grethlein favours Alfred Gell's concept of primary and secondary agency for illuminating the relationship between Odysseus and this object, Webb focuses on the ekphrastic character of Odysseus' description and the significance of his emphasis on the process of making the bed and chamber rather than solely on the finished object. For Canevaro, Odysseus' bed can be read in relation to the other objects that link him with different women, especially the raft he constructs to leave Calypso's island.

κολλητὰς δ᾽ ἐπέθηκα θύρας, πυκινῶς ἀραρυίας.
καὶ τότ᾽ ἔπειτ᾽ ἀπέκοψα κόμην τανυφύλλου ἐλαίης,   (195)
κορμὸν δ᾽ ἐκ ῥίζης προταμὼν ἀμφέξεσα χαλκῷ
εὖ καὶ ἐπισταμένως καὶ ἐπὶ στάθμην ἴθυνα,
ἑρμῖν᾽ ἀσκήσας, τέτρηνα δὲ πάντα τερέτρῳ.
ἐκ δὲ τοῦ ἀρχόμενος λέχος ἔξεον, ὄφρ᾽ ἐτέλεσσα,
δαιδάλλων χρυσῷ τε καὶ ἀργύρῳ ἠδ᾽ ἐλέφαντι·   (200)
ἐν δ᾽ ἐτάνυσσ᾽ ἱμάντα βοὸς φοίνικι φαεινόν.
οὕτω τοι τόδε σῆμα πιφαύσκομαι· οὐδέ τι οἶδα,
ἤ μοι ἔτ᾽ ἔμπεδόν ἐστι, γύναι, λέχος, ἦέ τις ἤδη
ἀνδρῶν ἄλλοσε θῆκε, ταμὼν ὕπο πυθμέν᾽ ἐλαίης.

What man has put my bed in another place? But it would be difficult for even a very expert one, unless a god, coming to help in person, were easily to change its position. But there is no mortal man alive, no strong man, who lightly could move the weight elsewhere. There is one particular feature in the bed's construction. I myself, no other man, made it. There was the bole of an olive tree with long leaves growing strongly in the courtyard, and it was thick, like a column. I laid down my chamber around this, and built it, until I finished it, with close-set stones, and roofed it well over, and added the compacted doors, fitting closely together. Then I cut away the foliage of the long-leaved olive, and trimmed the trunk from the roots up, planing it with a brazen adze, well and expertly, and trued it straight to a chalkline, making a bed post of it, and bored all holes with an auger. I began with this and built my bed, until it was finished, and decorated it with gold and silver and ivory. Then I lashed it with thongs of oxhide, dyed bright with purple. There is its character, as I tell you; but I do not know now, dear lady, whether my bed is still fixed in place, or if some man has cut underneath the stump of the olive, and moved it elsewhere. (*Od.* 23.184–204, trans. Lattimore 1967)

Although it is robustly material (hewn of olive wood, inlaid with gold, silver and ivory, and covered in purple oxhide), this description equally emphasises its cognitive characteristics: one would have to be a 'a very expert one' in order to remove it (or else a divinity) to match the skill (εὖ καὶ ἐπισταμένως, 197) with which it was constructed.[47] It is this combination that allows it to be a tangible token of identity,

---

[47] But as Webb 2018 perceptively explores in great detail, Odysseus' description of the bed's construction defies easy reconstruction in the audience's mind: 'The bed is distinguished by the difficulty the reader has in conceiving of it as a finished object and by the need to fill in the gaps and to propose means of articulating the discrete elements mentioned by Odysseus.'

a *sēma*, which, as Froma Zeitlin has characterised it, is 'both object and idea, both artifact and symbol' (1996: 29). And its construction bears hallmarks of the kind of *mētis* seen so far in this chapter: the repurposing and refashioning of the materials at hand to create something unique and uniquely tied to the person who crafted it, as Odysseus emphasises in saying 'I myself and no other man made it' (τὸ δ' ἐγὼ κάμον οὐδέ τις ἄλλος, 189). That Odysseus' description here is precipitated by Penelope's insinuation that the bed had been moved indicates his belief that he, his marriage bed and his marriage are one and the same.[48]

Indeed, the central presence and sturdiness of the tree was what compelled Odysseus to transfigure it into a component and symbol of his marriage (190–1). As Hermes stripped and whittled a stick of bay wood to fashion the fire-sticks, so too does Odysseus spend considerable effort stripping (ἀπέκοψα, 195), smoothing (ἀμφέξεσα, 196) and so reshaping the tree into a functional bedpost (ἐπὶ στάθμην ἴθυνα, / ἑρμῖν' ἀσκήσας, 197–8). And not only does he in this way transform the living tree into a permanent part of his marriage bed, but this is what provides the starting point for the bedroom itself as well as the rest of the bed's construction (ἐκ δὲ τοῦ ἀρχόμενος λέχος ἔξεον, 199). Odysseus' treatment of this tree typifies the kind of mind–material engagement elaborated by Malafouris, where the entanglement between Odysseus' plan (to craft a bed that would be a permanent symbol of his and his marriage's identity), technical expertise and the materiality and vitality of the olive tree together produces a bed that is a physical artefact as well as a steadfast and unique symbol of their marriage.[49] Each of the three – Odysseus' idea, his physical execution of the idea and the tree itself – is indispensable to the construction of the *lechos* and specifically Odysseus' desire to make it an entity 'fixed in place' (ἔμπεδος, 203).[50]

---

[48] cf. Canevaro 2018: 99: 'by the time Odysseus returns it [the bed] has become more than an abstract sign or representation: it embodies his marriage, and its physicality is key'. See also Zeitlin 1996: 42: 'the *sēma* that is *empedon* (i.e. the bed rooted in the earth) emerges as a *sēma empedon* (a valid sign). In these two junctures – the maker with his object, the words with their literal and figurative meanings – the system of reference gains a deeper coherence and closes in upon itself as securely as the chamber that Odysseus "built around the tree trunk".'

[49] cf. Webb 2018: 'The resulting object is a *sēma* of these actions – a visible and tangible trace of those gestures made, much as the *sēma* or tomb of the hero is a trace of the actions of his companions and a mark of his former presence at a particular point in time and space.' On the recurrence of olive wood as Odysseus' preferred medium for objects see Canevaro 2018: 154–5.

[50] cf. Grethlein 2020: 13: 'Through its stability, the bed gives substance to who Odysseus is; it materializes his identity as a husband. Fusing together bed and Odysseus, ἔμπεδος signals a close entanglement of man with thing.'

In contrast to his marriage bed's permanence, the bed that Odysseus fashions for himself in *Odyssey* 5 is born out of desperation and need, but still showcases his resourcefulness. Seeking shelter after his shipwreck, Odysseus spies 'two bushes growing in the same spot' (ἐξ ὁμόθεν πεφυῶτας, 5.477) that grow so closely and thickly together (ὡς ἄρα πυκνοὶ ἀλλήλοισιν ἔφυν ἐπαμοιβαδίς, 5.480–1) that they offer an impenetrable shelter. Odysseus is able to 'see through' the thick growth by recognising that there will be a protected place within. And the centrality of these plants to this temporary dwelling makes this another version of his marriage bed, whose tree-trunk post formed the centre around which the whole bedchamber is constructed. Here, however, the bed consists of the leaves piled beneath the close-growing branches of the bushes:

> ἄφαρ δ᾽ εὐνὴν ἐπαμήσατο χερσὶ φίλῃσιν
> εὐρεῖαν· φύλλων γὰρ ἔην χύσις ἤλιθα πολλή,
> ὅσσον τ᾽ ἠὲ δύω ἠὲ τρεῖς ἄνδρας ἔρυσθαι
> ὥρῃ χειμερίῃ, εἰ καὶ μάλα περ χαλεπαίνοι.   (485)
> τὴν μὲν ἰδὼν γήθησε πολύτλας δῖος Ὀδυσσεύς,
> ἐν δ᾽ ἄρα μέσσῃ λέκτο, χύσιν δ᾽ ἐπεχεύατο φύλλων.
> ὡς δ᾽ ὅτε τις δαλὸν σποδιῇ ἐνέκρυψε μελαίνῃ
> ἀγροῦ ἐπ᾽ ἐσχατιῆς, ᾧ μὴ πάρα γείτονες ἄλλοι,
> σπέρμα πυρὸς σῴζων, ἵνα μή ποθεν ἄλλοθεν αὕοι,   (490)
> ὡς Ὀδυσεὺς φύλλοισι καλύψατο.

And with his own hands Odysseus heaped him a bed to sleep on, making it wide, since there was great store of fallen leaves there, enough for two men to take cover in or even three men in the winter season, even in the very worst kind of weather. Seeing this, long-suffering great Odysseus was happy, and lay down in the middle, and made a pile of leaves over him. As when a man buries a burning log in a black ash heap in a remote place in the country, where none live near as neighbours, and saves the seed of fire, having no other place to get a light from, so Odysseus buried himself in the leaves. (5.482–91)

Odysseus' keen eye for material affordances becomes clear from the fact that he is able to instantly assess the potentialities of this resource in identifying the grove as sufficient for 'two men . . . or even three'. And like Hermes, who saw the tortoise as a potential instrument, Odysseus sees the heap of leaves as a source of warmth and comfort: it makes him glad (τὴν μὲν ἰδὼν γήθησε, 486).[51] That his

---

[51] cf. Mills 1981: 98, who observes that Odysseus, in contrast to Polyphemus, is 'a man who

burrowing into this makeshift bed is compared to a farmer stowing a firebrand in the ashes emphasises not only the straits in which Odysseus has found himself, but more importantly, draws attention to both his and the farmer's shrewd preservation of resources.[52] However, the fact that it is Odysseus who is both the farmer and the firebrand in this simile ('buried himself', καλύψατο) emphasises how Odysseus' situation necessitates that he treat himself as a valuable but perishable material.

If his marriage bed embodies a form of self-preservation as an extension of Odysseus and his marriage, the temporary bed he fashions here is likewise born out of the same aptitude for self-preservation, one that consists in his remarkable ability to create his own unique niche in whatever environment he finds himself in. And this particular example, in its portrayal of Odysseus' covering himself with the leaves, visualises another and equally important aspect of his *mētis* that we will explore in more detail next: his facility for disguising and concealing himself.

Each of the figures discussed so far – Prometheus, Hermes and Odysseus – deploys his *mētis* in ways that are remarkably in tune with the criteria that Clark and Chalmers (1998) use to define cognitive extension: the seamless cohesion between object and user, the personally tailored nature of mind-enhancing tools, and the severe impairment that would be caused by the removal of such props.[53] First, these characters are all fluent and swift with their respective forms of material engagement, drawing on this skill as naturally as Otto pulls out his notebook. Second, each of their creations is personally tailored and idiosyncratic, designed as they are from the materials at hand in order to fulfil highly specific roles. Third, and arguably most importantly, it has become clear that none of these figures could exist as figureheads of *mētis* if they were 'brains in vats' and so deprived of the ability to interact with their environs. For as I have endeavoured to show, these bearers of *mētis* do not just rely on material things as props, but extend this cognitive faculty through the kind of material engagement envisioned by Malafouris.

In the first section of this chapter, I introduced the notion of entanglement as a way to capture the convergences and mutual interactivity between the individuals who possess *mētis*, their productions and the intended targets of their ruses. While this section has focused more closely on the entanglement between the identities of

---

possesses an adaptive *technē*, that is, the ability to see the potential in things and adapt them for a particular need'.

[52] cf. Canevaro 2018: 140: 'But ultimately his craftsmanship and his control over created objects emerge triumphant as he acculturates the natural environment, using his hands to repurpose a pile of leaves into a rudimentary bed.'

[53] For discussion of these criteria in relation to Otto in particular see Clark 2008: 231.

Hermes and Odysseus and their respective creations, next we will turn to the media they rely on more often in order to deceive: speech and the body.

Social Media and the Embodiment(s) of *Poikilomētis*: A Viewing Guide

If *mētis*'s dexterity with material things prompts reconsideration of the boundaries between mind and world, descriptions of how the targets of *mētis*'s machinations detect these ruses can also provide a template for how to literally re-cognise the relations between cognition, bodies and things. For what we will find in this section is that deceptive behaviour becomes apparent as such to an interlocutor from their awareness of the exceptionally close connection between deceptive intentions, speech and body language at work in the attempt to deceive.

As Clark and Malafouris are well aware, neither extended cognition nor material engagement would be possible without the body.[54] And this confluence between the activities of body and mind finds particularly lucid expression in the forms of disguise that are the focus of this section. For if the 'embodied' component of '4E' cognition stresses how the particularities of the human body actively participate in thought, the characters endowed with *mētis* literalise this idea by exploiting the most familiar and at-hand materials available (bodily expressions) as constitutive elements of their ruses.[55]

Prometheus is nothing if not self-conscious about his intelligence. In the *Theogony*, Prometheus' trick with the sacrifice is presented as the reason for Zeus' jealousy over fire, and during this episode we are twice told how Prometheus 'did not forget his deceitful craft' (δολίης δ' οὐ λήθετο τέχνης, 547; οὐκ ἄρα πω δολίης ἐπελήθεο τέχνης, 560). This, combined with the repeated references to Prometheus' avowed intent to deceive (ἐξαπαφίσκων, *Theog.* 537; δολοφρονέων, *Theog.* 550) emphasises how Prometheus' ruse must be actively constructed as he goes along, a self-consciousness

---

[54] The role of the body is clearest in one of Malafouris's favourite examples of material engagement: that of the potter at a wheel. Most recently, he has characterised this interaction as a 'transactive ensemble between the affordances of the potter's body and the affordances of wet spinning clay' (2018: 766), an ensemble that he designates 'thinging': 'the notion of *thinging* suggests that only by looking at this performative transactional environment that permits and constrains movement (bodily and neural) can we ever understand how the potter's intention to act comes to life' (ibid.).

[55] Gesture is the focus of Clark 2007: 176–83, who draws on numerous neuroscientific studies of gesture to conclude that such bodily motions likewise form part of the machinery of extended cognition: 'Neural systems coordinate with, help produce, exploit, and can themselves be entrained by, those special-purpose bodily motions that constitute free gestures' (183).

that is also alluded to by the 'slight smile' that Prometheus emits while inviting Zeus to choose between the offerings (τὸν δ' αὖτε προσέειπε Προμηθεὺς ἀγκυλομήτης, / ἦκ' ἐπιμειδήσας, δολίης δ' οὐ λήθετο τέχνης·, *Theog.* 546–7). This emphasis on Prometheus' attention to his own thoughts well illustrates his heightened awareness of the integration between bodies, minds and things needed for his ruse to work.

Disguise is a favourite weapon of the figures characterised as *poikilomētis*, and it is one that likewise relies upon the kind of cognitive–material integration that has recurred throughout this chapter. The shifting, adaptable nature of *mētis* lends itself naturally to deception because it enables its users to adapt to their environments and conceal themselves within different forms, like the octopus blending with the rock that was so vividly described by Theognis: Odysseus disguises himself as a beggar, Athena assumes the form of a young herdsman in *Odyssey* 13, and Hermes cites his babyish appearance as proof of his innocence in the *Homeric Hymn to Hermes*. While Detienne and Vernant have attributed the propensity of *mētis* to assume disguises to the inherently unstable and changeable nature of this kind of intelligence, an aspect of these portrayals that repays greater attention is the fact that each figure's *mētis* becomes most apparent precisely when it fails. For it is when a disguise is recognised as such that the *mētis* of the individual comes to the fore: Athena, for instance, refers to Odysseus as *poikilomētis* just after he has claimed that he is a refugee from Crete (*Od.* 13.256–86), and Maia addresses Hermes as *poikilomētis* when she observes that he has been out all night (*Hymn. Hom. Merc.* 4.155).[56]

After the baby Hermes' nocturnal theft of Apollo's cattle, his mother Maia 'does not fail to notice' (μητέρα δ' οὐκ ἄρ' ἔληθε θεὰν θεός, 154) her son's trickery, and it is at this point that Hermes begins to rely on disguise more than machinations as his mother asks, 'What are you up to, <u>wily one</u>? Where are you coming back from in this hour of the night, clothed in shamelessness?' (Τίπτε σύ, <u>ποικιλομῆτα</u>, πόθεν τόδε νυκτὸς ἐν ὥρῃ / ἔρχῃ, ἀναιδείην ἐπιειμένε;, 153–5). In this instance, Maia recognises Hermes' *mētis* in the fact that he is not behaving like his (genuine) wily self, but is merely playing the role that is suggested by his physical appearance. The vocative ποικιλομῆτα thus marks Maia's recognition of Hermes' attempt to effect a disguise through his behaviour. For Hermes, his appearance and language are a medium not unlike the sticks and twigs he used in his other schemes, and he proves equally adept at manipulating these.

When Apollo comes upon Hermes playing up his babyhood and pretending to be asleep (239–42), he, like Zeus with Prometheus, 'knew and did not fail to recognise' (γνῶ δ' οὐδ' ἠγνοίησε Διὸς καὶ Λητοῦς υἱός, 243) Hermes as being 'wrapped in deceitful tricks' (παῖδ' ὀλίγον δολίης εἰλυμένον ἐντροπίῃσιν, 245). The narrator

---

[56] cf. Pucci 1977: 83–5.

dwells on Hermes' elaborate efforts to simulate an innocent child (e.g. in the description of his curling up and feigning sleep when Apollo enters the house at 240–1), and this characterisation not only lends a comic element to the confrontation between Hermes and Apollo, but also reveals Hermes' masterful command of his body language and behaviour.[57] However, Apollo is, like Maia, keenly aware (γνῶ δ' οὐδ' ἠγνοίησε, 243) of the affected quality of these gestures. In effect, Hermes attempts here to become a living *dolos*, enfolding himself in an innocuous exterior like those Prometheus used for his theft of fire and the ruse of the sacrificial portion.

In response to Apollo's accusation, Hermes in turn criticises Apollo for speaking to him 'harshly' (τίνα τοῦτον ἀπηνέα μῦθον ἔειπας; 261) and 'inappropriately' (ἀπρεπέως, 272). By making such a claim, he reveals his own mastery of social mores and conventions, and the formal qualities of his speech corroborate this effect. For as Thomas Van Nortwick (1975) has shown, Hermes' defence is not only a highly stylised piece of rhetoric, but paradoxically also aims to reproduce the sound of childish speech with its short sentences and simple syntax.[58]

Moreover, in an attempt to boost his credibility still further, Hermes also adopts a variety of distinctive facial movements:

ὡς ἄρ' ἔφη καὶ πυκνὸν ἀπὸ βλεφάρων ἀμαρύσσων
ὀφρύσι ῥιπτάζεσκεν ὁρώμενος ἔνθα καὶ ἔνθα,
μάκρ' ἀποσυρίζων, ἄλιον τὸν μῦθον ἀκούων

So he spoke, and with much rapid fluttering of his eyes and brow, he fidgeted, looking this way and that, whistling awhile, listening to Apollo's account as an idle one. (278–80)

Rather than perceiving effects like raised eyebrows and darting glances as genuine expressions of emotion, Apollo is aware that these are *affected* gesticulations.[59] Nevertheless, what these lengthy descriptions of Hermes' antics makes clear is how his *mētis* extends to all fronts (the form and content of his speech, his body language and behaviour as well as his material machinations), to the end of cultivating a bewildering array of impressions.

Whereas Apollo, the victim of Hermes' guile, is filled with consternation at

---

[57] cf. Richardson 2010 ad 227–92 and Vergados 2011: 104 n. 12: 'The poet of *Herm.* correlates the god's radiant look with his inventiveness.'

[58] Van Nortwick 1975: 93–5; cf. Richardson 2010 ad loc.

[59] Similarly, Alcinous at *Od.* 11.363–6 suggests that there is a distinctive visual quality of liars such that they can be identified from their appearance alone.

Hermes' ploy, Zeus, who is equally aware of Hermes' guilt, finds great amusement in watching Hermes' *mētis* at work:

ὣς φάτ' ἐπιλλίζων Κυλλήνιος Ἀργειφόντης·
καὶ τὸ σπάργανον εἶχεν ἐπ' ὠλένῃ οὐδ' ἀπέβαλλε.
Ζεὺς δὲ μέγ' ἐξεγέλασσεν ἰδὼν κακομηδέα παῖδα
εὖ καὶ ἐπισταμένως ἀρνεύμενον ἀμφὶ βόεσσιν.

Thus spoke Cyllenian Hermes, the slayer of Argus, winking, and he held his swaddling over his arm and did not cast it away. Zeus gave a great laugh upon seeing the wickedly crafty child well and deftly denying his guilt about the cattle. (387–90)

That Zeus here acts in his capacity as the arbitrator of the crime confirms Hermes' skill at creating a convincing impression of innocence. This is clear from the fact that he judges Hermes' antics as being 'well and deftly' (εὖ καὶ ἐπισταμένως) done. In particular, the adverb ἐπισταμένως suggests that Hermes effects deception as though it were an art form that can therefore be 'knowledgeably' executed, like Odysseus' description of his marriage bed's skilful construction (εὖ καὶ ἐπισταμένως καὶ ἐπὶ στάθμην ἴθυνα, *Od.* 23.197).[60] Moreover, that Zeus takes great pleasure in observing Hermes' deception at work indicates that deceit does not automatically entail a negative response, but that the artistry therein can be a source of pleasure and amusement.[61] Nor is Zeus' gleeful response here an isolated phenomenon: Athena, too, smiles at the convincing quality of Odysseus' speech, as we will see.

In the *Homeric Hymn to Hermes*' depictions of Hermes' speech and body language, it is possible to identify several perceptual characteristics of his *mētis* that bear similarity to the experiences of *poikilia* discussed in previous chapters. First, his *mētis* features prominently in his articulation of superficially apparent qualities (e.g. facial movements, the sound of his speech), analogous to the way in which we have seen that the *poikilia* of artefacts appears as the result of an artisan's manipulation of material surfaces. Second, in the same way that the apparition of *poikilia* reflects the skill of the artisan (one that is often manifested in the lifelike, vivid quality of imagery), so too does Hermes' *mētis* translate into a mastery of the ability to create convincing impressions in body and speech. Thus while we saw in the previous section how Hermes can leave the mark of his *mētis* on his physical environment by

---

[60] cf. Alcinous' praise of Odysseus' storytelling, which he characterises as being done ἐπισταμένως. It is for this reason that he says that Odysseus' words are like the songs of a skilled bard (μῦθον δ' ὡς ὅτ' ἀοιδὸς ἐπισταμένως κατέλεξας, *Od.* 11.368).

[61] cf. Pratt 1993: 67–71, 81–5.

transforming ordinary materials into marvellous inventions, with his own body and speech the god instead seeks to belie this cunning.

But just as even incredibly lifelike images are not genuinely alive, Hermes isn't fooling anyone with his impressions. This is precisely because everyone he encounters is able to perceive his behaviour as an extension of his *mētis* and not as a genuine indication of the innocence deceptively suggested by his appearance. What the epithet *poikilomētis* marks here, I suggest, is the dynamism and fluidity of Hermes' guile, which become apparent in his appearance and speech. His deceit, moreover, triggers a range of responses: Maia worries about the consequences of Hermes' shamelessness (ἀναδείην ἐπιειμένε, 156), Zeus laughs aloud in pleasure, while Apollo smiles softly, secure in his knowledge of Hermes' true nature.[62] That *mētis* is multivalent in its effects on others is an aspect that will be of special relevance in the case of a particularly divisive figure like Odysseus, who is likewise both lauded and condemned in ancient sources.[63]

While there is no question that lies are Odysseus' special bailiwick, it is equally clear that he is a master of disguise, as well. And Antenor's description of Odysseus in *Iliad* 3, where he depicts how Odysseus' speech and appearance interact, suggests that his ability to use the two in combination constitutes an integral part of his *mētis*. For this reason, Detienne and Vernant (1978) cite this passage (*Il.* 3.205–24) as a paradigmatic illustration of Odysseus' cunning. First, Helen identifies Odysseus as someone who 'knows all manner of deceits and clever wiles' (εἰδὼς παντοίους τε δόλους καὶ μήδεα πυκνά, 202), and as an example of this, Antenor recounts how Odysseus' foolish appearance was at odds with the power of his voice and speech:

ἀλλ' ὅτε δὴ πολύμητις ἀναΐξειεν Ὀδυσσεὺς
στάσκεν, ὑπαὶ δὲ ἴδεσκε κατὰ χθονὸς ὄμματα πήξας,
σκῆπτρον δ' οὔτ' ὀπίσω οὔτε προπρηνὲς ἐνώμα,
ἀλλ' ἀστεμφὲς ἔχεσκεν ἀΐδρεϊ φωτὶ ἐοικώς·
φαίης κε ζάκοτόν τέ τιν' ἔμμεναι ἄφρονά τ' αὔτως.

But when wily Odysseus stood up, he would stand there looking down with his eyes fixed on the ground, not moving his staff backwards or forwards, but holding it immobile, looking like such a witless fool that one would have thought him surly and someone entirely lacking in understanding. (216–20)

---

[62] See Pratt 1993: 73 n. 27. On the different significance allotted to smiling and laughter in Homeric poetry see especially Levine 1982, as well as Bungard 2011 on laughter in the *Homeric Hymn to Hermes* in particular.

[63] On the varying appraisals of Odysseus' cunning in post-Homeric literature, see especially Montiglio 2011: 1–19.

On this account, Odysseus' nonverbal gestures (his expression, posture and movements) would all lead a viewer to think he was foolish. But this is to heighten the contrast that emerges when Odysseus does speak, and Antenor is explicit about the effects of this juxtaposition:

ἀλλ' ὅτε ὅπα τε μεγάλην ἐκ στήθεος εἵη
καὶ ἔπεα νιφάδεσσιν ἐοικότα χειμερίῃσιν,
οὐκ ἂν ἔπειτ' Ὀδυσῆΐ γ' ἐρίσσειε βροτὸς ἄλλος·
οὐ τότε γ' ὧδ' Ὀδυσῆος ἀγασσάμεθ' εἶδος ἰδόντες

But when his great voice and words, like wintry snowflakes, came forth from his breast, it is at this time that no other mortal could contend with Odysseus, and then we did not marvel so at the way he looked. (221–4)

Significantly, Antenor does not allude to the contents of Odysseus' speech, but indicates that it was impressive simply in virtue of its formal characteristics: the aural 'greatness' of his voice and the intensity of his words. One way to interpret the snowflake simile is to understand this aspect of his speech as a reference to its dense, rapid quality, and thus as the embodiment of the 'clever wiles' (μήδεα πυκνά) already alluded to by Helen (202).[64] What is most striking, then, about Odysseus' speech is the paradoxical impression created by his doltish visual characteristics on the one hand and the impressive sound of his voice on the other. Analogous to the way in which Hermes' infant appearance belies his guile, so too does Odysseus' *mētis* seem to rely upon a similar manipulation of the expectations of his audience, who are led by his appearance to think that he is a fool. In short, the *mētis* of both Hermes and Odysseus consists, at least in part, in each figure's ability to conceal the fact of his own intelligence at will.

When Maia saw through Hermes' antics and addressed him as *poikilomētis*, so too does Athena use the vocative form of the epithet when Odysseus attempts to deceive her (*Od.* 13.258–86). Book 13 of the *Odyssey* presents a double disguise scene: Athena confronts Odysseus when she is in the guise of a young shepherd, and Odysseus pretends that he is a Cretan exile. When Athena informs Odysseus that he has reached Ithaca, he makes a conscious decision to conceal his identity,

---

[64] As Jonathan Ready 2011 has emphasised, the simile attempts to express an aural quality in terms of a visual idea. He suggests that the fact that snow similes are elsewhere used to describe violence (e.g. falling missiles at *Il.* 12.156–60) and flashing armour (*Il.* 19.357–61) indicates that we should interpret Antenor's simile as showing he views Odysseus' words in the assembly as 'mechanisms of force' (115).

which he achieves by suppressing his true elation at this news: 'But he did not speak the truth, but bit back his speech, always mulling inwardly in his crafty mind' (οὐδ' ὅ γ' ἀληθέα εἶπε, πάλιν δ' ὅ γε λάζετο μῦθον, / αἰεὶ ἐνὶ στήθεσσι νόον πολυκερδέα νωμῶν, 13.254–5). The phrase πάλιν . . . λάζετο, 'he bit back', indicates that Odysseus had been about to reveal his true identity, but his shrewd thinking (πολυκερδέα) prevents him from doing so. The fact that the verb used for 'mulling inwardly' (νωμῶν) can also refer to physical action (e.g. holding a spear at *Il.* 5.594, holding a sceptre at *Il.* 3.218) is suggestive of the way in which, as we have seen, Odysseus' cunning tends to manifest itself physically in the world. But in this instance, the narrator explicitly alludes to a disjunction between Odysseus' instinct (his expression of elation) and his cunning, cunning that in turn he must consciously deploy in order to conceal his true feelings and to produce the dissembling speech (ἔπεα πτερόεντα προσηύδα, 13.253).[65]

The speech that Odysseus offers in response is the first of the 'Cretan lies', a narrative that resurfaces in varying forms in Odysseus' encounter with Eumaeus (*Od.* 14.191–359) and Penelope (*Od.* 19.165–202, 221–48, 262–307, 336–42). In this story, which appears in its most abbreviated form in Odysseus' encounter with Athena, Odysseus claims that he is on the run because of his murder of Idomeneus' son Orsilochus (*Od.* 14.258–70). While Odysseus' Cretan lie allows him to conceal his identity from Eumaeus and even Penelope, Athena, as a goddess and as a divinity endowed with her own *mētis*, is obviously not taken in by his story. Before replying, she 'smiles and strokes him with her hand' (ὣς φάτο, μείδησεν δὲ θεὰ γλαυκῶπις Ἀθήνη, / χειρί τέ μιν κατέρεξε, *Od.* 13.287–8). Like Apollo's grin in response to Hermes' lies, here too Athena's smile conveys her sense of superior wisdom as she recognises the ruse, but also communicates amused affection. The latter is more forcefully expressed in her stroking Odysseus with her hand. This gesture, as Daniel Levine (1982) has shown in his analysis of the smile and stroking hand combination in the *Odyssey*, indicates an affectionate bond.[66] Moreover, that this is the only time

---

[65] Bowie 2013 ad 253–4 draws attention to how the description of Odysseus' change of mind creates a very unusual delay between the direct speech introduction formula (καὶ μιν φωνήσας . . . προσηύδα, 13.253) and the speech itself: 'this sudden breaking off from the expected speech mirrors and graphically conveys Od.'s own sudden change of mind not to speak the truth'.

[66] It is only in the *Odyssey* that characters evince both a smile (μείδησεν) and a caress (χειρί τέ μιν κατέρεξε): the two other examples are (1) Calypso's reaction to Odysseus' suspicion of her motives; and (2) Menelaus to Telemachus after the latter has refused to accept horses as a gift. As Levine 1982: 102 notes, each of these situations depicts 'a stronger character caressing a weak and dependent loved one', and so he sees the gesture as signifier of this kind of bond. Angus Bowie 2013 ad 287–8 offers a somewhat different but compatible

in the *Odyssey* that Athena is said to smile suggests that she does so in this instance precisely because their shared use of *mētis* allows her to take pleasure in witnessing its apparition.

Likewise does Athena's language allude to this bond, for she expresses admiration for Odysseus' skill at lying speech:

κερδαλέος κ' εἴη καὶ ἐπίκλοπος ὅς κε παρέλθοι
ἐν πάντεσσι δόλοισι, καὶ εἰ θεὸς ἀντιάσειε.
σχέτλιε, <u>ποικιλομῆτα</u>, δόλων ἆτ', οὐκ ἄρ' ἔμελλες,
οὐδ' ἐν σῇ περ ἐὼν γαίῃ, λήξειν ἀπατάων,
μύθων τε κλοπίων, οἵ τοι πεδόθεν φίλοι εἰσίν.
ἀλλ' ἄγε, μηκέτι ταῦτα λεγώμεθα, εἰδότες ἄμφω
κέρδε' ἐπεὶ σὺ μέν ἐσσι βροτῶν ὄχ' ἄριστος ἁπάντων
βουλῇ καὶ μύθοισιν, ἐγὼ δ' ἐν πᾶσι θεοῖσι
μήτι τε κλέομαι καὶ κέρδεσιν.

If there is someone who can surpass you, even when it is a god you meet, they must be cunning and knavish in every kind of guile. Bold man, <u>crafty-minded</u>, master of tricks, you will not cease from deception and deceitful words even in your own land, which are so dear to you. But come, let us talk no longer of these things, since we both of us know the cunning arts, with you being the best by far among mortals in counsel and speech, and I being famed for my cunning and craft among all the gods. (*Od.* 13.291–9)

In this speech, Athena, like Zeus in his interaction with Hermes, construes Odysseus' *mētis* as a particular kind of knowledge (εἰδότες ἄμφω, 296) that can therefore be used with greater and lesser degrees of skill. Athena and Odysseus are thus united by being 'the best by far' (ὄχ' ἄριστος, 297) in the realm of *mētis*. And in this context, the choice of the epithet *poikilomētis* (instead of αἰολομῆτις or πολυμῆτις, both of which also characterise Odysseus) takes on greater significance, because it suggests that this quality is part of what makes him such a good liar, together with being 'bold' (σχέτλιε, 293) as well as a 'master of tricks' (δόλων ἆτ', 293). But in spite of Odysseus' pre-eminent skill in cunning, Athena's appraisal of him here is not altogether a positive one. Angus Bowie (2013), for instance, has characterised

interpretation of this gesture: 'this affectionate gesture of smiling and reaching out to touch someone is used in *Od.* when that person has responded to a speech by treating it suspiciously or a bit too seriously'.

Athena's use of the epithet as a 'jesting insult' (ad 293).[67] Thus the precise force of the term as Athena uses it here is as ambiguous as the figure it describes, who can likewise use his *mētis* for good or ill.

Moreover, Athena's use of the epithet is, like Maia's in the *Homeric Hymn to Hermes*, a response to a *failed* attempt at deception. The *poikilia* of Odysseus' *mētis* thus becomes most apparent precisely when it fails to achieve its goal. But given Athena's emphasis on the dexterity with which Odysseus deploys his *mētis*, it becomes clear from this exchange that the corresponding ability to recognise *poikilia* in speech and behaviour is tantamount to being able to see through lies and ruses. This is because to do so is also to recognise a form of artifice at work, one that aims at creating a *realistic* impression, rather than a real (genuine) one. And the importance of this ability – to 'see through' others and be able to respond accordingly – is exactly what Theognis wished to instil in the example discussed at the opening of this chapter.

In this section, we have seen how the application of the epithet *poikilomētis* to Hermes and Odysseus underscores how the most basic elements of communication (speech, body language, physical appearances) can be manipulated in order to deceive. In this sense, these media function just as efficaciously as raw materials like dyes and paints in the kinds of illusory effects they produce, and Hermes and Odysseus exploit them as skilfully as they do the materials and techniques discussed in the second section of this chapter. For this reason, these examples of *mētis* at work provide a vivid illustration of a question that pervades theories of mind: namely, where does the mind end and the world begin? For we have seen in the cases of Hermes and Odysseus in particular that there is no clear-cut division between their devious intentions and the physical dimensions of their cunning, whether the latter consist in gestures or facial expressions or in hand-crafted objects.

However, it is this aspect (namely, that their cunning takes perceptible, physical form) that can also be their undoing. For this means that the *poikilia* of their cunning can be recognised by those who are aware of the permeable boundaries between mind and world that I have argued are fundamental to *mētis*. And it is in this way (i.e. through such re-cognising) that a would-be deceiver can be foiled and become disastrously entangled in their own *dolos*, an outcome that is most famously associated with Prometheus.

---

[67] Bowie 2013 ad 293 also notes the humour generated by Athena's use of an epithet conventionally restricted to the Homeric narrator, 'as if she knows the formulaic system and can make a jest about it'.

Conclusions

As punishment for his trickery, Zeus orders Prometheus to be fastened to a rock with unbreakable chains (δῆσε δ' ἀλυκτοπέδῃσι Προμηθέα ποικιλόβουλον / δεσμοῖς ἀργαλέοισι μέσον διὰ κίον' ἐλάσσας, *Theog.* 521–2). The protean and adaptable character of Prometheus' *poikilia* thus finds its juxtaposition in material that is fixed, immutable and inescapable. In this way, Prometheus' dexterity with material engagement reaches its ultimate end, as he becomes physically unable to escape the confines of the material and apply his cunning to his environment. And this image also provides a fitting way to end this chapter. At the outset, I indicated that the figure of the snare, *dolos*, and its accompanying effect of entanglement would link together the examples discussed here. This is due first and foremost to *mētis*'s penchant for literal entanglement in its ability to craft devices to ensnare their targets. And while Detienne and Vernant's study of *mētis* likewise placed the net or snare centre stage, my aim here has been to tease out the further strands of entanglement involved in *mētis*.

In the first section, I argued that Hesiod's portrayals of Prometheus' ruses depict the Titan's cunning as cognitively extended, specifically in his processes of material engagement. The next section likewise focused on the forms of material engagement associated with Hermes and Odysseus. Here, however, we saw how their creations were not exclusively *doloi*, but instead were objects that were fundamental to each figure's identity. Having established that each figure's epithet of *poikilomētis* reflects how his cunning extends into the material world, the third section turned to another domain closely associated with deception: disguise. I argued that each character's facility with lies and disguises is closely related to his canniness with crafting material things. In the context of deceptive confrontations, speech and body language become akin to the materials used in the construction of physical *doloi*. And it is through the recognition of *mētis*'s superlative ability to integrate body and mind that the deviousness of *mētis* is laid bare.

While the question of where the mind ends and the world begins has surfaced in previous chapters, here it has come to the fore because these examples portray objects and materials actively contributing to the construction of thought. For Hermes, Odysseus and Prometheus, their *mētis* is inextricable from their bodies as well as their material environs.[68] And it is for this reason, I suggest, that *poikilia*

---

[68] Thus Clark 2007: 164's characterisation of the extended cognitive system seems particularly apt to describe the workings of *mētis*, as comprised of 'inextricable tangles of feedback, feed-forward, and feed-around loops: loops that promiscuously criss-cross the boundaries of brain, body, and world'.

appears in the epithet afforded to each of them, since we have seen how this term is consistently associated with precisely the kind of mind–material interactivity that is so fundamental to *mētis*. And the next and final chapter will continue in this vein, focusing on the distinctive ways that women can use forms of *poikilia* to effect ruses and ensnare their targets as surely and inextricably as the chains fastening Prometheus to his rock.

6   The Materiality of Feminine Guile

WE HAVE ALREADY encountered a number of the extraordinary objects that populate Homeric epic, but one of the most powerful of these remains to be discussed: the *kestos himas* of Aphrodite that features in *Iliad* 14.[1] It is this garment that Hera must secure in order to seduce Zeus and so distract him from Poseidon giving aid to the Greeks. I begin with this object because its description equates the garment's material and aesthetic qualities with its profound emotional and cognitive effects. The *kestos himas*, in other words, is explicitly allotted agency.[2] And while this can be explained in terms of the magical powers that it is supposed to possess, the *kestos himas* nonetheless offers a particularly illustrative example of a pattern that will emerge from this chapter. For here we will find women deploying objects as ruses, but by comparison with those of the male figures discussed in the previous chapter, these tricks operate in a remarkably different way. Rather than fashioning at-hand objects and materials as extensions of their cunning, we will find women using precious artefacts because their intimate relationship with them entails that they are able to recognise a peculiar agency already *in* these objects. And this agency consists, as we will see, in the physically captivating quality of these objects, one that

---

[1] This garment has attracted much scholarly attention, both ancient and modern. Plutarch, for instance, discusses it at some length at *Quomodo adul.* 19e–20b, and Heraclitus finds in it an allegory for spring (*Homeric Problems* 39.7–8). Seminal articles devoted to the *kestos himas* include Bonner 1949, Brenk 1977 and Faraone 1990.

[2] On the *kestos himas* as a force of specifically feminine agency, see the rich discussion by Canevaro 2018: 216–22, who explores how this object relates to the other magical things wielded by divinities in early epic. As she summarises it, the *kestos himas* is 'a decorated object entangled with its decorations' (222).

makes them efficacious as traps, *doloi*.[3] Aphrodite's *kestos himas*, with its explicit allotment of powers, thus presents an extreme version of the kind of agency that inheres in the various feminine accoutrements I analyse in this chapter.

Hera and the *Kestos Himas*

On the pretence of needing Aphrodite's help to reconcile Oceanus and Tethys, Hera approaches Aphrodite and asks to be given 'love and desire, with which you subdue all men, mortal and immortal alike' (δὸς νῦν μοι φιλότητα καὶ ἵμερον, ᾧ τε σὺ πάντας / δαμνᾷ ἀθανάτους ἠδὲ θνητοὺς ἀνθρώπους, *Il.* 14.198–9). In response, Aphrodite offers up the *himas*, which she describes as the very embodiment of all things to do with affection:

> Ἦ, καὶ ἀπὸ στήθεσφιν ἐλύσατο κεστὸν ἱμάντα
> <u>ποικίλον</u>, ἔνθα δέ οἱ θελκτήρια πάντα τέτυκτο·
> ἔνθ' ἔνι μὲν φιλότης, ἐν δ' ἵμερος, ἐν δ' ὀαριστὺς
> πάρφασις, ἥ τ' ἔκλεψε νόον πύκα περ φρονεόντων.
> τόν ῥά οἱ ἔμβαλε χερσὶν ἔπος τ' ἔφατ' ἔκ τ' ὀνόμαζε·
> τῇ νῦν τοῦτον ἱμάντα τεῷ ἐγκάτθεο κόλπῳ
> <u>ποικίλον</u>, ᾧ ἔνι πάντα τετεύχαται· οὐδέ σέ φημι
> ἄπρηκτόν γε νέεσθαι, ὅ τι φρεσὶ σῇσι μενοινᾷς

> She spoke, and loosened the embroidered, <u>elaborate</u> belt from her chest, and there was wrought in it every kind of charm. In it was love, desire and allurement, which steals over the minds even of the wise. She put this in her hands and addressed her: 'Now place this <u>finely crafted</u> belt in your bosom, in which all things are wrought. I tell you that you will not come back unfulfilled as to whatever it is you so deeply desire.' (*Il.* 14.215–21)

This description immediately raises questions about the material dimensions of the *himas*. Aphrodite loosens it 'from her chest' but instructs Hera to place it 'in' or 'on' her 'lap' or 'bosom', although *kolpos* could equally refer to a fold in her garment as well as to a particular spot on her body. Nevertheless, the question remains as to what sort of garment this description means to portray. *Himas* is used elsewhere in Homer to refer to a chin-strap of a helmet (*Il.* 3.371, 3.375) or to any kind of leather

---

[3] In this sense, these objects represent particularly efficient versions of Gell's 'mind traps', where in the presence of an elaborately patterned surface 'we are drawn into the pattern and held inside it, impaled, as it were, on its bristling hooks and spines' (1998: 80).

strap (*Il.* 5.727, 22.397), so its placement around Aphrodite's chest suggests a saltire of the type for which there are Near Eastern comparanda.[4] While such interpretations focus on the meaning of *himas*, the term *kestos* has also elicited comment. One of the scholiasts on this passage, for instance, asserts that *kestos* is attributed to the belt specifically because of the fact that it is also described as *poikilos*.[5] H. A. Shapiro (1993) has interpreted this remark literally, proposing that the belt contained sewn (πεποικίλθαι) depictions of personifications of Love, Desire and Allurement. Thus while the *kestos himas* is emphatically material – passing as it does between the goddesses and occupying different places on each of their bodies – its physical character is decidedly fluid, not unlike that of the aegis discussed in Chapter 2.[6]

There is another way in which the *kestos himas* has an element of unreality and that is in the extraordinary powers attributed to it. For one, it contains 'every kind of charm' (ἔνθα δέ οἱ θελκτήρια πάντα τέτυκτο). Like Achilles' shield, then, the *kestos himas* contains a superfluity of things that are putatively impossible for a 'real' object. Moreover, embedded within it are 'love, desire and allurement' that are supposed to guarantee a particular cognitive impact: the *himas* will 'steal over' the mind of even a prudent person.[7] This qualification, 'even the mind of a prudent person', emphasises how the power of the *himas* exceeds any rational, intellectual faculty, even the sort of cunning explored in the previous chapter. That the garment literally embodies desire and allure and the like is signalled by the repetition of ἐνὶ . . . ἐν . . . ἐν (a repetition that also occurs in the description of the images in Achilles' shield), indicating that these feelings do not just exist outside the garment (i.e. as responses elicited *by* it), but inhere within it, whether as images (as in the shield) or as love charms.[8] The designation of the garment in terms of *poikilia* thus can be interpreted as a reference to the aspect of the garment's elaborate decoration as well as to the myriad effects generated *by* this quality (e.g. as in the English 'enchanting' or 'tantalising'). In this sense, the materiality of the *himas* provides a logic for the stupefying effects of desire that can afflict even the king of the gods. For its defining quality, *poikilia*, is like the *poikilia* of *poikilomētis* in that it marks the entangled quality of the *kestos*: it is both

---

[4] On the Near Eastern parallels for such a garment see especially Bonner 1949, Faraone 1990 and Janko 1992.

[5] 'The word for the *himas* is not *kestos*, but it is included because the garment is decorated' (οὐκ ἔστιν ὄνομα τοῦ ἱμάντος ὁ κεστός, ἀλλ' ἐπίθετον διὰ τὸ πεποικίλθαι, Scholia T ad Σ 214b, Erbse 1969: III.608).

[6] See especially Brouillet and Carastro 2018 on the agency and materiality afforded to the aegis and *kestos himas*, as well as Canevaro 2018: 206–17 on the similarities between these objects and their comparable roles in negotiating power relations among the Olympians.

[7] On the magical properties of this garment see especially Faraone 1990 and 1999: 97–110.

[8] On the significance of this repetition see also Canevaro 2018: 215–16.

material and cognitive, enacting the will of whoever wears it and generating love and desire from its target.

The characterisation of this garment in terms of its craftsmanship (as both 'embroidered' and 'finely crafted') further heightens the sense of agency belonging to the garment. For these qualifiers convey how it has been consciously and carefully constructed for a specific purpose and so is able to *act on* living beings. This is especially clear from the fact that it is said to contain *himeros*, desire, since this indicates that the *himas* will incite desire *in* Zeus (rather than in its wearer). Conversely, Aphrodite guarantees that the garment will fulfil 'whatever' Hera desires (οὐδέ σέ φημι / ἄπρηκτόν γε νέεσθαι, ὅ τι φρεσὶ σῇσι μενοινᾷς, 220–1). This is significant not only because Hera is borrowing it for a different purpose from the one she told Aphrodite, but also because Aphrodite stipulates that, even though it is her trademark garment, it will nonetheless act as an agent of the person wielding it.[9] Based on this description, multiple forms of agency appear to be distributed within the *kestos himas*: Aphrodite, as the owner of the garment and the patron goddess of the garment's effects; the various charms that give the garment its efficacy; the desires of the garment's wearer in the *kestos himas*'s capacity to accomplish 'whatever' that person wishes; and finally, the desire elicited by the target of the *kestos himas*'s charms.

Nor is Aphrodite's promise an empty one. When Zeus is confronted with the sight of his wife, the power of the *himas* is immediately confirmed, 'And when he saw her, thus did desire cloud over his shrewd wits' (ὡς δ' ἴδεν, ὡς μιν ἔρως πυκινὰς φρένας ἀμφεκάλυψεν, 14.294). While Aphrodite assured Hera that the *himas* would 'steal' the mind of its target, the sexual desire it elicits is here styled more as a kind of 'enshrouding' or 'clouding over' (ἀμφεκάλυψεν). This verb, with its associations with physical covering or veiling, is thus qualitatively similar to several of the ruses discussed in the previous chapter, where *mētis* found expression in the ability to craft material surfaces that conceal something within. Moreover, this formulation, with 'shrewd wits' (πυκινὰς φρένας) as the object of 'cloud over', reminds us that shrewdness itself is not infrequently conceptualised in terms of its density or thickness in archaic and classical thought. Helen describes Odysseus, for instance, as one who 'knows all manner of deceits and clever wiles (*mēdea pukna*)' (εἰδὼς παντοίους τε δόλους καὶ μήδεα πυκνά, *Il.* 3.202). And as promised in Aphrodite's characterisation of the *kestos himas*'s powers (its power to 'steal over the minds even of the wise', ἥ τ' ἔκλεψε νόον πύκα περ φρονεόντων, *Il.* 14.218), in this portrayal of its effects Zeus' 'shrewd wits' (πυκινὰς φρένας) are the target of desire.[10] By visualising

---

[9] cf. Canevaro 2018: 218, who discusses how the *kestos himas* is 'intrinsically linked' with Aphrodite.

[10] See also Walsh 1984 on the similar enchanting effect associated with song and music in

both desire and Zeus' intellectual acuity in similarly 'dense' or 'thick' spatial and material terms (with the 'clouding over' and 'pouring over' of desire), the mentally disconcerting effect of *eros* finds vivid and tangible expression as a force to rival Zeus' shrewdness.

Zeus himself testifies to how the cognitive impact of desire has the phenomenological character of a physical force. Upon seeing his wife, he is seized by a feeling like no other, 'For never yet has desire for any goddess or woman so overpowered me and poured all through my very core' (οὐ γὰρ πώ ποτέ μ' ὧδε θεᾶς ἔρος οὐδὲ γυναικὸς / θυμὸν ἐνὶ στήθεσσι περιπροχυθεὶς ἐδάμασσεν, 14.315–16).[11] The hapax περιπροχυθείς further underscores the overwhelming quality of his desire (ἔρος) as a physical phenomenon by visualising it as a force that 'pours all through' him and so affects him to his core (θυμός), which is itself bodily (ἐνὶ στήθεσσι). As we will see, there is reason to think that Zeus' impression of 'pouring' is more than a figure of speech. While the *kestos himas* is the final and crucial accessory that Hera must secure for her seduction and deception, she is also radiantly clothed and adorned, and in the next section we will find a correlation between the sensations of 'pouring' and 'melting' that accompany Zeus' feeling of overwhelming desire and the extraordinary radiance that Hera emanates.

Iliad 14's description of the *kestos himas* and its effects offer a clear departure from the last chapter's modes of deception. Whereas we saw Prometheus, Hermes and Odysseus adapting and manipulating at-hand materials (including their own bodies) in attempts at deceit, what we find in *Iliad* 14 and in the examples of feminine deception at stake in this chapter is a distinctive way of using objects, one that relies less on the canny crafting of materials and more on a kind of vitality unique to finely crafted objects. Rather than entangling themselves with things through their material engagement with them, the women of this chapter instead rely more on the capacity for objects to effect their own entanglements and, in so doing, enact each woman's deceptive plots. By concentrating narrowly on four accounts of feminine ruses, the continuities between their respective uses of material things will come into sharp focus. In this way, this chapter also circles us back to the first chapter's discussion of *poikilia* in fabric. This is because here, too, we will find that *poikilia* does not mark objects as 'merely' decorative, but instead encapsulates the captivating, ensnaring effect of highly wrought surfaces. And if we saw in the first chapter how

---

archaic and classical Greek thought, as well as Peponi 2012: 95–153 for discussion of the erotic desires and pleasures associated with music.

[11] See too Peponi 2012: 102–7's discussion of Zeus' response here, which she relates to the overwhelming desire that Apollo experiences at hearing Hermes' music in the *Homeric Hymn to Hermes*.

textiles could function as extensions of the women who made them, here too we will find women operating in close concert with their accoutrements: combining their awareness of how particular material qualities will impact their targets with words as carefully wrought as the objects each woman recruits in her deceit.

Goddesses in Disguise and Divine Assemblages

The *kestos himas* is but one of the objects that Hera recruits in order to make herself enticing to Zeus. Before she obtains this garment from Aphrodite, the narrator details at length her bathing and adornment. And the correlation between artifice and agency already apparent from the *kestos himas*'s description as 'embroidered' and finely crafted' as well as able to not leave 'unfulfilled whatever' is equally fundamental to the other accessories that Hera dons.[12] From robe to jewellery to sandals, all of these are extraordinarily radiant and beautiful. And the same superfluity of alluring garments and accessories – one that we have already seen in Chapter 3's discussion of Pandora – is likewise operative in Aphrodite's seduction of Anchises. Given the heterogeneous character of feminine adornment, this section therefore focuses on the agency afforded to *groups* of things. It places the notion of assemblage centre stage by considering episodes where particular effects and affects are generated only from configurations of different objects, both organic (e.g. skin, hair) and inorganic (armour, jewellery etc.).[13] Dress, which by definition always combines material objects with bodily matter, is naturally a domain in which assemblages are prominent. The examples in this section will thus demonstrate each goddess's awareness of how assemblages of objects can gain a degree of agency not accessible to any one thing alone.

We can gain a clearer perspective on how to approach these scenes of divine adornment by considering Jane Bennett's encounter with the vitality of a decidedly

---

[12] Lee 2015 is, to my knowledge, the most recent monograph devoted to ancient Greek dress, but see also the collection of essays in Llewellyn-Jones 2002.

[13] Here I rely on the particular definition of assemblage formulated by Bennett 2010: 23–4: 'Assemblages are ad hoc groupings of diverse elements, of vibrant materials of all sorts. Assemblages are living, throbbing confederations that are able to function despite the persistent presence of energies that confound them from within . . . Each member and proto-member of the assemblage has a certain vital force, but there is also an effectivity proper to the grouping as such: an agency *of* the assemblage' (emphasis in original). For a robust analysis of the effectivity of clothing in particular see especially Miller 2010: 12–41, who concludes that 'the concept of the person, the sense of the self, the experience of being an individual, are radically different at different times and in different places, partly in relation to differences in clothing' (40).

less glamorous kind of assemblage: the street refuse of Baltimore. Here is how she describes this incident:

> When the materiality of the glove, the rat, the pollen, the bottle cap, and the stick started to shimmer and spark, it was in part because of the contingent tableau that they formed with each other, with the streets, with the weather that morning, with me . . . But they *were* all there just as they were, and so I caught a glimpse of an energetic vitality inside each of these things, things that I generally conceived as inert. In this assemblage, *objects* appeared as *things*, that is, as vivid entities not entirely reducible to the contexts in which (human) subjects set them. (2010: 5, emphasis in original)

Her point here is that the specific combination of these items with each other, with her and with their surroundings creates a unique effect that would not be possible outside of this highly particular confluence of circumstances. Likewise, although Hera and Aphrodite employ objects that are individually spectacular, the effect achieved by their combination far exceeds the sum of their parts. And the language Bennett uses here and elsewhere – of shimmering, sparking and vividness – is especially pertinent to the passages I turn to next, where objects and bodies gain an extraordinary degree of brightness from assemblages of finery.[14]

A variety of terms denoting luminosity and shimmer proliferates in the description of Hera's preparations, a proliferation that emphasises that Hera desires above all to be spectacular:

ἀμβροσίῃ μὲν πρῶτον ἀπὸ χροὸς ἱμερόεντος (170)
λύματα πάντα κάθηρεν, ἀλείψατο δὲ λίπ' ἐλαίῳ
ἀμβροσίῳ ἑδανῷ, τό ῥά οἱ τεθυωμένον ἦεν·
τοῦ καὶ κινυμένοιο Διὸς κατὰ χαλκοβατὲς δῶ
ἔμπης ἐς γαῖάν τε καὶ οὐρανὸν ἵκετ' ἀϋτμή.
τῷ ῥ' ἥ γε χρόα καλὸν ἀλειψαμένη ἰδὲ χαίτας (175)
πεξαμένη χερσὶ πλοκάμους ἔπλεξε φαεινοὺς
καλοὺς ἀμβροσίους ἐκ κράατος ἀθανάτοιο.
ἀμφὶ δ' ἄρ' ἀμβρόσιον ἑανὸν ἔσαθ', ὅν οἱ Ἀθήνη
ἔξυσ' ἀσκήσασα, τίθει δ' ἐνὶ δαίδαλα πολλά·
χρυσείης δ' ἐνετῇσι κατὰ στῆθος περονᾶτο. (180)
ζώσατο δὲ ζώνῃ ἑκατὸν θυσάνοις ἀραρυίῃ,

---

[14] See also Grand-Clément 2016 on the aesthetic effects associated with the brilliance of gold and purple.

ἐν δ' ἄρα ἕρματα ἧκεν ἐυτρήτοισι λοβοῖσι
τρίγληνα μορόεντα· χάρις δ' ἀπελάμπετο πολλή.
κρηδέμνῳ δ' ἐφύπερθε καλύψατο δῖα θεάων
καλῷ νηγατέῳ· λευκὸν δ' ἦν ἠέλιος ὥς·   (185)
ποσσὶ δ' ὑπὸ λιπαροῖσιν ἐδήσατο καλὰ πέδιλα.
αὐτὰρ ἐπεὶ δὴ πάντα περὶ χροῒ θήκατο κόσμον
βῆ ῥ' ἴμεν ἐκ θαλάμοιο.

And first she cleansed every stain from her lovely skin, and anointed herself with rich, fragrant, ambrosial oil: such was the sweetness of its fragrance that, even if it were shaken in the bronze-floored house of Zeus, its smell would still reach earth as well as heaven. With this she anointed her beautiful flesh and combed her hair, and braided it, the shining, beautiful, and divine locks streaming from her immortal head. And she put about her an ambrosial robe, which Athena had made smooth for her with much effort, and she placed on it many baubles,[15] pinning gold brooches about her chest. And she girded herself with a belt fitted out with a hundred tassels, and in her pierced ears she placed earrings in the shape of three drops: much delight shone from these. And she, brilliant among goddesses, covered herself with a newly made, gorgeous veil that was as white as the sun. And she bound up her shining feet with lovely sandals. And then when she had placed every adornment about her body, she went from the chamber. (*Il.* 14.170–88)

The sensuous plenitude of Hera's seductive assemblage finds its corollary in the richness of its description, which is as lavish and ornate as the goddess's appearance. The effect of such profusion of detail is to underscore the composite and complex nature of this adornment. It is, as we will see, an assemblage that flattens the differences between body and clothing, skin and jewellery. Given this level of adornment, it is not surprising that Hera should be described here as 'brilliant among goddesses' (δῖα θεάων, 184). As Lilah Grace Canevaro (2018: 215) points out, this is the only time in the *Iliad* that this description is applied to Hera, which suggests that 'the adornment does seem to have elevated her beauty'. The extraordinarily radiant aspect of Hera's clothing and jewellery also recalls the blinding flashes of metal and armament discussed in Chapter 2. And Hera dresses for her seduction in just as

---

[15] In translating τίθει δ' ἐνὶ δαίδαλα πολλά, I follow the interpretation of Frontisi-Ducroux 1975: 49–50, who argues that the reference to the substantive *daidala* looks ahead to the earrings and brooches with which Hera adorns herself in the lines immediately following. Since *daidal/* is not used anywhere else in Homer to refer to textiles, this seems the most natural reading.

elaborate a type-scene as the arming scenes of the Homeric heroes discussed there.[16] Here, too, the sheer abundance of glittering surfaces and objects comprised by Hera's adornment presents her resulting form as an assemblage of objects chosen for their extraordinary sensory qualities.[17] In this way, the difference between Hera's body and her ornamentation is elided, as each element contributes equally to an overall effect of supernatural brightness.[18]

While visual characteristics predominate in this description, haptic and olfactory qualities also contribute. In particular, the description of her divine, ambrosial scent is distinctive because it locates in smell a physically pervasive quality that is of a piece with the visually radiant nature of her luminous clothing and jewellery.[19] So powerful is her fragrance that 'even if it were shaken in the bronze-floored house of Zeus, its smell would still reach earth as well as heaven' (*Il.* 14.172–4). The ambrosial oil thus has a rich potency that correlates with the theme of abundance and amplitude that runs throughout the whole description: Hera washes away 'every stain', dons 'every adornment', wears 'many baubles' as well as a belt decked out with a 'hundred tassels'. Hera's adornment exhibits on a larger scale the amplitude belonging to Aphrodite's *kestos himas*, which likewise is endowed with 'every charm'. It is only with such abundance that Hera's body can become as 'ambrosial' as her robe and fragrance.

While Hera clearly selects her clothing and jewellery with care, she is equally attentive to her body. Hera, in effect, treats her skin and hair as material that, like metal itself, requires considerable 'work' in order to achieve the desired appearance.[20] Just as her robe has been treated and smoothed by Athena herself (ὅν οἱ

---

[16] On this passage's similarity to arming type-scenes as well as to the descriptions of adornment that appear in the *Homeric Hymn to Aphrodite* and in the *Theogony*'s and *Works and Days*' portrayal of Pandora's creation, see Janko 1992: 173 ad 166–86.

[17] cf. Canevaro 2018: 214, who notes that in this description of Hera's adornment, 'objects come thick and fast'. This portrayal of divine adornment also typifies what Ruby Blondell 2013 has identified as a general principle of Greek feminine beauty: 'The most beautiful woman is the one with the best accessories' (7).

[18] See also Brouillet and Carastro 2018, who similarly draw attention to the agency exerted by the *kestos himas* as well as by the Homeric aegis.

[19] See too the beautification of Penelope by Athena at *Od.* 18.190–6, where the goddess uses the ambrosia of Aphrodite (cf. *Od.* 8.364–5, where Aphrodite herself is portrayed as anointing herself with this substance) to make Penelope taller and more beautiful, as well as more luminous than 'new sawn ivory' (καί μιν μακροτέρην καὶ πάσσονα θῆκεν ἰδέσθαι, / λευκοτέρην δ' ἄρα μιν θῆκε πριστοῦ ἐλέφαντος, *Od.* 18.195–6). On the ambiguities of ambrosia and nectar and their significance in demarcating divinities as such, see also Grand-Clément 2018.

[20] cf. Steiner 2001: 188 on Hesiod's depiction of Pandora's creation: 'the body must be

Ἀθήνη / ἔξυσ' ἀσκήσασα, 177–8), so Hera subjects herself to similar care. Her skin must be bathed and anointed so that it exudes fragrance; her hair is combed, braided and made to stream down from her head. With this pampering, Hera endows her body and hair with the same gleaming, glossy attributes that define her dress and jewellery. In this way, she succeeds in levelling the difference between her body and her adornment by making herself physically akin to an elaborately wrought artefact like her earrings or gown, or one like Pandora herself, who is, as we saw in the previous chapter, a living *dolos*.[21] Conversely, the fact that Hera's body and hair can take on such a vibrant character testifies to the liveliness of metal and fabric. Far from inert, passive matter, these media glitter with a vitality akin to that which Bennett detected on the streets of Baltimore.

As a result of Hera's brilliant beauty, Zeus claims to have never before experienced such an overwhelming 'pouring' of desire. And this sense of pleasure is one succinctly expressed in the allusion to the abundance of *charis* ('delight') that 'shone' from Hera's earrings (χάρις δ' ἀπελάμπετο πολλή), which conveys the idea that superlative beauty does not just exist *in* an object but instead extends outwards to captivate the senses.[22] As we saw in Chapter 2, metal provides a particularly vivid expression of the way that materials can give the appearance of vitality, but in the case of the divine seduction scenes at stake here, this vibrancy takes a palpably different form. Hera's earrings provide a case in point: these earrings, in exuding *charis* ('delight'), crystallise the pleasure Zeus feels in regarding Hera.[23] Hera thus proves

"worked" and enhanced from the outside in order to achieve maximum appeal and to acquire the status of an *agalma* or thing that gives delight'. In what follows, my interpretation is closely aligned with that of Steiner 2001, especially p. 195: 'a work of art does not owe its appeal to its resemblance to a living beloved, but the beloved instigates passion precisely because he or she displays the properties that belong to finely crafted objects'. But whereas her focus is on what these passages reveal about ancient Greek conceptualisations of the plastic arts, mine is on why certain materials gain greater vitality and agency in combination with one another and with living bodies.

[21] cf. Steiner 2001: 235: 'Just as armor need not so much cover the body as be identical with or even substitute for it, so, too, a woman's garments form one with what lies underneath, as though all elements of her appearance were the outcome of a single manufacturing process.'

[22] cf. MacLachlan 1993: 35 on Hera's earrings: 'the earrings' principal attraction, which accounted for their beauty, was their sparkle'. While *charis* can take many forms and is accordingly translated in a variety of ways (from 'grace' to 'charm' to 'favour'), as Bonnie MacLachlan 1993 has observed, it always refers to some reciprocal relation, where the term names the positive feeling attendant in an interaction between persons and gods or persons and objects: '*Charis* bound people together in the archaic Greek world, through the experience of pleasure' (ibid., 6).

[23] cf. Canevaro 2018: 215: 'this brilliance [of δῖος] is something in which the male gods are not well versed, and as such it may be expected to dazzle Zeus'.

herself every bit as adept as Hermes at manipulating materials, but her aim is not disguise. Instead, by assimilating herself to the beauty and radiance of her jewellery and so creating a sensuous spectacle, Hera's fabulous appearance simultaneously expresses and disguises her intentions: to hoodwink Zeus by seducing him.

Aphrodite's Seductive Assemblage in the *Homeric Hymn to Aphrodite*

Aphrodite employs much the same method in order to lure Anchises to bed, but in this case the goddess' aim is to conceal her divinity.[24] The depiction of Aphrodite's preparations for this encounter in the *Homeric Hymn to Aphrodite* also dwells upon the artificial aspects of her appearance: her clothing, jewellery and scent.[25] Significantly, however, her appearance is focalised both through the narrator in his description of her adornment and through Anchises. Whereas in Hera's adornment the focus is on how she tweaks and manipulates her appearance for optimal results, this *Hymn* relays in more detail the phenomenological character of this kind of elaborate get-up.

First, the narrator relates how the Graces bathe Aphrodite and anoint her with fragrant oil:

ἔνθα δέ μιν Χάριτες λοῦσαν καὶ χρῖσαν ἐλαίῳ
ἀμβρότῳ, οἷα θεοὺς ἐπενήνοθεν αἰὲν ἐόντας,
ἀμβροσίῳ ἑδανῷ, τό ῥά οἱ τεθυωμένον ἦεν.

And there the Graces bathed her and anointed her with divine oil, such as blooms on the bodies of the immortal gods, sweet oil that she had, and fragrant. (61–3)

This characterisation, like that of *Iliad* 14, stresses the sweetness of the oil's fragrance as well as its materiality, as something that can anoint the skin and so 'bloom' (ἐπενήνοθεν) on immortal bodies. Ambrosia's depiction here, however, draws greater attention to the amorphousness of this substance: it is both a fragrant vapour and a component of oil (which in turn enables it to anoint fabric as well as skin) in addition to being, of course, a substance that the gods consume.[26] This association

---

[24] See also Brown 1997 on what he terms 'the Pandora complex', which considers the prominence of gold in both Pandora's adornments and the *Homeric Hymns* devoted to Aphrodite (5 and 6) as expressive of male sexual and economic anxieties.

[25] See Richardson 2010 ad 58–67 and 87–90, who also notes the similarities between this passage and the portrayal of Hera in *Iliad* 14 (as well as of Aphrodite in *Hymn. Hom. Ven.* 6), and offers Near Eastern parallels for depictions of such elaborately adorned goddesses.

[26] On the distinctive appetites of the gods see most famously *Il.* 5.441–2: 'for they do not eat bread nor drink shining wine, on account of which they are bloodless and are called immor-

with divinity is reflected in the use of ambrosia as a preservative for human flesh, where its application can prevent a corpse from deteriorating (as at *Il.* 19.38–9, on Patroclus' body) or even make a mortal immortal (as in the *Homeric Hymn to Demeter* 235–40, where Demeter anoints the baby Demophon with an unguent of ambrosia). Ambrosia is thus a substance explicitly endowed with a supreme vitality that finds expression in its sweet fragrance and shining aspect.[27] Further, its material indeterminacy corresponds well to the variety of shapes and dispositions that the gods themselves can adopt, as Aphrodite presents herself here in the guise of a mortal maiden. The fluidity of ambrosia's form thus presents in microcosm the similar blurring between the objects and bodies operative in these divine adornment scenes.

Having dressed herself in beautiful clothing and adorned herself with gold (ἑσσαμένη δ' εὖ πάντα περὶ χροῒ εἵματα καλὰ / χρυσῶι κοσμηθεῖσα, 64–5), Aphrodite appears to Anchises in the likeness of a girl (παρθένωι ἀδμήτηι μέγεθος καὶ εἶδος ὁμοίη, 82). Unlike Hera's, the success of Aphrodite's seduction depends upon the successful concealment of her immortal identity: she adopts the appearance and stature of a mortal 'so that Anchises would not be afraid' (μή μιν ταρβήσειεν ἐν ὀφθαλμοῖσι νοήσας, 83). But despite the fact that Aphrodite assumes this form, Anchises experiences a sense of profound marvel at her appearance. The narration of the latter's perspective makes it explicit that what Anchises perceives are the stunning qualities of Aphrodite's assemblage of accoutrements, especially her 'dazzling necklaces' (ὅρμοι παμποίκιλοι):

> Ἀγχίσης δ' ὁρόων ἐφράζετο θάμβαινέν τε,
> εἶδός τε μέγεθός τε καὶ εἵματα σιγαλόεντα,
> πέπλον μὲν γὰρ ἕεστο φαεινότερον πυρὸς αὐγῆς,
> εἶχε δ' ἐπιγναμπτὰς ἕλικας κάλυκάς τε φαεινάς,
> ὅρμοι δ' ἀμφ' ἁπαλῆι δειρῆι περικαλλέες ἦσαν
> καλοὶ χρύσειοι <u>παμποίκιλοι</u>· ὡς δὲ σελήνη
> στήθεσιν ἀμφ' ἁπαλοῖσιν ἐλάμπετο, θαῦμα ἰδέσθαι.
> Ἀγχίσην δ' ἔρος εἷλεν, ἔπος δέ μιν ἀντίον ηὔδα·

And Anchises, looking at her, marked her well and marvelled at her form and stature and her shining clothes, for she was clad in a robe more radiant than a beam

---

tal' (οὐ γὰρ σῖτον ἔδουσ', οὐ πίνουσ' αἴθοπα οἶνον, / τοὔνεκ' ἀναίμονές εἰσι καὶ ἀθάνατοι καλέονται). See also Clements 2015: 50–1 on the indeterminacy of ambrosia, as well as Sissa and Detienne 2000: 78–80 on the centrality of ambrosia and nectar to divine vitality.

[27] cf. Clements 2015: 51: 'For in all these guises – as a solid, a liquid and a smell– its [ambrosia's] unique power is to negate the effects of temporality, to collapse time.' See also Onians 1951: 200–28 on the association of liquidity with human vitality.

of fire, and she had on twisted bracelets and shining earrings, and about her soft breast were exceedingly beautiful necklaces, lovely, golden, and <u>highly wrought</u>. And these shone like the moon about her tender chest, a wonder to behold. And desire took hold of Anchises, and he spoke to her. (84–91)

Whereas in Hera's seduction the audience is privy to the details of Hera's adornment prior to her encounter with Zeus, in the *Hymn* we gain this perspective from the viewpoint of Anchises. This description conveys how Aphrodite appears to Anchises as an amalgam of the dazzling qualities emanating from her jewellery and clothing (conveyed by σιγαλόεντα, φαεινότερον, φαεινάς, ἐλάμπετο), which in turn make her a 'wonder to behold' (θαῦμα ἰδέσθαι). More specifically, it is the '<u>highly wrought</u> necklaces' (ὅρμοι <u>παμποίκιλοι</u>) that seem to have the most striking visual effect, for the fact that these are the last item mentioned before Anchises is said to be over-whelmed with desire, coupled with the fact that they are 'exceedingly (*pam-*) highly wrought', suggests that these are a peculiarly affective component of her adornment.[28]

Moreover, the 'glowing' (ἐλάμπετο) and 'moonlike' (ὡς δὲ σελήνη) appearance of these necklaces 'around her soft breast' make Aphrodite a 'wonder to behold' (θαῦμα ἰδέσθαι), a phrase evocative of spectacular works of craftsmanship. Elsewhere in early hexameter, as we have seen, the phrase θαῦμα ἰδέσθαι most often designates products of craft: Hephaestus' automatic tripods at *Il.* 18.377; the palace of the Phaeacians at *Od.* 7.45; armour at *Il.* 5.725, 10.439; clothing at *Od.* 8.366, 13.108; Pandora at Hes. *Theog.* 575. Aphrodite, like Hera, excels at the 'craft' of adornment, so much so that she comes to resemble a marvellous artefact. Also significant is the fact that Aphrodite appears 'more radiant than a beam of fire' to Anchises, for this recalls the description of Achilles' armour with a similar phrase (ἀμφὶ δὲ χαλκὸς ἐλάμπετο εἴκελος αὐγῇ / ἢ πυρὸς αἰθομένου ἢ ἠελίου ἀνιόντος, *Il.* 22.134–5). The characterisation of Aphrodite's appearance with this kind of terminology suggests that Anchises' apprehension of Aphrodite here is phenomenologically akin to the perception of metal, as the luminosity of her skin, hair, clothing and jewellery merges together. And unlike, for instance, the epiphany of Demeter, where the goddess reveals herself in a flash of blinding light (*Hymn. Hom. Dem.* 275–80), Aphrodite's radiance here is specifically born out of her assemblage of accoutrements.

When Aphrodite reveals her divinity to Anchises, however, 'Beauty shone out from her cheeks' (κάλλος δὲ παρειάων ἀπέλαμπεν, 174) rather than her necklaces,

---

[28] cf. Putnam 1960: 81: 'They [the *hormoi*] receive the place of extreme importance in the catalogue of Aphrodite's garments and seem to be the most seductive, for they appear at the culminating point in the description, just before the poet tells us that love seized Anchises.'

and Anchises becomes afraid when he recognises her neck and eyes as divine (ὡς δὲ ἴδεν δειρήν τε καὶ ὄμματα κάλ' Ἀφροδίτης | τάρβησέν, 181–2). This change reveals a significant ontological difference between mortal and immortal bodies. Whereas divinities are recognisable as such from the epiphanic aspect intrinsic to their bodies, this effect can only be approximated in mortals with the help of jewellery and clothing crafted from precious materials. And conversely, the similar sheen imagined to inhere in both divine bodies and precious artefacts in turn suggests a similar ontology between them, one that consists in a particular kind of vitality that manifests itself in its entrancing effect on the human gaze.[29]

If divine beauty and radiance is a given, though, why does each narrator spend so much time elaborating each goddess's toilette instead of describing a brief touch-up, like that described at *Od.* 8.364–5, when Athena beautifies Odysseus? First and most significantly, cataloguing each one's accoutrements offers a justification for why both goddesses succeed in their ruses and conveys the overwhelmingly lavish quality of each one's appearance. Both Aphrodite and Hera prove to be adept at engineering assemblages of objects that together infuse their bodies with a dazzling vitality. Second, while Hera also has Aphrodite's *kestos himas* to guarantee her success, that she still takes pains to outfit herself with an array of spectacular objects makes it clear that her appearance is designed to be as beguiling and powerful as the charms contained within the *kestos himas*. The magical effects of this garment are thus correlated with the effects of extraordinary beauty, suggesting that the adornment of the feminine body – with or without such magical implements – functions as a kind of snare, *dolos*, like the one emblematised in the figure of Pandora.

Pandora as *Dolos*

The ensnaring effect of sexual desire is an idea that finds paradigmatic expression in the story of Ares and Aphrodite. In this narrative, the effect of Hephaestus' *dolos* and its 'unbreakable bonds' (δεσμοὺς ἀρρήκτους ἀλύτους, *Od.* 8.274–5) is to physically immobilise the pair caught in the sexual act. This paralysis is suggestive of the *amēchania*, 'helplessness', that accompanies Pandora, whom Hesiod describes as an 'irresistible snare' (αἰπύς δόλος, *Theog.* 589, *Op.* 83).[30] And Pandora is characterised

---

[29] cf. Steiner 2001: 97 n. 73: 'The beauty that Aphrodite displays in such superlative form has a different quality from her earlier allure: through the use of the predicative genitive in the description, the poet marks it out as no product of the external garments, cosmetics, or jewelry that the goddess wears, but as unimpeachably hers.'

[30] For the immobilising and intractable effects of *doloi* see Detienne and Vernant 1978: 21–3, 27–31 and 41–6.

as such because her beauty renders men helpless at the sight of her, which there-fore makes them susceptible to the 'dog's mind and thievish character' that her appearance belies (κύνεόν τε νόον καὶ ἐπίκλοπον ἦθος, *Op.* 67). The combination of her beautiful exterior and evil nature gives the archetypal woman her particular power because men, in their desire, will experience pleasure at the same time as they literally embrace their own destruction (τέρπωνται κατὰ θυμὸν ἑὸν κακὸν ἀμφαγαπῶντες, *Op.* 58). Men are literally unable to perceive anything in Pandora apart from the form of a 'beautiful, lovely form of a maiden similar in her face to the immortal goddesses' (ἀθανάτης δὲ θεῆς εἰς ὦπα εἴσκειν / παρθενικῆς καλὸν εἶδος ἐπήρατον, *Op.* 62–3) and in this way they succumb to the pitfalls of their own lust.

Analogously, the visually stunning appearances of Hera and Aphrodite both phys-ically and mentally overpower Anchises and Zeus. Desire 'takes hold of' Anchises (Ἀγχίσην δ' ἔρος εἷλεν, *Hymn. Hom. Ven.* 91) and Zeus is 'subdued by his longing' (ὕπνῳ καὶ φιλότητι δαμείς, 14.355; ἔρος . . . ἐδάμασσεν, 14.315–16). While the characterisation of desire in terms of physical force is a standard trope of archaic thought, the allusion to such effects gains additional potency in these episodes, where the subduing force of sexual attraction is a crucial element for ensuring the success of each goddess' ruse.

Not only is their yearning imagined as a physically overpowering sensation, there are profound cognitive effects, as well.[31] Zeus' mind is 'clouded over' (ὡς δ' ἴδεν, ὧς μιν ἔρως πυκινὰς φρένας ἀμφεκάλυψεν, 14.294), instantiating the effects of the *poikilos kestos* just as Aphrodite had described them (ἥ τ' ἔκλεψε νόον πύκα περ φρονεόντων, 14.217). Analogously, Anchises does not 'know clearly' (οὐ σάφα εἰδώς, 167) when he succumbs to Aphrodite's beauty. Here, too, *poikilia* plays a starring role as a quality of her golden necklaces (ὅρμοι δ' ἀμφ' ἀπαλῆι δειρῆι περικαλλέες ἦσαν / καλοὶ χρύσειοι παμποίκιλοι, *Hymn. Hom. Ven.* 88–9), making her a 'wonder to behold' (θαῦμα ἰδέσθαι, *Hymn. Hom. Ven.* 90). Both Zeus' and Anchises' responses to beauty are thus akin to the physical and intellectual paralysis (*amēchania*) that characteristically inheres in the *dolos*. And these passages also let us see in action a phenomenon first observed in Chapter 1. Like the elaborate ornamen-tation of the archaic korai I discussed there, which worked to slow down perception, the *poikilia* of Hera and Aphrodite has the power to stop spectators in their tracks.

Poikilia, by contributing in both instances to the arresting appearance of the god-desses, thus helps to ensure a failure of recognition: the man perceives only beauty, not guile, and so feels only desire.[32] In short, the beguiling visual artifice constituted

---

[31] Calame 1999 remains a foundational and comprehensive study of desire (*eros*) and its effects as portrayed across Greek literature.

[32] cf. Blondell 2013: 7: 'Aphrodite "deceives" people into going against their better judgment,

by each woman's assemblage works to conceal the layer of artifice that consists in the fact that neither woman is what she seems. And the strategy that we have seen in these portrayals of divine seductions – where each goddess relies on and exploits the strange and overwhelming vitality of beautiful objects – will likewise prove important in the next section, where Clytemnestra and Medea will instead use it for deadly purposes.

Killer Style and Tragic *Poikilia*: Clytemnestra and Medea

In Chapter 1, I argued that textiles and the manifestation of *poikilia* therein can function as forms of a distinctively feminine mode of extended cognition. As we will see here, however, it is not only by *making* textiles that women can assume agency: Clytemnestra and Medea exploit the special connection between women and textiles for nefarious ends.[33] Not only do Clytemnestra and Medea deploy richly decorated garments as agents of destruction, but this deployment reflects their keen awareness of the multifarious ways that material things can impact human perception and interpretation. If Hera and Aphrodite created assemblages of beautiful objects to stage their seductions, for Clytemnestra and Medea these objects themselves do the seducing.[34] The *poikilia* that surfaces so prominently in their respective traps encompasses not only the sensuous allure of the fabric, but the cunning that enables each character's deadly ruse to work. For both of these figures exploit the capacity for objects to be much more than they appear: this is what Bill Brown has described as the 'excess' of objects: 'You could imagine things . . . as what is excessive in objects, as what exceeds their mere materialization as objects or their mere utilization as objects – their force as a sensuous presence or as a metaphysical presence' (2001: 5). In each example, the material forms that *poikilia* assumes far exceed their status as 'mere' objects. Instead, it is the force they exert as sensuous or metaphysical presences that enables them to do their deadly work.

In the *Oresteia*, *poikilia* plays a crucial role as the defining characteristic of the garments with which Clytemnestra lures and then murders Agamemnon.[35] First,

---

by "persuading", "shrouding", or otherwise incapacitating their "wits" or good sense – in other words, inducing them to think the indulgence of the desire she inspires is right or good when it is really bad, wrong, or disastrous.'

[33] On the commodification of women themselves in Greek tragedy, see especially Wohl 1997.

[34] See also the essays collected in Telò and Mueller 2018 for analyses of a variety of materials and objects in the plays of Aeschylus, Euripides and Sophocles.

[35] cf. Noel 2013: 173: 'Through its malleability, the object [the textile-trap] becomes a metonym for the whole trilogy' ('Par sa malléabilité, l'objet devient alors une métonymie de la trilogie tout entière').

she entices him to trample upon this fabric before ensnaring and murdering him in another piece of *poikilos* material. As Oliver Taplin (1977: 314–15) has put it, 'Agamemnon walks over the rich tapestry-garment and into an inextricable richness of garment-net.' Each form of *poikilia* thus functions as a *dolos*, a snare or trap. Both pieces of *poikilia* are designated with a variety of different terms that makes it difficult to determine the precise nature of either (or indeed, whether or not they are the same piece of cloth), since they are variously characterised as mere fabric, with words like 'spreadable cloth' (πέτασμα, 909) and 'woven stuff' (ὑφάς, 949), but also and more specifically as 'clothing' (εἵματα, 921, 963) or robes (πέπλοι, 1126).[36] Like the ambrosia that featured so prominently in Aphrodite's and Hera's seductions, this central prop of the *Oresteia* is protean in a way that maps onto the varying ways that this fabric is perceived and used.[37]

Poikilia, however, is the adjective that characterises the fabric in each play of the trilogy. This consistency, in turn, reflects the intimate connection between the quality itself and the physical mechanism of Clytemnestra's trap: the visually captivating quality of the *Oresteia*'s textiles becomes a physically ensnaring force. While in the first chapter we saw how the *poikilia* of fabric could slow down or even arrest perception (on the model first proposed by Gell 1992 in his exploration of the 'technology of enchantment'), in the case of Clytemnestra as well as Medea we will see this effect concretised to its most extreme form.

As Melissa Mueller (2016a: 50) has observed, Clytemnestra never claims to have made the textiles that feature so prominently in the *Agamemnon*. Nonetheless, she emphatically asserts ownership over them by first ordering servants to strew Agamemnon's path with fabric:

> νῦν δέ μοι, φίλον κάρα,
> ἔκβαιν' ἀπήνης τῆσδε, μὴ χαμαὶ τιθεὶς
> τὸν σὸν πόδ', ὦναξ, Ἰλίου πορθήτορα.
> δμωιαί, τί μέλλεθ', αἷς ἐπέσταλται τέλος
> πέδον κελεύθου στορνύναι πετάσμασιν;
> εὐθὺς γενέσθω πορφυρόστρωτος πόρος

---

[36] cf. Mueller 2016a: 59's attractive interpretation of the ambiguities of the type of textile used in these scenes: 'we may wonder whether the "net" used for trapping Agamemnon is not the same cloth on which he stepped to enter his house, with the treading being a proleptic entangling and marking of Agamemnon as a walking corpse'.

[37] As will become clear, my interpretation of the *Oresteia*'s textiles is indebted to Mueller 2016a: 42–69's discussion of Atreid textiles, and my hope is to complement this study through my focus on *poikilia*.

Now, dear heart, come down from this carriage but do not let your foot, the sacker of Troy, touch the ground, my lord. Servants, why do you hesitate, when you've been tasked with strewing the ground of his path with fine fabrics? Let his path straight away be spread in purple. (905–11)

While the precise nature of the textiles with which Clytemnestra prepares his path and kills her husband has attracted a great deal of attention,[38] what is abundantly clear is that the cloth on which Agamemnon treads on his way into the house is valuable indeed and not designed to be laid underfoot. Not only is it *poikilos*, but also it has been treated with the most expensive dye, 'deep crimson' (πορφύρεος). For this reason, he hesitates before making his entry and chastises Clytemnestra for preparing his entry in this way:

καὶ τἄλλα μὴ γυναικὸς ἐν τρόποις ἐμὲ   (918)
ἅβρυνε, μηδὲ βαρβάρου φωτὸς δίκην
χαμαιπετὲς βόαμα προσχάνῃς ἐμοί,
μηδ' εἵμασι στρώσασ' ἐπίφθονον πόρον
τίθει· θεούς τοι τοῖσδε τιμαλφεῖν χρεών·
ἐν ποικίλοις δὲ θνητὸν ὄντα κάλλεσιν
βαίνειν ἐμοὶ μὲν οὐδαμῶς ἄνευ φόβου.
λέγω κατ' ἄνδρα, μὴ θεόν, σέβειν ἐμέ.   (925)
χωρὶς ποδοψήστρων τε καὶ τῶν ποικίλων
κληδὼν αὐτεῖ·

As to the rest, do not pamper me in the manner of a woman, nor gape at me with grovelling acclaim, falling to the ground as if I were some barbarian. Nor place envy in my way by strewing the ground with fabric.[39] For truly it is the gods that we should honour with such things. For a mortal man to tread upon beautiful and decorated textiles to me seems not at all without trepidation. I maintain that you should honour me as a man, not as a god. For my reputation resounds even without mats and fancy finery. (918–27)

---

[38] Indeed, as Oliver Taplin 1977: 314 has suggested, 'It may be no accident that the exact nature and function of the cloth are unclear.'

[39] On this translation of εἷμα see Denniston and Page 1957 ad 909, who note that the use of this term makes it clear that the reference to *petasma* at 909 (στρωννύναι πετάσμασιν) does not indicate 'carpets', but rather 'fabrics which are, or resemble, *clothing*' (emphasis in original). More recently, McNeil 2005 has suggested that the fabric is meant to represent a nuptial cloth.

The fact that Agamemnon refers to this cloth with the adjective *poikilos* multiple times (923, 926, 936) reflects the centrality of this quality to the ruse.[40] Clytemnestra, for her part, never refers to it in this way. By contrast, Agamemnon is revealed to be especially attentive to this quality and its multiple meanings. First, he recognises that such valuable textiles more properly belong to the gods (θεούς τοι τοῖσδε τιμαλφεῖν χρεών, 922). To step on them would therefore be to attract the ill will of the gods (μηδ' εἵμασι στρώσασ' ἐπίφθονον πόρον / τίθει, 921–2). Echoing Clytemnestra's characterisation of the fabric as a 'path', a *poros*, Agamemnon instead uses the term to suggest that the path points in a different direction, towards hubris. And in using the term 'way' (πόρος, 921), he also foreshadows the *lack* of a path or means of escape he will encounter inside the house as he becomes physically entangled in similarly rich fabric. His criticism also dwells on the textile's suggestion of effeminate (μὴ γυναικὸς ἐν τρόποις, 918) and barbaric luxury (μηδὲ βαρβάρου φωτὸς δίκην, 919). Finally, he insists that his reputation 'resounds' (αὐτεῖ) without the aid of such material finery. By reacting in this way, Agamemnon proves himself to be a deft interpreter of *poikilia*'s significance, rehearsing several of its associations that have been unpacked in past chapters: its costliness and aesthetic value, its proximity to the divine, its connotations of luxury, and finally, its special relationship with women. And while Clytemnestra focuses on the dye of the fabric (πολλῆς πορφύρας, 959), Agamemnon repeatedly uses the terminology of *poikilia* to highlight the entanglement of significations and material properties embodied in the textiles. In so doing, he reveals his awareness of the peculiar vitality invested in fabric, one that consists in its ability to substantiate excess and hubris and so attract envy.

In addition, Agamemnon recognises how the *poikilia* of the fabric makes it a tangible form of his household's wealth.[41] Accordingly, he remarks later, when he actually treads across this path, that he is 'destroying the wealth of his household with his feet' (δωματοφθορεῖν ποσὶν / φθείροντα πλοῦτον ἀργυρωνήτους θ' ὑφάς, 948–9). To trample this fabric underfoot is not only symbolically destructive, but also literally brings irrevocable damage to it and in this way actually depletes the house's wealth, in spite of Clytemnestra's claims to the contrary (958–62). The

---

[40] Morrell 1997: 141 n. 4 provides an excellent summary of the interpretative issues at stake in this scene and of the relevant scholarship, among which Fraenkel 1950: 2.441, Denniston and Page 1957: 151 and Goheen 1955 loom large. More recently, see Morrell 1997's own study of the cultural significance of fabric in the *Oresteia*, as well as Jenkins 1985, Crane 1993 and Lee 2004, who likewise aim to situate the scene within its historical context. See also Goldhill 1984: 66–81, who emphasises Clytemnestra's manipulation of signs and signifiers in this scene.

[41] cf. Mueller 2016a: 46: 'In societies where human hands laboriously produce every thread of a garment, clothing does not merely symbolize wealth – it *is* wealth' (emphasis in original).

fabric, in short, is anything but inert matter: not only does it materialise a multiplicity of meanings, but it is a fungible form of wealth that makes it directly correlated with Agamemnon's power.[42]

Agamemnon worries not only about the gods' perspective, but also about that of his compatriots (φήμη γε μέντοι δημόθρους μέγα σθένει, 'But truly the voice of the people has great power', 938). In order to counteract these qualms, Clytemnestra's task is to manipulate Agamemnon's own perception and interpretation of the garments. And she does so by appealing to his vanity and reframing the act as a reproduction of his conquest in Troy: 'What do you suppose Priam would do, if he had accomplished these things?' (τί δ' ἂν δοκεῖ σοι Πρίαμος, εἰ τάδ' ἤνυσεν; 935), to which Agamemnon concedes that such an act would certainly be something that Priam would do: 'Surely he would tread upon the elaborate finery' (ἐν ποικίλοις ἂν κάρτα μοι βῆναι δοκεῖ, 936).[43] While commentators have puzzled over why Agamemnon would commit an act that he himself acknowledges to be characteristic of a barbarian king, Agamemnon's motive becomes more intelligible if we take into account the connotations of foreign luxury that he recognised in the *poikilia* of the fabric. For when seen in this way, his gesture – at least from his perspective – becomes not one of emulating Priam, but one of subjugation, as he mars an object that so vividly exhibits the type of luxury associated with the East.[44]

That Agamemnon succumbs to this ploy testifies to the success of Clytemnestra's persuasion in making him regard the cloth in a different way. In this sense, the cloth, on Charles Segal's interpretation, becomes something else yet again: a 'tangible symbol' of Clytemnestra's rhetoric:

> The tapestry itself is a visual emanation and a tangible symbol of Clytemnestra's cloying, seductive rhetoric. It is itself the emblem and the instrument of disruption in the sign system on which all civilized order rests. Waste, pride, and luxury are as dangerous in speech as in the house and in the kingdom. (1981: 55)

---

[42] cf. Lyons 2003 : 116–19.

[43] See also McClure 1996, who identifies the affinities between binding spells and Clytemnestra's speech here.

[44] cf. Grand-Clément 2011, who interprets the *Oresteia*'s incorporation of *poikilia* as indicative of changing attitudes towards Eastern luxury in the wake of the Persian Wars: 'Les tissus multicolores se trouvent marginalisés, subissant le même sort que les tissus pourpres – auxquels ils correspondent bien souvent: ils symbolisent désormais l'*hybris* et la perfidie du Barbare' (476). See also Kurke 1992, who addresses the similar shift that occurs in attitudes towards *habrosunē*.

Clytemnestra's speech thus works in concert with the significance of the fabric's *poikilia* to ensure the success of her *dolos*. For it is by making him regard the act of trampling the fabric as an expression of his superiority that Clytemnestra succeeds in concealing from her husband the fact that his destruction of the *poikilia* of the garments in his path will find its corollary in the *poikilia* of the cloth with which she will ensnare and kill him. This garment is also described in terms of *poikilia*, and so conveys how Clytemnestra, like Agamemnon, is also guilty of subverting the normal function of such a precious textile.[45] While Agamemnon defaces the material with his feet, Clytemnestra manipulates it into a deadly *dolos*, an aspect to which she herself alludes in referring to this cloth as an 'evil wealth of garment' (πλοῦτον εἵματος κακόν, 1383).

The *poikilia* of the *Agamemnon*'s textiles thus embodies the multifarious forms and functions that this fabric assumes over the course of a single play. As a fungible form of wealth repurposed into a walkway (and a site of complex and contentious meaning), *poikilia* finally materialises the ensnaring effect that we also have seen in Aphrodite's and Hera's seductions. Textilic *poikilia* in the *Agamemnon* is thus a site of entanglement par excellence. Not only is it physically a snare, but its efficacy as such depends on the ways it is entangled with humans: humans and their propensity to be seduced by material luxuries; conversely, the capacity for humans to manipulate and so repurpose material objects in unanticipated ways; and finally, the polyvalence of things that becomes so visible in the multiple ways of viewing and interpreting that the *Agamemnon*'s *poikilia* invites.

In the *Libation Bearers*, Orestes imbues the fabric of *poikilia* with even greater complexity. Like his mother, Orestes is highly attuned to the literal entanglement effected by the fabric in spite of his absence from the event itself. He highlights how the fabric has been turned specifically into a *dolos* by observing that the robe is an instrument akin to that which a hunter would use (997–1004), and refers to it as both a net (ἄγρευμα, 998) and a trap (δόλωμα, 1003). Further proof of this facet of the textile comes from the appearance of the fabric itself, an aspect upon which Orestes dwells both here and in the *Eumenides*. This is because the colours within the fabric (πολλὰς βαφὰς) are now mingled with Agamemnon's blood, which mars it (φθείρουσα) as indelibly as did Agamemnon's feet on his entry (πολλὰς βαφὰς φθείρουσα τοῦ ποικίλματος, 1013). That Orestes uses the same verb as his father did, φθείρω (δωματοφθορεῖν ποσὶν / φθείροντα πλοῦτον ἀργυρωνήτους θ' ὑφάς, 948–9), to describe the fabric's stain draws attention to how, in both instances, contact with Agamemnon's body leaves an indelible, destructive mark

---

[45] cf. McNeil 2005: 11: 'Unfortunately, instead of restoring the marital bond with her *kharis*-gift, Clytemnestra perversely uses the cloth to cloak deceit and betrayal with feigned *kharis*.'

on the material, a permanent stain that in turn reflects the inextricable nature of the snare itself.

While Agamemnon left a physical trace of himself on the cloth, Clytemnestra is no less implicated in the deadly fabric. As Mueller (2016a: 63) has pointed out,

> When he first came on the scene, Orestes regarded Clytemnestra and Aegisthus as his father's killers. Now the fabric itself bears the brunt of his blame. The garment has gone from being a mere 'witness' to an agent of death.

And because the cloth provides such a vivid illustration of Clytemnestra's murder, Orestes is able to summon it as a witness to his mother's crime (μαρτυρέω, *Cho.* 1010, *Eum.* 461) and thus use it for his own defence in the *Eumenides*: 'But my black-hearted mother killed him, and covered him with a crafty snare, which remains to testify to his murder in the bath' (ἀλλά νιν κελαινόφρων ἐμὴ / μήτηρ κατέκτα, ποικίλοις ἀγρεύμασιν / κρύψασ', ἃ λουτρῶν ἐξεμαρτύρει φόνον, 460–2). Here, when he refers to the cloth not as a robe, but as the 'crafty snare' (ποικίλοις ἀγρεύμασιν) that his mother used to kill his father, Orestes emphasises to Athena how the fabric provides a visible testament of his mother's guile and treachery. The fabric thus acquires a new life in its role as forensic evidence, both standing in for Clytemnestra as the perpetrator of the crime and so also offering justification for Orestes' own act of vengeance.

The *poikilia* that surfaces at these crucial junctures throughout the *Oresteia* is one that encompasses and even capitalises upon the material and semantic variability that I have traced in the previous chapters. In this sense, this instantiation of *poikilia* harmonises with the examples discussed in Chapter 1, where I argued that the highly decorated surfaces of textiles cultivated an entrancing effect in viewers due in part to the variegated nature of visual perception itself. The dynamism of visual perception is thus reflected in the instability of *poikilia*'s meaning in the *Oresteia*. In the same way that the fabric is viewed and used in different ways over the course of the trilogy, so too does the use of language shift in relation to the textiles in the play: in Clytemnestra's deception, her speech, by convincing Agamemnon to view the act of treading on rich fabric in a different light, manages to conceal her intentions. Orestes, on the other hand, uses and points to the blood-stained fabric to illuminate clearly his mother's crime.

However, the fact that Clytemnestra does not lay claim to be the producer of the *Agamemnon*'s textiles makes her trap significantly different from the forms of feminine textile production adduced in Chapter 1. Whereas we saw there how the process of weaving invites and even necessitates a form of extended cognition, it is Clytemnestra's subversion of this idea that makes her deception and murder successful as well as poignant. Not only does she succeed in persuading Agamemnon to tread on material embodiments of wealth and luxury (and the product of women's hands), but she then deploys a textile form of *poikilia* as a medium through which she destroys her husband (rather than contributing to the household's wealth with the production of such goods). In so doing, Clytemnestra emerges as a figure not unlike Hermes, Odysseus and Prometheus, for she too inaugurates a new (albeit deadly) way of using a familiar material: she sees the potential for woven fabric to be entrancing as well as literally ensnaring. In the final example of this chapter, we will see an even cannier and more duplicitous manipulation of objects at the hands of Euripides' Medea.

Euripides' Medea provides a fitting capstone to this chapter because she is an expert in the sort of charms that we also saw in Aphrodite's *kestos himas*. But whereas that garment could merely 'steal over the minds even of the wise' (ἥ τ' ἔκλεψε νόον πύκα περ φρονεόντων, *Il.* 14.217), the diadem and robes that Medea sends to her husband's new bride Glaucē are decidedly more nefarious.[46] This is because of the potions, *pharmaka*, with which she treats them (τοιοῖσδε χρίσω φαρμάκοις δωρήματα, Eur. *Med.* 789). Like the ambrosia favoured by Aphrodite and Hera, *pharmaka* are ontologically fluid: they can be liquids or unguents, or equally they can be immaterial by taking the form of spells or magic. And just as ambrosia contributed to the radiance of each goddess, here too the gifts exhibit what the chorus calls a 'heavenly gleam' (ἀμβρόσιός τ' αὐγὰ, 983). Together, this combination of potions and divine radiance will prove fundamental to the success of Medea's ruse. And if ambrosia beautifies divine bodies and can even make mortal beings immortal, Medea's *pharmaka* are no less powerful, ensuring total destruction rather than preservation.[47]

Like Clytemnestra, Medea puts to work precious objects that she possesses but has not made herself.[48] In Medea's case, the robe and diadem form part of her inheritance. She indicates that they were gifts from her grandfather Helios (954–5), and as Mueller has argued, Medea's presentation of the gifts' lineage 'sets in motion the performance (by the objects) that will bring her back, closer to her original autonomy' (2001: 494). By presenting Glaucē with the robes as well as the deadly

---

[46] See also Jenkins 1985: 127–8 as well as Blundell 1998: 69–72 on the significance of Medea's use of a textile as a murder weapon.

[47] See also Euripides' conceptualisation of writing as a form of *pharmakon*, as in his fragmentary *Palamedes* (on which see especially Torrance 2010: 219–22). See too Rinella 2010: 214–20's discussion of Plato's depiction of *pharmaka* and its reception in Jacques Derrida's 'Plato's Pharmacy'.

[48] On Medea's masterful manipulation of the dynamics of reciprocity in this play, see especially Mueller 2001.

golden diadem under the pretence of adding to her dowry (φερνάς, 956), Medea's characterisation of her plot as a *dolos* is apt (ἀλλ' ὡς δόλοισι παῖδα βασιλέως κτάνω, 783). For in so doing, she subverts the practice of giving brides expensive articles of adornment, especially articles of clothing.[49] Given the desirability and material value of *poikilia* within the feminine wardrobe, articles described as such do feature as genuine gifts elsewhere (e.g. Sappho fr. 44, *Od.* 15.104–8), but Medea co-opts the allure of this quality in order to ensure the efficacy of her *pharmaka*.

When the messenger refers to these garments as '<u>enticing</u> (*poikilous*) robes' (1159), the adjective takes on double force, signifying not only the captivating appearance of the garments, but also the deadly *pharmaka* that are integrated within the fabric. Moreover, that *pharmaka* can refer to potions as well as to the kind of dyes that would impart to fabric the colourful appearance characteristic of *poikiloi peploi* lends a further, ominous layer to the word's significance here. What enables this poison to take effect is the irresistible visual allure the garments have for Glaucē, who 'could not restrain herself' from putting them on at once (ἡ δ', ὡς ἐσεῖδε κόσμον, οὐκ ἠνέσχετο, 1156), thereby bringing the poison into direct contact with her flesh. Medea's guile thus consists in her knowledge of magic as well as in her keen awareness of what will entice Glaucē. The messenger's recollection of Glaucē's delight in the gifts is a testament to the deadly accuracy with which Medea had predicted the princess's taste:

ἡ δ', ὡς ἐσεῖδε κόσμον, οὐκ ἠνέσχετο,   (1156)
ἀλλ' ἤνεσ' ἀνδρὶ πάντα, καὶ πρὶν ἐκ δόμων,
μακρὰν ἀπεῖναι πατέρα καὶ παῖδας σέθεν
λαβοῦσα πέπλους <u>ποικίλους</u> ἠμπέσχετο,
χρυσοῦν τε θεῖσα στέφανον ἀμφὶ βοστρύχοις   (1160)
λαμπρῷ κατόπτρῳ σχηματίζεται κόμην,
ἄψυχον εἰκὼ προσγελῶσα σώματος.
κἄπειτ' ἀναστᾶσ' ἐκ θρόνων διέρχεται
στέγας, ἁβρὸν βαίνουσα παλλεύκῳ ποδί,
δώροις ὑπερχαίρουσα, πολλὰ πολλάκις   (1165)
τένοντ' ἐς ὀρθὸν ὄμμασι σκοπουμένη.
τοὐνθένδε μέντοι δεινὸν ἦν θέαμ' ἰδεῖν·

And she, when she saw the attire, could not restrain herself, but agreed to everything her betrothed asked, and before your children and their father had gone far from the house, grabbed up the <u>elaborate</u> robes and put them on. And placing the

---

[49] cf. Scheid and Svenbro 1996: 60–82, as well as Lee 2004 and 2015: 207–11 and Lyons 2003.

golden crown about her locks, she arranged her hair before a gleaming mirror, grinning at the lifeless reflection of her body. And then, getting up from her seat, she paraded through the room, making a dainty stride with her snow-white foot, so delighting in the gifts, gazing again and again at the straight line of her leg. But after this there was an awful sight to behold. (1156–67)

On this account, Glaucē is so desirous of the robes and diadem that she can hardly wait to put them on and 'agrees to everything' (ἀλλ' ἤνεσ' ἀνδρὶ πάντα, 1157) in order to get her hands on them. Moreover, she is enchanted with her own appearance and is overwhelmed with joy (ὑπερχαίρουσα, 1165) at how she looks. At first, then, the scene resembles those discussed in the first section of this chapter, as the gifts achieve their desired effect of enhancing Glaucē's beauty. But it is precisely in doing so that the *pharmaka*, disguised within the *poikilia* of the robes, take hold. And they achieve their effect in a particularly perverse way, by inverting the norms of feminine adornment that we have seen already. First, rather than being situated 'about her flesh' (περὶ χροΐ) – a formulaic element of the dressing scenes discussed in the previous section – the robe instead 'eats into her white flesh' (λευκὴν ἔδαπτον σάρκα, 1189). Second, rather than enhancing her appearance, Medea's *pharmaka* ensure that the girl becomes 'unrecognisable to anyone but her father' (πλὴν τῷ τεκόντι κάρτα δυσμαθὴς ἰδεῖν, 1196). And the dazzling radiance of the diadem, the kind that made Hera and Aphrodite irresistible, is perverted into 'consuming fire' (παμφάγου πυρός, 1187) that destroys the princess's face.[50] Glaucē is thus literally consumed by her desire to possess the robes and beautify herself by wearing them.

What enables the robe to transform from a precious gift into a gruesome death-trap is thus a double kind of magic: the *pharmaka* that inhere in the fabric, unseen amidst its elaborate patterning and fine texture, as well as the allure of its beauty and *poikilia*. As the chorus observes at 983–4, the grace, *charis*, and radiance of the gifts will inevitably persuade the princess to put them on: 'Their charm and heavenly gleam will entice her to put on the gown and the circlet of fashioned gold' (πείσει χάρις ἀμβρόσιός τ' αὐγὰ πέπλον / χρυσότευκτόν τε στέφανον περιθέσθαι). Without the gifts' ability to exert this influence on their recipient, the *pharmaka* would be all but useless.

Medea's *dolos* does not just ensnare and destroy its victim, but does so in a way that reflects her intimate awareness of the fallibility of feminine vanity and desire.[51]

---

[50] cf. Segal 1996: 34: 'The "lifeless image" of her beauty that the girl sees reflected back to herself in her mirror when she first puts on the crown anticipates the total destruction of that beauty in a "spectacle" of horror.'

[51] cf. Medea's remarks to Jason at 964, where she persuades him to let her send the gifts

In this sense, her expertise in *pharmaka* and magic turns out to be only half the battle. She also emerges as an uncannily good reader of human nature in her accurate prediction of her gifts' effect on Glaucē, and later on her father. For as Medea stipulates in saying that the poison will destroy Glaucē and 'anyone who touches her' (κακῶς ὀλεῖται πᾶς θ' ὃς ἂν θίγῃ κόρης, 788), she indicates her awareness that Glaucē's father Creon will be unable to resist grabbing hold of his daughter in his agony (περιπτύξας χέρας, 1206). For this reason, Medea can be confident that her gifts will destroy father as much as daughter.

As this section has shown, to act as Clytemnestra and Medea do requires more than cunning. What we find in these examples, as well as in the depictions of seduction explored in the first section, is an intimate knowledge of the power of objects and their ability to guide humans to particular actions. In the case of Clytemnestra and Medea, however, the entanglement effected by their chosen objects is exploited for deadly ends. But they rely no less than Hera and Aphrodite on the vitality of things, a vitality that finds expression in the *poikilia* of the objects they deploy. For if Hera and Aphrodite seduce with the *help* of objects, Clytemnestra and Medea allow things to seduce all on their own and destroy their targets in the process.

Conclusions

The fact that Glaucē is said to admire the 'lifeless reflection' of her adorned body in the mirror (ἄψυχον εἰκὼ προσγελῶσα σώματος, 1162) offers a poignant reflection on the vitality of the *poikilia* we have examined in this chapter.[52] First, we explored the particular feminine allure of *poikilia* in Glaucē's delight at her own appearance. Second, the fact that the mirror is said to contain her 'lifeless reflection' is not only gruesome foreshadowing, but implicitly alludes to the vibrancy of metal and its capacity to seem simultaneously inert (in its hardness) as well as remarkably lively (in its luminosity).[53] However, its radiation of a lifeless likeness presages the deathly entanglement between human and material effected in Medea's *dolos*. Unwittingly, Glaucē becomes one with the alluring materials that had before only figuratively transfixed her, in a manner reminiscent of Agamemnon's demise. The princess and her father thus fall victim to the kind of cunning we have seen throughout this

---

because 'they say that gifts can win over even the gods' (πείθειν δῶρα καὶ θεοὺς λόγος). On Medea's powers of persuasion see especially Buxton 1982: 153–70.

[52] See also Shirazi 2018 on Euripides' representation of the interaction between women and their mirrors in *Hecuba*, with discussion of Glaucē and her mirror at pp. 107–9.

[53] cf. Shirazi 2018: 109: 'The mirror is an especially effective tool for suspense and reversal: not only is it *the* object of beautification par excellence, but as such, it evokes an idealized sensory *and* cognitive moment' (emphasis in original).

chapter, one that consists in each woman's keen attention to the agency of finely crafted objects. Finally, in the robe's disturbing transformation from luxurious, beautiful gift into a deadly agent of destruction, the *poikilia* of Glaucē's garment embodies the dynamism that gives *poikilia* such prominence in archaic and classical thought. As we saw in the first chapter, in textiles this dynamism imparts a scintillating aspect that propels and beguiles the viewer's gaze. And it is precisely this facet of *poikilia*, and each woman's attentiveness to this facet, that has enabled the success of each of the ruses discussed here.

Conclusions

TEXTILES, METALS, AUTOMATA, music and lyrics, ruses and traps: each chapter has explored one of *poikilia*'s domains to the end of uncovering the variety of ways that this quality brings together minds, bodies and things. The result is a kaleidoscopic view of the sensory and cognitive experiences that cluster around this term, a richness that testifies to *poikilia*'s peculiar vitality. As we have seen, this vitality cuts in two directions. On the one hand, *poikilia* exerts a powerful fascination in the archaic and classical poetic imaginary, alternately entrancing, beguiling, stunning and perplexing those who encounter its material manifestations. On the other hand, these portrayals are also a window into how the human mind and senses were thought to work. To conclude, then, I will look at Plato's portrayals of *poikilia* in the *Republic*, since these illustrate in microcosm the two facets of this concept that link together each of the preceding chapters: its profound effects on bodily and cognitive processes, and the permeability between mind and world suggested by these interactions.

In the Introduction, I invoked the shield of Achilles to introduce a number of the themes explored in individual chapters: Plato's multifarious vision of *poikilia* offers an apt place to conclude.[1] In Homer, *poikilia* was one of the qualities that made the shield wondrous, but Plato is a notorious critic of the pleasures afforded by *poikilia*'s sensuality. However, his treatment of *poikilia* in the *Republic* echoes and even elaborates

---

[1] On Plato's criticisms of musico-poetic *poikilia* in particular see especially Wallace 2009, as well as Halliwell's 1988 comment ad *Resp.* 10.604e1: 'The Platonic mentality favours simplicity, and deprecates variety as decadent, in everything, whether food, music, clothing, politics or morality' (140). On Plato's objections specifically to the *poikilos mimēsis* of *Republic* book 10 see Moss 2007.

upon several of the ideas that have recurred throughout this book: the influence of aesthetic experience on cognitive and emotional states, the shifting and variable nature of embodied experience, and the central role that material things play in shaping human conceptions of their own cognitive and perceptual architecture. And in using *poikilia* to formulate his own vision of the dynamics between body, soul and environment, Plato – the arch-critic of *poikilia* – will paradoxically turn out to be one of the most outspoken champions of the vitality of *poikilia*. For even as Plato excludes *poikilia* from the ideal state, this quality surfaces again and again in the vivid imagery with which the philosopher illustrates the vagaries of embodied human experience.

Within the *Republic* alone Plato repeatedly condemns musico-poetic forms of *poikilia* because of their impact on the soul. In so doing, he affirms the scintillating appeal of this quality that I explored most fully in Chapter 4, but he attributes the experience of *poikilia*'s pleasure to the irrational part of the soul. While visual forms of *poikilia* (e.g. textiles and paintings) are objectionable because they provide merely sensuous pleasure, it is in the performance of music as well as drama that *poikilia* has the most profound impact. It is in these contexts, moreover, that *poikilia* supposedly embodies unstable emotional states.[2]

First, in book 3, Socrates excludes *poikilia* from the category of orderly and proper rhythms (μὴ ποικίλους αὐτοὺς διώκειν μηδὲ παντοδαπὰς βάσεις, ἀλλὰ βίου ῥυθμοὺς ἰδεῖν κοσμίου τε καὶ ἀνδρείου τίνες εἰσίν, 399e9–400a2) precisely because rhythm and melody 'penetrate to the innermost part of the soul' (μάλιστα καταδύεται εἰς τὸ ἐντὸς τῆς ψυχῆς ὅ τε ῥυθμὸς καὶ ἁρμονία, 401d6). If previous chapters have illuminated powerful effects generated by *poikilia*, ranging from pleasure and enchantment to terror, Plato locates in this quality a direct conduit to the human soul.

For this reason, musical *poikilia* writ large ('the composition in all modes and metres', ἐν τῷ παναρμονίῳ καὶ ἐν πᾶσι ῥυθμοῖς, 404d12) must be eschewed so as to avoid the kind of ill effect associated with the decadent, Sicilian food that Plato invokes as an analogy (Σικελικὴν ποικιλίαν ὄψου, 404d2): 'In that case [musical *poikilia*], embellishment (ἡ ποικιλία) brought about licentiousness (ἀκολασίαν), and here illness is the result' (οὐκοῦν ἐκεῖ μὲν ἀκολασίαν ἡ ποικιλία ἐνέτικτεν, ἐνταῦθα δὲ νόσον, 404e2–3). While eating rich food engenders physical illness, so too is great variety in musical form supposed to bring about the psychic illness of *akolasia*, the licentiousness that fills the afflicted with 'insatiable appetites' (ἀπληστία) and forces them to wander in vain pursuit of their fulfilment (cf. *Resp.* 586a1–4).[3] This

---

[2] cf. Ferrari 1989 and Ford 2002: 217: 'The viewer of poetic imitations undergoes an almost physical change, as directly and inevitably as gymnastic exercise shapes the body.'

[3] cf. *Ti.* 87a5–6, where Timaeus uses *poikilia* to convey how humours, when trapped within

is an idea that surfaced most prominently in Chapter 6, where we saw Agamemnon and Glaucē consumed and destroyed by their appetites for *poikilia*. In this respect, their portrayals seem to fall into the category of the *poikilos mimēsis*, which book 10 explores and rejects.

As an example of a *poikilos mimēsis*, Socrates invokes Homeric and tragic representations of grieving heroes (605d). He dwells on the paradoxical combination of emotions that such spectacles invite, as audience members 'delight in' (χαίρομεν, 605d3) them at the same time as they 'suffer together with' (συμπάσχοντες, 605d4) these heroes as they weep and lament.[4] While this study has shown that such strong emotions in association with *poikilia* are not unique to Plato's conception, his point in invoking these responses is to claim that such portrayals appeal to the lower, irrational (ἀλόγιστον) part of the soul, as he goes on to explain (*Resp.* 604e1–7).[5]

Given that the pleasure of tragic performances is generated from the audience's ability to sympathise with the characters portrayed, it is therefore crucial for the *ēthos* portrayed to be 'easy to understand' (εὐπετὲς καταμαθεῖν). And the representation of volatile characters is the easiest to understand because most people are themselves just such characters in their own lives: the 'people of every sort' (παντοδαποῖς ἀνθρώποις) gathered in the theatre will only find intelligible and enjoyable a figure engaged in similarly 'irrational' activity. Plato's exegesis here recalls the dynamism of *poikilia* that has recurred throughout this book, for seeing a *poikilos mimēsis* is nothing if not a highly moving experience: it 'stirs up' and 'nourishes' the irrational part of the soul and thus enables it to compromise the workings of the rational faculty (τοῦτο ἐγείρει τῆς ψυχῆς καὶ τρέφει καὶ ἰσχυρὸν ποιῶν ἀπόλλυσι τὸ λογιστικόν, 605b3; cf. 606d4–8). And as we will see shortly, 'the people of every sort' that enjoy such spectacles are themselves a kind of *poikilia* that Plato conceptualises through the image of a 'multicoloured cloak'.

---

the body, upset the soul's movements and implant all kinds of undesirable conditions: 'And they [the humours] animate all manner of forms of bad temper and bad spirits, and bring to life rashness and cowardice, and also forgetfulness as well as stupidity' (ποικίλλει μὲν εἴδη δυσκολίας καὶ δυσθυμίας παντοδαπά, ποικίλλει δὲ θρασύτητός τε καὶ δειλίας, ἔτι δὲ λήθης ἅμα καὶ δυσμαθίας). This passage thus assigns a physiological aspect to the destructive movements of *poikilia* that find their counterpart in the *poikilia* of music and poetry.

[4] The bibliography on Plato's accounts of *mimēsis* is enormous. Although I am not dealing here with the philosophical problems at stake in this issue, I cite here a few philosophical analyses that have informed my interpretations: Belfiore 1984, Janaway 1995: 133–57, Halliwell 2009: ch. 2 and Moss 2007.

[5] On the apparent discrepancy between the tripartite division of the soul adumbrated in books 4 and 6 and book 10's division of the soul solely into 'rational' and 'irrational' elements, I have found Destrée 2011 particularly illuminating.

Multiplicity, changefulness, pleasure, passion: given these features that Plato recognises as fundamental to *poikilia*, it is little wonder that he opts to excise it. But it is also *poikilia*'s multifariousness that allows him to elaborate in vivid detail the problems that he sees in the democratic state. Take, for example, the infamous 'multicoloured cloak' that is introduced as an analogue for democracy in book 8:

ὥσπερ ἱμάτιον <u>ποικίλον</u> πᾶσιν ἄνθεσι <u>πεποικιλμένον</u>, οὕτω καὶ αὕτη πᾶσιν ἤθεσιν <u>πεποικιλμένη</u> καλλίστη ἂν φαίνοιτο. καὶ ἴσως μέν, ἦν δ᾽ ἐγώ, καὶ ταύτην, ὥσπερ οἱ παῖδές τε καὶ αἱ γυναῖκες <u>τὰ ποικίλα</u> θεώμενοι, καλλίστην ἂν πολλοὶ κρίνειαν.

'Just as a multicoloured cloak <u>brightly decorated</u> with all kinds of flowers, so this state <u>adorned</u> with all kinds of characters would appear to be the finest. Perhaps too', I said, 'many would judge it to be so, just as children and women do when they see <u>intricate fabric work.</u>' (557c5–9)[6]

This image of the cloak elaborately adorned with flowers recalls Chapter 1 and its focus on the textile patterns crafted for and by women, especially the description of Andromache's work with *poikilia* (ἐν δὲ θρόνα <u>ποικίλ</u>᾽ ἔπασσε, *Il.* 22.440–1). Moreover, this is an affinity that Plato recognises in his condemnation of the appeal of such an ornate aspect. For on this analogy, *poikilia* encapsulates the all-inclusive and motley nature of a state that panders to the will of the populace. *Poikilia* here thus has both literal and metaphorical force, (literally) typifying the tastes of the mob as well as (metaphorically) representing the variegated composition of democracy.[7] And the force of this image is to convey how, in the same way that only those with inferior or underdeveloped minds (i.e. women and children) would judge such an object as the many-coloured cloak to be the most beautiful, so too would the variegated, all-inclusive nature of the democratic state erroneously appear to be 'the finest' (καλλίστην) constitution to many people (καλλίστην ἂν πολλοὶ κρίνειαν).

This would be an erroneous judgement because *poikilia*, throughout this discussion, is used to characterise democracy as a state tantamount to anarchy, as Socrates makes explicit a little later on: 'It [democracy] seems it would be a pleasant (ἡδεῖα) constitution, anarchic and <u>richly varied</u> (ποικίλη), which doles out a kind of equality

---

[6] cf. the description of the decadent, 'inflamed city' (φλεγμαίνουσιν πόλιν, 373a1) in *Republic* 2 (372e–373c), where *poikilia* appears within a laundry list of the sorts of frivolous non-essentials that inhabitants of such a state would require.

[7] On this passage see also Villacèque 2010, who situates this metaphor and its anti-democratic rhetoric within the sociopolitical context of the post-Peloponnesian war.

to the equal and unequal alike' (558c2–4).[8] And if democracy is a form of *poikilia* because of its indiscriminate allotment of powers, this is so because the democratic state is supposed to function like the irrational and appetitive element of the soul.

In book 9, Socrates invokes a 'complex and many-headed animal (ἰδέαν θηρίου ποικίλου καὶ πολυκεφάλου, 588c7) to illustrate this appetitive component:

> πλάττε τοίνυν μίαν μὲν ἰδέαν θηρίου ποικίλου καὶ πολυκεφάλου, ἡμέρων δὲ θηρίων ἔχοντος κεφαλὰς κύκλῳ καὶ ἀγρίων, καὶ δυνατοῦ μεταβάλλειν καὶ φύειν ἐξ αὑτοῦ πάντα ταῦτα
>
> Now then, put together a single form of a complex many-headed animal, but with a circle of heads of both tame and wild beasts, capable of changing and growing these parts out of itself. (588c7–10)

Socrates formulates this creature in order to visualise (ἵνα εἰδῇ ὁ ἐκεῖνα λέγων οἷα ἔλεγεν, 588b11) the variety of desires and impulses contained within the sphere of the irrational part of the soul, the part associated with mixed pleasures and with intemperance, *akolasia*. This description is thus a sort of ekphrasis of the soul and so not unlike the shield of Achilles, as Socrates here 'fashions' (πλάττε) a creature just as fantastical as Hephaestus' shield imagery. But in this instance the function of the creature's multiplicity and *poikilia* is to delineate the irrationality of the appetitive element. Because it seeks only after bodily pleasures, it is not only multi-headed (πολυκεφάλου) but is also constantly and unpredictably shifting according to the ever-fluctuating needs and wants of the body. And it is this part that delights in and lusts after the sort of music and poetry that are ultimately excluded from the ideal state, a state which itself should not exhibit *poikilia* in any form.

For by admitting persons of all types and not making any attempt to restrain their individual impulses (557e–558a), the democratic state is for Plato the political counterpart of the individual who is entirely ruled by the appetitive and spirited elements of his soul. This is what Socrates indicates in book 8 by characterising the quintessential democratic man as the one who lives by his whimsy and 'enjoys the desire that each day happens to bring along'(διαζῇ τὸ καθ' ἡμέραν οὕτω χαριζόμενος τῇ προσπιπτούσῃ ἐπιθυμίᾳ, 561c7–8), which in turn is supposed to make him *poikilos*:

> οἶμαι δέ γε, ἦν δ' ἐγώ, καὶ παντοδαπόν τε καὶ πλείστων ἠθῶν μεστόν, καὶ τὸν καλόν τε καὶ ποικίλον, ὥσπερ ἐκείνην τὴν πόλιν, τοῦτον τὸν ἄνδρα εἶναι. ὂν

---

[8] καὶ εἴη, ὡς ἔοικεν, ἡδεῖα πολιτεία καὶ ἄναρχος καὶ ποικίλη, ἰσότητά τινα ὁμοίως ἴσοις τε καὶ ἀνίσοις διανέμουσα.

πολλοὶ ἂν καὶ πολλαὶ ζηλώσειαν τοῦ βίου, παραδείγματα πολιτειῶν τε καὶ τρόπων πλεῖστα ἐν αὐτῷ ἔχοντα.

'I certainly think', I said, 'this is a man of all sorts, full of so many characteristics, both fine and <u>varied</u>, just like that city. Many men and women would envy him his way of life with all the many examples of constitutions and traditions it contains.' (561e3–8)

The democratic man, and by analogy the democratic city (ὥσπερ ἐκείνην τὴν πόλιν), is thus envisioned as the embodiment of *poikilia* because both are receptive to impulses and desires of all sorts. For this reason, they, like the many-coloured cloak, present a desirable image (πολλαὶ ζηλώσειαν τοῦ βίου) because both the democratic man and the state admit all the features that are normally excluded from the life of a man or city that is ruled by reason, not passion and desire. And given the tyrannical character of the appetitive, it is thus because of the democratic appetite (*aplēstia*) for freedom (562b7–10) that the threat of the tyrant emerges. And the tyrant, in turn, can take power because he is surrounded by others who have also been driven mad by their appetites: the defining characteristic of the tyrant's soul (572e–573b).

Accordingly, the tyrant's group of sycophants is also described in terms of *poikilia*: 'Let's talk about the tyrant's camp once again, how he's going to provision (θρέψεται) this fine large <u>motley</u> (ποικίλον) crew constantly on the drift (οὐδέποτε ταὐτόν)' (λέγωμεν δὲ πάλιν ἐκεῖνο τὸ τοῦ τυράννου στρατόπεδον, τὸ καλόν τε καὶ πολὺ καὶ <u>ποικίλον</u> καὶ οὐδέποτε ταὐτόν, 568d5–8). It is precisely this quality of being 'constantly on the drift' or 'never the same' (<u>ποικίλον</u> καὶ οὐδέποτε ταὐτόν) that makes *poikilia* so disturbing to Plato and so tantalising in the earlier sources analysed in the preceding chapters.

The materiality of *poikilia* thus plays an active and fundamental role in shaping Plato's soul–state analogy. In spite of his condemnation of this quality, it is clear that *poikilia*'s various manifestations – whether in textiles, music or drama – are for Plato the very embodiment of changefulness and irrationality. In other words, the *Republic*'s invocations of *poikilia* offer a clear illustration of how material things can shape the mind: in this case, Plato's conception of the relationship between soul, world and state. From this brief overview of Plato's evocations of *poikilia* within the *Republic*, we can see how he layers images of *poikilia* to create a kind of Russian doll effect: *poikilia* (especially in music and theatre) is what the mob (the 'many-coloured cloak' of the democratic state) desires because such phenomena stimulate the irrational and appetitive element of the soul, which is in turn defined by its *poikilia* in its shifting lusts for sensuous pleasures. By tracking Plato's use of *poikilia* throughout the *Republic*, it thus becomes clear that he repeatedly invokes this imagery in order to depict how external, phenomenal qualities can become inner, embodied ones. For by focusing on *poikilia* in music and drama (both of which are able to powerfully affect and shape their audiences) as well as in the democratic state and soul, Plato illustrates the permeability of the soul and state in the very way that he recycles the terminology of *poikilia* throughout this work.

Plato's multifarious picture of *poikilia* not only corresponds to the variegated complexion of this concept that I have sought to illuminate in this book, but also finds a remarkable parallel in Clark's reflections on his own work: work that, as we have seen throughout this book, helps to shed new light on the place of *poikilia* in the archaic and classical poetic imaginary. In particular, Clark dwells on the multiplicity of cognitive models he has constructed over the years:

> What came next was, for me, a striking (almost psychoanalytic) moment of intel-lectual self-discovery. For each new framework . . . is really offering a new way of *seeing ourselves*, making everything spin, morph, and alter around some new central construct, be it distributed representation, coupling, decentralised control, offloading, or predictions. What I am selling, then, is really a succession of ways of understanding the mind – distinct perspectives each of which puts something new and potentially transformative at the centre of the cognitive universe. (2019: 294, emphasis in original)

As Clark makes explicit here, the various metaphors and analogies he has created over the years to capture mind–world interactions were not intended as substitutions for one another, but as fresh ways of looking at the same set of questions. I would argue that the same could be said of *poikilia*: that each of the chapters in this book has offered a new way of seeing humans in relation to the material world.

What unites the colourful spectrum of sensory and cognitive experiences we have analysed is a fascination with the nuances and complexities of mind–world encoun-ters. In this sense, the vision of *poikilia* formulated in the *Phaedo* encapsulates the variegated perspective on this concept that I have sought to construct. For when Socrates recounts the appearance of the divine world when seen from above – '[The hollows of the earth] furnish a certain appearance of colour as each one [colour] gleams amid the <u>variety</u> of other hues, such that it creates the impression of one continuous appearance of <u>variegation</u>' (χρώματός τι εἶδος παρέχεσθαι στίλβοντα ἐν τῇ τῶν ἄλλων χρωμάτων <u>ποικιλίᾳ,</u> ὥστε ἕν τι αὐτῆς εἶδος συνεχὲς <u>ποικίλον</u> φαντάζεσθαι, 110d1–3) – he could be describing the perceptual and phenomenolog-ical sphere of *poikilia* itself in all its scintillating complexity.

Bibliography

Ahmed, S. 2006. *Queer Phenomenology: Orientations, Objects, Others.* Duke University Press.

Aldrete, G. S., Bartell, S. M., and Aldrete, A. 2013. *Reconstructing Ancient Linen Body Armor: Unraveling the Linothorax Mystery.* Johns Hopkins University Press.

Allen, T. W., Halliday, W. R., and Sikes, E. E. 1936. *The Homeric Hymns.* 2nd edn. Oxford University Press.

Appadurai, A. 1986. *The Social Life of Things: Commodities in Cultural Perspective.* Cambridge University Press.

Athanassaki, L. 2012. 'Performance and Re-Performance: The Siphnian Treasury Evoked (Pindar's *Pythian* 6, *Olympian* 2, and *Isthmian* 2).' In Agócs, P., Carey, C., and Rawles, R. eds. *Reading the Victory Ode.* Cambridge University Press. 134–57.

Bader, F. 1987. 'La Racine de Poikilos, Pikros.' In Killen, J. T., Melena, J., and Olivier, J. P. eds. *Studies in Mycenaean and Classical Greek Presented to John Chadwick.* Universidad de Salamanca. 41–60.

Bakogianni, A., and Hope, V. M., eds. 2015. *War as Spectacle: Ancient and Modern Perspectives on the Display of Armed Conflict.* Bloomsbury.

Barber, E. 1991. *Prehistoric Textiles: The Development of Cloth in the Neolithic and Bronze Ages with Special References to the Aegean.* Princeton University Press.

Barrow, R. 2015. 'The Body, Human and Divine in Greek Sculpture.' In Destrée, P., and Murray, P. eds. *A Companion to Ancient Aesthetics.* Wiley-Blackwell. 94–108.

Beazley, J. D. 1986. *The Development of Attic Black Figure.* University of California Press.

Becker, A. S. 1990. 'The Shield of Achilles and the Poetics of Homeric Description.' *American Journal of Philology* 111 (2): 139–53.

—. 1995. *The Shield of Achilles and the Poetics of Ekphrasis*. Rowman & Littlefield.

—. 2003. 'Contest or Concert? A Speculative Essay on Ecphrasis and Rivalry between the Arts.' *Classical and Modern Literature* 23 (1): 1–14.

Belfiore, E. 1984. 'A Theory of Imitation in Plato's Republic.' *Transactions of the American Philological Association* 114: 121–46.

Bennett, J. 2001. *The Enchantment of Modern Life: Attachments, Crossings, and Ethics*. Princeton University Press.

—. 2010. *Vibrant Matter: A Political Ecology of Things*. Duke University Press.

—. 2012. 'Systems and Things: A Response to Graham Harman and Timothy Morton.' *New Literary History* 43 (2): 225–33.

Bergren, A. 2008. *Weaving Truth: Essays on Language and the Female in Greek Thought*. Center for Hellenic Studies.

Berleant, A. 1970. *The Aesthetic Field: A Phenomenology of Aesthetic Experience*. Thomas.

Berryman, S. 2003. 'Ancient Automata and Mechanical Explanation.' *Phronesis* 48 (4): 344–69.

—. 2009. *The Mechanical Hypothesis in Ancient Greek Natural Philosophy*. Cambridge University Press.

Bettini, M. 2008. *Voci: Antropologia Sonora del Mondo Antico*. G. Einaudi.

Bielfeldt, R. 2014. 'Gegenwart und Vergegenwärtigung: Dynamische Dinge im Ausgang von Homer.' In Bielfeldt, R. ed. *Ding und Mensch in der Antike: Gegenwart und Vergegenwärtigung*. Universitätsverlag *Winter*: 23–38.

—. 2016. 'Sight and Light: Reified Gazes and Looking Artefacts in the Greek Cultural Imagination.' In Squire, M. ed. *Sight and the Ancient Senses*. Routledge. 123–42.

—. 2018. 'Candelabrus and Trimalchio: Embodied Histories of Roman Lampstands and Their Slaves.' *Art History* 41 (3): 420–43.

Billings, J. 2018. 'Orestes' Urn in Word and Action.' In Telò, M., and Mueller, M. eds. *The Materialities of Greek Tragedy*. Bloomsbury Academic. 49–62.

Blondell, R. 2013. *Helen of Troy: Beauty, Myth, Devastation*. Oxford University Press.

Blundell, S. 1998. *Women in Classical Athens*. Bloomsbury Academic.

Boardman, J. 2001. *The History of Greek Vases: Potters, Painters and Pictures*. Thames & Hudson.

Boivin, N. 2008. *Material Cultures, Material Minds: The Impact of Things on Human Thought, Society, and Evolution*. Cambridge University Press.

Bolling, G. 1958. 'ΠΟΙΚΙΛΟΣ and ΘΡΩΝΑ.' *American Journal of Philology* 79 (3): 275–83.

Bonifazi, A. 2004. 'Communication in Pindar's Deictic Acts.' *Arethusa* 37 (3): 391–414.

Bonner, C. 1949. 'KESTOS IMAS and the Saltire of Aphrodite.' *American Journal of Philology* 70 (1): 1–6.

Bowie, A. M. 2013. *Odyssey: Books XIII–XIV*. Cambridge University Press.

Bradley, M. 2009. *Colour and Meaning in Ancient Rome*. Cambridge University Press.

Brenk, F. E. 1977. 'Aphrodite's Girdle: No Way to Treat a Lady *(Iliad* 14.214–223).' *The Classical Bulletin* 54: 17–19.

Briand, M. 2013. 'Vision Spectaculaire et Vision Imaginative dans la Poésie Mélique Grecque: Le Cas des Épinicies de Pindare.' *Pallas* 92: 115–31.

—. 2016. 'Light and Vision in Pindar's Olympian Odes: Interplays of Imagination and Performance.' In Cazzato, V., and Lardinois, A. eds. *The Look of Lyric: Greek Song and the Visual*. Brill. 1:238–54.

Brinkmann, V. 2007. *Gods in Color: Painted Sculpture of Classical Antiquity: Exhibition at the Arthur M. Sackler Museum, Harvard University Art Museums, in Cooperation with Staatliche Antikensammlungen and Glyptothek Munich, Stiftung Archäologie Munich, September 22, 2007–January 20, 2008*. Biering und Brinkmann.

Brinkmann, V., and Wünsche, R. 2004. *Bunte Götter: Die Farbigkeit Antiker Skulptur. Eine Ausstellung der Staatlichen Antikensammlungen und Glyptothek München in Zusammenarbeit mit der Ny Carlsberg Glyptotek Kopenhagen und den Vatikanischen Museen, Rom*. 2nd printing. Munich: Staatliche Antikensammlungen und Glyptothek.

Brockliss, W. 2018. '"Dark Ecology" and the *Works and Days*.' *Helios* 45 (1): 1–36.

Brøns, C. 2017. *Gods and Garments: Textiles in Greek Sanctuaries in the 7th to the 1st Centuries BC*. Oxbow Books.

Brouillet, M. forthcoming. '"Si Fort Résonna Arès": Retour sur le Corps des Dieux chez Homère.'

Brouillet, M., and Carastro, C. 2018. 'Parures Divines: Puissances et Constructions Homériques de l'Objet.' In *Dossier: Place aux Objets! Présentification et Vie des Artefacts en Grèce Ancienne*. Éditions de l'École des Hautes Études en Sciences Sociales. 85–106.

Brown, A. S. 1997. 'Aphrodite and the Pandora Complex.' *Classical Quarterly* 47 (1): 26–47.

Brown, B. 1996. *The Material Unconscious: American Amusement, Stephen Crane and the Economies of Play*. Harvard University Press.

—. 2001. 'Thing Theory.' *Critical Inquiry* 28 (1): 1–22.

—. 2003. *A Sense of Things: The Object Matter of American Literature*. University of Chicago Press.

—. 2015. *Other Things*. University of Chicago Press.

Budelmann, F. 2009. 'Introducing Greek Lyric.' In Budelmann, F. ed. *The Cambridge Companion to Greek Lyric*. Cambridge University Press. 1–18.

—. 2018. *Greek Lyric: A Selection*. Cambridge University Press.

Budelmann, F., and LeVen, P. 2014. 'Timotheus' Poetics of Blending: A Cognitive Approach to the Language of the New Music.' *Classical Philology* 109 (3): 191–210.

Budelmann, F., and Phillips, T. 2018. 'Introduction: Textual Events: Performance and the Lyric in Early Greece.' In Budelmann, F., and Phillips, T. eds. *Textual Events: Performance and the Lyric in Early Greece*. Oxford University Press. 1–27.

Bungard, C. 2011. 'Lies, Lyres, and Laughter: Surplus Potential in the *Homeric Hymn to Hermes*.' *Arethusa* 44 (2): 143–65.

Burnett, A. P. 1983. *Three Archaic Poets: Archilochus, Alcaeus, Sappho*. Harvard University Press.

—. 2005. *Pindar's Songs for Young Athletes of Aigina*. Oxford University Press.

Butler, S. 2015. *The Ancient Phonograph*. Zone Books.

Buxton, R. G. A. 1982. *Persuasion in Greek Tragedy: A Study of Peitho*. Cambridge University Press.

Calame, C. 1999. *The Poetics of Eros in Ancient Greece*. Trans. Janet Lloyd. Princeton University Press.

—. 2004. 'Deictic Ambiguity and Auto-Referentiality: Some Examples from Greek Poetics.' Trans. Jenny Strauss Clay. *Arethusa* 37 (3): 415–43.

Campbell, D. A. 1982. *Greek Lyric: Sappho Alcaeus*. Harvard University Press.

Canevaro, L. G. 2018 *Women of Substance in Homeric Epic: Objects, Gender, Agency*. Oxford University Press.

—. 2019. 'Materiality and Classics: (Re)Turning to the Material.' *Journal of Hellenic Studies* 139: 222–32.

Carpenter, T. H. 1986. *Dionysian Imagery in Archaic Greek Art: Its Development in Black-Figure Vase Painting*. Clarendon Press.

Cave, T. 2016. *Thinking with Literature: Towards a Cognitive Criticism*. Oxford University Press.

Chadwick, J., and Baumbach, L. 1963. 'The Mycenaean Greek Vocabulary.' *Glotta* 41: 157–271.

Chalmers, D. J. 2019. 'Extended Cognition and Extended Consciousness.' In Colombo, M., Irvine, E., and Stapleton, M. eds. *Andy Clark and His Critics*. Oxford University Press. 9–20.

Chantraine, P. 1968. *Dictionnaire Étymologique de la Langue Grecque: Histoire des Mots*. Klincksieck.

Chase, G. H. 1902. 'The Shield Devices of the Greeks.' *Harvard Studies in Classical Philology* 13: 61–127.

Chesi, G. M., and Sclavi, G. 2020. 'Pandora and Robotic Technology Today.' In Chesi, G. M. and Spiegel, F. eds. *Classical Literature and Posthumanism*. Bloomsbury Academic. 301–8.

Chua, L., and Elliott, M., eds. 2013. *Distributed Objects: Meaning and Mattering after Alfred Gell*. Berghahn Books.

Clark, A. 1997. *Being There: Putting Brain, Body, and World Together Again*. MIT Press.

—. 2003. *Natural-Born Cyborgs: Minds, Technologies, and the Future of Human Intelligence*. Oxford University Press.

—. 2007. 'Curing Cognitive Hiccups: A Defense of the Extended Mind.' *The Journal of Philosophy* 104 (4): 163–92.

—. 2008. *Supersizing the Mind: Embodiment, Action, and Cognitive Extension*. Oxford University Press.

—. 2009. 'Spreading the Joy? Why the Machinery of Consciousness Is (Probably) Still in the Head.' *Mind* 118 (472): 963–93.

—. 2010. 'Material Surrogacy and the Supernatural: Reflections on the Role of Artefacts in "Off-Line" Cognition.' In *The Cognitive Life of Things: Recasting the Boundaries of the Mind*. McDonald Institute for Archaeological Research. 23–8.

—. 2016. *Surfing Uncertainty: Prediction, Action, and the Embodied Mind*. Oxford University Press.

—. 2019. 'Replies to Critics: In Search of the Embodied, Extended, Enactive, Predictive (EEE-P) Mind.' In Colombo, M., Irvine, E., and Stapleton, M. eds. *Andy Clark and His Critics*. Oxford University Press. 266–302.

Clark, A., and Chalmers, D. 1998. 'The Extended Mind.' *Analysis* 58 (1): 7–19.

Clarke, M. 2004. 'The Semantics of Colour in the Early Greek Word Hoard.' In Cleland, L., Davies, G., and Stears, K. eds. *Colour in the Ancient Mediterranean World*. Archaeopress. 131–9.

Clarke, M. J. 1999. *Flesh and Spirit in the Songs of Homer: A Study of Words and Myths*. Oxford University Press.

—. 2005. 'On the Semantics of Ancient Greek Smiles.' In Cairns, D. ed. *Body Language in the Greek and Roman Worlds*. Classical Press of Wales. 37–54.

Clay, J. 1974. 'Demas and Aude: The Nature of Divine Transformation in Homer.' *Hermes* 102: 129–36.

Clements, A. 2015. 'Divine Scents and Presence.' In *Smell and the Ancient Senses*. Routledge. 46–59.

Collins, S. D., and Stauffer, D. 1999. 'The Challenge of Plato's *Menexenus*.' *The Review of Politics* 61 (1): 85–115.

Colombo, M., Irvine, E., and Stapleton, M., eds. 2019. *Andy Clark and His Critics*. Oxford University Press.

Cook, A. 2018. '4E Cognition and the Humanities.' In Newen, A., De Bruin, L., and Gallagher, S. eds. *The Oxford Handbook of 4E Cognition*. Oxford University Press. 875–92.

Coole, D., and Frost, S., eds. 2010. *New Materialisms: Ontology, Agency, and Politics*. Duke University Press.

Corsín Jiménez, A., and Nahum-Claudel, C. 2019. 'The Anthropology of Traps: Concrete Technologies and Theoretical Interfaces.' *Journal of Material Culture* 24 (4): 383–400.

Crane, G. 1993. 'Politics of Consumption and Generosity in the Carpet Scene of the "Agamemnon".' *Classical Philology* 88 (2): 117–36.

Culhed, E. 2014. 'Movement and Sound on the Shield of Achilles in Ancient Exegesis.' *Greek, Roman and Byzantine Studies* 54: 192–219.

Cunningham, V. 2007. 'Why Ekphrasis?' *Classical Philology* 102 (1): 57–71.

Cuomo, S. 2007. *Technology and Culture in Greek and Roman Antiquity*. Cambridge University Press.

Currie, B. 2012. 'Hesiod on Human History.' In Marincola, J. ed. *Greek Notions of the Past in the Archaic and Classical Eras*. Edinburgh University Press. 37–64.

—. 2013. 'The Pindaric First Person in Flux.' *Classical Antiquity* 32 (2): 243–82.

Cursaru, G. 2012. 'Les Sandales d'Hermès, III: Enquête sur les Traces des σάνδαλα dans l'Hymne Homérique à Hermès.' *Mouseion: Journal of the Classical Association of Canada* 1012 (1): 17–50.

D'Alessio, G. B. 1994. 'First-Person Problems in Pindar.' *Bulletin of the Institute of Classical Studies* 39: 117–39.

—. 2004. 'Past Future and Present Past: Temporal Deixis in Greek Archaic Lyric.' *Arethusa* 37 (3): 267–94.

Davison, J. A. 1959. 'Anacreon, Fr. 5 Diehl.' *Transactions and Proceedings of the American Philological Association* 90: 40–7.

Deacy, S., and Villing, A. 2009. 'What Was the Colour of Athena's Aegis?' *Journal of Hellenic Studies* 129: 111–29.

DeLanda, M. 2006. *A New Philosophy of Society: Assemblage Theory and Social Complexity*. Continuum.

—. 2016. *Assemblage Theory*. Edinburgh University Press.

Delcourt, M. 1982. *Héphaistos, ou, La Légende du Magicien*. Les Belles Lettres.

Deleuze, G., and Guattari, F. 1987. *A Thousand Plateaus: Capitalism and Schizophrenia*. Trans. Brian Massumi. University of Minnesota Press.

DeMarrais, E., Gosden, C., and Renfrew, C., eds. 2004. *Rethinking Materiality: The Engagement of Mind with the Material World*. McDonald Institute for Archaeological Research.

Dennett, D. 1991. *Consciousness Explained*. Little, Brown.

Denniston, J. D., and Page, D. 1957. *Aeschylus: Agamemnon*. Oxford University Press.

Destrée, P. 2011. 'Poetry, Thumos, and Pity in the Republic.' In Destrée, P., and Herrmann, F. eds. *Plato and the Poets*. Brill. 267–81.

Destrée, P., and Murray, P., eds. 2015. *A Companion to Ancient Aesthetics*. John Wiley & Sons.

Detienne, M., and Vernant, J.-P. 1978. *Cunning Intelligence in Greek Culture and Society*. Trans. Janet Lloyd. University of Chicago Press.

Devecka, M. 2013. 'Did the Greeks Believe in Their Robots?' *Cambridge Classical Journal* 59: 52–69.

Dewey, J. 1934. *Art as Experience*. Minton, Balch.

Dietrich, N. 2010. *Figur ohne Raum? Bäume und Felsen in der attischen Vasenmalerei des 6. und 5. Jahrhunderts v. Chr.* De Gruyter.

—. 2011. '"Archaischer Realismus": Archaische Plastik als Alternatives Konzept von Realismus im Bild.' In *Jahreshefte Des Österreichischen Instituts in Wien*. 13–46.

—. 2017. 'Framing Archaic Greek Sculpture: Figure, Ornament, and Script.' In Platt, V., and Squire, M. eds. *The Frame in Classical Art: A Cultural History*. Cambridge University Press. 270–316.

—. 2018a. 'Order and Contingency in Archaic Greek Ornament and Figure.' In Dietrich, N., and Squire, M. eds. *Ornament and Figure in Graeco-Roman Art: Rethinking Visual Ontologies in Classical Antiquity*. De Gruyter. 167–202.

—. 2018b. 'Viewing and Identification: The Agency of the Viewer in Archaic and Early Classical Greek Visual Culture.' In Kampakoglou, A., and Novokhatko, A. eds. *Gaze, Vision, and Visuality in Ancient Greek Literature*. De Gruyter. 464–92.

Dietrich, N., and Dietrich, N. 2015. 'Figure and Space in Vase Painting and in Architectural Sculpture: On the (Ir-)Relevance of the Medium.' *Tempo* 21 (38): 57–94.

Dietrich, N., and Squire, M. 2018. *Ornament and Figure in Graeco-Roman Art: Rethinking Visual Ontologies in Classical Antiquity*. De Gruyter.

Donohue, A. A. 2005. *Greek Sculpture and the Problem of Description*. Cambridge University Press.

Dougherty, C. 2001. *The Raft of Odysseus: The Ethnographic Imagination of Homer's Odyssey*. Oxford University Press.

Draycott, J. 2018. *Prostheses in Antiquity*. Routledge.

Dross-Krüpe, K., and Paetz gen. Schieck, A. 2014. 'Unravelling the Tangled Threads of Ancient Embroidery: A Compilation of Written Sources and Archaeologically Preserved Textiles.' In Harlow, M., and Nosch, M.-L. eds. *Greek and Roman Textiles and Dress: An Interdisciplinary Anthology*. Oxbow Books. 207–35.

Edmunds, S. T. 2012. 'Picturing Homeric Weaving.' In *Donum Natalicum Digitaliter Confectum Gregorio Nagy Septuagenario a Discipulis Collegis Familiaribus Oblatum*. Center for Hellenic Studies.

Edwards, M. W. 1991. *The Iliad: A Commentary*. Cambridge University Press.

Elsner, J. 2006. 'Reflections on the "Greek Revolution": From Changes in Viewing to the Transformation of Subjectivity.' In Goldhill, S., and Osborne, R. eds. *Rethinking Revolutions Through Ancient Greece*. Cambridge University Press. 68–95.

Erbse, H. 1969. *Scholia Graeca in Homeri Iliadem (Scholia Vetera)*. De Gruyter.

Essinger, J. 2007. *Jacquard's Web: How a Hand-Loom Led to the Birth of the Information Age*. Oxford University Press.

Fanfani, G. 2017. 'Weaving a Song: Convergences in Greek Poetic Imagery between Textile and Musical Terminology. An Overview on Archaic and Classical Literature.' In Gaspa, S., Michel, C., and Nosch, M.-L. eds. *Textile Terminologies from the Orient to the Mediterranean and Europe, 1000 BC to 1000 AD*. Zea Books. 421–36.

Fanfani, G., and Harlizius-Klück, E. 2016. '(B)Orders in Ancient Weaving and Archaic Greek Poetry.' In Fanfani, G., Harlow, M., and Nosch, M.-L. eds. *Spinning Fates and the Song of the Loom: The Use of Textiles, Clothing and Cloth Production as Metaphor, Symbol and Narrative Device in Greek and Latin Literature*. Oxbow Books. 61–99.

Fanfani, G., Harlow, M., and Nosch, M.-L. 2016. *Spinning Fates and the Song of the Loom: The Use of Textiles, Clothing and Cloth Production as Metaphor, Symbol and Narrative Device in Greek and Latin Literature*. Oxbow Books.

Faraone, C. 1987. 'Hephaestus the Magician and Near Eastern Parallels for Alcinous' Watchdogs.' *Greek, Roman and Byzantine Studies* 28: 257–80.

—. 1990. 'Aphrodite's ΚΕΣΤΟΣ and Apples for Atalanta: Aphrodisiacs in Early Greek Myth and Ritual.' *Phoenix* 44 (3): 219–43.

—. 1999. *Ancient Greek Love Magic*. Harvard University Press.

Fauconnier, G., and Turner, M. 2002. *The Way We Think: Conceptual Blending and the Mind's Hidden Complexities*. Basic Books.

Fearn, D. 2017. *Pindar's Eyes: Visual and Material Culture in Epinician Poetry*. Oxford University Press.

Felski, R. 2011. 'Context Stinks!' *New Literary History* 42 (4): 573–91.

Ferrari, F. 2010. *Sappho's Gift: The Poet and Her Community*. Trans. Benjamin Acosta-Hughes and Lucia Prauscello. Michigan Classical Press.

Ferrari, G. 1989. 'Plato and Poetry.' In Kennedy, G. ed. *The Cambridge History of Literary Criticism. Vol. 1: Classical Criticism.* Cambridge University Press. 92–149.

Finkelberg, M. 1998. *The Birth of Literary Fiction in Ancient Greece.* Oxford.

Fisher, N. 2015. 'The Pleasures of Reciprocity: Charis and the Athletic Body in Pindar.' In Prost, F., and Wilgaux, J. eds. *Penser et Représenter le Corps dans l'Antiquité.* Presses Universitaires de Rennes. 227–45.

Fitzgerald, W. 2016. *Variety: The Life of a Roman Concept.* University of Chicago Press.

Fletcher, J. 2009. 'Weaving Women's Tales in Euripides' *Ion.*' In Cousland, J. R. C., and Hume, J. R. eds. *The Play of Texts and Fragments: Essays in Honour of Martin Cropp.* Brill. 127–40.

Foley, J. M. 1999. *Homer's Traditional Art.* Penn State University Press.

Ford, A. 1992. *Homer: The Poetry of the Past.* Cornell University Press.

—. 2002. *The Origins of Criticism: Literary Culture and Poetic Theory in Classical Greece.* Princeton University Press.

Fowler, B. H. 1984. 'The Archaic Aesthetic.' *American Journal of Philology* 105 (2): 119–49.

Fowler, H. N. 1925. *Plato: Statesman, Philebus, Ion.* Harvard University Press.

Fraenkel, E. 1950. *Agamemnon.* Oxford: Clarendon Press.

Francis, J. A. 2009. 'Metal Maidens, Achilles' Shield, and Pandora: The Beginnings of "Ekphrasis".' *American Journal of Philology* 130 (1): 1–23.

Freeman, D. C. 1995. '"Catch[Ing] the Nearest Way": Macbeth and Cognitive Metaphor.' *Journal of Pragmatics* 24 (6): 689–708.

Frontisi-Ducroux, F. 1975. *Dédale: Mythologie de l'Artisan en Grèce Ancienne.* François Maspero.

—. 1995. *Du Masque au Visage: Aspects de l'Identité en Grèce Ancienne.* Flammarion.

—. 2002. '"Avec Son Diaphragme Visionnaire: Ἰδυίῃσι Πραπίδεσσι", *Iliade* XVIII, 481: À Propos du Bouclier d'Achille.' *Revue des Études Anciennes* 115: 463–84.

Gaifman, M., and Platt, V. 2018. 'Introduction: From Grecian Urn to Embodied Object.' *Art History* 41 (3): 402–19.

Gaifman, M., Platt, V., and Squire, M., eds. 2018. *The Embodied Object in Classical Antiquity: Art History.* Association for Art History.

Gell, A. 1992. 'The Technology of Enchantment and the Enchantment of Technology.' In Coote, J., and Shelton, A. eds. *Anthropology, Art and Aesthetics.* Clarendon Press. 40–67.

—. 1998. *Art and Agency: An Anthropological Theory.* Clarendon Press.

Gellar-Goad, T. H. M. 2017. 'Failure of the Textual Relation: Anacreon's Purple

Ball Poem (PMG 358).' In Park, A. ed. *Resemblance, Reality, and Tradition in Greek Thought*. Routledge. 46–64.

Gibbs, R. W., Jr. 2017. *Metaphor Wars: Conceptual Metaphors in Human Life*. Cambridge University Press.

Gibson, J. 1986. *The Ecological Approach to Visual Perception*. Lawrence Erlbaum.

Gildersleeve, B. 1885. *Pindar: The Olympian and Pythian Odes*. Harper & Brothers.

Goheen, R. F. 1955. 'Aspects of Dramatic Symbolism: Three Studies in the *Oresteia*.' *American Journal of Philology* 76 (2): 113–37.

Goldhill, S. 1984. *Language, Sexuality, Narrative: The Oresteia*. Cambridge University Press.

Gorman, R., and Gorman, V. B. 2014. *Corrupting Luxury in Ancient Greek Literature*. University of Michigan Press.

Gosden, C. 2004. *Rethinking Materiality: The Engagement of Mind with the Material World*. McDonald Institute for Archaeological Research.

Gottschalk, H. B. 1964. 'The *de Coloribus* and Its Author.' *Hermes* 92 (1): 59–85.

Grand-Clément, A. 2011. *La Fabrique des Couleurs: Histoire du Paysage Sensible des Grecs Anciens*. De Boccard.

—. 2015. '*Poikilia*.' In Destrée, P. and Murray, P. eds. *A Companion to Ancient Aesthetics*. Wiley-Blackwell. 406–21.

—. 2016. 'Gold and Purple: Brilliance, Materiality and Agency of Color in Ancient Greece.' In Goldman, R. B. ed. *Essays in Global Color History: Interpreting the Ancient Spectrum*. De Gruyter. 121–37.

—. 2018. 'La Saveur de l'Immortalité: Les Mille et Une Vertus de l'Ambroisie et du Nectar dans la Tradition Homérique.' *Pallas: Revue d'Études Antiques* (106): 69–83.

Grethlein, J. 2008. 'Memory and Material Objects in the *Iliad* and the *Odyssey*.' *Journal of Hellenic Studies* 128: 27–51.

—. 2011. 'Divine, Human and Poetic Time in Pindar, *Pythian* 9.' *Mnemosyne* 64 (3): 383–409.

—. 2016. 'Sight and Reflexivity: Theorizing Vision in Greek Vase-Painting.' In Squire, M. ed. *Sight and the Ancient Senses*. Routledge. 85–106.

—. 2017. *Aesthetic Experiences and Classical Antiquity: The Significance of Form in Narratives and Pictures*. Cambridge University Press.

—. 2018. 'Ornamental and Formulaic Patterns: The Semantic Significance of Form in Early Greek Vase-Painting and Homeric Epic.' In Dietrich, N. and Squire, M. eds. *Ornament and Figure in Graeco-Roman Art: Rethinking Visual Ontologies in Classical Antiquity*. De Gruyter. 73–96.

—. 2020. 'Odysseus and His Bed: From Significant Objects to Thing Theory in Homer.' *Classical Quarterly* 70: 1–16.

Grethlein, J., and Huitink, L. 2017. 'Homer's Vividness: An Enactive Approach.' *Journal of Hellenic Studies* 137: 67–91.

Gross, K. 1992. *Dream of the Moving Statue*. Penn State University Press.

Grusin, R. 2015. *Nonhuman Turn*. University of Minnesota Press.

Gurd, S. A. 2016. *Dissonance: Auditory Aesthetics in Ancient Greece*. Fordham University Press.

Hainsworth, B. 1993. *The Iliad: A Commentary. Vol. 3: Books 9–12*. Cambridge University Press.

Hall, E. 2006. *The Theatrical Cast of Athens: Interactions Between Ancient Greek Drama and Society*. Oxford: Oxford University Press.

—. 2018. 'Materialisms Old and New.' In Telò, M., and Mueller, M. eds. *The Materialities of Greek Tragedy: Objects and Affect in Aeschylus, Sophocles, and Euripides*. Bloomsbury Academic. 203–18.

Halliwell, S. 1988. *Plato: Republic 10, with Translation and Commentary*. Aris & Phillips.

—. 2009. *The Aesthetics of Mimesis: Ancient Texts and Modern Problems*. Princeton University Press.

—. 2011. *Between Ecstasy and Truth: Interpretations of Greek Poetics from Homer to Longinus*. Oxford University Press.

Hamilakis, Y. 2013. *Archaeology and the Senses: Human Experience, Memory, and Affect*. Cambridge University Press.

Hamilton, J. T. 2003. *Soliciting Darkness: Pindar, Obscurity, and the Classical Tradition*. Harvard University Press.

Haraway, D. 1991. 'A Cyborg Manifesto: Science, Technology, and Socialist-Feminism in the Late Twentieth Century.' In Haraway, D. *Simians, Cyborgs, and Women: The Reinvention of Nature*. Routledge.

Harman, G. 2011. *Quentin Meillassoux: Philosophy in the Making*. Edinburgh University Press.

Harrison, E. B. 1991. 'The Dress of Archaic Greek Korai.' In Buitron-Oliver, D. ed. *New Perspectives in Early Greek Art*. Yale University Press. 216–39.

Harvey, P., Casella, E. C., Evans, G., Knox, H., McLean, C., Silva, E. B., Thoburn, N., and Woodward, K., eds. 2013. *Objects and Materials: A Routledge Companion*. Routledge.

Haug, A. 2018. 'Ornament und Design: Attisch geometrische Figuralgefäße und Gefäße mit plastischem Dekor.' In Dietrich, N. and Squire, M. eds. *Ornament and Figure in Graeco-Roman Art: Rethinking Visual Ontologies in Classical Antiquity*. De Gruyter. 97–128.

Hausrath, A., and Hunger, H. 1970. *Corpus Fabularom Aesopicarum. Vols. 1.1 and 1.2*. Teubner.

Heath, J. 2005. *The Talking Greeks: Speech, Animals, and the Other in Homer, Aeschylus, and Plato*. Cambridge University Press.

Heffernan, J. A. W. 1993. *Museum of Words: The Poetics of Ekphrasis from Homer to Ashbery*. University of Chicago Press.

Heiden, B. 2010. 'Truth and Personal Agreement in Archaic Greek Poetry: The *Homeric Hymn to Hermes*.' *Philosophy and Literature* 34 (2): 409–24.

Hett, W. S. 1936. *Aristotle: Minor Works: On Colours. On Things Heard. Physiognomics. On Plants. On Marvellous Things Heard. Mechanical Problems. On Indivisible Lines. The Situations and Names of Winds. On Melissus, Xenophanes, Gorgias*. Harvard University Press.

—. 1957. *Aristotle: On the Soul, Parva Naturalia, On Breath*. Harvard University Press.

Hodder, I. 2012. *Entangled: An Archaeology of the Relationships between Humans and Things*. John Wiley & Sons.

Holmes, B. 2010. *The Symptom and the Subject: The Emergence of the Physical Body in Ancient Greece*. Princeton University Press.

—. 2015. 'Situating Scamander: "Natureculture" in the *Iliad*.' *Ramus* 44 (1–2): 29–51.

Hölscher, T. 2018. *Visual Power in Ancient Greece and Rome: Between Art and Social Reality*. University of California Press.

Hubbard, T. K. 1992. 'Nature and Art in the Shield of Achilles.' *Arion: A Journal of Humanities and the Classics* 2 (1): 16–41.

Hunzinger, C. 2015. 'Wonder.' In Destrée, P. and Murray, P. eds. *A Companion to Ancient Aesthetics*. Wiley-Blackwell. 422–37.

Hurwit, J. 1977. 'Image and Frame in Greek Art.' *American Journal of Archaeology* 81 (1): 1–30.

—. 1992. 'A Note on Ornament, Nature, and Boundary in Early Greek Art.' *Bulletin antieke Beschavung* 67: 63–72.

Hutchinson, G. O. 2001. *Greek Lyric Poetry: A Commentary on Selected Larger Pieces*. Oxford University Press.

Ihde, D., and Malafouris, L. 2019. '*Homo Faber* Revisited: Postphenomenology and Material Engagement Theory.' *Philosophy and Technology* 32 (2): 195–214.

Ingold, T. 2010a. 'The Textility of Making.' *Cambridge Journal of Economics* 34 (1): 91–102.

—. 2010b. 'Transformations of the Line: Traces, Threads and Surfaces.' *Textile* 8 (1): 10–35.

Iovino, S., and Oppermann, S., eds. 2014. *Material Ecocriticism*. Indiana University Press.

Irwin, E. 1974. *Colour Terms in Greek Poetry*. Hakkert.

Janaway, C. 1995. *Images of Excellence: Plato's Critique of the Arts*. Oxford University Press.

Janko, R. 1992. *The Iliad: A Commentary. Vol. IV: Books 13–16*. Cambridge University Press.

Jenkins, I. D. 1985. 'The Ambiguity of Greek Textiles.' *Arethusa* 18 (2): 109–32.

Johannsen, N. 2012. 'Archaeology and the Inanimate Agency Proposition: A Critique and a Suggestion.' In Johannsen, N., Jessen, M. D., and Jensen, H. J. eds. *Excavating the Mind: Cross-Sections through Culture, Cognition and Materiality*. Aarhus University Press. 305–47.

Johannsen, N., Jessen, M. D., and Jensen, H. J., eds. 2012. *Excavating the Mind: Cross-Sections through Culture, Cognition and Materiality*. Aarhus University Press.

Johnston, S. I. 1995. 'The Song of the Iynx: Magic and Rhetoric in *Pythian* 4.' *Transactions of the American Philological Association* 125: 177–206.

Jong, I. J. F. de. 2011. 'The Shield of Achilles: From Metalepsis to *Mise en Abyme*.' *Ramus* 40 (1): 1–14.

Jouanna, J. 1999. 'Le Trône, les Fleurs, le Char et la Puissance d'Aphrodite (Sappho I, v. 1, 11, 19 et 22): Remarques sur le Texte, sur les Composés en -Θρονος et sur les Homérismes de Sappho.' *Revue des Études Grecques* 112 (1): 99–126.

Kahn, C. H. 1963. 'Plato's Funeral Oration: The Motive of the *Menexenus*.' *Classical Philology* 58 (4): 220–34.

Karakasi, K. 2003. *Archaic Korai*. J. Paul Getty Museum.

Karanika, A. 2014. *Voices at Work: Women, Performance, and Labor in Ancient Greece*. Johns Hopkins University Press.

Keesling, C. 2009. 'Finding the Gods: Greek and Cypriot Votive Korai Revisited.' In Mylonopoulos, J. ed. *Divine Images and Human Imaginations in Ancient Greece and Rome*. Brill. 87–103.

Keesling, K. 2003. *The Votive Statues of the Athenian Acropolis*. Cambridge University Press.

Kei, N. 2011. '*Poikilia* et *Kosmos* Floraux dans la Céramique Attique du VI et du V Siècle.' In Bodiou, L., Gherchanoc, F., Huet, V., and Mehl, V. eds. *Parures et Artifices: Le Corps Exposé dans l'Antiquité*. L'Harmattan: 233–53.

Kenaan, V. L. 2008. *Pandora's Senses: The Feminine Character of the Ancient Text*. University of Wisconsin Press.

Kerch, T. M. 2008. 'Plato's *Menexenus*: A Paradigm of Rhetorical Flattery.' *Polis: The Journal for Ancient Greek Political Thought* 25 (1): 94–114.

Keuls, E. C. 1997. *Painter and Poet in Ancient Greece: Iconography and the Literary Arts*. De Gruyter.

Kidd, S. E. 2019. *Play and Aesthetics in Ancient Greece*. Cambridge University Press.

Kindt, J. 2006. 'Delphic Oracle Stories and the Beginning of Historiography: Herodotus' *Croesus Logos*.' *Classical Philology* 101 (1): 34–51.

Kirichenko, A. 2016. 'The Art of Transference: Metaphor and Iconicity in Pindar's *Olympian* 6 and *Nemean* 5.' *Mnemosyne* 69 (1): 1–28.

Kirk, G. S., Raven, J. E., and Schofield, M. 1983. *The Presocratic Philosophers: A Critical History with a Selection of Texts*. Cambridge University Press.

Köhnken, A. 2005. 'Obscurity and Obscurantism: How to Read Pindar.' Edited by John T. Hamilton. *International Journal of the Classical Tradition* 11 (4): 602–6.

Kokolakis, M. M. 1980. 'Homeric Animism.' *Museum Philologum Londiniense* 4: 89–113.

Krentz, P. 1993. 'The *Salpinx* in Greek Warfare.' In Hanson, V. D. ed. *Hoplites: The Classical Greek Battle Experience*. Routledge. 110–20.

Kurke, L. 1991. *The Traffic in Praise: Pindar and the Poetics of Social Economy*. Cornell University Press.

—. 1992. 'The Politics of Ἁβροσύνη in Archaic Greece.' *Classical Antiquity* 11 (1): 91–120.

—. 2013. 'Imagining Chorality: Wonder, Plato's Puppets, and Moving Statues.' In Peponi, A. E. ed. *Performance and Culture in Plato's Laws*. Cambridge University Press. 123–70.

—. 2015. *Pindar's Material Imaginary: Dedication and Politics in Olympian 7*. UCL Department of Greek and Latin.

Kurke, L., and Neer, R. 2019. *Pindar, Song, and Space: Towards a Lyric Archaeology*. Johns Hopkins University Press.

Lachenaud, G. 2013. *Les Routes de la Voix: L'Antiquité Grecque et le Mystère de la Voix*. Belles Lettres.

Lakoff, G., and Johnson, M. 1980. *Metaphors We Live By*. University of Chicago Press.

Langer, S. 1953. *Feeling and Form: A Theory of Art Developed from Philosophy in a New Key*. Scribner's.

Lapatin, K. 2015. *Luxus: The Sumptuous Arts of Greece and Rome*. J. Paul Getty Museum.

Lather, A. 2016. 'Sense and Sensibility: The Experience of *Poikilia* in Archaic and Classical Greek Thought.' Dissertation: University of Texas at Austin.

—. 2017. 'The Sound of Music: The Semantics of Noise in Early Greek Hexameter.' *Greek and Roman Musical Studies* 5 (2): 127–46.

—. 2019. 'Pindar's Water Music: The Acoustics and Dynamics of the *Kelados*.' *Classical Philology* 114 (3): 468–81.

Latour, B. 2013. *An Inquiry into Modes of Existence*. Harvard University Press.

Lattimore, R. 1951. *The Iliad of Homer*. University of Chicago Press.

Lauwers, J., Schwall, H., and Opsomer, J. 2018. *Psychology and the Classics: A Dialogue of Disciplines*. De Gruyter.

Lawler, L. 1948. 'On Certain Homeric Epithets.' *Philological Quarterly* 27: 80–4.

Ledbetter, G. M. 2003. *Poetics before Plato: Interpretation and Authority in Early Greek Theories of Poetry*. Princeton University Press.

Lee, M. 2004. '" Evil Wealth of Raiment": Deadly Πέπλοι in Greek Tragedy.' *The Classical Journal* 99 (3): 253–79.

—. 2005. 'Constru(ct)ing Gender in the Feminine Greek *Peplos*.' In Cleland, L., Davies, G., and Llewellyn-Jones, L. eds. *The Clothed Body in the Ancient World*. Oxbow Books. 55–64.

—. 2015. *Body, Dress, and Identity in Ancient Greece*. Cambridge University Press.

Lefkowitz, M. 1991. *First-Person Fictions: Pindar's Poetic 'I'*. Oxford University Press.

Lessing, G. E. 1984. *Laocoön: An Essay on the Limits of Painting and Poetry*. Trans. Edward Allen McCormick. Johns Hopkins University Press.

LeVen, P. 2013. 'The Colours of Sound: *Poikilia* and Its Aesthetic Contexts.' *Greek and Roman Musical Studies* 1 (1): 229–42.

Levine, D. B. 1982. 'Homeric Laughter and the Unsmiling Suitors.' *The Classical Journal* 78 (2): 97–104.

Liebert, R. S. 2017. *Tragic Pleasure from Homer to Plato*. Cambridge University Press.

Lissarrague, F. 1990. *L'autre Guerrier: Archers, Peltastes, Cavaliers dans l'Imagerie Attique*. La Découverte.

—. 2008a. 'Corps et Armes: Figures Grecques du Guerrier.' In Dasen, V., and Wilgaux, J. eds. *Langages et Métaphores du Corps dans le Monde Antique*. Presses Universitaires de Rennes. 15–27.

—. 2008b. 'Le Temps des Boucliers.' *Images Re-vues: Histoire, Anthropologie et Théorie de l'Art* , special issue 1.

—. 2018. 'Armure et Ornement dans l'imagerie Attique.' In Dietrich, N. and Squire, M. eds. *Ornament and Figure in Graeco-Roman Art: Rethinking Visual Ontologies in Classical Antiquity*. De Gruyter. 129–41.

Liveley, G. 2006. 'Science Fictions and Cyber Myths: Or, Do Cyborgs Dream of Dolly the Sheep?' In Zajko, V., and Leonard, M. eds. *Laughing with Medusa: Classical Myth and Feminist Thought*. Oxford University Press. 275–94.

Llewellyn-Jones, L. 2002. *Women's Dress in the Ancient Greek World*. Duckworth.

Lobel, E., and Page, D. L. 1955. *Poetarum Lesbiorum Fragmenta*. Clarendon Press.

Loney, A. C. 2014. 'Hesiod's Incorporative Poetics in the *Theogony* and the Contradictions of Prometheus.' *American Journal of Philology* 135 (4): 503–31.

Lorimer, H. L. 1950. *Homer and the Monuments*. Macmillan.

Lovatt, H. 2013. *The Epic Gaze: Vision, Gender and Narrative in Ancient Epic*. Cambridge University Press.

Lundborg, G. 2013. *The Hand and the Brain: From Lucy's Thumb to the Thought-Controlled Robotic Hand*. Springer.

Lyons, D. 2003. 'Dangerous Gifts: Ideologies of Marriage and Exchange in Ancient Greece.' *Classical Antiquity* 22 (1): 93–134.

McClure, L. 1996. 'Clytemnestra's Binding Spell (*Ag.* 958–974).' *The Classical Journal* 92 (2): 123–40.

McNeil, L. 2005. 'Bridal Cloths, Cover-Ups, and *Kharis*: The "Carpet Scene" in Aeschylus' *Agamemnon*.' *Greece & Rome* 52 (1): 1–17.

Mack, R. 2002. 'Facing Down Medusa (An Aetiology of the Gaze).' *Art History* 25 (5): 571–604.

Mackay, E. A. 2010. *Tradition and Originality: A Study of Exekias*. Archaeopress.

MacLachlan, B. 1993. *The Age of Grace: Charis in Early Greek Poetry*. Princeton University Press.

Malafouris, L. 2013. *How Things Shape the Mind*. MIT Press.

—. 2018. 'Bringing Things to Mind: 4Es and Material Engagement.' In Newen, A., De Bruin, L., and Gallagher, S. eds. *The Oxford Handbook of 4E Cognition*. Oxford University Press. 755–72.

—. 2019. 'Mind and Material Engagement.' *Phenomenology and the Cognitive Sciences* 18 (1): 1–17.

Malafouris, L., and Renfrew, C., eds. 2010. *The Cognitive Life of Things: Recasting the Boundaries of the Mind*. McDonald Institute for Archaeological Research.

Mandoki, K. 2007. *Everyday Aesthetics: Prosaics, the Play of Culture and Social Identities*. Ashgate.

Manetti, G. 1993. *Theories of the Sign in Classical Antiquity*. Indiana University Press.

Manieri, A. 1998. *L'Immagine Poetica nella Teoria degli Antichi: Phantasia ed Enargeia*. Istituti Editoriali e Poligrafici Internazionali.

Marconi, C. 2017. 'The Frames of Greek Painted Pottery.' In Platt, V., and Squire, M. eds. *The Frame in Classical Art: A Cultural History*. Cambridge University Press. 117–53.

Maslov, B. 2015. *Pindar and the Emergence of Literature*. Cambridge University Press.

Mattusch, C. C. 1980. 'The Berlin Foundry Cup: The Casting of Greek Bronze Statuary in the Early Fifth Century B.C.' *American Journal of Archaeology* 84 (4): 435–44.

—. 2014. *Enduring Bronze: Ancient Art, Modern Views*. Getty.

Maurizio, L. 1993. *Delphic Narratives: Recontextualizing the Pythia and Her Prophecies*. Princeton University Press.

—. 1995. 'Anthropology and Spirit Possession: A Reconsideration of the Pythia's Role at Delphi.' *Journal of Hellenic Studies* 115: 69–86.

Meillassoux, Q. 2008. *After Finitude: An Essay on the Necessity of Contingency*. Trans. Ray Brassier. Continuum.

Meineck, P. 2012. 'The Embodied Space: Performance and Visual Cognition at the Fifth Century Athenian Theatre.' *New England Classical Journal* 39: 1–47.

Meineck, P., Short, W. M., and Devereaux, J. 2018. *The Routledge Handbook of Classics and Cognitive Theory*. Routledge.

Miller, A. M. 1993. 'Pindaric Mimesis: The Associative Mode.' *The Classical Journal* 89 (1): 21–53.

Miller, D. 2010. *Stuff*. Polity.

Mills, D. H. 1981. 'Odysseus and Polyphemus: Two Homeric Similes Reconsidered.' *The Classical Outlook* 58 (4): 97–9.

Minchin, E. 2001. 'Similes in Homer: Image, Mind's Eye, and Memory.' In Watson, J. ed. *Speaking Volumes*. Brill. 25–52.

—. 2019. 'Odysseus, Emotional Intelligence, and the Plot of the *Odyssey*.' *Mnemosyne* 72 (3): 351–68.

Montiglio, S. 2011. *From Villain to Hero: Odysseus in Ancient Thought*. University of Michigan Press.

Morizot, Y. 1974. 'À Propos de la Représentation Sculptée des Vêtements dans l'Art Grec.' *Revue des Études Anciennes* 76 (1): 117–32.

Morrell, K. S. 1997. 'The Fabric of Persuasion: Clytaemnestra, Agamemnon, and the Sea of Garments.' *The Classical Journal* 92 (2): 141–65.

Morris, S. P. 1992. *Daidalos and the Origins of Greek Art*. Princeton University Press.

—. 1995. *Daidalos and the Origins of Greek Art*. 2nd printing. Princeton University Press.

Morton, T. 2012. 'An Object-Oriented Defense of Poetry.' *New Literary History* 43 (2): 205–24.

Moss, J. 2007. 'What Is Imitative Poetry and Why Is It Bad?' In Ferrari, G. ed. *The Cambridge Companion to Plato's Republic*. Cambridge University Press. 415–44.

Most, G. 1997. 'Hesiod's Myth of the Five (or Three or Four) Races.' *Proceedings of the Cambridge Philological Society* (43): 104–27.

—. 2006. *Hesiod: Theogony, Works and Days, Testimonia*. Harvard University Press.

—. 2012. 'Poet and Public: Communicative Strategies in Pindar and Bacchylides.' In Agocs, P., Carey, C., and Rawles, R. eds. *Reading the Victory Ode*. Cambridge University Press. 249–76.

Mueller, M. 2001. 'The Language of Reciprocity in Euripides' Medea.' *American Journal of Philology* 122 (4): 471–504.

—. 2010. 'Helen's Hands: Weaving for *Kleos* in the *Odyssey*.' *Helios* 37 (1): 1–21.

—. 2016a. *Objects as Actors: Props and the Poetics of Performance in Greek Tragedy*. University of Chicago Press.

—. 2016b. 'The Disease of Mortality in Hesiod's *Theogony*: Prometheus, Herakles, and the Invention of *Kleos*.' *Ramus* 45 (1): 1–17.

Munson, R. V. 2001. *Telling Wonders: Ethnographic and Political Discourse in the Work of Herodotus*. University of Michigan Press.

Mylonopoulos, J. 2009. *Divine Images and Human Imaginations in Ancient Greece and Rome*. Leiden: Brill.

Nagy, G. 1996. *Poetry as Performance: Homer and Beyond*. Cambridge University Press.

—. 2002. *Plato's Rhapsody and Homer's Music: The Poetics of the Panathenaic Festival in Classical Athens*. Cambridge University Press.

—. 2012. *Homer the Preclassic*. University of California Press.

Neer, R. 2002. *Style and Politics in Athenian Vase-Painting: The Craft of Democracy, circa 530–470 BCE*. Cambridge University Press.

—. 2010. *The Emergence of the Classical Style in Greek Sculpture*. University of Chicago Press.

—. 2018a. 'Ornament, Incipience and Narrative: Geometric to Classical.' In Dietrich, N. and Squire, M. eds. *Ornament and Figure in Graeco-Roman Art: Rethinking Visual Ontologies in Classical Antiquity*. De Gruyter. 203–40.

—. 2018b. 'Amber, Oil, and Fire: Greek Sculpture beyond Bodies.' *Art History* 41 (3): 467–91.

Newen, A., Bruin, L. D., and Gallagher, S., eds. 2018. *The Oxford Handbook of 4E Cognition*. Oxford University Press.

Nightingale, A. 2018. 'The Aesthetics of Vision in Plato's *Phaedo* and *Timaeus*.' In Kampakoglou, A., and Novokhatko, A. eds. *Gaze, Vision, and Visuality in Ancient Greek Literature*. De Gruyter. 331–53.

Noë, A. 2004. *Action in Perception*. MIT Press.

—. 2012. *Varieties of Presence*. Harvard University Press.

Noel, A.-S. 2013. ' Le Vêtement-Piège et les Atrides: Métamorphoses d'un Objet Protéen.' In Le Guen, B., and Milanezi, S. eds. *L'Appareil Scénique dans les Spectacles de l'Antiquité*. Presses Universitaires de Vincennes. 161–82.

—. 2018. '"Prosthetic Imagination" in Greek Literature.' In Draycott, J. ed. *Prostheses in Antiquity*. Routledge. 159–79.

Nooter, S. 2017. *The Mortal Voice in the Tragedies of Aeschylus*. Cambridge University Press.

—. 2019. 'The War-Trumpet and the Sound of Domination in Ancient Greek Thought.' *Greek and Roman Musical Studies* 7 (2): 235–49.

Norwood, G. 1945. *Pindar*. University of California Press.

Onians, R. B. 1951. *The Origins of European Thought: About the Body, the Mind, the Soul, the World, Time and Fate*. Cambridge University Press.

O'Regan, J. K., and Noë, A. 2001. 'A Sensorimotor Account of Vision and Visual Consciousness.' *Behavioral and Brain Sciences* 24 (5): 939–73.

Osborne, R. 1998. *Archaic and Classical Greek Art*. Oxford University Press.

Osborne, R., and Tanner, J. 2008. *Art's Agency and Art History*. John Wiley & Sons.

Østergaard, J. S., and Nielsen, A. M. 2014. *Transformations: Classical Sculpture in Colour*. Ny Carlsberg Glyptotek.

Padel, R. 1992. *In and Out of the Mind: Greek Images of the Tragic Self*. Princeton University Press.

Pavlou, M. 2010. 'Pindar *Nemean* 5: Real and Poetic Statues.' *Phoenix* 64 (1/2): 1–17.

Pelliccia, H. 1991. 'Anacreon 13 (358 PMG).' *Classical Philology* 86 (1): 30–6.

—. 1995. *Mind, Body, and Speech in Homer and Pindar*. Vandenhoeck & Ruprecht.

Peponi, A.-E. 2004. 'Initiating the Viewer: Deixis and Visual Perception in Alcman's Lyric Drama.' *Arethusa* 37 (3): 295–316.

—. 2012. *Frontiers of Pleasure: Models of Aesthetic Response in Archaic and Classical Greek Thought*. Oxford University Press.

—. 2016. 'Lyric Vision: An Introduction.' In Cazzato, V., and Lardinois, A. eds. *The Look of Lyric: Greek Song and the Visual*. Brill. 1–15.

Petridou, G. 2015. *Divine Epiphany in Greek Literature and Culture*. Oxford University Press.

Petropoulos, J. C. B. 1993. 'Sappho the Sorceress: Another Look at Fr. 1 (LP).' *Zeitschrift für Papyrologie und Epigraphik* 97: 43–56.

Petrovic, A., Petrovic, I., and Thomas, E., eds. 2018. *The Materiality of Text: Placement, Perception, and Presence of Inscribed Texts in Classical Antiquity*. Brill.

Pfeijffer, I. L. 1999. *Three Aeginetan Odes of Pindar: A Commentary on Nemean V, Nemean III, and Pythian VIII*. Brill.

—. 2000. 'Playing Ball with Homer: An Interpretation of Anacreon 358 PMG.' *Mnemosyne* 53 (2): 164–84.

Pierre, M. 2009. 'Couleur, Mensonge, et Rhétorique: La Cosmétique de l'Orateur chez Cicéron et Quintilien.' In Carastro, M. ed. *L'Antiquité en Couleurs: Catégories, Pratiques, Représentations*. Jérôme Millon. 179–87.

Platt, V. 2011. *Facing the Gods: Epiphany and Representation in Graeco-Roman Art, Literature and Religion*. Cambridge University Press.

—. 2018. 'Of Sponges and Stones: Matter and Ornament in Roman Painting.' In

Dietrich, N. and Squire, M. eds. *Ornament and Figure in Graeco-Roman Art: Rethinking Visual Ontologies in Classical Antiquity*. De Gruyter. 241–78.

Platt, V., and Squire, M., eds. 2017. *The Frame in Classical Art: A Cultural History*. Cambridge University Press.

Porter, J. I. 2010. *The Origins of Aesthetic Thought in Ancient Greece: Matter, Sensation, and Experience*. Cambridge University Press.

—. 2013. 'Why Are There Nine Muses?' In Butler, S., and Purves, A. eds. *Synaesthesia and the Ancient Senses*. Acumen. 9–26.

—. 2016. *The Sublime in Antiquity*. Cambridge University Press.

Postrel, V. 2013. *The Power of Glamour: Longing and the Art of Visual Persuasion*. Simon and Schuster.

Power, T. 2011. 'Cyberchorus: Pindar's Κηληδόνες and the Aura of the Artificial.' In Athanassaki, L., and Bowie, E. eds. *Archaic and Classical Choral Song: Performance, Politics and Dissemination*. De Gruyter. 67–113.

Pratt, L. 1993. *Lying and Poetry from Homer to Pindar*. University of Michigan Press.

Prier, R. A. 1989. *Thauma Idesthai: The Phenomenology of Sight and Appearance in Archaic Greek*. Florida State University Press.

Pucci, P. 1977. *Hesiod and the Language of Poetry*. Johns Hopkins University Press.

Purves, A. 2015. 'Ajax and Other Objects: Homer's Vibrant Materialism.' *Ramus* 44 (1–2): 75–94.

—. 2019. *Homer and the Poetics of Gesture*. Oxford: Oxford University Press.

Putnam, M. 1960. '*Throna* and Sappho 1.1.' *The Classical Journal* 56 (2): 79–83.

Race, W. H. 1983. 'Negative Expressions and Pindaric ΠΟΙΚΙΛΙΑ.' *Transactions of the American Philological Association* 113: 95–122.

—. 1997a. *Pindar: Nemean Odes, Isthmian Odes, Fragments*. Harvard University Press.

—. 1997b. *Pindar: Olympian Odes, Pythian Odes*. Harvard University Press.

Rackham, H. 1932. *Aristotle: Politics*. Harvard University Press.

Rasmussen, T., Spivey, N., and Spivey, N. J. 1991. *Looking at Greek Vases*. Cambridge University Press.

Ready, J. L. 2011. *Character, Narrator, and Simile in the Iliad*. Cambridge University Press.

Renfrew, A. C., and Zubrow, E. B. W., eds. 1994. *The Ancient Mind: Elements of Cognitive Archaeology*. Cambridge University Press.

Richardson, N. J. 2010. *Three Homeric Hymns: To Apollo, Hermes, and Aphrodite : Hymns 3, 4, and 5*. Cambridge University Press.

Richter, G. M. A. 1968. *Korai: Archaic Greek Maidens: A Study of the Development of the Kore Type in Greek Sculpture*. Phaidon.

Ridgway, B. S. 1977. 'The Peplos Kore, Akropolis 679.' *The Journal of the Walters Art Gallery* 36: 49–61.

—. 1993. *The Archaic Style in Greek Sculpture*. Ares.

Rinaudo, M. 2009. 'Sviluppi Semantici e Ambiti d'Uso di Ποικίλος e Derivati da Omero ad Aristotele.' In Berardi, E., Lisi, F. L., and Micalella, D. eds. *Poikilia: Variazioni sul Tema*. Bonanno. 25–64.

Rinella, M. A. 2010. *Pharmakon: Plato, Drug Culture, and Identity in Ancient Athens*. Lexington Books.

Riskin, J. 2016. *The Restless Clock: A History of the Centuries-Long Argument over What Makes Living Things Tick*. University of Chicago Press.

Rosen, R. 2013. 'Plato, Beauty and "Philosophical Synaesthesia".' In Butler, S., and Purves, A. C., eds. *Synaesthesia and the Ancient Senses*. Acumen. 89–102.

Rosenmeyer, T. G. 1966. 'Alcman's *Partheneion I* Reconsidered.' *Greek, Roman and Byzantine Studies* 7: 321–59.

Rudolph, K. 2016. 'Sight and the Presocratics: Approaches to Visual Perception in Early Greek Philosophy.' In Squire, M. ed. *Sight and the Ancient Senses*. Routledge. 36–53.

Saito, Y. 2007. *Everyday Aesthetics*. Oxford University Press.

Scarry, E. 1999. *Dreaming by the Book*. Princeton University Press.

Scheid, J., and Svenbro, J. 1996. *The Craft of Zeus: Myths of Weaving and Fabric*. Harvard University Press.

Schibli, H. 1990. *Pherekydes of Syros*. Oxford University Press.

Schlesier, R. 2011. 'Aphrodite Reflétée: À Propos du Fragment 1 (LP/V) de Sappho.' In *Dans le Laboratoire de l'Historien des Religions: Mélanges Offerts à Philippe Borgeaud*. Editions Labor et Fides. 416–29.

Schmitz, T. 2013. 'Erzählung und Imagination in Sapphos Aphroditelied (Frg. 1 V).' In Dunsch, B., Schmitt, A., and Schmitz, T. eds. *Epos, Lyrik Drama: Genese und Ausformung der Literarischen Gattungen: Festschrift für Ernst-Richard Schwing Zum 75. Geburtsag*. Universitatsverlag Winter. 89–103.

Scully, S. 2003. 'Reading the Shield of Achilles: Terror, Anger, Delight.' *Harvard Studies in Classical Philology* 101: 29–47.

Seaford, R. 2004. *Money and the Early Greek Mind: Homer, Philosophy, Tragedy*. Cambridge University Press.

Segal, C. 1981. *Tragedy and Civilization: An Interpretation of Sophocles*. Harvard University Press.

—. 1992. 'Signs, Magic, and Letters in Euripides' Hippolytus.' In Hexter, R. and Selden, D. eds. *Innovations of Antiquity*. Routledge. 420–56.

—. 1996. 'Euripides' *Medea*: Vengeance, Reversal and Closure.' *Pallas* 45: 15–44.

—. 1998. *Aglaia*. Rowman & Littlefield.

Shapiro, H. A. 1993. *Personifications in Greek Art: The Representation of Abstract Concepts, 600–400 B.C.* Akanthus.

Shelmerdine, C. W. 1985. *The Perfume Industry of Mycenaean Pylos.* Astrom Editions.

Sheppard, A. 2015. 'Imagination.' In Destrée, P., and Murray, P. eds. *A Companion to Ancient Aesthetics.* John Wiley & Sons. 354–65.

Shirazi, A. 2018. 'The Other Side of the Mirror: Reflection and Reversal in Euripides' *Hecuba.*' In Telò, M., and Mueller, M. eds. *The Materialities of Greek Tragedy: Objects and Affect in Aeschylus, Sophocles, and Euripides.* Bloomsbury Academic. 97–112.

Sigelman, A. C. 2016. *Pindar's Poetics of Immortality.* Cambridge University Press.

Sissa, G., and Detienne, M. 2000. *The Daily Life of the Greek Gods.* Stanford University Press.

Skarsouli, P. 2009. 'S'Interroger sur la Relation entre Couleurs et Mots: Le Terme *Pharmakon* chez Empédocle.' In Carastro, M. ed. *L'Antiquité en Couleurs: Catégories, Pratiques, Représentations.* Jérôme Millon. 165–76.

Sluiter, I., and Rosen, R. M. 2012. *Aesthetic Value in Classical Antiquity.* Brill.

Snell, B. 1953. *The Discovery of the Mind: The Greek Origins of European Thought.* Trans. T. G. Rosenmeyer. Blackwell.

Snodgrass, A. M. 1967. *Arms and Armor of the Greeks.* Johns Hopkins University Press.

Spelman, H. 2015. 'Alcaeus 140.' *Classical Philology* 110 (4): 353–60.

—. 2017. 'Sappho 44: Trojan Myth and Literary History.' *Mnemosyne* 70 (5): 740–57.

—. 2018. *Pindar and the Poetics of Permanence.* Oxford University Press.

Spiegel, F. 2020. 'Malfunctions of Embodiment: Man/Weapon Agency and the Greek Ideology of Masculinity.' In Chesi, G. M., and Spiegel, F. eds. *Classical Literature and Posthumanism.* Bloomsbury Academic. 267–73.

Spivey, N. 1995. 'Bionic Statues.' In Powell, A. ed. *The Greek World.* Routledge. 442–59.

—. 1996. *Understanding Greek Sculpture: Ancient Meanings, Modern Readings.* Thames & Hudson.

Squire, M. 2013. 'Ekphrasis at the Forge and the Forging of Ekphrasis: The "Shield of Achilles" in Graeco-Roman Word and Image.' *Word & Image* 29 (2): 157–91.

—, ed. 2016. *Sight and the Ancient Senses.* Routledge.

Stafford, B. M. 2007. *Echo Objects: The Cognitive Work of Images.* University of Chicago Press.

Stager, J. M. S. 2016. 'The Materiality of Color in Ancient Mediterranean Art.'

In Goldman, R. B. ed. *Essays in Global Color History: Interpreting the Ancient Spectrum.* De Gruyter. 97–120.

Stanford, W. B. 1936. *Greek Metaphor: Studies in Theory and Practice.* Blackwell.

—. 1967. *The Sound of Greek.* University of California Press.

—. 1981. 'Sound, Sense, and Music in Greek Poetry.' *Greece & Rome* 28 (2): 127–40.

Starr, G. G. 2013. *Feeling Beauty: The Neuroscience of Aesthetic Experience.* MIT Press.

—. 2015. 'Theorizing Imagery, Aesthetics, and Doubly Directed States.' In Zunshine, L. ed. *The Oxford Handbook of Cognitive Literary Studies.* Oxford University Press. 246–68.

Stehle, E. 1996. 'Sappho's Gaze: Fantasies of a Goddess and Young Man.' In Greene, E. ed. *Reading Sappho: Contemporary Approaches.* University of California Press. 193–225.

Steiner, D. 1986. *The Crown of Song: Metaphor in Pindar.* Duckworth.

—. 1993. 'Pindar's "Oggetti Parlanti".' *Harvard Studies in Classical Philology* 95: 159–80.

—. 2001. *Images in Mind: Statues in Archaic and Classical Greek Literature and Thought.* Princeton University Press.

—. 2007. 'Feathers Flying: Avian Poetics in Hesiod, Pindar, and Callimachus.' *American Journal of Philology* 128 (2): 177–208.

Stieber, M. 2004. *The Poetics of Appearance in the Attic Korai.* University of Texas Press.

Stocking, C. H. 2017. *The Politics of Sacrifice in Early Greek Myth and Poetry.* Cambridge University Press.

Strassler, R. B., ed. 2009. *The Landmark Herodotus: The Histories.* Trans. Andrea Purvis. Anchor.

Summers, D. 1999. 'Pandora's Crown: On Wonder, Imitation, and Mechanism in Western Art.' In Platt, P. G. ed. *Wonders, Marvels, and Monsters in Early Modern Culture.* University of Delaware Press. 45–75.

Swift, E. 2009. *Style and Function in Roman Decoration: Living with Objects and Interiors.* Ashgate.

Swift, L. 2015. 'Lyric Visions of Epic Combat: The Spectacle of War in Archaic Personal Song.' In Bakogianni, A., and Hope, V. M. eds. *War as Spectacle: Ancient and Modern Perspectives on the Display of Armed Conflict.* Bloomsbury. 93–109.

—. 2016. 'Visual Imagery in Parthenaic Song.' In *The Look of Lyric: Greek Song and the Visual.* Brill. 255–87.

Tanner, J. 2006. *The Invention of Art History in Ancient Greece: Religion, Society and Artistic Rationalisation.* Cambridge University Press.

Taplin, O. 1977. *The Stagecraft of Aeschylus: The Dramatic Use of Exits and Entrances in Greek Tragedy*. Clarendon Press.

—. 1980. 'The Shield of Achilles within the *Iliad*.' *Greece & Rome* 27 (1): 1–21.

Telò, M., and Mueller, M., eds. 2018. *The Materialities of Greek Tragedy: Objects and Affect in Aeschylus, Sophocles, and Euripides*. Bloomsbury Academic.

Thomas, O. 2018. 'Hermetically Unsealed: Lyric Genres in the *Homeric Hymn to Hermes*.' In Budelmann, F., and Phillips, T. eds. *Textual Events: Performance and the Lyric in Early Greece*. Oxford University Press. 173–88.

Thompson, E. 2007. 'Look Again: Phenomenology and Mental Imagery.' *Phenomenology and the Cognitive Sciences* 6 (1–2): 137–70.

Torrance, I. 2010. 'Writing And Self-Conscious *Mythopoiēsis* in Euripides.' *The Cambridge Classical Journal* 56: 213–58.

—. 2013. *Metapoetry in Euripides*. Oxford.

Troscianko, E. 2014a. 'Reading Kafka Enactively.' *Paragraph* 37 (1): 15–31.

—. 2014b. *Kafka's Cognitive Realism*. Routledge.

Tuck, A. 2009. 'Stories at the Loom: Patterned Textiles and the Recitation of Myth in Euripides.' *Arethusa* 42 (2): 151–9.

Turkeltaub, D. 2007. 'Perceiving Iliadic Gods.' *Harvard Studies in Classical Philology* 103: 51–81.

Turkle, S., Resnick, M., Donath, J., Fischer, M. M. J., Gardner, H., Jenkins, H., Keller, E. F., Medina, E., Mitchell, W. J., and Pinch, T., eds. 2014. *Evocative Objects: Things We Think With*. MIT Press.

Uhlig, A. 2018. 'Noses in the Orchestra: Bodies, Objects, and Affect in Sophocles' *Ichneutae*.' In Telò, M. and Mueller, M. eds. *The Materialities of Greek Tragedy*. Bloomsbury Academic. 153–68.

Van Noorden, H. 2014. *Playing Hesiod: The 'Myth of the Races' in Classical Antiquity*. Cambridge University Press.

Van Nortwick, T. 1975. 'The Homeric Hymn to Hermes: A Study in Early Greek Hexameter Style.' Dissertation: Stanford University.

—. 2009. *The Unknown Odysseus: Alternate Worlds in Homer's Odyssey*. University of Michigan Press.

Vergados, A. 2011. *The Homeric Hymn to Hermes: Humour and Epiphany*. Oxford University Press.

—. 2013. *The Homeric Hymn to Hermes: Introduction, Text and Commentary*. De Gruyter.

Vernant, J.-P. 1991. *Mortals and Immortals: Collected Essays*. Edited by Froma I. Zeitlin. Princeton University Press.

—. 2011. 'Semblances of Pandora: Imitation and Identity.' Trans. Froma I. Zeitlin. *Critical Inquiry* 37: 404–18.

Villacèque, N. 2010. 'De la Bigarrure en Politique (Platon *République* 8.557C4–61e7).' *Journal of Hellenic Studies* 130: 137–52.

Wace, A. J. B. 1948. 'Weaving or Embroidery?' *American Journal of Archaeology* 52 (1): 51–5.

Wallace, R. 2009. 'Plato, *Poikilia*, and New Music in Athens.' In Berardi, E., Lisi, F. L., and Micalella, D. eds. *Poikilia: Variaizioni sul Tema*. Bonanno. 201–13.

Walsh, G. B. 1984. *The Varieties of Enchantment: Early Greek Views of the Nature and Function of Poetry*. University of North Carolina Press.

Webb, R. 2009. *Ekphrasis, Imagination and Persuasion in Ancient Rhetorical Theory and Practice*. Ashgate.

—. 2018. 'Odysseus' Bed: Between Object and Action.' In *Dossier: Place aux Objets! Présentification et Vie des Artefacts en Grèce Ancienne*. Éditions de l'École des Hautes Études en Sciences Sociales. 65–83.

Webster, T. B. L. 1954. 'Personification as a Mode of Greek Thought.' *Journal of the Warburg and Courtauld Institutes* 17 (1/2): 10–21.

Weiss, N. 2018. 'Speaking Sights and Seen Sounds in Aeschylean Tragedy.' In Mueller, M., and Telò, M. eds. *The Materialities of Greek Tragedy: Objects and Affect in Aeschylus, Sophocles, and Euripides*. Bloomsbury Academic. 169–84.

Wells, J. B. 2009. *Pindar's Verbal Art: An Ethnographic Study of Epinician Style*. Harvard University Press.

West, M. L. 1966. *Hesiod's Theogony*. Clarendon Press.

—. 1978. *Works & Days*. Clarendon Press.

—. 2003. *Homeric Hymns, Homeric Apocrypha, Lives of Homer*. Harvard University Press.

West, S. 1987. 'Herodotean Autopsy.' Edited by O. Kimball Armayor. *The Classical Review* 37 (1): 6–8.

Whitley, J. 2013. 'Homer's Entangled Objects: Narrative, Agency and Personhood In and Out of Iron Age Texts.' *Cambridge Archaeological Journal* 23 (3): 395–416.

Wickkiser, B. L. 2010. 'Hesiod and the Fabricated Woman: Poetry and Visual Art in the *Theogony*.' *Mnemosyne* 63 (4): 557–76.

Wilamowitz, U. 1922. *Pindaros*. Weidman.

Wohl, V. 1997. *Intimate Commerce: Exchange, Gender, and Subjectivity in Greek Tragedy*. University of Texas Press.

Wollheim, R. 1980. 'Seeing-as, Seeing-in, and Pictorial Representation.' In Wollheim, R. ed. *Art and Its Objects*. Cambridge University Press. 205–26.

Woodbury, L. 1979. 'Gold Hair and Grey, or the Game of Love: Anacreon Fr. 13:358 PMG, 13 Gentili.' *Transactions of the American Philological Association* 109: 277–87.

Yatromanolakis, D. 2009. 'Alcaeus and Sappho.' In Budelmann, F. ed. *The Cambridge Companion to Greek Lyric*. Cambridge University Press. 204–26.

Young, D. C. 1983. 'Pindar, Aristotle, and Homer: A Study in Ancient Criticism.' *Classical Antiquity* 2 (1): 156–70.

Zanker, A. T. 2019. *Metaphor in Homer: Time, Speech, and Thought*. Cambridge University Press.

Zanker, G. 1981. '*Enargeia* in the Ancient Criticism of Poetry.' *Rheinisches Museum für Philologie* 124 (3/4): 297–311.

Zeitlin, F. I. 1996. *Playing the Other: Gender and Society in Classical Greek Literature*. University of Chicago Press.

Zorach, R., and Phillips, M. W. 2016. *Gold: Nature and Culture*. Reaktion Books.

Index Locorum

Aeschylus
  Agamemnon
    37–8, 117
    905–11, 212–13
    909, 212
    918–27, 213–14
    921, 212
    935–6, 215
    938, 215
    948–9, 214
    949, 212
    958–62, 214
    959, 214
    963, 212
    1062, 125
    1126, 212
    1383, 216
  Eumenides
    460–2, 217
  Libation Bearers
    195, 116
    232–3, 61
    997–104, 216
    1010, 217
    1013, 216
  [*Prometheus Bound*]
    24, 26
    110–11, 168
    308, 168
    506, 168
Aesop
  Fable 12, 164n4
Alcaeus
  fr. 69.6–8, 164
  fr. 93.1, 160
  fr. 140
    3–5, 91
    5–10, 92–3
    6–7, 91
  fr. 345, 158n87
Alcman
  Partheneion 1
    64–9, 137–8
    70–2, 138
Anacreon
  PMG 358, 138–9, 150
Apollodorus
  Bibliotheca 1.45.2–3, 167n15
Apollonius
  Argonautica 4.1645–7, 68n14, 80n45
Aristides
  Oration 28.57, 143n55

Aristophanes
    Birds, 248–9, 158n87
    Clouds, 449, 135n30
    Knights
        196, 123
        269, 135n30
    Peace, 1174, 133n27
    Wasps, 645, 174n30
Aristotle
    De Anima, 420b5–6, 110
    [*De Coloribus*]
        793b9–12, 159n91
        794a32–794b7, 23–4
    Metaphysics 982b12–13, 126
    Meteorologica
        375a6–8, 22
        375a22–8, 22–3
    Politics
        1253b33, 108n32
        1253b33–1254a2, 109
    Rhetoric
        1411b31–1412a8, 79–80
        1412a3–4, 80
Bacchylides
    2.12, 154
    3.97–8, 159n89
Critias
    DK 26, 33–4, 26
Cypria
    fr. 4, 1–6, 128n6
Democritus
    B 154 DK, 159n89
Dionysius of Halicarnassus
    De Compositione Verborum 23,
        160n92
Empedocles
    DK B 23, 55–6, 59, 163
Euripides
    Electra, 333–5, 118n49
    Hecuba, 836–40, 118–19
    Helen

        262–3, 55–6
        1096, 26
    Heracles 376, 160
    Hippolytus
        417–18, 117
        865, 118n48
        877–80, 118n48
        1074–5, 117
        1076–7, 117–18, 124
    Ion, 1417–25, 61–2
    Iphigenia in Tauris
        50–2, 119
        1245, 160
    Medea
        783, 219
        788, 221
        789, 218
        954–5, 218
        956, 219
        983, 218
        983–4, 220
        1156–67, 219–20
        1162, 221
        1187, 220
        1189, 220
        1196, 220
        1206, 221
    Phoenissae, 469–72, 124
Heraclitus
    Homeric Problems 39.7–8, 196n1
Herodotus
    Histories
        2.125.6, 125
        2.148.1–2, 98–100
        2.148.3, 98
        2.148.6, 95, 100–1
        7.11.2, 123
        8.19.6, 174n30
Hesiod
    Theogony
        27, 148

Hesiod *(cont.)*
  151–2, 69
  187, 69
  212, 78
  367, 154n80
  511, 168
  521, 168
  521–2, 194
  537, 171, 185
  539, 170
  540–1, 170, 171
  546–7, 186
  547, 185
  550, 185
  551–2, 171
  555, 171
  560, 185
  563, 69
  566, 168
  567, 168
  570, 108
  570–90, 104–7
  572, 108
  580, 108
  589, 104, 108, 209
Works and Days
  42, 169
  50, 168
  57, 169, 170
  58, 210
  60–83, 119–21
  62–3, 210
  67, 210
  77–8, 170
  83, 170, 209
  94–8, 170
  103–4, 121
  109, 68
  112, 68
  143–6, 68
  147–8, 78

  148–9, 69
  150–1, 68–9
  203–8, 158
Homer
Iliad
  1.104, 73
  2.450–2, 88
  2.455–8, 88
  2.490, 85
  2.781–3, 74–5
  3.64, 79
  3.125–8, 58–9, 60
  3.202, 179, 189, 199
  3.205–24, 189–90
  3.218, 191
  3.236–43, 61n78
  3.327, 66
  3.337, 91
  3.371, 197
  3.375, 197
  4.44, 66
  4.226, 66
  4.432, 66
  4.489, 89
  5.1–2, 88
  5.4, 88
  5.239, 66
  5.292, 80
  5.295, 89
  5.335–40, 79
  5.401, 59, 128n7
  5.441–4, 206n26
  5.504, 75
  5.594, 191
  5.725, 208
  5.727, 198
  5.735=*Il.* 8.386, 20, 30, 57–8
  5.738–9, 65
  5.741–2, 72
  5.749–51=8.393–5, 112n38
  5.784–6, 85

5.900, 59, 128n7
6.48, 68
6.205, 68
6.234–6, 69n17
6.288, 39n35
6.294–5, 21, 44
6.469–70, 91
6.503–14, 90–1
6.504, 66
7.222, 89
8.19, 68
8.558, 82
9.214, 59
9.389, 79
10.75, 66
10.149, 66
10.315, 68
10.322, 66
10.379, 68
10.393, 66
10.439, 208
10.501, 66
10.504, 66
11.16, 70
11.18, 70
11.20–3, 71
11.24–5, 70
11.29–31, 70
11.32, 72
11.33–5, 70, 78n39
11.36–7, 71, 72
11.38–40, 71
11.42, 91
11.44–5, 69, 70
11.46–7, 71
11.241, 78
11.242–3, 78
11.574, 79n41
12.167, 89
12.208, 89
12.295, 78

12.338, 74
12.396, 66
13.20–2, 67
13.130–5, 81
13.136–42, 82
13.139, 84
13.152, 81
13.153–4, 82
13.244, 84
13.340–4, 69, 76, 77, 78
13.536, 66
13.837, 76
14.170–88, 202–5
14.198–9, 197
14.215–21, 197–8
14.217, 210, 218
14.218, 199
14.220–1, 199
14.294, 199, 210
14.315–16, 200, 210
14.355, 210
14.420, 66
14.431, 66
15.20, 68
15.230, 65
15.309–10, 65–6
15.317, 79n41
15.371, 66
15.453, 144
15.542, 79n41
15.603, 88
15.623, 88
16.133–4, 66
16.138, 91
16.672, 78
17.210–14, 89
17.424–5, 75, 84
17.425, 74, 75
17.594–6, 65–6
18.130–1, 78
18.217–18, 84

Homer *(cont.)*

18.218, 84
18.219–23, 83
18.225–7, 84n52, 88
18.289, 68
18.370–1, 67
18.372–80, 112–13, 175
18.377, 208
18.380, 115
18.409, 175
18.412, 175
18.416–21, 114
18.468, 175
18.469, 113
18.469–77, 111–12
18.470, 175
18.474–5, 87
18.478–609, 6–13, 14–16
18.516–19, 93–4
18.519, 84
18.549–50, 102
18.590, 66
18.599–601, 86
18.600, 174
19.13–19, 13, 87
19.16–17, 73
19.38–9, 207
19.362, 69
19.362–3, 73–4
19.363, 69, 74
19.373–4, 13, 69, 87
19.375–8, 87
19.384–6, 86
19.386, 90
19.404, 89
19.407, 144n56
21.168, 79n41
22.134–5, 87–8, 208
22.136, 88
22.397, 198
22.440–1, 20, 59, 128, 226

22.447–8, 61
22.509, 89
24.20–1, 65
24.341, 68

Odyssey

3.2–3, 75
3.492, 66
4.70–5, 68
4.150, 73
5.38, 68
5.101, 82
5.234, 174
5.241–61, 179
5.477, 183
5.480–1, 183
5.482–91, 183–4
6.232–4, 170
6.235, 170
7.45, 208
7.91, 79
7.91–4, 107n29
7.94, 79
7.107, 39n35
8.274–5, 209
8.364–5, 204n19, 209
8.366, 208
8.443–5, 180
8.447–8, 180
8.507, 168
8.512–13, 168
8.515=4.277, 168
8.555–9, 115
8.562–3, 115
8.564–9, 115
10.239, 84n54
11.368, 188n60
13.108, 208
13.253, 191
13.254–5, 191
13.256–86, 186, 190
13.287–8, 191

13.291–9, 192
14.191–359, 191
15.106–8, 21, 44, 219
15.145, 66
18.190–6, 204n19
19.18, 76n34
19.40, 79n42
19.137, 56
19.165–202, 191
19.221–48, 191
19.227–31, 101–2
19.258–70, 191
19.262–307, 191
19.336–42, 191
19.446, 73n26
21.52, 39n35
23.184–204, 180–2
23.197, 188
Homeric Hymn to Aphrodite
61–3, 206
64–5, 207
82–3, 207
84–91, 44–5, 207–8
88–9, 210
90, 210
91, 210
167, 210
173–5, 79n42
174, 208
181–2, 209
Homeric Hymn to Apollo
234, 144
322, 171
442, 79n42
444, 79n42
Homeric Hymn to Demeter
70, 73
188–9, 79n42
235–40, 207
275–80, 208
277–8, 39n35

Homeric Hymn to Helios 9–11, 73n27
Homeric Hymn to Hermes
38, 178
41–2, 178
43–6, 178
47–51, 178
49, 178
52, 178
55, 178
79–86, 175–6
108–14, 173–5
153–5, 186
154, 186
155, 186
156, 189
219–26, 177
239–42, 186
243, 186, 187
245, 186
261, 187
272, 187
278–80, 187
348–9, 177
387–90, 188
483, 178–9
487, 178–9
488, 179
511–12, 173
Homeric Scholia T ad Σ 214b, Erbse 1969:
    III.608, 198n5
Ibycus fr. 36a, 158n87
IG II 6, 1, 261.17–18, 21
IG II 754.8–9 = Michel, no. 819, 8–9,
    21
Pindar
    fr. 52.1–2, 73n27
    fr. 179, 154n79
    fr. 194, 26n12, 143–4
    Isthmian 3/4.36, 141
    Nemean 4.14–16, 153
    Nemean 5

Pindar *(cont.)*
  26–32, 152
  42, 152, 153
 Nemean 8
  13–16, 154
  14–15, 26n12
 Nemean 9.54, 148n63
 Nemean 10.36, 45
 Nemean 11.18, 148n63
 Olympian 1
  25–32, 147–9
  36, 148
  47, 148
  52, 148
  105, 148n63
 Olympian 2.83–6, 125
 Olympian 3.3–9, 156–8
 Olympian 4.2–3, 160
 Olympian 5.21, 148n63
 Olympian 6
  1–2, 151
  3–4, 151
  86–7, 26n12, 150–1,
   152
  91, 151
  105, 151
 Olympian 10.98, 148n63
 Olympian 13.52, 174n30
 Paean 6.17–18, 144
 Pythian 1.9, 159
 Pythian 4
  213–17, 156
  249, 160
 Pythian 6.2, 148n63
 Pythian 8.44–7, 146
 Pythian 9
  3–4, 148n63
  77–8, 149–50
  89–90, 148n63
 Pythian 10
  39, 154

  46, 160
  46–50, 147
Plato
 Cratylus 388b–c, 110
 Hippias Major 298a1–3, 24
 Ion 534e, 125
 Laws 644d7–8, 126n62
 Menexenus
  97d, 109
  234c7–235a2, 122
  235a9–235b1, 122
  235b6–7, 122
 Phaedo 110d1–3, 229
 Phaedrus
  229d–e, 105n18
  234d1, 122n57
  242d7, 122n57
  242e1, 122n57
  275b–c, 117n46
 Philebus 12c5–9, 140–1
 Protagoras 328d3, 122n57
 Republic
  372e–373c, 226n6
  373a1, 226n6
  399e9–400a2, 224
  401d6, 224
  404d2, 224
  404d12, 224
  404e2–3
  529d6–7, 25, 26
  557c5–9, 226
  557e–558a, 227
  558c2–4, 226–7
  561c7–8, 227
  561e3–8, 227–8
  562b7–10, 228
  568d5, 125
  568d5–8, 228
  572e–573b, 228
  586a1–4, 224
  588b11, 227

588c7–10, 227
592c8–d2, 25
604e1–7, 225
605b3, 225
605d3–4, 225
Theatetus 155d3, 126
Timaeus
39d1-2, 25n11
39d10, 25n11
87a5–6
Plutarch
Quaestiones convivales 703a,
169n18
Quomodo adulescens poetas audire debeat
19e–20b, 196n1
Pratinas *TrGF* 3, 157n85
Sappho
fr. 1.1–2, 127–8
fr. 39
133n27, 135
fr. 44.8–10
135–6, 219

fr. 58.25, 134
fr. 98a–b, 133
Shield of Heracles
160, 72
145, 72
236, 72
423, 66
Sophocles
Oedipus the King, 130, 123
Trachiniae
212, 154
673, 102
677, 103
693–4, 103
697–8, 103
702, 103
1118–19, 124
1120–1, 124
Theognis
1.213–18, 162–3
1.602, 160
1.624, 174n30

Subject Index

Achilles, 21–2, 51–3, 73, 83–5
  armour of, 66–7, 78, 85–90, 208
  shield of, 6–13, 45, 93–4, 198, 227
Acropolis Korai, 29–55, 63, 105, 210
  as *agalmata*, 21, 29, 44, 55, 63
  Kore 594, 34, 40–4
  Kore 674, 34
  Kore 675, 34–44
  Kore 682, 34–9
  Peplos Kore, 30–3
adornment
  and *poikilia*, 18n1, 25, 147–9, 208, 210,
    226
  of women, 44–5, 104–7, 137–8, 201–9,
    219–20
  see also Agalma
Aegis, 65–6, 72, 198
affordances, 9, 69, 172, 175, 183
Agalma (precious offering), 137–8,
  154
  and armour, 90–3
  and Pandora, 106n25, 204n20
  see also Acropolis Korai
Agamemnon, 73
  armour of, 70–2, 78
  murder of, 211–18

Amasis painter, 48–50
Andocides and Lysippides painters, 52–4
Andromache
  weaving of, 20, 55, 57, 59–61, 128, 226
  wedding gifts of, 135–6, 137–8
animals, 30–3, 47, 89, 105, 107–8, 177,
  227
  birds, 158–60, 162
  octopodes, 162–4
  serpents, 89, 160
Aphrodite, 79–80, 120, 127–9, 131–3, 156,
  204n19, 209, 221
  kestos himas, 196–201, 204, 218
  seduction of Anchises, 44–5, 206–9, 210,
    212
assemblage
  in armour, 71–2, 77
  in clothing, 202–11
  theories of, 71, 201–2
Athena, 104–5, 217
  relationship to Odysseus, 170–1, 186, 188,
    190–3
  relationship to weaving, 20, 30, 44, 57–8,
    120, 203–5
  role in battle, 65–6, 70–1, 72, 84, 88,
    93–4

automata, 17, 95, 97, 105, 115–22
ancient theorisations of, 79–80, 108–10, 114
Hephaestus' creation of, 109, 111–19

Bennett, Jane, 4, 16n35, 64, 97n5, 103n14, 201–2
Brown, Bill, 2, 7n14, 96–7, 99, 103, 211

chorus/*choros*, 14–16, 137–8, 141n46, 152–3
Clark, Andy, 229
cognitive 'props', 110–11, 130–1, 149, 166–8
extended mind, 5–6, 57, 97, 110–11, 165, 185
clothing *see* adornment; weaving
colour
Aristotle's theory of, 22–4, 26, 160
in painting, 45–56
in sculpture, 29–44
see also polychromy
craftsmanship
as metaphor, 26, 58, 130, 142–4, 150, 151, 157, 160–1
in painting, 51–4
as simile, 15–16, 54–6
see also Daidalos/Daidalos; Hephaestus; weaving

Daidalos/Daidalos, 14–16, 101–2, 118–19
dance, 86–7, 144, 157–8; *see also* chorus/*choros*
Dennett, Daniel, 28, 36–8
desire
as force, 45, 80, 105, 120, 197–200, 205, 208, 209–11, 227–8
in relation to objects, 116, 121, 127, 132–8, 219–20

Enactive Perception *see* Noë, Alva
entanglement, 8, 71, 80, 82, 165–7, 182, 184, 194, 200, 214, 216, 221

Exekias, 21, 48, 51–2
Extended Cognition, 56, 62–3, 97, 194–5, 211, 217–18; *see also* Clark, Andy

fire
destructiveness of, 72–3, 87–90, 220
relationship to craft, 104, 112, 168–70, 173–5, 183–4, 185, 208
fragrance, 7, 39, 203–4, 206

Gell, Alfred, 36, 62, 197n3, 212
gold, 8, 11, 21, 45, 65, 67–9, 77, 79, 93–4, 101–2, 107, 114, 136, 137–8, 139, 144, 146, 151, 170–1, 181, 207–8, 210, 219, 220
Gorgon, 62, 71, 72, 147

hands, 15, 20, 30, 54–6, 57–9, 61, 63, 69, 79, 86–7, 105, 118, 163, 174–5, 183, 191, 197
Helen, 179, 189, 199
beauty of, 55–6
weaving, 55, 58–61
Hephaestus, 7–16, 65, 66, 67, 87, 93, 97, 108–15, 118, 170, 175, 178, 209, 227; *see also* Achilles: shield of; automata
Hera, 196–206, 208, 209, 210, 221
deception of Zeus, 196, 199–200
role in battle, 70, 71, 85
Hermes, 164–6, 172–9, 184–5, 186–9, 193–4

jewellery, 45, 136, 201, 203–6, 208–9

lies, 120, 147–9, 189, 191, 193
lifelikeness, 7, 8, 14, 16, 54–5, 82, 93–4, 95, 101–2, 114, 163, 169, 188
luxury, 134, 214–15
lyre, 157, 160, 173, 178–9

Malafouris, Lambros, 6, 57, 69, 167–8, 169, 182

Neer, Richard, 30, 33, 52, 93
Noë, Alva, 5, 19, 27–8, 62

Odysseus
  brooch of, 101–2
  cunning of, 3, 164–6, 168–9, 170–1, 172,
    179–84, 186, 189–93, 199, 218

Pandora, 103–8, 114, 119–22, 169–70, 201,
    205, 208, 209–10
paradox, 10, 12–13, 65, 82–3, 87, 93,
    98–101, 103, 105–6, 118, 187, 190, 224,
    225
Penelope, 56, 180–2, 191, 204n19
pleasure, 13, 24, 38–9, 78, 87, 92, 129,
    135–6, 138, 140–1, 142–3, 148, 151,
    153–5, 156, 160n92, 170, 178, 188–9,
    192, 205, 210, 223–5, 226, 227
polychromy, 24–5, 54–9, 67, 158–9, 162–4,
    216–17, 219, 225–6, 229
Prometheus, 164–73, 175, 176, 178, 184–5,
    185–6, 187, 193–5, 200, 218

sandals, 68, 139–40, 157–8, 173, 175–8, 201,
    203
Scarry, Elaine, 89, 130–1, 137, 145
skin/flesh
  animal, 49, 65, 67, 135, 137, 160
  divine, 79, 80, 201, 203, 204–5, 206–7,
    208
  human, 66, 72, 77, 79, 80, 84, 86, 87, 92,
    94, 106, 114, 219–20
Stafford, Barbara Maria, 26–7, 36, 62–3
Starr, Gabrielle, 38–9, 145–6

stars, 21, 25, 26, 34, 36, 44, 52, 66–7
stones/rocks, 7, 82–3, 102, 163, 165, 167,
    169, 174, 181, 186, 194

texture(s), 7, 29, 34, 38–9, 40, 62, 65, 160,
    220
thauma/wonder, 8, 12–13, 45, 93, 95–107,
    113, 119, 123, 125–6, 147, 208, 210
Thing Theory see Brown, Bill
tools, 5, 57, 97, 108–12, 114–15, 121, 125,
    151, 167, 169, 174–5, 179, 184
traps, 104–5, 106, 108, 122, 165, 167, 171,
    197, 211, 212, 216, 217, 220, 223

vision, 24, 64, 71, 72, 73, 76, 87–8, 91, 92,
    103, 146–7, 199, 210, 220
  and imagination, 61, 113, 131n18, 145,
    161
  theories of, 12–13, 20, 27–8, 38–9, 73
  see also desire
vital materialism see Bennett, Jane
vividness, 36, 54–5, 80, 96, 129, 131n18,
    132, 134, 135, 139–40, 145, 147, 150,
    151, 161, 202; see also vision

weaving, 18, 20–1, 28, 46, 56–9, 60–3,
    128–9, 176, 217–18
  relationship to poetry, 58, 26n12, 150–2
  technologies of, 59–60

Zeus, 65, 68, 74–5, 76, 82, 84, 88, 105, 106,
    108, 120, 121, 159, 167, 168, 169–72,
    185–6, 188, 189, 194, 196, 199–200,
    205–6, 210

CPSIA information can be obtained
at www.ICGtesting.com
Printed in the USA
BVHW011502300422
635719BV00002BA/42